STALIN'S FOLLY

Books by Constantine Pleshakov

THE TSAR'S LAST ARMADA:
The Epic Voyage to the Battle of Tsushima

THE FLIGHT OF THE ROMANOVS
A Family Saga (with John Curtis Perry)

INSIDE THE KREMLIN'S COLD WAR
From Stalin to Khrushchev (with Vladislav Zubok)

STALIN'S FOLLY

THE TRAGIC FIRST TEN DAYS OF WORLD WAR II ON THE EASTERN FRONT

CONSTANTINE
PLESHAKOV

HOUGHTON MIFFLIN COMPANY
BOSTON • NEW YORK
2005

Visit our Web site: www.houghtonmifflinbooks.com.

Library of Congress Cataloging-in-Publication Data

Pleshakov, Konstantin.
Stalin's folly : the tragic first ten days of World War II on the Eastern front / Constantine Pleshakov.
p. cm.
Includes bibliographical references and index.
ISBN 0-618-36701-2
1. World War, 1939–1945—Campaigns—Eastern Front. 2. Stalin, Joseph, 1879–1953. I. Title.
D764.P5317 2005 940.54'217—dc22
2004065133

Printed in the United States of America

Book design by Victoria Hartman
Maps by Jacques Chazaud

MP 10 9 8 7 6 5 4 3 2 1

For Lenya Serebriakov,
who joined me in a rip tide on a Long Island beach;
without his being there, I probably would have told the
June 22 story to horseshoe crabs — not to mention
the redemption of my still precariously young twins,
Anton and Anya, who watched my plight from the shore,
and my mother, Elza, unaware, four thousand
miles away from us that day

ACKNOWLEDGMENTS

I owe the completion of this project to a number of people and want to express my gratitude to each.

To my family — my mother, Elza Bilenko, and my kids, Anton Pleshakov and Anya Pleshakova. Life in general and writing in particular make sense only when one can share.

To my agent, Susan Rabiner. Without Susan, this book would never have been conceived or, of course, placed.

To Joyce Seltzer, of Harvard University Press, who helped me find Susan.

To Eric Chinski, who enthusiastically welcomed me to Houghton Mifflin.

To the editor of this book, Amanda Cook at Houghton Mifflin, who patiently dealt with Stalin's follies and a very tense author who sometimes despaired of interpreting them. To Liz Duvall, who trimmed the book beautifully, and Erica Avery, for all the inquiries.

To Sarah McNally, for her inspiring interest in my writing.

To Edwina Cruise, for laughs and tears.

To Tania Babyonysheva, for insights.

To Sasha Sumerkin, for wisdom and magic.

Special thanks to Bill and Jane Taubman, John Curtis Perry, Marty and Susan Sherwin, and Stephen Jones for their generous and invaluable help in the Kafkaesque Pleshakov Denial Case.

To Joan Cocks, Lev B. Doubnitsky, Leonid Kolpakov, Slava Mogutin, Katia Ozhegova, Katia Yegorova, and Sasha Zotikov, for involvement and support.

To my 2003 Critical Social Thought 350 class at Mount Holyoke College — Alima Bucciantini, Megan Chabalowski, Dori Cohen, Noelle Danian, Amelia (Miles) Goff, Naomi Goldberg, Hannah Hafter, Clodagh Kosior, Laura Norton-Cruz, Clare Robbins, and Sarah (Serafina) Youngdahl-Lombardi — for stimulation.

CONTENTS

LIST OF MAPS

STALIN'S FOLLY

PROLOGUE

Joseph Stalin was an insomniac, often staying up until dawn. But on the evening of June 21, 1941, the absolute ruler of what had once been the czar's immense realm retired uncharacteristically early.

The preceding day had been stressful. Reports of German plans to attack the Soviet Union had been reaching him all day, from many sources. Only a few days before, he hadn't believed such reports. He had not doubted that Hitler would one day turn his rapacious leer on the Soviet Union, but in Stalin's mind that would not happen before spring 1942, after Britain was on its knees. The German General Staff, he believed, would not allow Germany to be bogged down once again, as it had been in 1914, in a two-front war. By then Stalin's own plan, which he had kept secret thus far even from the majority of his generals, would be in place. It called for a full-scale attack on the Germans, one that would allow the Soviet Union to acquire even more of Eastern Europe and join it to the Red empire.

Until mid-June, Stalin had felt fairly secure, and if anything had made him uneasy, it was not the German lines rapidly unfurling along the Soviet Union's western border but the pestering of his two top military commanders, People's Commissar of Defense Semen Timoshenko and the stubborn and outspoken chief of the general staff, Georgy Zhukov.

While the timing of a German attack was settled in Stalin's mind, the generals were far less sanguine. By his order they had developed the top-secret plan to launch the Red Army's offensive down the road, but they also knew that if Germany attacked now, the plan would be irrelevant, and there was no defensive strategy to fall back on, because the dictator deemed such a precaution unnecessary. It was a potentially catastrophic scenario, as the two generals continually reminded him.

Stalin had withheld from them the alarming information he was receiving from his spies in Europe — information that consistently predicted an imminent German attack — but they were receiving sufficiently unnerving reports of their own from the frontier. At least ten German planes were crossing the Soviet border daily, some penetrating 30 miles into Soviet territory. One of the planes had not turned around until it reached Moscow, 650 miles inside the border, where it safely and impudently landed, presumably having reconnoitered the most likely route for the German ground troops from the frontier to the Soviet capital. Timoshenko and Zhukov agreed that intrusions like this unambiguously pointed at Hitler's intention to strike soon. On June 13 they started pressing Stalin to allow them to put the troops on the western border on high alert. "Let's talk about this later," the dictator said, brushing them off.

But in a few days the generals returned, even more determined, and asked for an aggressive regrouping of troops and even a mobilization of reservists.

"Do you understand that this would mean war?" Stalin exploded.

The generals kept silent, and in that meaningful silence Stalin toned down his anger and matter-of-factly asked, "How many divisions do we have in the west?"

"One hundred forty-nine."

"See, this should be enough. The Germans do not have that many."

But Zhukov had his answer ready. "According to our intelligence, a German division has fourteen to sixteen thousand men, and ours just eight thousand."

Stalin became exasperated. "You cannot always trust the intelligence," he snapped.

Zhukov and Timoshenko didn't dare to object, but privately they agreed that this remark was preposterous. However, the cruel irony was that Stalin had a point: because they were denied access to most spy cables, the generals didn't know that spies had already warned of German invasion, first as early as July 1940, then in the first weeks of 1941, then again in April. Now, distrustful by nature, the dictator simply dismissed the spies' warnings as stupidity or, worse, treason.

Throughout the first weeks of June he had met Zhukov's and Timoshenko's pleas with immense irritation and tried to see as little of the generals as possible. However, he had now lost all peace of mind. Spy cables from Bucharest or Helsinki could be ignored, but the concentration of Wehrmacht troops along the border and the presence of Luftwaffe planes in Soviet airspace were hard facts.

Twenty-two months earlier, in August 1939, Stalin had allied himself with Hitler by signing the Soviet-German nonaggression pact. So far the alliance had paid off. Hitler had allowed Stalin to occupy Estonia, Latvia, Lithuania, and the areas of Poland, Romania, and Finland that had been part of the old czarist empire. Eastern Poland had been particularly useful property to acquire, since it pushed the Soviet border 200 miles west.

But annexing territory and gaining control over it are two different matters. Stalin was well aware that the newly acquired territories swarmed with anti-Soviet elements. His police had been working hard, shooting some suspects and sending others to the gulag, but Stalin knew that those who hadn't yet been uprooted would gladly cooperate with the Germans, maybe even operate a sabotage ring at the rear of the Red Army.

He himself had created an even more serious problem. With the annexation of eastern Poland, the Soviet Union had dismantled the fortifications along its original border. But now, twenty months later, the new fortification line was nowhere near finished.

One of the things Stalin admired about Hitler was his audacious nature. If Hitler was indeed planning to strike now, he had picked his moment well, attacking when the Soviet Union was extremely vulnerable.

After much hesitation, on the evening of June 21, Stalin called a secret meeting to put the finishing touches on the preemptive strike plan. The revised plan called for launching an attack within a couple of weeks.

At 8 P.M., with the conference still in progress, he received an urgent call from Zhukov. A German noncommissioned officer had crossed the border to report to the Soviet command that Germany would strike in the small hours of June 22. If the deserter was right, Stalin had less than eight hours to prepare for the onslaught. But when Timoshenko and Zhukov walked into his office fifty minutes later, they found a leader still reluctant to believe that an attack was imminent.

"Could this be a German provocation rather than a real attack?" Stalin asked yet again.

They demurred. "No, we believe the deserter is telling the truth."

Stalin could have cursed the wily Hitler for outfoxing him. He could have cursed himself for ignoring the present danger because he was consumed with carrying out his secret plan in the future. In a moment of courageous leadership, real or fueled by bravado, he could have said, "We will resist them to the last man. Do whatever you have to do to repulse any attack." Instead, locked in the doubt that had prevented him from treating previous reports seriously, he asked, of no one in particular, "What do we do now?"

His question was met with silence — not surprisingly, given the fact that telling Stalin something he did not want to hear often resulted in a one-way ticket to the gulag. However, when Timoshenko judged that enough time had passed, he answered the question bluntly. "We should put the troops at the western border on high alert."

Stalin then learned that Timoshenko and Zhukov had already prepared a preliminary plan for just such a move. Whether he liked it or not, his generals were preparing for war.

"Then read it!" he said with a snort, referring to the document they held in their unsteady hands.

He didn't like the plan. Not at all. He acknowledged that some sort of trouble on the border was possible, but he still could not believe it meant war. Perhaps Hitler was probing to test Soviet readiness for war.

Perhaps he intended to stage a skirmish to use as leverage in future diplomatic bargaining. But war? A war on Soviet soil before Britain had fallen? It just didn't seem possible. His judgment had been right so far, and he would trust it.

The troops' commanders, he announced, were to be informed that a sudden German attack could occur on June 22 or 23 after an unspecified "provocation." Therefore, the troops were to move closer to the border and stay on high alert throughout the night. If a German incursion was detected, however, they were "not to yield to any provocation," in order to prevent "big complications" — in other words, all-out war. In effect, Stalin immobilized his armed forces, since any prompt response to the German attack could be interpreted as falling into Hitler's trap.

Driving back to the People's Commissariat of Defense, Zhukov and Timoshenko didn't exchange a single word, locked in their own thoughts about their predicament. The mighty German war machine was about to attack the Soviet Union, and Stalin had tied their hands.

The two generals chose to spend the night in Timoshenko's office. No officer of the Commissariat of Defense or General Staff was allowed to leave his desk, whether he was on duty that night or not. But at 11 P.M., Stalin headed home, believing that his order had taken care of the situation. Shortly after midnight it would have reached all military district headquarters, and from there it would go to every unit of the Red Army. Or so he thought. Stalin and his top generals did not know that communications in the west had already been disrupted by German saboteurs, acting on Hitler's order on the evening of June 21 to launch a full-scale attack against the Soviet Union the following morning.

▪ ▪ ▪

Almost five hours after Stalin left his office, at 3:45 A.M., General Vlasik, the head of his personal security, awakened him, telling him an urgent call was waiting. Stalin, it was noted, took three minutes to pick up the receiver.

Zhukov was on the phone. He anxiously reported that German planes were bombing all the major Soviet cities along the western border.

Stalin did not respond. All Zhukov could hear was his breathing.

"Did you understand what I said?"

More silence. Finally Stalin asked, "Where is the people's commissar of defense?"

"Talking to the Kiev Military District. I am asking for your permission to open fire to respond."

"Permission not granted," Stalin said. "This is a German provocation. Do not open fire or the situation will escalate. Come to the Kremlin and summon the Politburo."

Zhukov could scarcely believe what he was hearing. The Germans were attacking the Soviet Union, yet the leader of the country was claiming that it was a provocation and postponing critical decisions.

When Zhukov and Timoshenko reached the Kremlin at 5:45 A.M., they found just three others there: the spymaster Lavrenty Beria, the ideological watchdog Lev Mekhlis, and Stalin's always dutiful deputy, Vyacheslav Molotov. Stalin was pale. He was sitting at the table fingering his pipe. The pipe wasn't even filled with tobacco.

"Could this be a provocation on the part of the German generals?" he asked.

"The Germans are bombing our cities in Ukraine, Byelorussia, and the Baltics," Timoshenko responded. "This doesn't look like a provocation."

"When German generals need to set up a provocation," Stalin said, "they will bomb even their own cities . . . Call the German embassy immediately," he ordered.

The embassy was ready for the call. The diplomat on duty said that the ambassador, Count von Schulenburg, had an important statement to make to His Excellency, the people's commissar of foreign affairs, Mr. Molotov.

Shortly after Molotov left to meet with Schulenburg, Zhukov's deputy, General Vatutin, sent word that German troops had started crossing the border. The invasion begged for an immediate response, but Stalin still delayed. "Let's wait for Molotov," he stubbornly muttered.

In a few minutes Molotov slunk into the room, looking shaken. "The German government has declared war on us," he said. Taking his seat at the conference table, he failed to mention that when von Schulenburg had made the fateful announcement, he himself had squeaked, "What have we done to deserve this?"

By Stalin's lights, they had done nothing whatsoever to deserve it. On the contrary, for twenty-two months, since the start of the war in Europe, the Kremlin had been going out of its way to cajole Berlin, as if appeasement had not already been tried at Munich and shown to be ineffective in satiating Hitler's appetite. Only a few days earlier Stalin had shipped nine tons of strategic raw materials — copper, nickel, tin, molybdenum, and wolfram — to military plants in Germany. He had personally authorized German officers to investigate Soviet border areas, allegedly to find the graves of German soldiers lost during World War I, ignoring the repeated warnings of Zhukov and Timoshenko that these trips were logistical intelligence-gathering missions.

Now, having heard the declaration of war, Stalin sank lower in his chair. Although he said nothing, no one else stepped in. Nobody in the room seemed to know what to do next.

▪ ▪ ▪

Just as every American of an older generation remembers where he or she was when John Kennedy's assassination was reported, every elderly Russian remembers where he or she was when the news about the German attack was announced. My family members were among the first in the country to be informed. They knew that war had started even before Joseph Stalin did.

That was not because of some special privilege. My grandparents were not Red moguls but engineers. They were simply unfortunate enough to be employed by a power plant in Sevastopol, located at the tip of the Soviet Union in the Black Sea. Sevastopol was the first Soviet city to be attacked by the Luftwaffe, and the warning my family received was not the Soviet government's statement, delivered nine hours later, at noon, but the German bombs that hit the city at 3:15 in the morning.

My grandmother, Anna Fedorovna Zimina, was a tough woman. A farm girl born in the southern Russian steppes, she left home at the age of ten and went to a big city to enroll in school. At twenty she was already an engineer at a major coal mine, one of the first female professionals in the field. She saw many horrific things: during the civil war, the Communists slaughtered her father in the family's back yard; a few years later, during Stalin's collectivization, the family was thrown out of its house and robbed of all its possessions; at the peak of the Great Terror, she herself was accused of sabotage and nearly lost her life. But no matter how dramatic or appalling these episodes were, none, she said, could compare to what she saw during the Second World War.

By a sheer miracle her family survived the destruction of their house in Sevastopol by a German bomb. When the Soviets were evacuating the city, Anna and her husband were ordered to blow up the power plant at which they worked, but before they could carry out this order the Red Army fled, thus delivering them (and the power plant) into the hands of the Germans. During the German occupation, my grandmother cooked potato peels she stole from the Wehrmacht soldiers; she searched for her sister in the city's ruins; she crossed the Crimean mountains in wintertime, carrying seventy pounds of flour on her back. When her mother died of cancer, she had to dig the grave herself. She refused to go to Germany to provide slave labor and was nearly shot by a German officer for her stubbornness. Once, she and her six-year-old daughter — my mother, Elza — were machine-gunned by Romanian soldiers. (Fortunately for me, Hitler's allies from the chaotic Balkans were tipsy, so they missed.) For my grandmother, two words summed up all these horrors: June 22.

World War II left scars all over Europe, North Africa, the Middle East, the Pacific, and even, remarkably, the Caribbean. Some nations were more traumatized than others, of course. We children who lived in the western part of the Soviet Union in the 1960s knew that we were growing up on an immense battlefield. Twenty years after the war, our soil still readily yielded shrapnel, cartridges, and torn panzer armor. The bullies of my childhood carried German knuckledusters, and occasionally the local newspaper reported the death of a teenager who had discovered a grenade in the woods and attempted to detonate it. In the Black Sea, fishermen's nets regularly caught rusty, spiky mines still floating in the water. Even as late as the 1990s, a hike in the woods practically anywhere between Moscow and the western border took you over wartime trenches; though plowed away in the fields, they remained in the forests. If you cared to, you could easily work out how many machine guns or pieces of artillery had been used there a half-century earlier, because the trenches had been custom-made to accommodate every precious item of scarce weaponry.

▪ ▪ ▪

The ten days following June 22, 1941, changed the Russian people in ways that they have not yet come to terms with. Those days supplied the nation with a nagging feeling of failure, which is one of the reasons that the term "World War II" is used in Russia exclusively by historians and speechwriters, when everyone else still refers to the conflict as "the war."

Consider the following: In the first three weeks of war, twenty-eight Soviet infantry divisions were destroyed, and those that survived lost half or more of their men. In the first twenty days, the Soviets lost one in five soldiers stationed near the front — approximately 600,000 men, out of roughly 3 million. In the vicinity of Minsk alone, 328,898 Soviet soldiers were taken prisoner of war. Tens of thousands remained missing.

To this day, no one knows how many Soviet lives were lost in regaining this ground. In 1945, when the Allies were victorious, Stalin set the figure at 10 million. His successor Nikita Khrushchev liberally added 10 million more. Under Mikhail Gorbachev the official figure jumped to 27 million; some independent estimates now put it at 50 million. It may be that the accurate figure will never be known. Between 1941 and 1945, nobody kept track of the dead, either at the forward positions or in the struggling rear. After the war, attempts to reconstruct what had happened would have been seen by the authorities as subversive, such was the Soviet tyranny over information — and history.

According to even the most conservative estimates originating in the Russian General Staff, however, the Soviet Union lost between 8.6 and 11.4 million soldiers (Hitler lost 3.25 million combatants in both the west and the east). A further 5.8 million Soviet soldiers were captured by the Nazis, to be used as slave labor in concentration camps; at least 3 million of these died. Although Britain and France entered the war two years earlier and Britain was subjected to extensive German bombing, neither they nor the United States lost anywhere near the number of soldiers and civilians who died defending the Soviet Union. The total figures for both civilian and military casualties for France, Britain, and the United States are 810,000, 388,000 and 295,000, respectively — in other words, 1.9, 0.8, and 0.4 percent of their populations. The official Soviet figure of 27 million casualties corresponds to about 13.6 percent. It is also known that 1,710 Soviet cities and towns and 70,000 villages were destroyed or severely damaged, as were 40,000 hospitals, 84,000 schools, and 43,000 libraries — a scale of devastation unparalleled in modern history.

Of course, war statistics are about not only the dead but the living. Twenty-nine million Soviets fought at one point or another at the front, including 800,000 women. All came back with physical or mental wounds that would never fully heal; all were exposed to the criminal ineffectiveness of the regime; all returned exhausted and disillusioned. Some belonged to units that lost more than half their tanks to clogged engines and bad roads before they even contacted the enemy, others to units that were tossed around for days by incompetent generals before they were finally allowed to die for the motherland. Some lost their families in blazing military compounds at the front line, because no evacuation of civilians had been sanctioned.

Life at the rear was almost as horrific. The collapse of the Soviet military allowed the Germans to advance 350 miles east in the first ten days and bring under their control a number of the best industrial and farming areas of the Soviet Union. By the end of June 1941, 20 million Soviets were living on territory controlled by the German Reich. Jews and Communists were arrested and taken to execution sites, and others had to face the protracted agony of famine and racial harassment, to say nothing of calamities such as epidemics and extreme cold. Hitler had forbidden the administrators of the occupied territories to provide the local population with health care and education. He planned to send German settlers to the fertile lands of Ukraine. As for Russia itself, he intended to turn it into a wasteland, with probably one exception: he wished to have a reservoir built where St. Petersburg stood.

The war's impact on Soviet society lingered long after Hitler's defeat. During the war Stalin's regime proved staggeringly inept at everything except crushing domestic dissent and using millions as cannon fodder, and that is why the Soviets entered the postwar world feeling at once betrayed by their leaders and thoroughly intimidated by them. The age-long Russian gap between the rulers and the ruled widened, resulting in renewed passivity among the people and reinvigorated impunity within the system.

The Kremlin successfully used the June 22 trauma to keep its people at bay: no matter how extreme the food shortages or how absent the civil liberties, Soviet citizens were constantly reminded that war was much worse. A whole industry of war movies, songs, and novels sprang to life and were unabashedly exploited by the government to make excuses for its numerous inadequacies. The 27 million lives lost during the war became mere propaganda, manipulated to cajole the living into obedience.

The war also killed Soviet feminism. Before the war women had been aircraft pilots and cabinet ministers; after 1945, despite the fact that nearly a million women had fought at the front and millions of others had labored alongside men, they were sent back to the kitchen. The sense of military male camaraderie forged during the war years took the nation back to its old patriarchal ways. In turn, Joseph Stalin, who had partly abandoned Communism for the sake of Russian nationalism during the war, discarded feminism as an un-Russian, alien notion.

The war also exacerbated the already serious drinking habits bred into Russian culture over many cold winters. True, Russians have never been known for moderation when it comes to alcohol. But at Stalin's personal order, 28 million men were given a glass of vodka a day for four years, thus ensuring that the next generation would be fully trained to function in an inebriated nation.

The scars of war still prevent Russians and Eastern Europeans from coming to terms with each other in the twenty-first century. Lithuanians, Ukrainians, Poles, and others recall that Moscow dismembered

Eastern Europe in its businesslike partnership with Hitler in 1939–1940 and then occupied it completely in 1944–1945, while Russians reproach Eastern Europeans for sabotaging the Soviet war effort in June 1941. To many Ukrainians, the urban guerrillas of the Organization of Ukrainian Nationalists who attacked Soviet troops in Lvov on June 24, 1941, look like freedom fighters; to many Russians, they continue to be seen as despicable pro-Nazi terrorists.

Because the Soviet people were not sufficiently informed about the responsibility of their own leaders for the June 22 catastrophe and because they had suffered so much from the ensuing invasion, they were easily led at the end of the war into a fierce xenophobia. The impact on Russia's foreign policy continues to this day, and can best be seen in the country's staunch opposition to NATO's expansion in Eastern Europe. The punch line of a recent anti-NATO editorial reads: "We will not let another June 22 happen."

▪ ▪ ▪

The first ten days of war in the Soviet western borderland were among the most devastating of World War II. The Germans advanced as much as 150 miles in the south and 350 miles in the north. So great was the advantage conceded to the Germans that it was not until the end of 1944, just months before the end of the war, that the front between the two armies was back at the preattack line of June 21.

Nonetheless, the story of how and why this advantage was given to the Germans has remained largely untold. Why? Because while the Communists remained in power, they did not want it discussed and so did not make the necessary documentation available. Thus, most of those who have written about the Russian experience during World War II have had to focus their narratives on a number of episodes in which Soviet troops behaved gloriously, such as the battle of Stalingrad and the siege of Leningrad.

With the collapse of the Soviet Union in 1991, however, Russians began reevaluating their past and deconstructing numerous ideological myths, distortions, and untruths. While historians were unearthing copious documents in the archives, families of dead marshals were publishing their uncensored memoirs, and veterans were providing uncensored oral histories, the tragic events of 1941–1945 became the subject of many heated debates. This new material has already significantly enriched a number of books on Leningrad and Stalingrad and can now be put to use to tell the real story of the ten days following June 22, 1941.

The variety of new sources is truly impressive. Among the most important are cables from Soviet spies and diplomats around the world, classified Politburo documents, General Staff and police memorandums, Stalin's office logs (which are incredibly helpful, dryly registering the meetings that some generals chose so conveniently to forget), high command orders and decrees, and the authentic memoirs and notes of Politburo member Anastas Mikoyan, Marshal Georgy Zhukov, Admiral Nikolai Kuznetsov, Marshal Matvei Zakharov, Marshal Konstantin Rokossovsky, and a number of lesser generals and state functionaries. Such evidence was overwhelmingly important when researching this book, making it possible to disprove the conventional wisdom on a number of key points.

It is now clear that Stalin was indeed preparing a preemptive strike against Germany, a subject long debated by historians. Though no smoking gun has been found in the archives yet — no document signed by Stalin naming the date of the attack — the new evidence demonstrates that the leader of the Soviet people started planning as early as the summer of 1940 and hoped to launch the invasion by the summer of 1942. We now have access to a succession of war plans drafted between August 1940 and May 1941 and also a number of top-secret Party and army directives. In light of this, the tantalizing hints of a preemptive strike that have been torturing historians for decades finally make perfect sense.

Contrary to popular belief, Stalin did not sink into criminal passivity in the spring of 1941, refusing to act on reports of the concentration of German troops on the border. He was aware of the danger, but he continued to believe that Hitler would not be able to strike before the summer of 1942. Thinking that he still had time, he kept postponing the final war preparations. It was not until Japan's foreign minister, Yosuke

Matsuoka, visited Moscow and signed a neutrality pact in April, thus securing the Soviet Union's eastern flank, that Stalin ordered preparations for a preemptive strike. This happened between April 15 and May 5, but it was already too late; his indecisiveness cost the nation dearly, as the Red Army got caught in a strategic limbo between offense and defense and consequently was ready for neither.

The value of the 1941 intelligence reports warning of the imminent German attack now has to be reevaluated. Some of them did guess the date of the invasion more or less correctly — but the same sources had been predicting it for about a year, and the flow of outrageously misleading telegrams announcing German attack as early as the summer of 1940 had made Stalin skeptical about the reliability of intelligence in general.

Close study of the documents related to the debacle of June 1941 leads us to conclude that the overall efficiency of Stalin's regime has been grossly overrated. No institution in the country functioned effectively on the eve of war: the army had no reserve command posts, the Kremlin had no underground bunker, the railroads couldn't keep track of the military echelons, the defense industry didn't know how to make time bombs. Even Stalin's police, normally described as the perfect instrument of intimidation and control, failed to intercept German commandos who managed to paralyze the Red Army by interrupting almost all cable communications in the western part of the country on the night of June 21.

It is very clear now that during the catastrophe in the western borderlands, no senior officer suggested withdrawing the retreating Soviet armies to the rear, as the Russian generals had done in 1812, when the country had also found itself overwhelmed — that time by Napoleon's invasion. It appears that everyone at the top willingly agreed with Stalin's assessment that a planned withdrawal equaled surrender. As for the strategic value of the horrific bloodbath in the west, sometimes called a fighting retreat, it was ultimately worthless. Drained by meaningless resistance and counterstrikes ordered by Stalin, the Soviet armies disintegrated in a matter of days and left the hinterland unprotected. That led to the loss of Ukraine and the northern Caucasus and allowed the

Germans to reach the Volga River. The disastrous routing of the Southwestern Front in Ukraine, after the devastated army group was forced to counterattack, was the culmination of that strategic madness.

We now know the true degree of Stalin's withdrawal from state affairs after the start of the war. It used to be claimed that he either sank into depression or never abandoned the helm. Neither is true; he kept the helm precariously unstable. He was absent from his Kremlin office for just two days, June 29 and June 30, yet his usual wartime office hours, during which he was technically in, look shockingly short and generally misconceived. When the first battle reports arrived in Moscow in the morning, the dictator was fast asleep. By the time he reached the Kremlin, in the late afternoon or evening, the Germans had advanced 30 miles and his instructions, based on the morning reports, had become irrelevant.

People's Commissar of Defense Timoshenko and Chief of General Staff Zhukov did their best on the eve of the invasion to persuade Stalin that the attack was imminent, but new sources suggest that their performance during the first ten days of war was poor. In most cases they fulfilled their roles as yes men, lecturing the field commanders on the merits of the suicidal counterstrikes ordered by Stalin. In the next three years Zhukov became *the* Soviet World War II hero, and in May 1945 his troops took Hitler's lair in Berlin, yet it is now clear that the traditional interpretation of Zhukov as a sage of the Red Army, a brilliant strategist, and an honest soldier has been far too generous. The suicidal mission of the Southwestern Front troops that he supervised in June 1941, which he kept bragging about after the war, is a good example. Endowed with outstanding willpower, considerable talent, and amazing ruthlessness, Zhukov deservedly presided over the assembly of marshals, but neither he nor the lesser stars, from Timoshenko to the gulag survivor Konstantin Rokossovsky, was blessed with empathy or sensibility. Men of steel, they might have won the right to be reincarnated as monuments, but definitely not as icons.

Another inevitable conclusion of any study of the newly available sources is that the Great Terror of 1937–1939 was completely rational from Stalin's perspective. It has traditionally been argued that the prewar purge that killed about 35,000 Red Army officers was one of the reasons for the terrible defeats of the summer of 1941. This is surely true, as the troops were consequently led by inexperienced and often ill-prepared commanders. But the purge was also the source of the Soviet regime's strength. Without that seemingly irrational terror, which had killed people virtually at random, a military coup d'état or a popular revolt against Stalin would almost certainly have occurred in the first days or weeks after the German invasion. Hundreds of thousands, if not millions, had grievances against the system — the best proof being the 300,000 soldiers who joined General Andrei Vlasov's Russian Liberation Army, a collaborationist military force formed by the Nazis among the Soviet POWs. Without a doubt, many joined such units simply to escape the Nazi concentration camps, but it is indisputable that to many others the German invasion looked like a chance to topple Stalin. Not only Vlasov but quite a few Red Army generals collaborated with the Germans — men like Major General Pavel Bogdanov, a veteran who had temporarily lost his Party membership during the Great Terror for having had a sexual relationship with a typist "who had direct connections to three enemies of the people." In June 1941 he commanded the Forty-eighth Division on the Northwestern Front, which was decimated in three days. In the POW camp he immediately turned in two commissars, who were subsequently shot; later on he joined the Second Russian Squad of the SS.

The list of generals like Bogdanov is rather long, proving that many military professionals were willing to fight the despotic regime of Stalin and his Party — but only after they were out of its reach, on German terrain. The Great Terror saved the dictator and his system; instead of collapsing in the summer of 1941, as it should have, it survived for another fifty years.

The consequences are painful to contemplate. In 1941, no force in the world was more dangerous than Hitler's juggernaut, but the continued existence of Stalin's regime resulted in enormous suffering across the world when Stalin unleashed a new round of purges in the Soviet Union and then spread his government's misery to Poland, Hungary, Czechoslovakia, Bulgaria, Romania, Yugoslavia, Albania, North Korea, and China. At the same time, if the Soviet people had not recovered from the enormous advantage Stalin gave the invading Germans in June 1941, the result would have been catastrophic. A victory over the Soviet Union would have left Hitler's armies free to reach the Middle East and, after that, India, and in a matter of months to join ranks with the Japanese in the Pacific. The Allies could then anticipate their joint attack on the United States — an enormous challenge to withstand, even for such a powerful nation. It is therefore not surprising that Winston Churchill, despite his intense dislike of Communism, declared Britain's support for the Soviet Union in its most desperate hour.

Still, Stalin's great folly in these first ten days made Hitler's triumph very likely. Thanks to the whimsical mindset of the Red dictator in June 1941, the world came very close to one of the greatest calamities in history.

1

WAR GAME

January 2, 1941: The Kremlin

The end of 1940 was grim. Two armies, one clad in gray, the other in khaki, were destroying the Old World. They had thrown themselves at Europe abruptly and ferociously, like ants attacking a cake left on a garden table. And like ants, they arrived in geometrically impeccable columns, never questioning their right to devour the trophy.

The ants were of two different species. The grays took orders from the German Führer, Adolf Hitler; the khakis closed ranks around the Soviet leader, or *vozhd,* Joseph Stalin. Having been dismissed by cultured European politicians, cartoonists, and sketch writers as pests that could be stamped out by the civilized world in a flash, the ants had proved their worth by 1940.

France crumbled under the wheels of German tanks in less than three weeks. The British force on the continent, expected to save the day, was decimated at Dunkirk. As headlines shouted about the impending demise of these two great powers, pillars of the West since the days of the Crusades, smaller European nations such as Belgium, Holland, Denmark, Poland, Czechoslovakia, and Norway wriggled under German occupation, their cries unheard by the panicking world.

At the other end of the continent, the Red Army grabbed Lithuania, Latvia, and Estonia and tore away chunks of Poland, Finland, and Romania.

In both the west and the east, killings were performed speedily and expertly: troops swept through the ancient cities, blind to decorum, and the punitive squads followed immediately to scavenge, to cleanse, to kill. Hitler's men looked for Jews and Communists; Stalin's went for the "exploiting classes."

The proud and elaborate European order, which had taken centuries to create, was smashed in less than a year, because the two armies acted in accord. Hitler let Stalin do what he wanted to on the fringes of Europe, and Stalin turned a blind eye to the plight of the West and even reined in his fifth column abroad, the fanatically anti-Nazi Comintern. But this was not a partnership of equals — Hitler snatched the best pieces, and Stalin collected the crumbs. Kaunas was a poor match for Paris, the port of Riga didn't fare nearly as well as that of Rotterdam, and Romanian Cabernet hardly deserved the name when compared to the French varieties.

At the end of 1940 a weird lull fell over Europe. The two armies had reached an impasse. Germany's hunger could not be sated by the annexation of the few lesser countries, like Yugoslavia and Greece, that were still stubbornly maintaining their sovereignty. The Germans had to launch a spectacular conquest to justify their roll across Europe; that was what all other empires had done at the peak of their might, and that was what Adolf Hitler had promised the German people.

They had few options. One was to invade Britain, another the Middle East; yet another was to strike at the Soviet Union. At the end of 1940 nobody knew which path Hitler would choose.

Virtually every person in the Soviet Union had heard about *Mein Kampf,* Hitler's manifesto, published years before and now distributed to German newlyweds as a state gift. In the book Hitler promised the Germans virtually unlimited living space, *lebensraum,* on the immense plains between the Danube and the Urals, which now belonged to the Union of Soviet Socialist Republics, formerly the Russian Empire. Since

August 1939 the two countries had been allies, but few Soviets doubted that the deal would be short-lived. They also knew that almost every prominent general in the USSR had been shot during the Great Purge, and the talent and vigor of the men who replaced them had yet to be tested.

No matter how much the newspapers bragged about the prosperity of the Communist motherland, people knew that just ten years before, few households had had electricity and people had been signing papers with an X because they couldn't read or write. The workers building power plants, factories, and dams still lived in wooden shacks and muddy holes. In 1932 the government ordered so much grain from Ukraine, with its unsurpassed black earth, that its people suffered a fierce famine. Meanwhile, Germany was a nation of science, efficiency, and advancement.

None of this bode well for the nations that had been forcibly herded into the Union of Soviet Socialist Republics over the course of the past twenty-three years. The Red Army, whose soldiers were drafted from urbane Leningrad and arrogant Moscow, demure Byelorussia and warlike Chechnya, Islamic Uzbekistan and Buddhist Buryatia, froze in suspense, anticipating the *vozhd*'s instructions. But as yet no order had come its way.

▪ ▪ ▪

In the fall of 1940 the Soviet people discovered that their woods were studded with an amazing number of mushrooms. Highly prized as a delicacy by both rich and poor, mushrooms rarely survived the month of September, since they were enthusiastically picked and then pickled, boiled, fried, dried, and sautéed. However, in 1940 the mushrooms were so plentiful that no matter how many were gathered, many more sprang forth — not just the uninspiring yellow chanterelles and the barely edible scarlet russulas, but also the czar of the forest, the delicious and beautiful King Boletus.

In a country devastated by economic barbarism and political ineptitude, such a surprising harvest should have been a welcome supplement to a meager diet. It wasn't. Every adult in that superstitious land knew that the unusual abundance of mushrooms meant just one thing: war.

▪ ▪ ▪

In the early evening of January 2, 1941, the generals were summoned to the Kremlin.

The order came without warning. The generals were important, and so was their mission in Moscow — they were attending an annual conference — yet nobody was sure whether the "heir of Lenin," the "genius of all times and peoples," Iosif Vissarionovich Stalin, would deign to see them.

Regardless of the awe the leader inspired in their hearts, the generals knew that he must have been alarmed by what was happening in the west of the country. The strongest army in the world, Hitler's Wehrmacht, rustled and coiled along the border like a gigantic serpent, and it was hard to believe that its intentions were peaceful.

The very fact that they had been summoned to the conference indicated that the *vozhd* was concerned about the state of the army. Conferences of military leaders were held annually, but this assembly was extraordinary. Usually the gatherings were attended by district commanders, their commissars, and chiefs of staff, but this time they were joined by a number of army, corps, and even division leaders, and the meeting was to be followed by a comprehensive strategic game.

The generals were uneasy. The most recent execution of military leaders had occurred less than two years before. All of the participants in the conference had benefited from the carnage, as the murders had created lucrative vacancies. However, they could not be sure that the butchery would not resume, this time destroying them as it had destroyed their predecessors.

Also, they were confused. Throughout the 1930s they had been taught that Nazism was a belligerent and therefore dangerous ideology. Now, however, their country was bound to Nazi Germany by a pact and also by the joint conquest of Eastern Europe.

Throughout the conference week, five reports and fifty presentations were made. One report definitely stood out: that supplied by the commander of the Kiev Military District, Army General Georgy Zhukov, on "The Nature of Modern Offensive Operation." Zhukov thought big. In his view, to win a war, an army group had to use at least eighty-five rifle divisions, four mechanized corps, two cavalry corps, and thirty air force divisions. In all, Zhukov suggested, a strike would involve about 1.5 million men, 8,000 aircraft, and 5,000 tanks.

Nobody had ever fought a war like that. Whether the generals agreed with Zhukov or not — and some found his presentation presumptuous — he inspired respect. The man was remarkably vigorous, ambitious, and blunt, qualities all but lost to the army in the recent purge. He looked like he had stepped in from another, happier age, when ingenuity and risk-taking were still the marks of the military man.

Zhukov was not the only star of the conference. The commander of the Western Military District, Colonel General Dmitry Pavlov, also delivered a rousing report. Pavlov compared tank operations of World War I to those currently unfolding in Europe. The differences were staggering. During the Battle of the Somme, Pavlov said, tanks had advanced two and a half miles in three hours, and that had been trumpeted as a major success. In May and June 1940, however, the German panzers had crushed all of France in seventeen days. Pavlov sounded motivated and keen, and his presentation was well received. In a way, his report complemented Zhukov's, advocating aggressive use of modern weaponry, but after Pavlov spoke the two generals began to look at each other apprehensively, as their rivalry became clear.

On New Year's Eve the junior corps and division commanders were sent back home. Senior generals started preparing for the strategic game, which would pit the "Reds" against the "Blues" — or the Soviets against the Germans. Unexpectedly, before they began, the generals were told that Stalin required their presence.

▪ ▪ ▪

By 1941 the Kremlin was four and a half centuries old. The Italian architects invited to build it must have felt overwhelmed by the task. For starters, the grand prince of Moscow, Ivan III, needed a castle that could withstand any deadly attack, and Muscovite Russia was endowed with unfortunate strategic terrain: it was remarkably flat, with no significant natural obstacles to deter an enemy's onslaught. It was also landlocked by three assertive powers, Sweden, Poland, and the Ottoman Empire. The Ottomans' vassals, the Crimean Tatars, looted Russia every spring, so they knew their way to Moscow well; they had recently pillaged and burned the Russian capital. So, among other things, the Kremlin had to be fireproof.

Ivan wanted the new castle to inspire artistic respect too. After the collapse of Byzantium, he had married its heiress, Zoë Palaiologos, and he regarded himself as a successor to the glamorous rulers of Constantinople. In other words, the fortress had to look like a palace. There had never been a shortage of land in Russia, so the prince designated a huge chunk of it for this project, which made the architects' task even more challenging.

After their initial frustration, the Italians performed valiantly. The new fortress was virtually impenetrable. Its walls were thirty feet high and ran for almost a mile and a half, forming a firm ring atop a hill. That made the Kremlin one of the largest structures in Europe. It was among the gloomiest, too. The red brick with which it was built looked dull even on a sunny day, and its towers were extremely tall and loomed menacingly over the city. Its roofs were shaped like nomadic tents, giving the aura of a military camp. For security reasons the castle was built as a huge triangle, so that the sentries on its towers would have a good view of the walls, but its shape was uncompromisingly sharp. On maps the Kremlin looked like a pointed tooth biting into Moscow's flesh.

Ironically, given the monolithic nature of the word *kremlin* today, every major Russian city used to have such a structure. A kremlin — the word means "citadel" in Russian — crowned a hill on a riverbank, and each time nomads attacked from the steppes or a rival prince from the woods, the townsfolk sought shelter behind its walls. There they could count on two things, water and prayer, for every kremlin had a church and a well. As for other essentials, like food and cover, these were reserved for the prince and his army.

Gradually kremlins became extinct. The Kremlin devoured them. The rulers of Moscow crushed their opponents and destroyed their castles. Peter the Great, the illustrious westernizer, wanted every Russian city to look like Amsterdam, so kremlins had to be torn down to provide the space needed for baroque chapels and neoclassical mansions. Two centuries after Peter, the Bolsheviks launched their own orgy of reconstruction when revolution delivered Russia into their hands. Kremlins gave way to factories, streetcars, and Marxist statues. But the Moscow kremlin was spared: it became the seat of a government that was afraid of its own people and therefore used the Kremlin's protective walls and watchtowers to powerful effect.

Few at the time of the revolution knew that Lenin was more coward than hero. Politically courageous, he simply could not handle physical danger. As soon as the civil war started, he fled the front in Petrograd (as St. Petersburg was then called). A hastily commandeered train took him and his accomplices to Moscow, where cars rushed them to the Kremlin. Lenin didn't like what he saw. The walls were indeed high and thick, but the structure was populated by a coterie of palace servants, priests, monks, and nuns. Lenin firmly ordered them out. He also called for the destruction of the monasteries and Romanov monuments on the grounds and gleefully participated in the demolition himself.

Soon the citadel was spacious and quiet. The only intruding sound was the cawing of crows. In 1918, Russians were dying of starvation and there was not much for the crows to scavenge in the garbage bins of Moscow. But food could always be found in the Kremlin. Scanning the citadel for leftovers, hundreds of birds assembled on its spires. The guards started shooting them, but the noise upset Lenin even more than the crows' noise, and the hunt was called off.

Uninterested in luxuries that he could easily afford, Lenin lived in a tiny apartment with his wife and sister. His tastes were spartan, and the apartment looked like a ward in an orphanage: tidy, gray, minimalist, with narrow and bumpy iron beds, crippled tables, and shabby chairs. Lenin didn't spend much time there anyway, preferring his study, which was conveniently located just across the hallway. That was where he did all his writing and worked for the survival of his new utopian state.

At night the Kremlin felt particularly eerie. When the crows were asleep and few people and cars were around, the citadel was completely silent. The steps of a bodyguard pacing the cobblestone yard produced an alarming echo. The engine of an automobile roared like a highland brook. The Kremlin's palaces were abandoned, its churches locked, its past discarded. With its svelte white bell towers resembling lilies and its golden church domes like thistle globes, the citadel bore the look of a petrified garden.

In the days of the czars, every Muscovite could see the ruler. All anyone had to do was go to the Kremlin on a big church holiday — the czar would be there, spectacular in his golden robes studded with jewels, possibly even distributing candies and linen scarves to the faithful. By the 1940s, though, very few people had access to the Kremlin. Its image was printed on countless posters, stamps, and postcards, but for most people the place was unreal, much like the mysterious demigod who now inhabited it.

▪ ▪ ▪

The generals walked into Stalin's office at 7:30 P.M. Even the few who had seen the *vozhd* in person couldn't take their eyes off the man. From a distance — say, in a convention hall — Stalin looked unimposing: a short, stooping, thickset, visibly aged man. But in a smaller space he was an overwhelming presence. The first thing people noticed was his bright light-brown eyes, which were nearly yellow: weirdly intense, discomforting, almost animalistic in their quiet alertness. All his other features — his low brow, thick hair, mustache, pockmarks — seemed to fade away in the enigmatic glow of his eyes.

The *vozhd* spoke slowly, quietly, and clearly, carefully punctuating each sentence with a pause, almost never sitting down while he talked but wandering around like a restless beast. Occasionally he would stop directly in front of a visitor, deliberately entering his private space and staring him right in the eye.

By Soviet standards, Stalin's office was large, its walls richly paneled with oak, the table covered by an ostentatious green cloth. Portraits of Marx, Engels, and Lenin were the sole decorations on the bare walls. The furniture was uncomfortable, and Stalin's desk was littered with piles of papers and maps. The only organized objects were the telephones and a bunch of freshly sharpened colored pencils. Those close to Stalin knew that he preferred blue ones.

That night the *vozhd* was in a bad mood. He barely nodded to the generals before embarking on a long and scathing criticism of their leader, Semen Timoshenko, the people's commissar of defense. Stalin announced that he had spent the whole night of December 30 going through a draft of Timoshenko's speech, editing it line by line, only to find that Timoshenko had presented the unsanctioned version the following day. Now all his corrections were useless. "Timoshenko has made a mistake," he snarled.

Each time the *vozhd* became angry, he got noticeably pale and his eyes grew cold. Few dared to contradict him at those moments. The generals could not understand what had annoyed him so much, since Timoshenko's concluding remarks at the conference had been extraordinarily cautious. In all likelihood, Stalin had something else on his mind.

After lecturing the generals on the virtues of respect and discipline, the *vozhd* finally asked, "When is the game?"

"Tomorrow morning," Timoshenko answered, visibly unnerved.

"All right, go ahead . . . But do not let the commanders relax . . . Who will be playing for the Blues and who for the Reds?"

"Army General Zhukov will be playing for the Blues, Colonel General Pavlov for the Reds."

Even Stalin must have appreciated the casting of the rival generals in these roles, but he didn't let on if so. At 9:45 the generals left the Kremlin, feeling intimidated and depressed. The encounter had made Georgy Zhukov all the more determined to win the following day. He was a Soviet poster boy, and as such, he couldn't afford to fail.

January 3–13: General Staff, Moscow

When Georgy Zhukov was nine, he spent a night in a cemetery on a bet. The Kaluga province, where he was born in 1896, was one of the poorest in Russia. The family had meat only at Christmas and Easter, and their house was so old that one day its roof collapsed.

Like every other child in the village, Georgy started working in the fields when he was seven. He didn't complain, because everyone around him worked until completely exhausted. In fact, his mother often lifted 170-pound sacks of grain all by herself.

The boy was obstinate. No matter how hard his father beat him, he never apologized for misbehaving. Once, after a particularly severe beating, he spent three days hiding in the fields, angry and rebellious; when he finally returned, his father beat him again.

For three years Georgy went to a local church school. He was an excellent student, but there was no way he could continue his education. Food at home was scarce, so when he was eleven his father sent him to Moscow to work for a furrier.

Moscow made the boy speechless. It was fast and noisy and mean. On his first day there, in a stampede to enter a streetcar, he was hit so hard on the nose by a fellow passenger's heel that blood poured out. In retrospect, that was a fitting introduction to his new life.

The furrier's shop opened at six in the morning and closed at eleven at night. Apprentices like Georgy slept on the floor, and at mealtime they were the last ones permitted to approach the pot; usually by then no meat was left. Each time an apprentice did something wrong, he was thrashed. Sometimes the boys were beaten just because the furrier was in a bad mood, and occasionally the beating was so hard that they had ringing in their ears for the rest of the day. The furrier took real pleasure in watching pain: often he forced two boys to lash each other with branches of honeysuckle, the particularly hard wood used to straighten furs. When the furrier felt good about life — which was rare — he took the apprentices to a mass in the Dormition Cathedral, in the Kremlin. The cathedral was famous for its choir, and a visit there was regarded as a special treat.

Georgy remained restless. He discovered reading and enrolled in an evening school. When he turned fifteen, he was allowed a ten-day leave to visit home. He hadn't seen his family for four years. His parents had aged and looked very old, and life in the village was just as miserable as it had ever been. The teenager knew he would never go back.

Three years later, an angry young man from another poor country shot the Austrian archduke, and a world war began. In Moscow it started with the looting of German and Austrian stores. Zhukov felt intoxicated by the patriotic sentiment that enveloped the city and for a while toyed with the idea of enlisting, but he was in love, and he was finally making some money, so he procrastinated. But in August 1915 he was drafted.

Although short, Zhukov was handsome. The czarist army was very concerned with appearances, and since it would have been a waste to keep such a good-looking young man in the infantry, he was sent to an elite dragoon unit. In September 1916 he found himself on the front line in the southwest. He fought in a number of battles, was seriously shell-shocked, spent two months in a hospital, and then returned to the front. By the time the revolution swept away the monarchy in 1917, he was already a noncommissioned officer with two Saint George crosses — a rare distinction for someone from the lower classes.

At first Zhukov did not want to get involved with politics. He joined the Red Army only in August 1918, when the country was already engulfed in an atrocious civil war. One of Lenin's slogans was "Those who have been nothing will become everything," and that told Zhukov all he needed to know, and it resonated with millions of other peasants' and workers' children. No matter how badly equipped the Reds were and how infinitely more sophisticated the antirevolutionary Whites were, Lenin's message earned him victory. In the fall of 1920, the last White unit left European Russia for Istanbul to join a flock of desperate exiles. Fighting continued on the periphery of the empire, but by the mid-1920s the Communist victory was secure.

Lenin's plan for Russia, making it a kind of perpetually expanding anthill, was dreadful. Communist ants were to become identical, unsentimental, hardworking, and fierce. They were to value equality and the joys of labor above anything else, and they were expected to be violent yet disciplined. Having taken revenge on those who were privileged inside the country, they were supposed to proceed to Berlin, Paris, and New York to establish the anthill ways there and turn these cities into Moscow's franchises. That was called world revolution.

Zhukov enthusiastically joined in the great utopian enterprise. During the following ten years he was busy with studying, being promoted, and starting a family. Meanwhile, Stalin succeeded Lenin and quickly got rid of all the other Party leaders. Leon Trotsky, the founder of the Red Army and the most illustrious of Stalin's rivals, was exiled; others were transferred to ridiculously unimportant jobs. None were imprisoned — yet.

Still, the nation was quickly forgetting the meaning of the word *dissent.* Experimental artists got no commissions, writers who didn't subscribe to the Party line couldn't publish, and it became impossible to travel abroad without the Party's permission. Newspapers switched from news to brainwashing and from criticism to flattery. Dissenting intellectuals and the bourgeoisie were arrested and sent to labor camps.

Officers like Zhukov couldn't care less. They didn't go to art shows, read very few books, distrusted foreign cultures, believed in discipline, and applauded class revenge. They had starved as children and thought that it was high time somebody paid for that injustice.

Yet the next campaign Stalin launched, collectivization, was extreme by almost any measure. Richer peasants, or people who were denounced by neighbors as richer peasants because they had a second cow or an extra shed, were detained and then shipped east and north by cattle car. In the wilderness, the trains stopped and unloaded millions of men, women, and children. Sometimes they were given spades to dig holes for themselves, and sometimes they weren't. Nobody knew how many died, and nobody bothered to count. In place of private farms, worthless collectives, the pitiful *kolkhozes,* were supposed to power the economy.

The vast majority of Red Army cadres were peasants' sons. They knew the principles of village politics better than they knew the work of Marx or Clausewitz. Even if they were happy to see the end of more prosperous people who had battered them in their youth, they knew that rural communities were run by envy, suspicion, and malice, opening the way to an enormous abuse of power. They still had families in the countryside, and the stories of collectivization were appalling. Nonetheless, they remembered Lenin's motto and preferred to tolerate the ills of Party rule for the sake of the class retribution they called justice.

Liberally using slave labor, Stalin proceeded to industrialize the country. The process was hasty, violent, and ugly. Many projects were undertaken against common sense; costs and mistakes were ignored.

Each accomplishment was attributed to the *vozhd*, who was now hailed as the father of the Soviet people. Nonetheless, in a few years the nation was benefiting from the electricity, railroads, dams, automobiles, and aircraft provided by industrialization.

Everybody had to go to school now, and the conscripts Zhukov was overseeing were considerably better educated than those of his own draft class. They could all read and write, some could explain the law of gravity and recite Pushkin or even Walt Whitman, and many believed in the bright future. They were sure that the Party was doing the right thing and that the rest of the world would soon join the grand Communist endeavor.

▪ ▪ ▪

Nineteen thirty-seven became synonymous with the Great Terror. Purges had started much earlier, but that year they reached mind-boggling proportions. Zhukov might not have known enough about any purged civilians, like the former head of the government, Alexei Rykov, or the ex-chairman of the Comintern, Grigory Zinoviev, to regret their deaths, but he had met many of the purged military leaders personally and was sure that none of them could have been spying for Britain or Germany, let alone intending to blow up the Kremlin. If Stalin's rationale for killing the wise men of the Party remained unclear to Zhukov, he could see that the *vozhd* was motivated by fear, suspicion, and vengefulness when he purged the generals. Some of the executed men had long wished Stalin ill and some had been too close to the Party's old guard, particularly Trotsky, but all were potentially dangerous, for they commanded soldiers with rifles. An avid student of history, the *vozhd* kept reminding his colleagues that the French Revolution was followed by a coup d'état staged by a cocky general. He wanted no daring military leaders left. Rumor had it that as early as 1925 he had killed the greatest of them, Mikhail Frunze, by means of unnecessary surgery for a stomach ulcer.

A military professional like Zhukov knew that Marshal Mikhail Tukhachevsky and Stalin had been angrily debating for years over which of them had been responsible for a humiliating defeat at the doorstep of Warsaw in 1920, when Tukhachevsky had been a twenty-seven-year-old front commander and Stalin a forty-one-year-old Party emissary. Zhukov could also see how the charismatic Marshal Vassily Bliukher, a legendary civil war hero who until recently had been commanding troops in the Far East, could be regarded by Stalin as a budding Napoleon. However, outside the range of top commanders, logic failed. Stalin didn't even know most of the military leaders who were now being arrested and shot. Among them were 3 deputies of the people's commissar of defense; the people's commissar of the navy; 16 military district commanders; 5 fleet commanders; 8 directors of military academies; 33 corps commanders; 76 division commanders; 40 brigade commanders; and 291 regiment commanders.

All in all, in a little over a year, 35,000 Red Army officers were purged. Hundreds of scientists and weapons designers were arrested as well, suspected of having ties with the purged marshals. Among them were the leading aircraft makers Tupolev, Petlyakov, and Myasishchev and the rocket scientists Kleimenov, Langemak, and Korolev. However, an exception was made for some: Langemak was shot, but Tupolev was sent to a prison/think tank, Central Design Office No. 29.

The massacre of the military cadres looked like sheer madness, particularly when Europe was headed for another war. However, the Great Purge eliminated not only the elite but millions of rank-and-file Soviets. Some of them were children of landlords and factory owners, but the majority were ordinary people with no history of exploiting others. They were either snatched at random or reported by colleagues, friends, neighbors, or family members who coveted their apartments or their jobs or their spouses — or people who simply didn't like the way they dressed. It was enough to be noticed wrapping fish in a newspaper carrying Stalin's portrait to be arrested and disappear forever. Wives turned in their husbands; sons informed on their fathers. Torture broke even the stubbornest people, making them sign all the libelous papers accusing others of nonexisting conspiracies.

Vassily Bliukher was tortured so badly that when his wife eventually saw him in prison (she had been arrested too), she did not recognize him at first, for in her words, he looked "as if he had been driven over by a tank." On the eve of his arrest, Bliukher had told her, "There can be no person who wouldn't break down during interrogation. When they start twisting your arms and legs, you will sign anything."

The people's commissar of the interior, Lavrenty Beria, butcher and rapist, beat the marshal personally with a rubber stick in the splendor of his Lubyanka office, yelling, "Tell me how you sold out our Far East to the Japanese!"

Bliukher, virtually insane from pain, screamed, "Stalin, can you hear how they torture me!"

Then his torturers tore one of his eyes out of its socket and threw it into his palm.

All over the country people spent sleepless nights waiting for a knock on the door. Usually the police made arrests in the wee hours of the morning. They arrived in small teams, normally not more than three, and often recruited a female neighbor or a hotel maid to announce a cable. The person on the other side of the door invariably clung to the impossible hope that it was indeed a telegram from his uncle in Saratov or a cousin in Khabarovsk, announcing a death in the family or a forthcoming wedding, and released the lock. The agents would walk in, make the arrest, and, in the case of military personnel, take any medals and insignia from the person's coat. Then they would tell the man to turn over his Party card and any other identification and to put on some clothes. After that they threw him into a car and drove to the local prison, which, if he lived in Moscow, was the infamous Lubyanka or Lefortovo or Butyrki.

In those days the prisons contained few real felons, and as a rule the detainee found himself in a cell with others like himself. Usually these men told him that they had already signed all the slanderous reports admitting their involvement in terrorist activities and espionage and turning in dozens of others. Some had done so after torture, others because of fear of pain. Some, having adopted the perverted logic of the dungeons, explained that the more innocent people they turned in, the better: the absurd numbers of detainees, they argued, would sooner or later open Stalin's eyes to the dire injustice of the police. Few seemed to doubt Stalin's good will.

Very quickly the detainee was taught the ropes. Torture was ferocious, and occasionally he was brought back into the cell on a stretcher. He was given several days to recuperate and then returned to the torture chamber. The interrogators said that he had to admit his involvement in a conspiracy, but that was a pure formality. They were interested in any piece of paper naming other people, but because only a spy or a terrorist could know about other spies and terrorists, the admission of the detainee's own guilt had to come first.

In the cell a newcomer was given the worst place, next to the stinking toilet, but as the days passed and other people left the cell to be shot or exiled, he moved farther and farther away from it, until he reached the wall with the window. A seasoned inmate always found it easy to tell how much time this or that person had spent in jail. The cells were overcrowded; instead of twenty-five people they easily held more than seventy. The daily walk never lasted longer than half an hour, and sometimes it was as short as ten minutes.

After the detainee signed all the required papers or the interrogators gave up on him, he was taken to a courtroom, where three officers held a hearing on his case for four or five minutes. If he was an important person, he was told that he would be shot as a traitor. If not, he was informed that he would spend fifteen years in a labor camp and five additional years in exile.

Soon the detainee was taken to a train station and bundled into a cattle car along with thousands of others. The train carried them across the Volga River into the eastern wasteland, where Siberia lay.

In Siberian jails the detainee first met real felons — murderers, pimps, and burglars. They were almost as heartless as the police and stole all his money and sometimes even his clothes or shoes. In Vladivostok he was put on an old boat, and the ship, rocking on rough seas, took him to the land of desolation sitting across the strait from Alaska: the deadly Kolyma.

▪ ▪ ▪

Almost all the division commanders under whom Zhukov had served were shot. A few times he was accused of having been friendly with enemies of the people, and he survived, as he himself believed, by sheer miracle. Yet the Great Purge created critical vacancies, and he acquired his first important command — of the Third Cavalry Corps — after the arrest of a friend. Amid the continuing carnage, he soon won another enviable job, as deputy commander of the Western Military District, but it made him nervous — the post was too conspicuous, and he had every reason to suspect that he would suffer the same fate as his predecessors. However, in 1939 he was rewarded with a plum assignment. Mongolia, the only Soviet vassal at that time, was under Japanese attack, and after a series of embarrassing defeats, Stalin was looking for a new commander in chief in the eastern steppes. Zhukov was happy to go. He hoped that the mission would save his life.

The fighting in Mongolia was fierce but limited, and soon the Japanese withdrew. Stalin liked easy victories. The insignificant clashes were praised by the newspapers as major battles, and the commander of the Soviet troops was hailed as a military genius.

Stalin received Zhukov in the Kremlin. He listened to his excited report benevolently, and he liked the man, who was both opinionated and straightforward. Eventually he entrusted him with command of the Kiev Military District, on the western frontier.

Zhukov returned from the Far East too late to participate in the Polish occupation but just in time to lead Soviet troops in the annexation of eastern Romania, which had been gained from Bucharest through diplomacy. Zhukov's men didn't have to shed blood, but they did manage to grab some machinery that the Romanians tried to evacuate. Stalin liked Zhukov's thrift.

By early 1941, Zhukov and others in the military were cautiously optimistic. The *vozhd* himself had announced that many people had been arrested unlawfully in 1937, and he had the chief of police, Nikolai Yezhov, shot. The new appointee, Lavrenty Beria — brought to Moscow from Stalin's native Georgia at the end of the carnage — was a man of abundant cruelty and few principles. Even so, after 1939 the purge ground to a halt. A number of generals, like Zhukov's classmate Konstantin Rokossovsky, were released from the dungeons. A career military man still walked on eggshells, but at least he could now feel hopeful.

■ ■ ■

On January 3 the war game that had drawn so many to Moscow began. In the first exercise, the Blues — the Germans — attacked Byelorussia and the Baltics. Zhukov, assisted by fourteen other generals, represented the Wehrmacht. In the second exercise, played on Ukrainian terrain, Zhukov and Pavlov switched sides. Zhukov gave Pavlov a hard time, particularly when Zhukov played for the Germans. Having concentrated his troops in a mighty fist, he crushed the defenses of the Reds and moved deep inland.

When the game was over, the generals lingered in Moscow, anticipating another meeting with Stalin. The invitation arrived only two days later, on January 13. Heading for the Kremlin, Zhukov had no idea what Stalin's reaction to the success of the Blues would be. In January 1941, he still knew too little about the *vozhd.*

A.k.a. Dzhugashvili

Iosif Vissarionovich Stalin had created so many myths about himself that at some point he probably became confused about his own true identity. In people's eyes, he had no nationality, no homeland, no family, and virtually no past. In a word, he was almost divine. His biographies dripped with praise for his wisdom and stature but provided very few details about his life. If Stalin could have erased his past altogether, he would have done so, for he hated almost everything about it.

His father was a village cobbler in the mountains of Georgia, a peripheral Russian colony in the Caucasus. The father clearly disliked his son, and when he was drunk beat the boy with a ferocity that suggested that more than Oedipal malice was at stake. People said that the son, Iosif Dzhugashvili, had been born out of wedlock.

The mother was stern, pious, and possibly unloving. She battered her husband when he stumbled home drunk and beat her son for his mischievous ways. For the child's own good, as she saw it, she sent him to a seminary. He didn't believe in God, and he felt that he would fail in the climb to the top of the church hierarchy. His ambition was to become a poet, yet the few who saw his verse were unimpressed. Classmates and teachers found him stupid.

His future did not look promising. He would probably be assigned to some small parish in the highlands and languish there, flattering the landlord and the local garrison commander and traveling miles to give the last rites, only to have the peasants pay him with fruits and chickens. To build a career in the Eastern Orthodox Church, a person had to have money or connections, or at least social skills. The teenage Stalin had none of these. He felt exploited, abandoned, and alienated, so when he read Marx, he felt as if he had found God.

Marx was one of the most prolific writers of his age, but he was hardly the Stephen King of political philosophy, since he lacked King's clarity. He contradicted himself constantly, so that his words were embraced by both Iosif Dzhugashvili in Georgia and Left Bank intellectuals in Paris. There were just two undeniable tenets to Marxist doctrine: capitalism was bad, and the working class was good. The rest of his hodgepodge of thought was open to interpretation. Russian radicals guided by Lenin came out with their own Marxist blueprint: building a conspiratorial party; organizing the working class; staging a violent revolution; founding a proletarian state; purging the upper classes; expanding worldwide. Iosif Dzhugashvili gladly subscribed to that, because the blueprint promised extensive revenge against the "haves."

Every revolutionary had an alias, sometimes several. Iosif Dzhugashvili was known as Koba, after a Robin Hood kind of outlaw in a nineteenth-century Georgian novel, or Stalin, "the man of steel." Both aliases betrayed his lack of taste. More sophisticated people used unpretentious combinations of syllables for their aliases, like Lenin or Trotsky.

The first twenty years of Stalin's revolutionary career didn't prove as rewarding as he had hoped. The leaders of the Party didn't notice him, no matter how hard he tried to please them. For a while Lenin could not remember his name and referred to him as "that charming

Georgian" (when he needed to, the generally sullen and rude novice could be disarmingly amiable). He went to a number of Party conventions, but he felt so intimidated by the well-read highbrows who hadn't been spanked as children and whose fathers had read Homer to them that he rarely dared to open his mouth.

He spent a few months in Europe and hated every minute of it. He didn't speak a word of German or French and was too proud to learn, although in principle he was a proficient linguist; his Russian, though heavily accented, was rich, idiomatic, and precise. When he turned thirty, he learned that his father had been stabbed to death in a pub brawl. As for his mother, she might as well have been dead too, for he almost never visited her.

His career started gaining momentum only after the revolution. When Lenin was assembling the first Soviet government, he decided he needed a special department to deal with ethnic minorities. A principled believer in affirmative action, he thought that such a department had to be led by a non-Russian. Stalin won by default. In the first Bolshevik government he was made a people's commissar of ethnicities.

He didn't tame ethnic strife, but he did make a number of influential friends within the Party and, later, after being dispatched to the front as a political watchdog, within the army. At the front he was merciless to cowards and turncoats, causing Lenin to remark pensively, "This chef is going to cook spicy dishes only."

In 1922, Stalin was appointed general secretary of the Party. Everybody acknowledged that he was a very good administrator, and that was what the position required. A general secretary monitored all mundane activities, much as an office manager does in a corporation today. Renowned leaders such as Trotsky, Zinoviev, Kamenev, and Bukharin hardly noticed Stalin. They shaped the Party's policies, and he made sure the policies were implemented. But Stalin was quickly gaining political ground. After Lenin suffered a stroke, Stalin had him securely isolated in the quiet of a suburban estate and happily plunged into politics.

Lenin was not a softhearted person, yet even to him Stalin's methods looked harsh, authoritarian, and oppressive. Suddenly it dawned on the dying man that he had unwittingly entrusted the Party to a

Frankenstein's monster. He wrote a letter to the forthcoming Party congress demanding Stalin's removal, calling the man "too rude." When he learned that Stalin had used barnyard language to scold his wife for letting him work, Lenin sent him a furious letter severing all personal ties. He contacted Trotsky, asking that Stalin immediately be removed. In a few days, though, he had another stroke and lost the ability to speak. His demand was kept secret from the Party, and Trotsky and others didn't pursue the matter. To them, Stalin seemed innocuous.

Lenin died in January 1924, and his anointed disciples immediately started a feud. Even then they didn't take Stalin seriously. Trotsky sneeringly dismissed him as "the Party's most brilliant mediocrity." But it took only a year for Stalin, in an ad hoc coalition with Zinoviev and Kamenev, to get rid of Trotsky. Eleven months after that, together with Bukharin, he ousted Zinoviev and Kamenev. Three years after that, he sacked Bukharin and discovered that he no longer had any rivals.

The Bolshevik old guard remained a painful reminder of his undistinguished past, however. No matter how great his achievements were — like eliminating private property in the countryside by killing several million peasants, or forcibly industrializing the country with the use of strategically placed labor camps — the old snobs refused to give him credit.

In 1932, Stalin experienced a personal crisis involving his wife, Nadezhda ("hope"). She was twenty years his junior, the daughter of friends, and as a child she had often sat on his lap. He enjoyed the friendship, and after his first wife died, he married the pretty teenager. But she didn't prove to be the wife he had hoped for. She wanted a career of her own, felt offended by his bad manners, and was definitely against his philandering. After he publicly advised her to mind her own business, she shot herself in their Kremlin apartment. It was a huge embarrassment. Notwithstanding the efforts of the police, the country found out about the incident, and some even called Stalin a murderer.

■ ■ ■

Though he had become an absolute ruler, the indispensable *vozhd* of the Soviet people and the world proletariat, Stalin knew that he had many enemies. The intelligentsia longed to speak freely, the old Party cadres bemoaned his dictatorship, the workers complained about red tape and poor pay, the peasants wanted their land back. An organized opposition was bound to emerge — unless the country was completely frozen in terror.

On December 1, 1934, a popular Party leader, Sergey Kirov, was shot dead in Leningrad. Ordered and orchestrated by Stalin, the assassination was trumpeted as a plot organized by his old adversaries Zinoviev and Kamenev. After that, not only Zinoviev and Kamenev but all the wise old men of the Party were put on trial, indicted as foreign spies and terrorists, and shot.

That was largely an act of vengeance, as Zinoviev, Kamenev, and others had been broken men for almost a decade. However, Stalin still had a bona fide enemy — Trotsky, who was exiled but by no means subdued and was now openly calling for a popular revolt against him. Because Trotsky was the founder of the Red Army, the officers' corps had to be weeded heavily.

In Stalin's eyes, society was conspiratorial by definition. Trotsky, in Mexico, could suddenly push a button and get a response from even the most insignificant and remote part of his vast network. That required a gargantuan purge. Trotsky knew the deputy people's commissar of defense, Tukhachevsky; Tukhachevsky was friendly with Corps Commander A; Corps Commander A had a brother, Regiment Commander B; Regiment Commander B was on good terms with his chief of artillery, C; C patronized a young lieutenant, D — and that was why all of them had to be taken to the dungeons.

However, limiting the purge to Trotsky's circle or even to the army didn't make much sense, as every execution created potential avengers. Lieutenant D could have a devoted brother or a determined girlfriend or a bunch of idealistic classmates. Those potential security risks had to be taken into account too, and that meant that terror had to strike at random, knocking out not just the likely traitors but free will as such.

In the Great Terror, at least 5 million people were arrested. Two hundred were executed daily in Lubyanka prison alone. The *vozhd* killed those who could betray him and those who were close to those who could betray him. He killed people who one day might think of betraying him. He killed almost everybody of high rank and their families, so there would be no one to retaliate. He killed people who had relatives abroad. He killed former czarist officers. He killed children of aristocrats, priests, and shopkeepers. He killed Ukrainians who insisted on speaking Ukrainian and Russians who insisted on teaching Dostoyevsky. He killed police officers so they wouldn't get the wrong idea about their place in society. He killed people who read the Bible or the Koran, but he also killed people who read only Stalin. He killed people who failed to report political jokes and people who reported them. He killed people in their nineties and people in their teens. He killed Russians and he killed Georgians. He killed marshals, pilots, housewives, journalists, plumbers, people's commissars of the interior (two of them), writers, gardeners, spies, fishermen. The dreadful progress of his ax seemed irrational, but it was not. He pursued a clear goal: to reach a point where nobody in the country, be it a miner or a marshal, could be certain whether he would see the dawn. After he reached that point, he stopped. Then, instead of killing people, he sent them to the eastern wilderness, where the gulag camps were waiting for them. There the enemies of the people dug soil for gold, felled trees, and built railroads.

These prisoners grew so essential that they effectively became a second working class. Some apparatchiks got confused about the identity of this new proletariat and suggested that the gulag prisoners with excellent forced-labor records could be released before their jail term expired. Stalin said that that was impossible. "We will disrupt the camps' functioning," he explained matter-of-factly. "Of course, these people would be glad to be released, but this would be bad for the economy . . . The best would be released and the worst would stay."

To him, the discussion seemed childish. It highlighted the stupidity of the people he was working with, but he was not disappointed — that was exactly the kind of person he wanted to have around. He had already been forced to shoot the first generation of the bright children of the revolution, and he was not going to raise a new one. He firmly preferred mediocrity to meritocracy. That was the only way he felt safe.

▪ ▪ ▪

He felt safe but hardly happy — he was a hard-drinking, celibate, friendless bachelor, a collector of wristwatches, a man who appreciated long weekends and solitude. His children had carved out lives of their own, and he rarely saw them. Shortly before his mother died, he went to see her in Georgia, and she said to him, "Still, it's a pity you didn't become a priest."

He turned into an avid reader, preferring the masters of bitter sarcasm, Gogol and Chekhov. He had all but banned Dostoyevsky as "reactionary," but privately he admired him as a "great psychologist." Sometimes he went to a Russian opera such as *Boris Godunov,* or a modern Soviet play, and almost every night he watched movies in a private screening room in the Kremlin. That and drinking parties with the people he despised were the only pleasures he was left with.

He had mixed feelings about his official residence. In part he liked the Kremlin: it was secure, and no other leader in the world enjoyed so much protection. President Roosevelt's White House was separated from the city by a simple iron fence. Churchill's residence at 10 Downing Street was basically a townhouse. Even Hitler's lair in Berlin was nothing but a plain, though oversized, building. Stalin lived in a castle the size of a town.

He also liked the fact that he walked along corridors used by Czar Ivan the Terrible, a point he explicitly made to foreign guests so he could enjoy their shock and disgust. The bogeyman of Russian history, Ivan — whose guards had carried smelly dogs' heads and brushes, the symbols of purge, attached to their saddles — was his role model.

However, the Kremlin was loaded with disturbing memories. His wife had shot herself there. Lenin and other wise men of the Party who had been disdainful and hostile toward him had also once made the citadel their home. So while Stalin kept an apartment in the Kremlin and held office hours there, he spent his nights at one of his two dachas in the suburbs. These didn't have the Kremlin's fortified walls, but he felt comfortable in them. There he hosted late-night feasts for the Politburo, and there he had his repose. He needed a cozy place to claim as his own — he knew he was getting old.

In his later years, Stalin became invincible, invisible, and infallible, like the Holy Ghost. Praise and flattery were his favorite potions, and he couldn't do without them. Yet flattery and praise were changing him. Drunk with his own lies, he was losing his sharp political instincts. In his comfortable dictatorial nirvana, he forgot that the world was not an illusion and lost sight of what was real and what was false.

▪ ▪ ▪

On August 19, 1939, Stalin called an urgent Politburo meeting. There he told the Party leaders that he had chosen to side with Hitler. According to Stalin, Hitler had proposed a deal and was now sending his foreign minister, Joachim von Ribbentrop, to Moscow. This was a shock to the Politburo. The Soviet Union's official line had been profoundly anti-Nazi, and Stalin had called Hitler the worst manifestation of capitalism. For some time Moscow had been involved in tentative negotiations with London and Paris about an anti-German alliance, though no understanding had been reached because the prospective partners were too distrustful of one another.

Since his days in the seminary Stalin had acquired a taste for Manichaean debate, in which black and white intermingled, sometimes opposing, sometimes embracing, but in the end the white always prevailed. That was what he called Marxist dialectics. Each time, confronting a difficult issue, he applied this soothing method to justify compromises, retreats, and even losses. That day he could not have been less interested in persuading the frightened Politburo functionaries — any of whom he could make disappear with a wave of his finger — that his course was the right one. In all likelihood, he was trying to persuade himself.

The ultimate goal of the Soviet Union had always been to launch a world revolution, and that day Stalin began by saying that no Communist party in Western Europe could come to power in peacetime. "The dictatorship of such a party," he emphasized, "can become possible only in the case of a big war." That made sense. The people in the room remembered that Lenin's revolution had succeeded largely because the deprivations of World War I had made it the only viable option for millions of hungry Russians.

Stalin then informed the Politburo that Germany had suggested the Soviet Union could occupy eastern Poland, the three Baltic countries, and eastern parts of Romania. Hitler had also agreed to the Soviet Union's sphere of influence in the rest of Romania, Bulgaria, and Hungary.

Having dangled the expansionist lure, the *vozhd* returned to larger issues. It was likely, he said, that Germany would lose the war. In principle, its defeat could result in its Sovietization. However, if the war was short, Britain and France would have enough resources to intervene militarily and crush a Communist government in Berlin. So, he argued, the Soviet Union had to do everything possible to prolong the war and exhaust the Western powers. He believed that siding with Hitler would serve that purpose. If the war was long and difficult enough, he went on, it could eventually lead to the victory of the French Communist Party and the Sovietization of France as well.

Stalin admitted that it was possible for Hitler to win the war, in which case Germany would probably be too drained and too involved with monitoring France and Britain to attack the Soviet Union anytime soon. At the same time the defeated nations, like France, would develop strong left-leaning resistance movements, and thus world revolution would still eventually prevail.

It is unclear whether Stalin himself believed this exceedingly optimistic analysis, but four days later Ribbentrop landed in Moscow, where he and his Soviet counterpart, Vyacheslav Molotov, signed a pact dividing Eastern Europe.

When Hitler attacked Poland a week later, Stalin sent his troops there too. The Polish armed forces had been devastated by the Wehrmacht, and the Red Army didn't have to do much fighting. The *vozhd* was worried about potential resistance, though, and had his troops round up about 250,000 Polish soldiers and officers. Several months later, 15,000 officers were secretly shot and buried in the woods.

After Poland had been reapportioned by diplomacy, raped by war, and pacified by executions, Stalin lunged at Finland. The tiny nation put up a brave resistance and the Red Army advanced with great difficulty, but in the end Finland was forced to cede its southern provinces. In 1940, Stalin annexed Estonia, Latvia, and Lithuania and parts of Romania.

Notwithstanding these grand acquisitions, Stalin remained nervous. Hitler was winning the war in the West quickly and easily. It was becoming evident that the Wehrmacht was not exhausted at all and that the Soviet Union could well be Germany's next target. But it also seemed that Hitler was unsure about how to proceed. He clearly lusted after the British and French colonies and thought it might be worth using the alliance with Stalin to march as far east as India.

In November 1940, Molotov went to Berlin to talk to the Führer. Hitler proposed partitioning the British Empire. To that end, he envisaged a pact of four — Germany, Italy, Japan, and the Soviet Union, all vowing "to respect each other's natural interests," which in Stalin's case involved the Persian Gulf and the Arabian Sea coast.

It was then that Stalin became confused and overambitious, demanding from Hitler the whole of Finland, Romania, and Bulgaria and also pieces of Turkey, Hungary, and Iran. Czarist Russia had never controlled those vast, strategically important areas, and it was clear that Stalin wanted a dominant position in continental Eurasia. That looked like a huge stretch, but the blunder was understandable. Before siding with Hitler, the *vozhd* had never been a player on the world scene. The Communists had lived in virtual isolation from the rest of the world, and their rulers lacked experience. Also, what was happening in Europe seemed so extraordinary that every wild scheme now seemed feasible.

World War I had lasted four years, but very little territory had changed hands. German and Allied forces had fought for months for pitiful amounts of land, and no major capital had fallen. World War II was quite different. All traditional notions of power disintegrated, glamorous cities fell, and several countries disappeared from the map. Drugged by the orgy of destruction, Stalin thought he could get away with almost anything.

His demands looked outrageous to Hitler, however. The Führer believed he was the only one entitled to megalomania. Molotov was dismissed with deliberate coldness. As for a formal reply to Stalin's proposal, it never arrived.

▪ ▪ ▪

In January 1941, Stalin was still eagerly awaiting Hitler's response, so every week he felt increasingly uneasy. He knew that the Red Army was inadequately equipped and poorly trained, as its difficult victory over tiny Finland had proved. What was worse, he couldn't quite trust its generals. No matter how many people he killed or how many upstarts he brought in, no matter how fiercely he shuffled and reshuffled the military cadres, he could not achieve the ideal balance between loyalty and talent. He kept a close eye on his generals, knowing that they kept a close eye on him.

January 13: The Kremlin

When Georgy Zhukov walked into the Kremlin meeting room, he discovered that the other people there included not only the game participants but also the five top Red Army commanders: Kliment Voroshilov, Semen Budenny, Grigory Kulik, Semen Timoshenko, and Boris Shaposhnikov. These men had survived the purge and had been invited by the *vozhd* to enhance the importance of the forum. Each carried inch-wide stars, the marshal's proud insignia, on the collar and sleeve of his tight khaki tunic. They were the only men of that rank left in the country. Each time the five gathered together, the physical eccentricities they painstakingly cultivated in an effort to be easily identifiable on propaganda posters and postcards were highlighted in a ludicrous way.

The man with the glistening shaved head was the people's commissar of defense, Semen Timoshenko, whom Zhukov knew and understood best. Like Zhukov, Timoshenko was a peasant's son, a World War I veteran, a civil war cavalry commander, and a recent beneficiary of the Great Purge. He had led the Red Army to its thorny victory over Finland in 1940, and for that Stalin had rewarded him with his current post. Timoshenko was a gifted man, but he was not quite up to the task of directing 600,000 army groups. He had been an ideal military district chief, commanding 30,000-man corps, knowing his terrain as a farmer knows his back yard, and spending nights binge drinking with timid peasants and unpretentious local Party leaders. Also, he had seen too many careers collapse in a matter of minutes to afford himself the comfort of speaking up. The tension between professionalism and discretion pained him, and Timoshenko was never at peace with himself.

The man with the carefully trimmed English-style mustache was Kliment Voroshilov, or, as the whole country affectionately called him, Klim. Pictures of his pink, puffy, cheerful face, with its little eyes and piggy nose, adorned almost every office in the country. If Stalin was referred to as the father of the Soviet people, Voroshilov was called the first marshal. All major victories in the civil war were now falsely attributed to him, and he was fallaciously praised as one of the revolutionaries who had toppled the last czar and as a disciple of Lenin, though he was neither. Voroshilov mania had engulfed the whole country: two towns, several villages, and a few mountain peaks were named after him. At military training lessons in schools, children competed for the title of Voroshilov Shot. At least there was some truth in this title — Klim Voroshilov was a poor strategist and a low-key revolutionary, but he did shoot well. In fact, when a new heavy tank was named KV, it raised many eyebrows, since it was common knowledge that the marshal distrusted advanced weaponry.

During the Great Purge, Voroshilov, then the people's commissar of defense, eagerly sent hundreds of senior officers to the police dungeons, but in 1940 he lost his post: the war with Finland killed his career. Feeling absolutely overwhelmed by modern warfare, he counted every minute of it and in his final report to the Party didn't hesitate to say that the war had lasted "104 and a half days." His inability to lead the troops became obvious even to Stalin, and the *vozhd* fired him. Yet he didn't execute the hapless marshal,who had been a trusted friend since the civil war.

The man with the grotesque eight-inch mustache of a cinema villain was Semen Budenny, the most extraordinary commander during the civil war. A Cossack by birth, he became one of the best soldiers in the czarist army during World War I, winning the rare title of Full Saint George Cavalier, which meant that he proudly carried all four degrees of the Saint George Cross and four degrees of the Saint George's Medal on his barrel chest. Known as the scourge of the Whites, Budenny was recklessly brave and addicted to the thrill of hand-to-hand combat. He was endowed with the instincts of a killer, always knowing how to overwhelm an enemy in the middle of the night or during a fierce snowstorm, winning battles not through knowledge or planning but with gusto and by sheer force of will. However, after 1937 he was little more than a familiar face on a poster. After Stalin sent Budenny's wife, a Bolshoi opera singer, to prison, the marshal was a broken man.

The stooping dwarf with a sour face was Grigory Kulik, a friend of Voroshilov's and Budenny's. He was a military nonentity but a gifted sponger. He had benefited enormously from the purges and now held the joint positions of chief of the Main Artillery Directorate and deputy people's commissar of defense. When he couldn't understand a new project — and more often than not he couldn't — he labeled it sabotage. Pompous, loud, and unpredictable, he kept his subordinates in a permanent state of fear. His motto was "Either jail or medal."

Collectively, the three marshals were known as "cavalrymen." With dismay they watched the emergence of new weapons that they couldn't handle and the rise of younger generals with whom they couldn't compete. Their only true capital was Stalin's friendship. Having transferred the key military jobs to younger people, the *vozhd* still valued the cavalrymen's experience, and he shared their nostalgia for the days of the civil war, when they had been young and warfare had been simple.

The sick-looking man with his hair parted down the middle and the out-of-date glasses was Marshal Boris Mikhailovich Shaposhnikov, a former czarist colonel. Ignorant Great Terror upstarts now commanding armies were amazed by his phenomenal memory and his command of every strategic detail. He would shower a general from Central Asia with questions like "What is the condition of the railway between Samarkand and Termez? What is your plan for the railway bridge across the Amu Daria at Charzhou?" and even "Is the tavern at the seventy-fifth kilometer of the Samarkand-Termez road still in business?" In

1937, Stalin appointed him chief of the General Staff. Shaposhnikov was the only military leader whom the *vozhd* respectfully addressed by his patronymic, Boris Mikhailovich, and he allowed him to smoke in his study. Nonetheless, he fired him after the Finnish war, even though Shaposhnikov's performance had been beyond reproach. As the *vozhd* calmly explained, the people needed another scapegoat besides Voroshilov. The justification struck insiders as odd: Voroshilov had been fired three months earlier, and it was doubtful that Stalin gave a damn about public opinion.

Soft and considerate by nature, Shaposhnikov treated Stalin as yet another czar. In the presence of the *vozhd* the marshal felt totally intimidated, and he rarely dared to oppose the vulgar and aggressive cavalrymen either. He realized that people treated him as a maverick or as a relic of a bygone age; neither was flattering.

The conference started badly for the generals. Chief of General Staff Kirill Meretskov, who had replaced Shaposhnikov less than six months before, was even more afraid of Stalin than his predecessor was. The report he had to deliver was a tricky one. The grand strategic game had in fact ended in an impasse. The Blues, led by Zhukov, had crushed the defenses of the Reds, but their offensive had been brought to an artificial halt, so, technically speaking, the results of the clash remained inconclusive. Now the leaders of the People's Commissariat of Defense faced a daunting task: they had to alert Stalin to the Red Army's vulnerability without sounding alarmist.

Only Shaposhnikov was clever enough to pull it off. He and his disciples had drafted a report that was masterfully evasive, and it had to be presented carefully and precisely if its fastidious wording was to carry any meaning. A misread term or an omitted sentence would reduce the clever phrasing to mere gibberish — and that was what began happening now. Tense and anxious, Meretskov started to improvise, and the smart treatise turned into drivel. Realizing that his labors had been in vain and that the carefully nuanced paper was beyond salvation, Marshal Shaposhnikov looked heartbroken. His head jerked in a nervous tic as he shyly eyed Stalin, desperately trying to figure out how he would react.

It didn't take long for the *vozhd*'s anger to descend. Stalin liked to intimidate people, and he didn't like blathering generals. He started interrupting Meretskov with caustic remarks. Meretskov eventually had to admit that the results of the game had been uncertain.

That made Stalin fume with rage. "The Politburo wants to know who won," he said.

But Meretskov had no ready answer to give and was too unnerved to come up with a suitable response. Stalin showered him with more contemptuous remarks and then switched his attention to the commander of the Reds, General Pavlov.

"How come the Reds had a hard time?" he asked, with great displeasure.

The straightforward and easygoing Pavlov decided to crack a joke. "Bad luck happens even in games," he said.

Stalin had never liked other people's jokes. "A military district commander," he lectured, "has to master the art of war. He has to make the right decision, no matter what the situation is. You have failed this time . . . Who else wants to report?"

As the commander of the Blues, Zhukov knew he was entitled to a comment and raised his hand. There was not much he was willing to add to the dangerous win-or-lose issue, but that night he had a clear agenda of his own: to try to win Stalin's trust, or at the very least his attention. That was a dangerous endeavor, but the meeting also provided a once-in-a-lifetime chance, and the general chose to take the risk. He decided he would hint at the real cause of the Reds' misfortune: their main force was deployed in the wrong way. Because the game reflected the actual deployment of Red Army troops in the borderlands, the matter had to be addressed urgently.

Notwithstanding the new era of bombers and tanks, Europeans still believed in fortifications, despite their poor performance in recent battles. The Maginot Line, built by the French, had failed to deter the Germans; the Mannerheim Line, built by the Finns, hadn't stopped the Red Army. Both had been flawed. The Maginot Line didn't cover the Belgian border, and the Mannerheim neglected territories north of Lake Ladoga. In both cases the gaps had proved fatal.

With the occupation of Poland and the Baltics, the Soviet Union's frontier had rolled 100 to 250 miles west, and its initial chain of forts, known as Stalin's Line, had been rendered ineffective to protect the newly acquired territory. New fortifications were being built along the new border, and Zhukov was among those who thought that was a misguided effort. Now he openly challenged the wisdom of the project.

Zhukov understood that a modern defense line could not be a twentieth-century version of China's Great Wall. It couldn't be designed as a huge fortress, firmly barring any invasion, because no matter how thick its ramparts, sooner or later they would disintegrate under enemy bombs and artillery fire. Rather, the complicated system of forts, pillboxes, and trenches should be viewed as a secure base for ground troops to counterattack an enemy that was already overextended. When designing such a network, military planners should make sure the troops had enough space for tactical maneuvers between the fortifications and the enemy lines. Also, if the fortifications were placed too close to the enemy, aircraft and artillery could devastate them in the first minutes of war, depriving the defenders of shelter, arms, and supplies.

Stalin's decision to put the new defense line right on the border looked unbelievably foolish to Zhukov. He couldn't say so bluntly, but he was shockingly audacious in expressing his doubts. Knowing that he had nothing to lose, he continued by saying that the deployment of the main force was very insecure in general. The troops had also been placed too close to the border, where they could be heavily hit by a sudden German attack. One area of Pavlov's military district, the Belostok salient, looked especially vulnerable, as the Red Army could easily be trapped by the attacking Germans.

Every military professional knew what Zhukov was referring to. A salient — a triangular piece of land protruding into enemy territory — could be both a blessing and a curse. An army positioned in a salient could deliver a daggerlike strike at the enemy to overwhelm and eventually disband his troops, but if the enemy struck first, he could surround and seal off the salient, turning it into a lethal pocket. The Belostok area was a classic salient: narrow, long, and strategically located, a centerpiece of the pending Soviet-German clash.

Zhukov's forceful argument came as a blast in the stagnant Kremlin air. It had been a while since a general had dared to doubt the wisdom of Stalin's decisions. The remarks caused an uproar. Pavlov venomously said that in Zhukov's military district the fortifications were being built right on the border as well. Voroshilov angrily advised Zhukov to mind his own business. Others joined in. In the heat of the debate, random issues came up, and Marshal Kulik, switching to a matter dear to his heart, suggested that the artillery should be pulled by horses, not cars, and as for tanks, their significance was greatly overrated. Stalin rudely cut them all off, even Kulik.

It was clear that Stalin's bad mood had been aggravated by Zhukov's remarks, though they made perfect sense. Preparing for defensive warfare, a country never put its fortifications right on the border and never placed its army in narrow strips of territory like the Belostok salient, where it could be easily strangled by the enemy. Only a few people in the room knew that Stalin's real plan was to skip defensive war altogether and strike at Germany first.

▪ ▪ ▪

Joseph Stalin had many skeletons in his closet, but in January 1941 the preemptive war plan was his best-guarded secret. We do not know whether he had the idea himself or got it from one of his generals — maybe the brilliant Shaposhnikov — but in any case it was the most ambitious scheme of his reign thus far.

In strategic terms, an attack on Hitler looked both feasible and desirable. By striking first, the Soviet Union would not only defeat Hitler's army but also acquire more territory in Eastern Europe without any diplomatic bargaining. That was an opportunity not to be missed. Stalin was sure that the Führer was still focusing on Britain, leaving his eastern flank relatively weak. Only after Germany finished in the west, Stalin argued, would Hitler send the bulk of his troops to the Soviet Union's border. He didn't believe that Hitler would risk a war on two fronts, and common sense supported that view, since such a strategic arrogance had cost Germany a catastrophic defeat in World War I. British defenses were still sturdy, and Stalin thought that Britain wouldn't fall before the summer of 1942. What he said sounded quite rational. Only a madman would open another theater of war with the first one still in dispute.

Though Stalin knew the Red Army wasn't perfect, he was impressed that it had won a number of recent conflicts with minimal casualties. In Mongolia, Zhukov's troops had lost only 8,000 men. The difficult victory over Finland cost the nation 85,000 lives — a lot by European standards, but just a fraction for a nation that had lost 13 million in the civil war twenty years earlier. The occupation of eastern Poland, the Baltics, and eastern Romania had been quick and nearly bloodless.

German victories in Europe looked dazzling, but only one of the conquered nations, France, had once had a substantial army, and Stalin did not hold it in high regard. In other words, the Wehrmacht's might hadn't yet been truly tested, and it could well prove to be weaker than German propaganda claimed. The German occupation of Western Europe had demanded immense resolve and nerve, but not necessarily a top-notch army.

Stalin believed that there was no such thing as an impossible plan, as long as the timing was right and the enterprise was entrusted to the right sort of people. However, finding the latter continued to be a problem. The cavalrymen were devoted — particularly Voroshilov, whom he had first met as a roommate at a Party congress in Stockholm in 1906, where both felt depressed and alienated by a rich Western city sparkling with electricity. Twelve years later, during the civil war, the two had met again, in Tsaritsyn, and again felt united, this time by fear. The fighting was fierce, the Whites were just 10 miles away, the cannon blasts shattered windows in the Red headquarters, and at night the steppes blazed with orange light as the city's suburbs went up in flames. There the two met the Red hound, Semen Budenny, and piggybacked on his success.

Stalin and Voroshilov remembered very well the battle they had watched from the top of a hill at Novy Oskol. Through their binoculars they could see Budenny leading his troops toward General Mamontov across an immense snowy field. The First Cavalry Army was moving in a huge uninterrupted mass, known in military parlance as a lava, its men riding every known breed of horse and wearing the wildest assembly of clothes, from czarist army coats and mountaineers' fur cloaks to German and English military uniforms and Ukrainian embroidered shirts. Some had pointed woolen helmets on their heads. Medieval in look and designed by the last czar's generals to connect to ancient Russia, the hats had been appropriated by the Red riders, and Bolshevik propaganda unabashedly referred to them as "Budenny helmets." Most riders were Russian or Ukrainian, but there were also Jews, Kalmyks, Germans, Tatars, Latvians, Serbs, Hungarians, and others. That combination had never been seen before.

That day the Red Army's attack looked overpowering and unavoidable, like a real volcanic eruption. After Stalin and Voroshilov left the safety of the observation spot, they fell silent. The snow beneath the hill was red with the blood of dead soldiers and horses. It was a graphic scene, and both later admitted that it had been one of the most powerful moments of their lives.

But how could Stalin now entrust Voroshilov, who could barely read a map, with planning an incursion into Europe? How could he let Budenny lead a panzer armada? They were both relics of the past, like the precious sabers and daggers at Voroshilov's dacha, which he had collected from the White officers he had killed.

Voroshilov's successor in the People's Commissariat of Defense, Timoshenko, lacked the intellectual luster to do the job. Marshal Shaposhnikov was another matter. Stalin respected his education and erudition and was slightly intrigued by him. The *vozhd* was surreptitiously fascinated by the cultured world of old Russia, to which he had never had access, and for him Shaposhnikov epitomized a place where fathers never beat their sons and tablecloths were always clean. Few people knew that Stalin's favorite play was not some revolutionary blockbuster but the ideologically dubious *Days of the Turbins,* by Mikhail Bulgakov, which extolled a group of young White Army officers and the middle class in general. Although far less challenging authors had been detained and shot, Bulgakov was allowed to survive the purges. As for his play, Stalin saw it no fewer than fifteen times.

Like a model middle-class person, Shaposhnikov was tactful and delicate to the point of being ridiculous, addressing his subordinates as "My dear." He thought it improper to sit in Stalin's presence, so, since his health was always poor, he occasionally sneaked out of the dictator's office into the adjoining waiting room to relax in a chair for a few minutes. In Stalin's eyes, these old-fashioned manners guaranteed that Shaposhnikov was gifted *and* loyal and therefore could be asked to develop the preemptive-war blueprint.

However, if Shaposhnikov was to be the driving force behind the plan, he would need an executor, a trusted but relatively junior person who would look up the maps, check out the logistics, and take notes during important meetings. Stalin chose a young general, Alexander Vasilevsky, one of Shaposhnikov's disciples in the General Staff. He had always liked the officers Shaposhnikov trained; they were businesslike, precise, and hardworking. "Well, now, let's listen to the Shaposhnikov school!" the *vozhd* would say benevolently.

Vasilevsky had another big advantage in Stalin's eyes: he could be blackmailed into total obedience and secrecy. Like many other young people in the Soviet Union, he was ashamed of his father, who was a priest — that fact alone could damage the son's career. He himself had gone to a seminary, another biographical blemish he aspired to conceal. Determined to succeed, he cut all ties with his parents, but after fifteen years the old man, reduced to poverty, sent the son an awkward letter asking for an allowance. Terrified, Vasilevsky didn't write back. Instead he informed the General Staff's Party cell secretary that the rebellious parent had started pestering him with unwanted correspondence.

The incident was reported to Stalin. Soon, at a lavish dinner table where several Politburo members were seated, the dictator proposed a toast to Vasilevsky. Having overwhelmed the young general, he embarrassed him even more by asking slyly, "You graduated from a seminary but didn't become a priest. Why?"

Totally shaken, Vasilevsky responded that this had never been his wish.

"I see, I see," Stalin said with a smirk. "This had never been your wish. I understand. Well, Mikoyan and I" — he referred to a Politburo member with seminary on his curriculum — "actually wanted to become priests, but for some reason they didn't want us. We still have no idea why."

After enjoying the mirth caused by this self-deprecating remark, he continued: "Can I ask you, why are you not sending money to your father? And what about your brothers too? As far as I know, one is a doctor, another is an agronomist, the third one is a pilot, an officer who makes good money . . . I think if you all had been helping your parents, your father would have dumped his church long ago."

Vasilevsky nervously responded that he had severed ties with his family and thought that a religious father and a job with the General Staff were incompatible.

Stalin loved his fear. "Get in touch with your parents immediately," he advised the frightened man. "And start sending them money. Tell your Party cell secretary I've authorized that."

In the summer of 1940, under Shaposhnikov's guidance, Vasilevsky started work on the preemptive strike plan. The first memo was ready in mid-August and was signed by Shaposhnikov and Timoshenko. Politically, its wording was very careful, starting with the presumption that Germany could strike first. However, in the rest of the document the generals abandoned that supposition. The main task they envisaged for the Red Army sounded heavily preemptive: "to defeat the German forces concentrating in East Prussia and around Warsaw" and then to capture East Prussia and move on into northern Poland.

Unexpectedly, the *vozhd* rejected the draft. If the Red Army was to strike preemptively, it had to do so where German troops were most concentrated, to disable the Wehrmacht in the first days of war. Shaposhnikov thought that Hitler would place his main force in the north, pushing all the way through Lithuania at Riga and Minsk and eventually aiming at Moscow and Leningrad. Stalin argued that Hitler's main force would be deployed in the south; in his view, Germany craved Ukraine, with its wheat fields, coal, and iron. Therefore, Stalin said, the Red Army had to attack from Ukraine, not Lithuania or Byelorussia. Shaposhnikov stubbornly held his ground. In a few days, Stalin replaced him with the cowardly Meretskov.

Vasilevsky was told to rewrite the draft. Barely a month later, on September 18, 1940, Timoshenko and the new chief of general staff, Meretskov, sent it to Stalin. Now the document suggested two potential offensive corridors, one in the south and one in the north. Such strategic ambiguity made practical planning impossible, and in October, under Stalin's pressure, Timoshenko and Meretskov canceled the attack in the north altogether and agreed that the Red Army should strike in the south.

Now the army was expected "to cut Germany off from the Balkans in order to deprive it of paramount economic resources and to energetically influence the Balkan countries as far as their participation in war is concerned." This formula meant that Romania and Bulgaria, and probably Hungary and Yugoslavia, would cease to exist.

However, after October the top-secret deliberations came to a halt. The preemptive war remained a researched option, not a definitive plan. Having received the blueprints of the operation, Stalin still couldn't make up his mind whether he wanted to attack Germany soon or in a few years. In November, People's Commissar of Foreign Affairs Molotov went to Berlin, where Hitler suggested joint military action against Britain and Stalin replied with his list of desired territories. Although no response was forthcoming from Berlin, Stalin thought there was still a chance that Hitler would agree to his demands and that the alliance would continue as long as it took to dismember the colonial empires of Britain and France.

Nonetheless, Stalin hoped that sooner or later he would command an all-out war against Germany. He couldn't decide on the date or even the year of the preemptive war, but the basic elements had been ordered. Fortifications were to be built right on the border and would be used as the base of aggression, and the troops would assemble in a number of salients like the one in Belostok.

Now, on the evening of January 13, one of his generals had dared to criticize these decisions, oblivious of the preemptive strike plan and therefore ignorant of the underlying rationale. A few days earlier, that same general, playing for the Germans in a strategic game, had horned in on the Red Army's vulnerabilities, which resulted from Stalin's grand design, and crushed it. How could Stalin be sure that Hitler wouldn't do the same?

He didn't know Zhukov well, yet that night he was impressed. None of the people involved in the preemptive strike planning were daring enough. Timoshenko kept his thoughts to himself, Meretskov rambled,

Shaposhnikov just looked scared. The General Staff had seen three chiefs in three years — Marshal Alexander Yegorov, a civil war hero, dismissed in 1937 and shot two years later, then Shaposhnikov, now Meretskov — and none of the leaders really suited Stalin's tastes and goals. Once again, how did one combine daring and devotion?

Presumably consumed by these thoughts, Stalin offered some closing remarks. Usually he was a good speaker — logical, persuasive, and consistent. But that night his ruminations were remarkably confused, as his mind probably was. He kept jumping from one subject to another, and ended up discussing dried bread. War was imminent, he said, and the country had to stock up on food supplies. Dried bread was terrific, he thought, light and durable; the last czar's government had stocked it for the army during World War I. "A little tea with rusk," he earnestly said, "is already something." It sounded ridiculous, of course, but nobody dared remind him that meager food rations on the front had been one of the main reasons for the czarist government's collapse twenty-four years earlier.

Finally the *vozhd* moved to what really preoccupied him: cadres. His last comment was ominous. "The problem is," he said, "we don't have a real chief of general staff. Meretskov has to be replaced."

Everybody looked at the victim. Meretskov was dumbfounded but of course did not say a thing.

After a meaningful pause, the *vozhd* added, "The generals can leave now."

The following day Zhukov was brought to the Kremlin, where he was told that Stalin wanted him in Moscow as chief of general staff.

2

ON THE EVE

General Zhukov

In the Red Army, the chief of general staff was probably more important than the people's commissar of defense, as the latter remained in Stalin's shadow, something of a deputy, a figurehead, often a scapegoat. The chief of general staff had to do the real work, whereas the people's commissar had to clear decisions with Stalin.

Now Zhukov's top priority was the preemptive strike plan. He must have been shocked when he learned of its existence. At the same time, the strategic elements that had seemed so preposterous in a defensive position — the fortifications placed dangerously close to the border, the troops in a treacherous salient — finally came together in a logical design.

Stalin's military appointments of the previous year also started to make sense. As early as the summer of 1940, the *vozhd* had decided that the Red Army would now be led by generals familiar with the terrain of Ukraine. Timoshenko had commanded the Kiev Military District, and First Deputy Chief of General Staff N. F. Vatutin, Chief of the Mobilization Department N. L. Nikitin, and General Staff Commissar S. K. Kozhevnikov had all served in the south as well. Now Zhukov, another former commander of the Kiev district, brought a new team of southerners with him.

But the plan itself remained in draft form, because Stalin refused to finalize it. Meanwhile, there was no backup defensive scenario, no Plan B, in the event that Germany struck first. As a result, both the country and the army were caught between offense and defense — in effect, nowhere.

The situation was unacceptable, particularly in light of the fact that Zhukov believed the conflict would begin much sooner than Stalin thought. Soviet representatives returning from Germany reported both astonishing military technology and a nation determined to win the fight — disciplined, vigilant, aware. The condescending Germans let the Soviets see the famous aircraft plants of Heinkel and Junkers, Tempelhof Airport, and the Air Force Ministry. The country was ready for British air raids, the only real challenge to Germany so far, and it was obvious. At night all the windows in the capital of the Third Reich were darkened, and the blue lamp at the entrance of the Kaiserhof Hotel, where foreign visitors stayed, was the only source of light downtown. Airspace over Germany was closely monitored by the Luftwaffe. It looked like the Royal Air Force didn't have a chance of disrupting that meticulous order.

Throughout the spring Soviet spies kept reporting that German troops were concentrating along the border, and some went so far as to suggest that Hitler would attack in the coming weeks. Zhukov and Timoshenko, however, received only those communications that Stalin chose to share. When they asked him why, he laconically answered, "You will be told everything you will need to know."

But if the spies' reports remained off-limits, Zhukov had complete access to the intelligence sent by army commanders stationed on the frontier, and those cables looked alarming. On April 16, for example, six German planes violated Soviet airspace, obviously for reconnaissance purposes. Meanwhile, in accordance with a previous agreement, Soviet trains continued to take precious raw materials like copper and nickel, crucial for the German war effort, to the Third Reich, as if nothing suspicious were happening.

Zhukov found the situation disheartening. He wasn't fanatical about Communism, like Molotov, Stalin's alter ego, who was the head of government and also the people's commissar of foreign affairs; nor was he cynical about it, like police chief Beria. But the fact that Stalin had chosen to promote him suggested that the system did work on some level: a self-made prodigy, an exemplary "have-not," had been elevated to one of the most important posts in the country. He had hoped to find a wise mentor in Stalin, thinking that together they would make a difference and prepare the troops for war. But after only a few weeks on the job he found himself frustrated.

Very soon it became obvious to Zhukov that Stalin trusted nobody, that he chose to ignore other people's opinions and placed blind hope in his own instincts. The people he depended on were unworthy. Molotov was a hard-nosed ideologue who was now expected to handle the intricacies of diplomatic negotiation, although he knew nothing about the outside world and couldn't speak any foreign language. The cavalrymen were pathetic yet dangerous. Insulted by their loss of influence, they were ready to stab new appointees like Zhukov in the back. As for the military advice they could give Stalin, it was equal to sabotage, for to them a modern panzer armada looked the same as a civil war–type cavalry band. Beria, who ran a vast empire of police, border guards, prisons, labor camps, domestic informants, and foreign spies, was the person Zhukov hated most, and he half suspected that Beria was already accumulating an incriminating file on him. Yet Stalin trusted all those people more than he trusted his own chief of general staff. Instead of becoming the leader's right hand, Zhukov found himself a mere gearshift between the enigmatic *vozhd* and the halting Red Army, the gearshift that would be held accountable for every slip. What was particularly unsettling was that he was getting no guidance at all, and as a result the army was paralyzed.

The only promising development was that Zhukov found sympathy and support from the people's commissar of defense, Semen Timoshenko. With their nearly identical backgrounds and career paths and their shared disdain of Stalin's strategic ability, the two now acted as a team, beating off the cavalrymen's venomous criticisms and Beria's machinations and trying to alert Stalin to the disturbing developments on the border. Zhukov quickly became the leader; in him, ambition ruled everything, survival instinct included, and he prodded the more cautious Timoshenko to speak up.

Of course, there were limits to Zhukov's candor. He hadn't shared with Stalin the most shocking discovery of all. After he moved to Moscow and gained access to comprehensive information previously unavailable to him, he came to the conclusion that the nation was wholly unprepared for war, offensive or otherwise.

Numerically, the Red Army looked fine. It had 4,826,900 men, with 2.9 million already stationed along the western border. However, numbers could be misleading. Without modern weapons, these hundreds of thousands of soldiers and officers were nothing but cannon fodder.

In a paranoid society run by incompetent ideologues, it took an eternity for a new weapon to be approved (or rejected) by the government. Sometimes the weapon-makers had time to develop a better version before the initial one had gone through the necessary commissions, committees, boards, and councils. As the paperwork crawled from one desk to another, the army struggled with outdated equipment.

The Soviet Union had many more tanks and aircraft than the Germans: 14,200 Soviet tanks against 3,350 German ones, and 9,200 Soviet aircraft against Germany's 2,000. However, simple numerical superiority remained a mantra without meaning. Of the 14,200 tanks, 10,500 were outmoded T-26s and BT-7s, poorly designed and cheaply built. The newly released medium T-34 and heavy KV were superb, but the army had just 1,861 of them, and only 1,475 T-34s and KVs were placed in the west. German tanks did not look particularly impressive to the Soviet experts visiting German factories, and they were even less well regarded by Soviet veterans of the Spanish civil war. The two armies had clashed in Spain between 1936 and 1939, when Stalin had dispatched his tanks and aircraft to support the left-wing Republican government and Hitler had sent his men and weapons to reinforce General Franco. The veterans reported that even the outmoded T-26s were better than German T-Is and T-IIs. The German panzers had weaker guns and thinner armor, they said. Newer German models like the T-III and T-IV sported thicker armor and better guns, but they still didn't stand a chance against the cutting-edge T-34s and KVs. A T-34's armor was

45mm thick (versus 20–30mm). As for the KV's 75mm armor, it was virtually impenetrable to German artillery.

No doubt that sort of analysis made the *vozhd* feel good. The problem was that a purely technical comparison was just as meaningless as a numerical one. The Soviet tank corps, in theory superior to Germany's, was vulnerable for a number of reasons.

Just as captains trained in the days of sail distrusted steamships, Stalin, a veteran of the civil war, in which the cavalry had ruled, had major misgivings about tanks. He was enthusiastically supported by Voroshilov, Budenny, and Kulik. All were inclined to view tanks as auxiliary weapons operating in smaller units, as they had in the days of their youth. As a result, Soviet tanks remained dispersed, in theory strengthening every army unit but in reality wasting their potential. Stalin and the cavalrymen refused to admit that even newer, technologically superior tanks could not win the battle if they were spread too thinly.

Meanwhile, the German panzers that had defeated France, to say nothing of smaller nations like Belgium and Poland, crawled in armadas, like migrating reptiles. As late as 1940 Stalin sanctioned the creation of mechanized corps bound together by tanks, but by the beginning of 1941 the Red Army had just nine of those. In March, with great difficulty, Zhukov persuaded Stalin to form twenty more. By and large, Soviet tank corps were a work in progress.

Nazi Germany was not nearly as organized and disciplined as German propaganda insisted, yet it was more orderly than Stalin's Soviet Union. The German T-I and T-II tanks might have been a poor match even for older Soviet ones, but Hitler's vehicles were well built and well maintained. Soviet weapons designers were better than their German counterparts, but the workers who built the tanks and the soldiers who maintained them were underpaid and unskilled. It didn't matter that a Soviet T-26 was a better tank than a German T-I; what mattered was that generally only 80 percent of the tanks of a Soviet mechanized corps were operational at any given time, and the troops constantly had to deal with breakdowns.

Still, the new generation of Soviet tanks were armed with an awesome weapon, a 76mm USV-39 gun. The gun spat shells that pierced armor at a distance of 2,000 yards, and its German counterparts didn't do nearly as well. That potentially made USV-39 the winning weapon. But Stalin's artillery commander, Kulik, thought that bigger shells were always better. He insisted on equipping the tanks with 107mm guns instead. The bigger artillery shell didn't automatically guarantee better results, however, and it was unclear whether the weapons designers would be able to create a gun powerful enough to work at the same great distance as the lighter USV-39 could.

When the people's commissar of armaments, Boris Vannikov, complained to Stalin, the *vozhd* disagreed, saying, "One-hundred-seven-millimeter guns are very good. I still remember their performance during the civil war."

Vannikov couldn't believe his ears. Stalin knew even less about artillery than Kulik did. The 107mm gun in question had yet to be developed; the artillery piece Stalin had in mind was a World War I relic that shared nothing with the new gun save its caliber.

But that was the end of the discussion. The tank makers were instructed to bypass the excellent USV-39 and start working immediately on the 107mm gun instead. The hot-tempered Vannikov said that that was equal to disarming. This remark was reported to Stalin, and though he did not act on it immediately, few people doubted that Vannikov would have to pay for it.

Another revolutionary weapon, the first Soviet rocket, BM-13 — a.k.a. *katiusha,* or "Little Catherine" — also looked too unorthodox to Stalin and Kulik, and again the army was ordered to ignore it. In general, Soviet artillery was not as precise, powerful, or devastating as the German artillery. This placed huge restrictions on the use of panzers and aircraft. A superb tank armed with a poor gun was nothing but a moving target. A fleet of aircraft without reliable ground defense could easily be scattered by enemy fighters.

Aircraft fascinated the dictator, but he was suspicious of every new design, and at least 80 percent of his nation's military planes remained outmoded, lacking the most important asset of all, speed. Among Soviet aircraft, only two kinds of fighters, the YAK-1 and the LaGG-3, could be considered modern. The German Me-110 was infinitely better.

Conservatism ruled, and only 15 percent of pilots had been trained to fly at night. The average pilot had spent just twelve hours in the air between January and March 1941, and very few had been exposed to flying at high altitude. The aircraft, runways, and hangars had not yet been camouflaged. In the spring of 1941, planes sat parked in handsome geometrical configurations up and down the western border, as if daring the Germans to come and destroy their peaceful symmetry.

The air force's shortcomings would be most obvious in the event of a panzer war. A German tank couldn't destroy a Soviet KV, but if the Soviet air force lost the aerial battle, the Luftwaffe would flatten the superb Soviet machines on the ground.

Even before the war began, the Red Army was losing two or three aircraft a day to fatal accidents, which meant an annual loss of 600 to 900 planes. The accidents were not properly investigated, either. When Junior Lieutenant Koshlyak, of the Twenty-ninth Air Force Division, had an emergency landing in the wilderness in winter, deep snow prevented him from reaching any settlement, so he spent at least eight days in his aircraft's cabin before he finally died, desperate and alone, leaving a bitter note behind. His wrecked aircraft was discovered only accidentally, much later. When Stalin was told of the episode, he seemed very annoyed.

Meanwhile, the foundation of every military operation, communications, was a mess. Roads in Byelorussia and Ukraine were full of bumps, crevices, and potholes. Many bridges could not sustain the weight of a tank or even a piece of artillery. German railroads along the border could handle 220 trains a day, Soviet railroads 84 at most.

Radio transmitters remained scarce. The Baltic Military District had just 52 percent of the required number, the Kiev Military District 30 percent, the Western Military District 27 percent. Officers distrusted radios as too avant-garde and preferred cable communications, from telephone to telegraph. They said the airwaves weren't secure — anyone, they insisted, could intercept the exchange. Wires and cables were tangible, solid, and looked spy-proof. Few of them ran underground, however, and none were patrolled.

Another problem stemmed from the annexations of 1939–1940.

The new frontier areas remained quietly but persistently hostile to the Soviets. The western borderlands — the Baltics, Byelorussia, and Ukraine — had been in and out of the Russian sphere of influence for centuries, and Latvia, Lithuania, and Estonia had enjoyed a brief period of independence in the interwar years before being annexed by the Soviets in 1940. Western Ukraine and Byelorussia had been part of Poland. Now, with the exception of a few Party hacks, people there legitimately regarded the Red Army soldiers as intruders. Once Timoshenko and Zhukov watched a Goebbels propaganda film about the Wehrmacht's arrival in the Balkans, in which people enthusiastically welcomed the Germans and young women served them wine and flowers. Timoshenko loudly swore at the "forgery," but the Soviet generals knew that many people in the western part of the country would be only too happy to greet Hitler's army in the same way.

As Zhukov had begun to realize, the biggest problem of all was the cadres. The Great Purge had eliminated the cream of the officer corps, and 70 percent of the current commanders had been holding their jobs for less than two years. That basically meant that by 1941, regiments were led by men who had recently been lieutenants and armies by those who had been colonels.

Of the 225 regimental commanders, not a single one had gone to a military academy. One of them, when invited by an inspecting general to discern the depth of a ravine marked on a map, answered, "I cannot read the map. I will find out when we get there." The ravine proved to be thirteen feet deep and to contain a treacherous brook that would delay the unit's progress for several hours.

Badly educated upstarts couldn't take proper care of the modern weapons either. Inspection of the Red Army's First Mechanized Division found 60 out of 196 submachine guns broken.

Zhukov found it particularly ominous that the upstarts had infiltrated the strategic command. The most outrageous case was Pavel Rychagov, who was commanding the air force at the age of twenty-nine. The commander of the Kiev Military District, General Kirponos, had just two years earlier been a colonel in charge of a provincial military school.

Each military unit had a political officer, one of the notorious commissars, who had almost as much power as the commander. This resulted in immense confusion and often proved disastrous in time of war, since strategy had never been one of the commissars' strong points. In many cases uneducated and naive, these men were equally useless as ideological instructors. Once a commissar asked a soldier during a political class, "Tell me, how does the Soviet Union stand?" and when the soldier failed to understand the question, the commissar explained that the correct response should have been "The Soviet Union stands like a proud rock surrounded by the capitalist world."

▪ ▪ ▪

In the spring of 1941, the Soviet Union resembled not a proud rock but an arrested construction site, with millions of workers and foremen frozen in bewilderment. As late as mid-April, even top military leaders like Zhukov and Timoshenko were unsure what kind of warfare they were supposed to be preparing for, offensive or defensive.

A leader preparing to strike at a strong, aggressive adversary always operates under the threat of being forestalled. Indeed, if the enemy attacks while troops are still assembling, he will catch them in a moment of profound vulnerability: they won't have established proper fortifications, their army groups will be disunited (since they will still be marching to the front), their aviation units won't have functional airfields to use, and their tanks will need repairs after a long march. It is extremely difficult for a modern army preparing for an offensive attack to shift to a defensive posture at short notice, and while it regroups the adversary has an excellent chance of battering it, if not destroying it altogether.

With the exception of a few top commanders, the Soviet army still thought it was expected to defend the country, not strike first. More remarkably, while plans for a preemptive strike were sketchy, plans for defense were nonexistent. There were no reserve command posts, no backup communication lines, no alternative defensive positions marked out, no meeting points for retreating units. Usually in anticipation of an attack army engineers prepare all major communication arteries on the frontier for speedy and effective destruction. Bridges are layered with explosives, railroads and highways are secured with mines. Nothing of the sort was done in the spring of 1941, although nobody, including Stalin, could rule out a German attack.

To Zhukov's consternation, elements of the two opposing strategies, each of which required painstaking logistics, now intermingled, creating irreconcilable conflicts in military planning. Zhukov was most concerned about the fortifications. The old defense line, built from 1929 to 1935 along the initial Soviet-Polish border, had been all but abandoned, its guns removed, its garrisons mostly relocated, its warehouses quickly depleted of their stock, while the new one — on the current border, 150 to 200 miles farther west — was still under construction and still awaiting guns, soldiers, and supplies. If that were not enough, there were 30- to 40-mile gaps between the new forts, and construction was proceeding slowly. If the Red Army was getting ready for defense, the old fortifications should have been kept intact, at least for a while, and the new ones built at a comfortable distance from the current border. If the army was preparing to attack, as the new contour of fortifications indicated, the new forts had to get guns, personnel, and ammunition immediately.

Given the short range of Soviet aircraft, the air force needed new bases on the recently occupied territories. If the planes were to launch an assault, they had to be placed close to the border; if they were to help defend against an invasion, they needed to be deeper inland. Eastern Poland was occupied in September 1939. For a year and a half the pilots procrastinated. Stalin ordered the construction of new airfields only in February 1941 — and he wanted them very close to the border. Naturally, by April many were still under construction, so the existing ones remained overcrowded and undersupplied — easy prey for the Luftwaffe. Equally vulnerable were warehouses and fuel depots, also built right on the frontier to supply the army's preemptive strike.

Another issue was where to deploy the main force. A country facing the possibility of a powerful invasion rarely places the bulk of its force on the border, where it might be overwhelmed and destroyed, leaving the hinterland unprotected. Normally the main force is located a few hundred miles inland, which gives it freedom to maneuver, and the frontier is manned with just the first echelon of defense. Marshal Shaposhnikov, a shy but stubborn classicist, proposed to deploy the main force along the old fortification line, with a smaller force in the newly conquered territories. Stalin disagreed. However, if Stalin was seriously considering a preemptive strike, the troops along the western border needed reinforcements urgently. As it was, their ranks remained too thin for a successful assault.

If withdrawn to the rear, where it could flex its considerable muscle, the Red Army's main force would be able to resist a German attack. If reinforced with men and weapons, it would be able to evolve into a viable attack machine. Placed on the border as it was, it was good for neither, but was as weak and vulnerable as a molting crustacean.

Worse, the placement of Soviet troops was built around two salients that protruded west — one in Byelorussia, another in Ukraine. If Stalin ordered an offensive strike, each salient would serve as a thrust into Germany. But if the Germans forestalled him, the salients would become lethal traps for the Red Army.

In the absence of an overarching political decision, any serious and decisive military buildup was impossible. Indeed, the *vozhd* could not make up his mind, and the Red Army's leaders remained suspended in tired anticipation.

Stalin

Stalin spent the first weeks of spring in mental agony. He fully intended to strike at Germany first — hence the fortifications, airfields, and warehouses on the border, hence the troops in the western salients. However, he knew that for an attack to succeed, he would have to move a huge number of reinforcements to the frontier area. He would then reach the point of no return — he would be forced to forsake the defensive option altogether. Was it a good time for a preemptive strike or not? He needed to predict Hitler's next moves, and he felt he could not do so.

In February, German troops landed in North Africa. In April, they invaded Yugoslavia and Greece. That seemed to indicate that the

Führer had decided to deal with British colonies and allies in the eastern Mediterranean first, which was very good news for Stalin. With any luck, German troops would get mired in the Middle East. Even if they were victorious, it would take them several months to establish firm control over the rough and vast terrain. From Egypt, Hitler would probably proceed farther east, to the British colonies in Palestine, Transjordan, and Iraq, or to French Syria. In principle, from there his troops could march on to Iran, Afghanistan, and India. Also, Hitler had told Molotov the previous November that Germany wanted to acquire colonies in Africa, and Egypt would be a natural base for the implementation of that plan.

However, Stalin's intelligence — which was arguably the best in the world, as its recruits believed not in cash but in ideals — reported that Germany was plotting the imminent invasion of the Soviet Union.

Stalin didn't trust spies. Having himself betrayed many people, employers and patrons included, he saw no reason to believe that others wouldn't do the same to him, particularly if those others were liars by profession. His distrust also made sense from another, more objective perspective: spies had been promising a German attack for several months now, and each warning had proved false. On July 23, 1940, they reported that Germany would attack in just a few days and supported their forecast with meticulous enumeration of the German units arriving in Poland from the western front. In October they promised that an attack would occur in the first weeks of 1941, or not later than April. In December they said that "the war will be declared in March." How was that misleading data different from, say, a cable from "Zakhar" of April 11, 1941, quoting a source at the Luftwaffe headquarters who promised that Hitler would attack as soon as he crushed resistance in Yugoslavia and Greece?

On April 3 the prime minister of Great Britain, Winston Churchill, sent a private warning to Stalin about the impending German aggression. Churchill was very proud of his chivalrous act, but the warning ultimately did more harm than good. Churchill had been among Communism's staunchest opponents for more than twenty years, and understandably his warning raised suspicions about his possible motives.

Britain's position was desperate, and it would only be natural for the prime minister to do everything he could to drag Stalin into an alliance against Germany. Stalin was equally suspicious of other warnings he was receiving from the West, like the ones from the American undersecretary of state, Sumner Welles, and from the Yugoslavian ambassador to Moscow, Milan Gavrilovic. All these men had their own agendas, and the last thing Stalin wanted was for the Soviet Union to confront Germany before he was ready.

He had no confidant with whom to discuss any of this. Since the death of his wife, no woman had occupied a special place in his life, he had no friends, and as for his colleagues, they had mediocre minds, as had been his wish. The diplomatic corps had been devastated by the 1937 purge, and the person in charge of international policies, Vyacheslav Molotov, had been in the job just two years. Molotov had no command of foreign languages, no expertise in the outside world, and no real interest in his job. Lavrenty Beria, who commanded a blossoming web of agents abroad, had been a mere provincial police general before the Great Purge and had no idea how to run an international spy ring or, even more important, how to interpret and assess the information acquired. Those who could have helped both Molotov and Beria, educated and sophisticated men who had created both the Soviet foreign service and the worldwide Soviet intelligence network, now lay in common graves in prison yards.

Stalin couldn't even discuss the details of his preemptive strike plan with his generals. Brilliant strategists like Tukhachevsky, whom he had ordered shot, had been obsessed with the idea of leading the Red Army into Europe and would have enthusiastically joined in his great enterprise, contributing the knowledge and daring he so desperately needed. But they were dead, just like the diplomats and spymasters, and he couldn't possibly get sound advice from people like Voroshilov and Budenny, for whom the center of the world lay in the southern Russian steppes; they would have been literally lost in the confining European world of small countries and odd borders. Marshal Shaposhnikov was well versed in the art of war and European politics, but he lacked vision. The new star, Zhukov, was a man of formidable character, but his intellect still remained untested. Moreover, he was starting to look too opinionated. It was Zhukov who kept pestering the *vozhd* to pay attention to the concentration of the German troops on the border and the numerous violations of Soviet airspace. And it was becoming increasingly clear that Zhukov was influencing Timoshenko, who was growing equally alarmist.

Stalin's reservations were particularly painful as they went hand in hand with his paranoid visions of conspiracy and treason, which always ended in his own demise. The premonitions were becoming so overpowering that occasionally he was compelled to share them with somebody. Once, while taking a number of military leaders to dinner in his private quarters in the Kremlin and passing a large number of police officers defending a dense network of corridors, he suddenly said, "See how many of them are there? Each time I take this corridor, I think, which one? If this one, he will shoot me in the back, and if it is the one around the corner, he will shoot me up front. Yes, each time I pass them I get these thoughts." The terrified commanders didn't know what to say and proceeded to the table in silence.

Obsessed with grim thoughts about sedition, the *vozhd* decided he hadn't weeded out all potential traitors yet. Two years had passed since the previous cleansing, and some generals were already getting dangerously audacious. One of these was Lieutenant General Pavel Rychagov, commander of the Red Army's air force and Stalin's favorite.

At a conference with top military leaders, Stalin mentioned that the air force was sustaining far too many fatal accidents. It was true, but Rychagov thought the criticism was unfair. Barely thirty years old, a lieutenant only four years earlier, the boyish-looking young man didn't know how to behave. But he knew that the *vozhd* had a soft spot for reckless pilots, and thinking himself immune to Stalin's wrath, he jumped up, purple in the face from rage, and almost shouted, "Of course we will continue to have many accidents as long as you keep making flying coffins!"

Shocked silence fell over the room. Stalin, who had been pacing, stopped a few steps away from the young general and stared at him. Then he went back to his silent prowling. Finally he observed in a quiet voice, "That was the wrong thing to say!"

Rychagov, paralyzed by belated fear, didn't move. In a few moments the *vozhd* once again stopped in front of him and repeated even more calmly, "That was the wrong thing to say." And, after a pause, "The meeting is adjourned."

In a week Rychagov was arrested.

Stalin's mind worked systematically. A thing always belonged to a group. After Rychagov's arrest, the whole air force command was doomed.

The tension was becoming too much for the *vozhd.* Just like his father, he tried to calm himself by drinking heavily. In the past, at parties, he had let people choose how much they drank — or whether they wanted to drink at all. The feasts at his dacha had been reasonably joyful, if never relaxed. Now the host remained gloomy, drinking one glass of wine after another and making sure everybody else kept up with him. The dignitaries complained, since many of them could not stand alcohol and knew that by dawn they would be in the bathroom, being violently ill. They said among themselves that Stalin was turning them into a crowd of drunkards, but the resourceful Beria urged his colleagues to yield, saying, "Let's get drunk as soon as we can. The sooner we get drunk, the sooner he will let us go."

▪ ▪ ▪

In April, Japan's foreign minister, Yosuke Matsuoka, arrived in Moscow. The Soviet Union and Japan were slated to sign a nonaggression pact, much like the German-Soviet pact negotiated nineteen months earlier. On the face of it, Stalin should have felt reassured that the Axis powers had accepted him as a partner. But the world situation was growing increasingly complex.

Before coming to Moscow, Matsuoka had visited Berlin. Stalin would have paid dearly to learn what Hitler had told him. Japan had occupied the coastal areas of China and tried to penetrate Eurasia's heartland — it was during that effort that its troops clashed with the Red Army in Mongolia — and it was clear that the expansion would continue, but Stalin couldn't be sure what direction that would take. The *vozhd* was very concerned about the Soviet Union's eastern flank and had to keep a strong army group there to deter a potential Japanese strike. Would Japan be bold enough to attack the Soviet Union, or would it invade the British colonies in Southeast Asia, such as Singapore?

When they met, Matsuoka told Stalin that he wanted to meet Zhukov. Stalin smirked; obviously Matsuoka had been impressed by the general's performance in Mongolia. The dictator instructed Zhukov to be "nice" to the visitor, but Matsuoka stuck to the usual meaningless pleasantries during their conversation, saving matters of substance for the *vozhd*. That conversation took place on April 12 in the Kremlin.

As many other foreign leaders did in those days, the Japanese spoke openly about the impending war between Germany and the Soviet Union. But unlike others, he had spoken to Hitler just days earlier. "Though Japan is Germany's ally," he said, "this does not mean Japan will engage the Soviet Union in the event of war. To the contrary, if something happens between the Soviet Union and Germany, Japan would like to mediate."

How was Stalin expected to interpret that? Had Hitler told Matsuoka that he would attack the Soviet Union in the next few months? Or was Matsuoka consciously planting disinformation? Perhaps it was a sincere pledge on Matsuoka's part. As far as Stalin knew, Hitler had been unaware of Japan's intention to sign a neutrality pact with the USSR as recently as a few weeks before. Did that mean that the Axis was heading for a rift?

In addition to mediating any crisis with Germany, the Japanese foreign minister said, Japan would support the Soviet Union if Stalin decided to strike at the British colonies in the Middle East. It was time to put an end to British rule in Asia, Matsuoka declared, and he pledged his country's forbearance if Stalin entered Karachi. That jibed with what Hitler had told Molotov in Berlin the previous November. Did that mean that Germany would not attack the Soviet Union after all and that Moscow, Tokyo, and Berlin could instead launch a joint war against Britain in Asia?

On the one hand, a neutrality pact with Japan offered peace on Stalin's eastern flank, which meant that the *vozhd* could focus all his attention on Europe. On the other hand, how could he trust Tokyo when he didn't trust Berlin? His two top commanders, Zhukov and Timoshenko, thought that Hitler was preparing to launch an attack on the Soviet Union in spite of the 1939 nonaggression pact.

Even if Zhukov and Timoshenko were right and Hitler was going to ignore the pact, the truce between the two countries had already lasted for nineteen months. It was highly unlikely that Matsuoka would sign a neutrality pact only to toss it aside a few weeks later. If a Soviet-Japanese truce could last for nineteen months, Stalin's eastern flank would surely be secure until the end of 1942.

Stalin felt that his reasoning was sound, and he signed the pact. He was so elated that he went to the railway station to see Matsuoka off. After shaking hands with stunned railway personnel and frightened travelers, he threw his arm around the neck of the German military attaché in Moscow, Colonel Krebs, and playfully asked, "We are going to remain friends, aren't we?"

This lighthearted affability, totally uncharacteristic of the *vozhd*, was a deliberate act of reassurance for Berlin. In fact it was part of a grand smokescreen Stalin was starting to build. Shortly afterward he informed his generals that he had decided to proceed with the preemptive strike against Germany.

The Preemptive Strike

It had taken Stalin about nine months to make this decision. The days of equivocation had come to an end.

Matsuoka's visit had been a pivotal moment in the *vozhd*'s journey. He perceived a growing rift between Germany and Japan, and he believed that Japan would not attack the Soviet Union in the next year and a half. This provided him a critical window of opportunity. Whether Zhukov and Timoshenko were right or wrong about Hitler's intentions, Stalin decided he would strike soon, while his eastern flank was safe and the Wehrmacht was still tied up in the eastern Mediterranean and North Atlantic.

On May 5, Stalin appointed himself chairman of the Council of People's Commissars — in effect, prime minister. Until then he had been just the general secretary of the Party, providing guidance and criticism but never being directly responsible for what the government did, so that he could always distance himself from its inadequacies and blunders. Now, seventeen years into his rule, he was finally willing to assume full responsibility. The rationale for the *vozhd*'s assumption of total control, as it was announced to the nation, sounded ominous, built around key words like "strained international relations" and "defense."

The same day, May 5, the *vozhd* gave a speech at the Red Army academies' commencement in the Kremlin. "Is the German army invincible?" he asked. As usual, he answered the question himself: "There is no such thing as an invincible army." Yet he didn't want to ease the commanders' vigilance and pointedly called the Wehrmacht the best force in the world. To defeat the Germans, he continued, an army had to be nourished, unlike the French army, which had been defeated a year earlier. In France, "Girls wouldn't even marry a soldier," he remarked with sincere indignation. But, he noted emphatically, the army *was* nourished by the people and the government of the Soviet Union.

At the banquet following these remarks, a tipsy major general, choking with loyalty and still unable to sense a change in the wind, toasted Stalin's "peace-loving policy." Irritated by the man's stupidity, the *vozhd* objected.

"Let me introduce a correction here," he said. "A policy promoting peace did secure peace for our country. It was a good thing. For a while we emphasized the need for defense — until we rearmed our troops and gave them modern weaponry. Now, with the army restructured and possessing equipment for modern combat — now that we have become strong — it is time to go from a posture of defense to one of attack."

The tipsy major general wasn't the only person in the room who had been confused by Stalin's speech at the commencement, which hinted at a break with the past but failed to address the issue of aggression directly. Only now, after the *vozhd*'s "correction," did the graduates understand. The mood in the room immediately changed, as the officers felt a surge of excitement, energized by the leader's promise of an imminent and no doubt victorious assault.

Meanwhile, Timoshenko, Zhukov, Zhukov's deputy, Vatutin, and Shaposhnikov's favorite disciple, Vasilevsky, were working on the war plan. They did not share the graduates' enthusiasm, however. For them, Stalin's painful vacillation continued. The principal decision had been made — the Soviet Union would strike first — but when they talked to the *vozhd* about specifics, he was vague. He honestly believed that he had until the summer of 1942, so detailed planning could wait. All he wanted now was another broad blueprint.

Also, preparing a war plan for Stalin was always a nightmare. His chronic suspiciousness and strong opinions were difficult enough, but what made the generals feel really desperate was that he didn't seem to realize that he lacked the most basic military skills. He was unable to read maps correctly. He noticed things like distances and the locations of cities, but he never paid attention to the terrain. In his view, the difference between the green and brown areas on the map that denoted valleys and hills, the arcane marks indicating marshes and forests, and the thin blue threads announcing the presence of rivers were insignificant. His armies were to march from point A to point B in a straight line, following a precise schedule.

That schedule was ready by May 15. It was a fifteen-page memo in black ink in Vasilevsky's handwriting, addressed to Stalin and carrying a warning in its upper right-hand corner: "Top Secret. Very Urgent. Exclusively Personal. The Only Copy."

Both Timoshenko and Vasilevsky had worked on drafts of the plan, but it was Zhukov's first chance to leave his imprint on history. Having exhibited a passion for grandiose assaults virtually unprecedented in the Red Army, in his report "The Nature of the Modern Offensive Operation" and then again during the strategic game of January, he now made sure the first-strike document envisaged a grandiose assault.

The generals knew that the *vozhd* favored the south as the major strategic theater — he coveted the Balkans, and he also expected to find Hitler's main force there. For that reason, the document suggested striking from Ukraine and defeating the Germans' main force in southern Poland. The Kiev Military District, transformed into a group called the Southwestern Front, was to lead the attack, its troops striking at Krakow. In accordance with Zhukov's megalomaniacal tendencies, the Southwestern Front was to send about 1 million men and 8,000 tanks

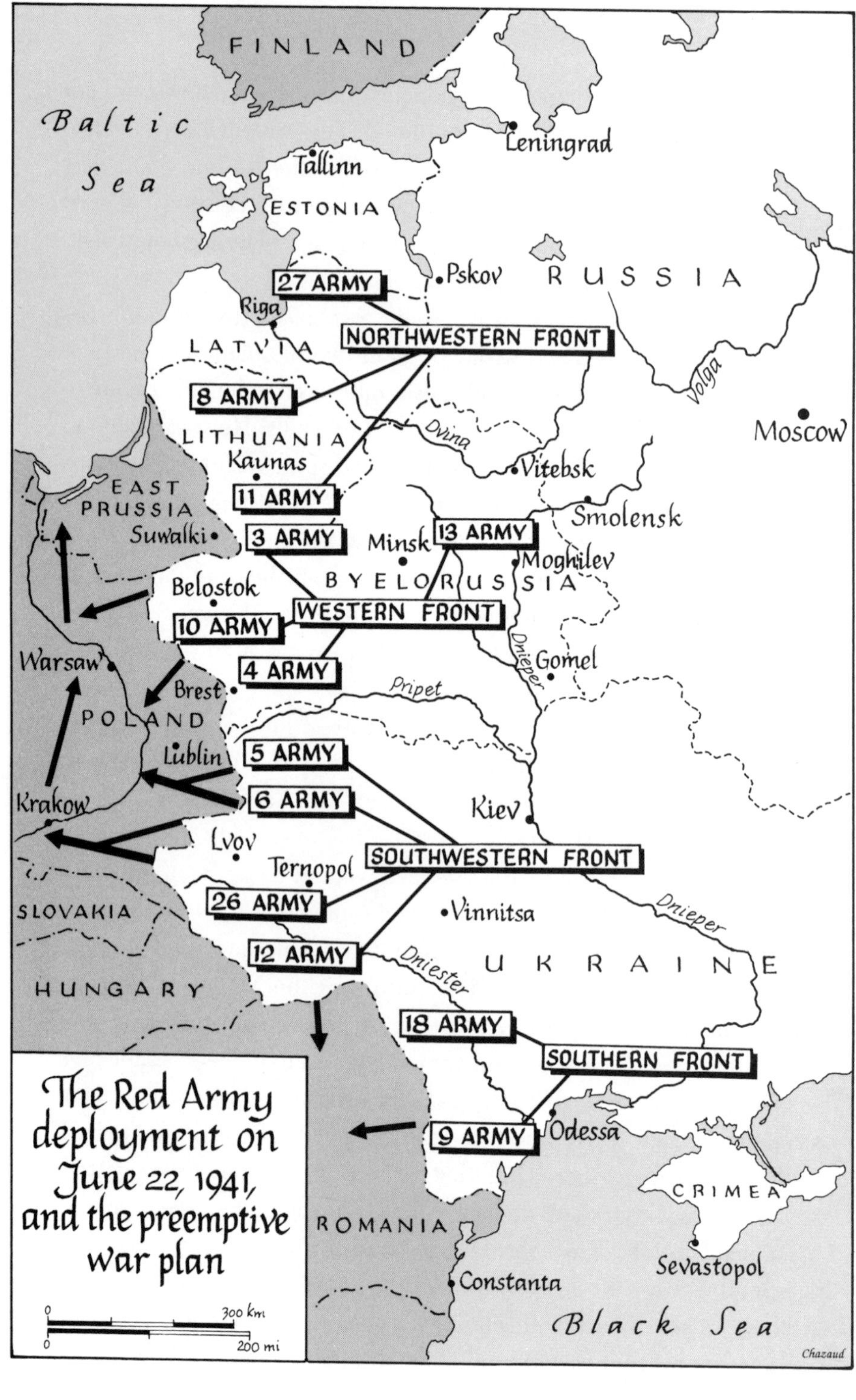

The Red Army deployment on June 22, 1941, and the preemptive war plan

into battle. Romania would also be invaded. In the north, the Western Military District, now the Western Front, was to hit Warsaw.

In thirty days the Red Army had to reach a line running from Ostroleka, in Poland, via the Narew River, to Lowicz, Lodz, Kluczbork, Opole, and the Czech city of Olomouc. That would take Stalin's soldiers into the heart of Europe. The southernmost point of advance, Olomouc, was just 270 miles from Munich and 100 miles from Vienna. Progress in the north was planned on a more modest scale, as the Western Front would not be as strong as the southwestern one. Its troops were expected to stop at Ostroleka; from there, they would turn north to occupy eastern Prussia and the rest of Poland. The plan didn't suggest what would happen next, since Stalin himself was obviously in doubt. He probably hoped that Hitler could be forced to sign a peace treaty and yield the whole of Eastern Europe. In any case, it was far too early to plan an attack on the core of the Third Reich.

The plan was a direct successor to the three previous drafts, but it differed from them in two important respects: it openly advocated a preemptive strike ("it is necessary to deprive the German command of all initiative, to preempt the adversary and to attack"), and it unambiguously favored Ukraine as the main springboard of aggression.

The assault required an enormous amount of preparation. The Southwestern Front had just four armies out of the envisaged eight, although all four — the Fifth, Sixth, Twelfth, and Twenty-sixth — were already very close to the border. The Western Front looked almost ready for its mission — three armies out of the four suggested in the blueprint, the Third, Fourth, and Tenth, stood at the frontier, and the Thirteenth was being assembled in the rear — but according to the plan, the Soviet high command also had to have five armies in strategic reserve, stationed 150 to 400 miles inland. That reserve still had to be created.

For that purpose, the generals suggested secretly mobilizing reservists under the smokescreen of "training exercises" and quietly sending a number of armies now stationed in the east to the planned war theater. The air force needed more planes along the frontier as well. The plan also noted that it was time to start working on the rear, establishing new hospitals and depots.

No date was given for the attack, but the document suggested finalizing preparations in 1942. That gave the Red Army about a year to get ready. Immediately after the plan was completed in mid-May, though, Stalin launched an aggressive military buildup. In all likelihood he had been unnerved by Rudolf Hess's surprising defection to Britain.

An eccentric maverick, Hess presided over the Nazi Party and had long been Hitler's most trusted associate. In the spring of 1941, feeling alienated from the Führer by the ascendancy of new favorites and clearly experiencing a severe mental disorder that made him talk to "supernatural powers," Hess developed the bizarre idea of unilaterally arranging peace with Britain to ease the strain on the Führer and the German people. A former air force pilot, he flew to the British Isles in a twin-engine plane and parachuted into Scotland on May 10, intending to negotiate a deal with the British government. Enraged, Hitler declared him legally insane. The British made him a prisoner of war, but conspiracy theories sprang up all over the world.

Since Stalin had always subscribed to that mode of thinking, he was alarmed, suspecting that Hitler and Churchill were indeed negotiating a peace. Reinforcing his suspicions, Soviet spies in London reported that Hess wanted to forge an Anglo-German alliance because it would allow Britain and the Third Reich to strike at the Soviet Union together. Stalin should have been reassured when, on May 20, the Germans landed on Crete and quickly defeated British troops there — hardly a way to promote a joint anti-Soviet endeavor. But he was not.

Stalin believed more strongly in conspiracy theory than in Marxism-Leninism. His own ascent to power during the 1920s had been achieved through deceit and scheming, and in 1939 he had successfully conspired with Hitler to divide Eastern Europe. Now he smelled a rat. He simply couldn't believe that the second in command of the Nazi Party had just flown a plane to Britain to negotiate an alliance with London because he was insane. He wasn't sure who had dispatched Hess on his mission, Hitler or a bunch of anti-Hitler plotters — perhaps some old-school German generals eager to get rid of the Anglophobic Führer, sign peace with the capitalist government of Britain, and then attack the USSR. A few times Stalin had hinted in the presence of Zhukov and Timoshenko that German generals could be involved in just such a conspiracy.

Hess's defection was the second pivotal moment that spring. After it happened, Stalin decided to accelerate war preparations. Whatever precipitated Hess's flight, he was now no longer sure he had until the summer of 1942. The Red Army had to be able to move sooner than that.

He notified his defense industry that starting on June 25, it had to begin producing fifty military aircraft a day instead of twenty. Five armies started secretly moving west: the Sixteenth, Nineteenth, Twentieth, Twenty-first, and Twenty-second. The Sixteenth, Nineteenth, and Twenty-first were heading to the southwest to be deployed 100 to 300 miles from the border and later to join the first wave of attack. The Twentieth and Twenty-second were sent to Byelorussia, 250 to 300 miles from the frontier, to establish the high command reserve. The armies were to be in position by July 10. Two more armies — the Twenty-fourth and Twenty-eighth — were to redeploy soon after. The move was to remain top-secret.

By May 20, Timoshenko and Zhukov had sent the commanders of the frontier military districts vague directives developed by Vasilevsky, like all the drafts of the preemptive war plan. The directives alerted the generals to the possibility of war but never mentioned the preemptive strike or the coming reinforcements. The commanders were expected to deliver a "detailed plan to defend the frontier" by May 25. The only hint of the planned aggression was in clause II.4: "If the situation is favorable, all the defending troops and reserves of the armies and the district" had to be ready to launch "energetic blows" at the order of the high command. However, the precise phrasing of the clause differed, depending on the front. The Western Military District, which was given an auxiliary role in the preemptive strike, had "to be ready to launch energetic blows." However, the Kiev Military District, which was expected to strike at southern Poland, and the Odessa Military District, which was to attack Romania, received a more vigorous version. The Kiev Military District was ordered to "be ready to launch energetic blows to devastate enemy troops, transfer hostilities on its territory, and reach advantageous positions there." The Odessa Military District also had to be ready to transfer hostilities on enemy territory and take advantageous positions there. However, its "energetic blows" had to be "short-range," probably because Romania was small.

The relocation of seven armies to the west wouldn't solve the problem of manpower, however; at least two more were needed. Also, many existing units were heavily understaffed. In May and June, 800,000 reservists were quietly drafted. All military schools were ordered to finish early that year so the young lieutenants could be sent west.

The accelerated buildup suggested that the army would be ready to strike by midsummer. The seven armies were expected to be in place by July 10, and although the last date for the reservists' draft was set for August 25, the majority would be assembled by June 1.

In total, almost 3 million soldiers were deployed between the Baltic and the Black Sea. That figure included eleven police regiments charged with imposing order on the territories that were to be occupied. The frontier military districts were starting to move troops closer to the border. The commanders of those districts were ordered to begin preparing combat headquarters. By June 25, the Baltic Military District had to have moved to Panevezys, the Western Military District to Obuz Lesny, the Kiev Military District to Ternopol, and the Odessa Military District to Tiraspol. The new locations were just under 100 miles from the proposed front line. Soon the districts were to be renamed "fronts," as the tentative war plan envisioned. The existence of a front unambiguously implied war. The Russian language had no word for a front-line mega-unit during peacetime; only a fighting army could have such a thing.

In all likelihood, fewer than ten people knew about these measures in their entirety. Three million servicemen had no idea that very soon they would find themselves on a front line, and even the military district headquarters were unaware of the overall strategic design. Since the grand military conference of December and January, the Red Army's top officers hadn't met as a group, so there had been precious few opportunities for rumors to spread. But at the end of May an urgent summons was sent out: the *vozhd* would be holding a top-secret meeting in his Kremlin study on May 24.

It was common practice for Stalin to divide meeting participants into groups and give each a separate briefing. True to form, on May 24 he divided the attendants into three clusters. At 6 P.M., Molotov and Timoshenko walked in. Ten minutes later they were joined by Zhukov and Vatutin (Stalin no doubt separated Timoshenko and Zhukov to sow discord between them). Another forty minutes passed before sixteen more generals joined them: the commander of the air force, P. F. Zhigarev; the commanders of the frontier military districts, Pavlov, Kuznetsov, Kirponos, Popov, and Cherevichenko; and their commissars and air force commanders. The meeting lasted for two and a half hours. Its agenda is still unknown, but probably Stalin informed the generals about the preemptive strike plan during this gathering.

Around the same time he started "cleansing" the newly conquered territories in the west, ordering the police to accelerate purges in Lithuania, Latvia, and Estonia. Several categories of people were to be arrested automatically: members of all "counterrevolutionary" parties; former policemen; former landowners, capitalists, and bureaucrats; former officers of Polish, Lithuanian, Latvian, Estonian, and White Russian armies; and felons. They were to be sent to labor camps for five to eight years and then kept in Siberia for twenty more. Their families were also to be deported, to spend twenty years in Siberia as well. All in all, at least 170,000 men and women in the Baltics fell victim to this eleventh-hour purge.

▪ ▪ ▪

If the Soviet Union was going to strike anytime soon, Stalin knew, the nation's spirits needed to be boosted. The concept of offensive warfare certainly wasn't new to the Soviets. For the last several years Stalin had been repeating the mantra that the Red Army would fight any war "with minimal losses and on enemy's territory." Boys and girls who competed for the title of Voroshilov Shot grew up with the idea, and the military subscribed to it too. When Chief of General Staff Marshal Yegorov proposed preparing a reserve command post for the western war theater in 1937, Marshal Voroshilov accused him of being a defeatist who didn't believe in Stalin's doctrine of offensive war. Yegorov and other defeatists were shot, and since then nobody had dared to dispute Stalin's wisdom.

But the nation, like the army, was confused by the ad hoc alliance with Germany. After the pact was signed in 1939, many relaxed, believing there would be no war. According to the official line, a "war with minimal losses" waged on enemy territory would take place only after the Communist motherland was attacked. Each time Stalin ordered the army to cross the border, he had to justify it. The pretext usually involved the oppressed desires of the working class in the attacked country or the provocations of its capitalist rulers. But this time Stalin decided to exploit the powerful anti-Fascist sentiment that had built up during the 1930s, only to be abandoned abruptly in 1939.

As early as April 24 he called the writer Ilia Erenburg, one of the few urban bohemians who had been allowed to survive the purges. Erenburg was an intellectual, well connected in Europe, who willingly let Stalin use him for propaganda missions abroad. He had recently found himself in the doghouse, though. A Francophone, he had published an anti-Nazi novel, *The Fall of Paris,* inspired by the occupation of France, and its last part was so violently antagonistic to Germany that the censors had banned it. Now Stalin suggested that Erenburg start marketing the book aggressively. Soon the stunned author was reading the banned portions of his novel to the People's Commissariat of Foreign Affairs, the General Staff, and the People's Commissariat of the Interior.

On May 15, Andrei Zhdanov, a dependable high-ranking ideologue, informed Soviet filmmakers that the Soviet Union would "keep propagating socialism." That implied war ahead. In the beginning of June, the chief of the Red Army Propaganda Directorate, A. S. Shcherbakov, issued a directive to that effect. War against capitalist countries was inevitable, it said, and it was the Soviet Union's duty to initiate it, "to spread socialism." The pathetic president of the USSR, the chairman of Stalin's legislature, Mikhail Kalinin, addressed the graduates of Lenin Military Academy on June 5, saying that "war is the time when you can expand communism." By June 20, the Red Army Propaganda Directorate had prepared a secret document aimed at the officer corps. It was quite explicit, saying that it was useless to build defenses against the German juggernaut, as the example of a number of European countries had proved, and that the Soviet Union would therefore "apply an offensive strategy" against Germany.

The Premonitions

Very soon word of the impending attack reached the outside world. Despite Stalin's efforts to root out all treasonous elements, foreign countries obviously still had eyes and ears in the Soviet Union. Already, on May 9, the newspaper *Izvestiya* had published a governmental refutation drafted by Stalin personally, calling reports in the foreign press of the concentration of Red Army troops along the western border "totally fantastic." But no matter how tightly controlled the information was, it was simply impossible to conceal preparations for the preemptive strike or limit knowledge of it to the top ten or twenty military leaders. People flying from Siberia or Central Asia to Moscow could easily see numerous military trains on the ground, heading west. Several generals from the eastern part of the country were spotted in Moscow in field uniforms. Military district headquarters in the west were hastily preparing for relocation to battle posts. An army private or a regimental commander might remain ignorant of all this, but hundreds of senior officers did pay attention and, piecing together the many clues, started whispering to one other that a full-scale war was on the way.

Infuriated, the *vozhd* decided that he had been betrayed. In mid-June, at a meeting in his Kremlin study, he suddenly said, "Shtern has proved a scum." That was his way of informing the top leaders of the country that a prominent general, the commander of the Red Army Air Defense, Colonel General Grigory Shtern, had been arrested. If the arrest of Air Force Commander Pavel Rychagov several weeks earlier had been something of a whim, Shtern's arrest signaled that the machine of terror had been restarted in earnest. The dismayed people's commissar of the navy, Kuznetsov, thought, "Today it is Shtern, tomorrow it could be me." The Politburo economist Voznesensky, sitting next to him, hastily and loudly pronounced Shtern "a swine."

Shtern was arrested on June 7. Under torture he admitted to having been a German spy since 1931. Next was another senior air force officer, Lieutenant General Y. V. Smushkevich. After that the purge spread quickly. Lavrenty Beria tortured the generals personally. Among the arrested was the commander of the Baltic Military District, Colonel

General A. D. Loktionov. By June 16, having been tortured but still unwilling to confess, he wrote a letter to the government asking to be allowed to "die an honorable death." He signed it "former Colonel General Loktionov." Not everyone had this kind of resolve. Rear Admiral Konstantin Samoilov, head of naval schools, arrested on June 18, admitted that as early as 1922 the Persian consul in Baku had recruited him to work for French intelligence.

The June purge was one of Joseph Stalin's most ominous acts. Unleashed in the midst of battle preparations, the arrests looked particularly insane. About three hundred people were arrested, among them twenty-two bearers of the highest military decoration in the country, the golden star of a Hero of the Soviet Union.

Tormented by paranoia, suspecting that his military leaders were selling his war plans to the Germans — or possibly preparing a coup — Stalin oversaw the massacre. Rychagov's silly comment about the Kremlin forcing his men to pilot "flying coffins" had triggered it, and now the purge engulfed those close to Rychagov (first the air force command and aircraft makers, among them the deputy people's commissar of the aviation industry, Vassily Balandin); those who, like Rychagov, had fought as Soviet "volunteers" in Spain, where they could have been recruited by Trotsky or foreign intelligence (like Smushkevich); and those who, again like Rychagov, had defied Stalin or his lieutenants.

Among the latter was People's Commissar of Armaments Vannikov. Stalin had never forgiven him for his comment about "disarming" the army on the eve of war, when tank armaments were being debated. Yet on June 15, Stalin unexpectedly announced that Vannikov's chief opponent, the Red Army artillery supervisor Marshal Kulik, would have to step down too. Kulik was Stalin's pet, and though he was not arrested, the whole establishment was overcome with fear: it looked like another Great Purge was beginning.

▪ ▪ ▪

Meanwhile, more and more reports about a possible German invasion were reaching Stalin's desk. "Zeus," stationed in Sofia, reported a concentration of German motorized divisions along the Soviet border on

May 14. On May 19, "Dora" cabled from Zurich to say that plans for the attack had been finalized. On May 20, "Extern," from Helsinki, confirmed as much. On May 28, "ABC," in Bucharest, testified that the war would start in June. "Mars," in Budapest, gave the date of the invasion as June 15. "Ramzai," in Tokyo, reported the same date. Knowing that Stalin didn't believe the warnings, the analysts at the intelligence agency filed the cable from "Ramzai" — in real life an idealistic German Communist, Richard Sorge, who had led a precarious existence in Japan befriending German diplomats and Japanese officials — in the "folder of dubious and misleading reports." It was obvious that spies now irritated Stalin more than air force commanders. After receiving a memo from a Soviet source at German air force headquarters warning that war could start at any time, he wrote in the margin: "Maybe we should tell this 'source' to go fuck himself. He's not a source but a liar."

But it wasn't just spies who were delivering daily reports of suspicious behavior on the part of the Germans. Troops on the border were joining the chorus. A few months earlier, German border sentries would jump to attention and salute if they spotted a Soviet officer. Now they deliberately ignored the Red Army commanders. More important, German planes were constantly violating Soviet airspace. Between June 10 and 19, the frontier was violated no fewer than eighty-six times; on June 20 and 21, fifty-five times. Each time the aircraft flew at least 20 or 30 miles deep.

Even the servile and opportunistic Beria, who normally told Stalin only what he wanted to hear, reported that the Germans had dispatched numerous saboteurs to Ukraine, Byelorussia, and Lithuania. The saboteurs crossed the border individually or in small groups and carried radio transmitters, weapons, currency, and Soviet passports. Some of them were former White Army officers who had fought against the Reds in the same region twenty years earlier. In May the border guards captured 353 men trying to cross the border; in the first ten days of June, 108. It was unclear how many had made it through undetected. On June 11, Beria's men discovered a telephone cable on the bottom of the San River; the Germans had been monitoring Red Army phone conversations.

Each time Stalin was confronted with such information, he said — sometimes with irritation, sometimes with forced calm — "Hitler and his generals are not so foolish as to start a two-front war. The Germans broke their neck on this in World War I. Hitler would never risk such a thing."

However, the *vozhd* felt that he and Hitler were now locked in a tight race. The first to accumulate enough troops to strike would in all likelihood win the war. He had accelerated his preparations only a few weeks earlier. Even if his spies continued to be wrong about the date of the German invasion — they now said mid-June — it was clear that Hitler had already sent a mighty army to the border. The months of hesitation, during which Stalin hadn't been able to make up his mind about what kind of war he was willing to fight, looked as if they would cost the country dearly.

Military developments abroad remained difficult to interpret. The British had evacuated Crete, having lost about 15,000 men. London suspected that the Germans could now land in Syria and Malta. The latter was already effectively blockaded by the German air force and could no longer be used by the British navy as a major base. The Luftwaffe attacked the Suez Canal from recently acquired bases in the Dodecanese, and Rommel's panzer armada was just 450 miles west of it. The sole British success in recent months had been the sinking of the predatory German battleship *Bismarck* in the North Atlantic.

It was hard to tell what all this meant for the Soviet Union. Britain had been so weakened that some thought Hitler might discard it as a major opponent and consequently risk a two-front war. His powerful push in the eastern Mediterranean could, however, signify his intention to grab the Middle East first.

It was a truism that any large-scale attack on Russia had to take place in the late spring or early summer to finish the campaign before winter struck. Mud season, occurring in both spring and fall, made most of the roads impassable, narrowing the window even more. If Hitler was going to strike in 1941, he had to do it soon, so as to finish the main part of the campaign before September. In 1812, Napoleon had struck on June 24.

Yielding to immense stress, Stalin's mind started wandering, or at least that was his generals' impression. On June 7 he told Kuznetsov to put antisubmarine nets in the Kerch Strait, which led from the Black Sea to the Sea of Azov, and to cover the town of Batumi in the Caucasus with naval ships. The Sea of Azov didn't have a single important target, and Batumi had no particular significance, except that Stalin had spent part of his youth there. The directive seemed to reflect his fear of an imminent German attack, but if he was concerned about the safety of the Soviet coast, why didn't he order similar measures for important locations like Leningrad and Riga?

If the *vozhd*'s wavering upset Admiral Kuznetsov — who held a relatively inconsequential job as commander of the navy in a landlocked nation — it tortured the two generals bearing full responsibility for the army, Timoshenko and Zhukov. By June 1941, Timoshenko, who had then spent a year in the halls of power, was utterly exhausted, and with each week he sank deeper and deeper into fatalism and depression. Zhukov, brought to Moscow only five months earlier, was a changed man too. His initial zeal had receded, his fear of Stalin had grown, and he had to acknowledge that he was just a lackey.

However, he was a thinking lackey. Zhukov knew that Hitler was winning the race for the first strike. The army divisions so desperately needed on the frontier were still inching across the Russian plains. The military plants still had to increase the production of modern aircraft and tanks. The reservists still had to reach their destinations. Hitler's Wehrmacht, in contrast, looked fit. In Zhukov's view, the frontier military districts had to be put on combat alert immediately. But Stalin kept saying that that was too risky, since Hitler might become alarmed and actually order an attack.

As time went by, Zhukov felt that Stalin increasingly resented him. It almost looked like the *vozhd* regretted his decision to bring him to Moscow. He dismissed Zhukov's concerns as overblown and saw him as little as possible.

Some exchanges with the *vozhd* were virtually unbearable, hinting at a disturbed mind, or at least one trapped in its own delusions. At the end of May, Stalin told Zhukov and Timoshenko that the German government sought permission to locate the graves of German soldiers who had died in Russian territory during World War I. "Make sure they do not dip deeper than the border areas," he directed. "Tell the military districts to maintain direct contact with our border guards. The border guards already have their instructions."

Timoshenko and Zhukov looked visibly shocked, and the ideologue Andrei Zhdanov ironically said, "It looks like our comrades have been upset by the German government's request. Perhaps you want to say something?"

"The Germans are going to research the areas where they plan to strike," Zhukov said. "And as for the grave search, it is a blatant lie."

Timoshenko added, "The Germans have been violating our airspace too often recently. And they fly deep into our territory. Zhukov and I think we should start shooting the German planes down."

Stalin emphatically disagreed. "The German ambassador has explained that their air force has too many youngsters who are not well trained yet. Young pilots can easily lose their way. The ambassador has asked us to ignore the wandering planes."

Zhukov and Timoshenko indignantly countered by saying that the German pilots wandered over the most important Soviet military targets and descended very low, so that they could see every detail.

"Well," Stalin said, "then we should urgently prepare a note and tell Hitler to curb his generals' license. I am not sure he knows about that."

In another conversation, when Zhukov voiced his continued concern about the accumulation of German troops on the border, Stalin again chose to reassure him. The Soviet ambassador to Germany, he said, had spoken confidentially with Hitler, who had said, "Please do not worry when you hear about the concentration of our troops in Poland. They are going there for massive training before major strikes in the West."

Stalin's behavior was more and more erratic. He worried about irrelevant defense precautions like the nets in the Kerch Strait, and he allowed the Germans to violate Soviet airspace in critically important areas. He suspected that Hitler had sent Hess to England to negotiate peace, and yet he believed Hitler when he said that German pilots violated Soviet airspace only because they were young and untrained.

To Zhukov and Timoshenko, the contradictions were glaring. Sometimes it looked as if the *vozhd* was consumed by anxiety, but occasionally they got the impression that Stalin had a strange trust in Hitler and believed his most blatant lies.

Kremlin insiders knew that the *vozhd* regarded Hitler as the only person on earth who matched his greatness — Hitler was an alter ego, a soulmate in an odd way. Both had come to power in an elaborate coup, both had rid themselves of rivals, both had crushed the dissent of minorities and weaker neighbors. Sometimes it seemed that Hitler was the only human being Stalin truly respected. Back in 1934, when Hitler had massacred his own party's old guard, the *vozhd* had muttered, "Hitler, what a lad!" The *vozhd* feared his military leaders, and now, projecting his paranoia onto Hitler's situation, he started worrying that German generals could be conspiring against the Führer. This perverse relationship probably explained his bizarre trust in an enemy he was about to attack.

In mid-June, German diplomats and their families started leaving Moscow. Soviet agents in the embassy reported that the Germans were sending diplomatic files to Berlin or destroying them — a typical procedure for an embassy preparing to evacuate. Stalin remained unconvinced, and the frustrating process continued: the Germans kept piling up troops on the border, Stalin kept refusing to put the Red Army on combat alert, and Soviet trains continued to take strategic raw materials to the Third Reich.

On June 13, Timoshenko and Zhukov called Stalin from Timoshenko's office. Keeping their pact of friendship and refusing to let Stalin play them off each other, they did their best to persuade him that Hitler could forestall him. That day they were both particularly worried. For two days the *vozhd* had been receiving no one. Now they formally sought his permission to put the frontier military districts on combat alert. Zhukov couldn't hear Stalin's response, so after Timoshenko put the receiver down, he asked, "Well?"

"He told me to check tomorrow's newspaper," said Timoshenko angrily. Out of sheer desperation, he added, "Come on, let's go have some dinner."

The next day, June 14, *Izvestiya* did carry a prominent government statement. Like the one in May, it dealt with "rumors" about the forthcoming war between the Soviet Union and Germany. It announced that Germany had never demanded territorial concessions from the Soviet Union, that Germany was scrupulously observing the nonaggression pact, that the Soviet Union was also observing the pact, and that a number of Soviet units had been relocated closer to the border purely for training purposes.

Timoshenko and Zhukov were appalled. Whatever it was — diplomacy, propaganda, or mere stupidity — it was going to have a devastating effect on the army. How could the commanders be expected to boost morale when the government was telling the world that Germany was still the Soviet Union's best friend?

Judging by Stalin's schedule, the *vozhd* was nearly in hiding. In the first half of June, he spent eight days away from his office, and between June 11 and 18 he didn't grant Timoshenko and Zhukov a single audience. This outraged the generals. Whether they were right or wrong in sounding the alarm, they still needed daily contact.

They didn't know why he was avoiding them. He could have been angered by their nagging, he could have been confident that everything was fine, or he could have been planning to have them both arrested. Zhukov felt particularly vulnerable, as several generals rounded up in the June purge had been his subordinates.

Brought together by anxiety and fear, Zhukov and Timoshenko decided to hold their ground. As soon as they had a chance to see the *vozhd*, they told him once again that the troops had to be put on combat alert. Stalin exploded, saying that doing so would mean war. At the same time he reluctantly admitted that the situation was becoming more untenable by the day. Concerned about the safety of his air force on the border, he finally ordered all aircraft to be painted with matte camouflage by July 20. The runways were to be disguised as well. However, those were stopgap measures.

Exasperated and tired, he finally told Molotov to go to Berlin and talk to Hitler. Molotov urgently tried to get in touch with the German government. Berlin didn't respond.

The Evening of June 21

On Thursday, June 19, Stalin skipped his office hours once again. He was away from his desk for forty-three hours, but he finally returned to the Kremlin shortly before 8 P.M. on Friday, June 20. There he received another warning. His old colleague Mikoyan, in charge of foreign trade, informed him that a group of twenty-five German vessels had suddenly left the port of Riga without completing the loading and unloading of goods.

Stalin said they were free to do as they wished, but he sensed that something was up. He called General Ivan Tiulenev, head of air defense of the Moscow Military District, saying, "Situation has become unsteady. Boost your air defense readiness to seventy-five percent."

However, he did not call Timoshenko or Zhukov. He did not want to provoke the Germans by putting his border troops on combat alert.

The next day, Saturday, June 21, he realized he had to do something more. His instinct was telling him that inaction would be perilous.

The first measure he took was largely symbolic: he had a number of popular poets taken to the Radio Committee and ordered to compose bellicose anti-Nazi songs. The second step was real: Soviet diplomats in Berlin were instructed to visit Foreign Minister Ribbentrop right away and ask him to explain the concentration of German troops on the border. The German Foreign Ministry replied that Ribbentrop was out of town. All queries throughout the day were met with the same response. Now truly alarmed, Stalin called an urgent meeting.

The night was sultry, hot and windless. The Kremlin trees stood motionless in the heat, their leaves flaccid, and people gulped for air in their offices.

Stalin came to the Kremlin late. His closest associate, Molotov, walked into his study at 6:27 P.M., but the meeting didn't start until 7:05. Among the participants were Beria, Voznesensky, a Party manager named Malenkov, Kuznetsov, Timoshenko, the head of the Mobilization Department, Safonov, and, unexpectedly, the Soviet naval attaché in Germany, Captain Mikhail Vorontsov. Vorontsov had arrived from Berlin just a few hours earlier, and his boss, Kuznetsov, had persuaded Stalin to invite him to give the most recent, alarming report. Vorontsov firmly believed that Germany would attack soon. In a private conversation with Kuznetsov, he had plainly stated, "It's war!"

Zhukov was not invited. Perhaps Stalin didn't want the advice of the opinionated chief of general staff that night, or perhaps he needed to have him monitoring reports from the border at the central command post.

The meeting lasted for seventy minutes. The transcript is still not available, but in all likelihood Stalin ordered the preemptive strike — maybe in a matter of days, perhaps in a matter of a week or so. All western military districts were to organize into fronts immediately. The three strategic areas would be getting supervisors from Moscow, and the toughest general, Zhukov, would be sent to the strategic centerpiece, Ukraine, to supervise the Southwestern Front. Although Stalin was angry over Zhukov's stubborn nagging, he grudgingly admitted that the general had a stamina the others lacked. Zhukov had also exhibited a strong taste for ambitious tasks, as his input into the preemptive plan had proved in May. Although the dictator was still apprehensive about the general's zeal and initiative, he nevertheless decided to put both talents to use.

Zhukov's predecessor, Meretskov, was to represent Stalin in Leningrad, coordinating all military activities in the north. Timoshenko was to go to the Western Front in Minsk, accompanied by a top Party apparatchik, Lev Mekhlis. A group of generals from the Moscow Military District was dispatched to the Southern Front on the Black Sea coast.

The four armies slowly moving westward from the interior — the Nineteenth, Twentieth, Twenty-first, and Twenty-second — were given to the High Command Reserve. Though Marshal Budenny, the brightest star of the civil war, did not attend the meeting, he was appointed its commander, with headquarters at Briansk, a town 400 miles from the border, right in the center of the western strategic terrain. The majority of troops were supposed to reach their new locations by the end of the month, although the overall relocation wouldn't be completed before July 10.

The four armies were to form a north-to-south line across Byelorussia and Ukraine from Vitebsk to Kremenchug, Vitebsk lying parallel to eastern Prussia, Kremenchug parallel to Hungary. The armies were to strike "upon a special order of the high command." Another army moving westward, the Sixteenth, was to join the Southwestern Front.

Stalin's state of mind was probably reflected in whom he invited to attend this critical meeting on the evening of June 21. Out of nine people present, only two, Timoshenko and Kuznetsov, were military professionals. Two were diplomats, one was a policeman, one an economist, and three were Party apparatchiks. Stalin didn't even invite his loyal cavalrymen, even though Budenny was to be given a critical assignment. But he let the insignificant Captain Vorontsov attend the top-secret discussion.

At 8 P.M., while the meeting was still in progress, Zhukov called. A defector had crossed the border and informed the local Soviet command that war would start at dawn on June 22 — in other words, in just six to eight hours. Stalin told the general that he would see him and Timoshenko in forty-five minutes.

▪ ▪ ▪

When the generals walked into his Kremlin office at 8:50 (Timoshenko had excused himself thirty-five minutes earlier for a short conference with Zhukov), they found a few others in the room: Molotov, Beria, Malenkov, the hastily summoned Budenny, and Captain Vorontsov, who by now must have been terrified. In contrast to his usual poise, Stalin looked very nervous. He asked whether the warning could be a German provocation. No, Timoshenko and Zhukov said, they were sure the defector was telling the truth. The troops at the western border had to be put on combat alert immediately, they insisted. Stalin seemed unconvinced.

His concerns were obvious. Barely an hour earlier he had ordered an enormous strategic shakeup to prepare the army for a first strike. Now, having finally ordered his troops to mobilize, the last thing he wanted was for Hitler's army to strike first. If the Red Army was put on combat alert, the Germans would notice immediately, and that could provoke them into instant action. But if Hitler had already ordered an attack, Stalin didn't want his troops to be caught unawares.

To his immense displeasure, Timoshenko and Zhukov had already prepared the draft of a directive alerting the troops. It sounded too belligerent to him. He still didn't believe that Hitler was ready for an all-out war. Therefore he started dictating the order himself.

Hours later, the troops' commanders would be informed that a German attack could occur on June 22 or 23, after an unspecified "provocation." The army was to be prudent in its response in order to prevent "big complications" — in other words, war. In Stalin's words, they were "not to yield to any provocation." The troops were to move closer to the border and stay on high alert throughout the night.

▪ ▪ ▪

Nobody except the eight dignitaries conferring in Stalin's study knew about the directive yet. Even Stalin's omnipotent secretary, Poskrebyshev, didn't know. He had seen Timoshenko and Zhukov entering the *vozhd*'s room, and he knew that Stalin was very agitated, but he could only guess why.

Sitting under a photograph of the young Stalin in a Budenny helmet, Poskrebyshev tried to figure out what was going on. In spite of the open window, the air was still exceptionally hot and muggy. Poskrebyshev nervously sipped mineral water and whispered to people he trusted that the Germans could strike at any minute.

At ten o'clock the storm came. In the bright midsummer dusk, harsh winds created small tornadoes of dust on the sidewalks, and curtains framing the open windows billowed. In the next moment thunder struck, and a torrential rain flooded Moscow.

▪ ▪ ▪

Zhukov and Timoshenko were dismissed at 10:20 P.M. They left in silence, their minds racing. The directive they were taking with them was disastrous. It was bound to confuse the generals on the border. No one would be able to decide where a provocation ended and war began. Nothing had been said about the use of fire. Suppose the Germans did strike that night — could the Soviet artillerymen shoot at their tanks? Could they shoot down German aircraft that crossed the border?

The two generals had been too timid during the meeting with the *vozhd* to insist on the necessary clarifications. Worse, the directive was signed by them, not by Stalin, so they would be held accountable for the chaos that would almost inevitably ensue.

When the car stopped in front of the Commissariat of Defense, the two men decided that they would meet ten minutes later in Timoshenko's office. By then many officers had already assembled outside Timoshenko's door, anticipating the crisis and hoping to be helpful. Carrying various files and maps that the people's commissar of defense would need, they exchanged agitated whispers. Everyone could feel the tension in the air.

As for Stalin, he spent just forty minutes more in his office, conferring with Molotov, Beria, and, of all people, Captain Vorontsov. Earlier that night Molotov had arranged an urgent meeting with the German ambassador, Count von Schulenburg. When Molotov asked about the rumors of impending war, Schulenburg said that he was unable to give any answer. In Berlin, Ribbentrop was still unavailable. The situation was dire, but at eleven o'clock the *vozhd* left for his dacha.

■ ■ ■

At about midnight, another defector, a German soldier of the Seventy-fourth Infantry Division, quietly slipped into the water and swam across the river to the Soviet side of the border west of Vladimir Volynsky. He reported that the invasion would start at 4 A.M.

The commander of the Kiev Military District, Kirponos, communicated the soldier's information to Zhukov. At 0:30 A.M., Zhukov called Stalin.

"Did you send the directive to the military districts?" Stalin asked. Zhukov said he did. That was the end of the exchange.

3

THE ATTACK

General Pavlov, Minsk

Discreetly and effectively blockaded by German saboteurs on the night of June 21, the Red Army frontier units never received Stalin's directive. Their inland headquarters did — but not until three o'clock in the morning. As Zhukov and Timoshenko had predicted, the directive caused immense confusion. What should the commanders expect — border clashes or war? If they were not supposed to yield to provocations, should they react at all? A few generals called the People's Commissariat of Defense for clarification. Should they open fire if the Germans crossed the border? they asked. No, Timoshenko responded, opening fire would mean yielding to the German provocation. But most military leaders held Moscow too much in awe even to ask for clarification.

Among those was Dmitry Pavlov. In June 1941, General Pavlov commanded the Western Military District, one of the two most important districts in the country. Stalin personally favored the Kiev Military District, farther south, but the Western Military District had an important role in the first-strike plan: to take eastern Prussia and Warsaw. As far as defending the country went, the Western was second to none: it barred the way to Moscow.

Pavlov's career had been dazzling. Like many others he had fought for the Republican cause in Spain, but unlike many he had survived the return to the USSR. After the Republicans lost to Franco, Stalin ordered a purge of Spanish civil war veterans. Some were accused of ineffectiveness, some of cowardliness, all of state treason, because Stalin's mortal foe, Trotsky, had been dispatching men to Spain too, and Stalin suspected that some of his envoys were recruited to work for the brilliant exile.

Miraculously, Dmitry Pavlov wasn't blacklisted. On the contrary, Stalin showered him with honors and important assignments. Pavlov was doggedly loyal, straightforward, and cheerful. Among his most important sayings were "Never mind — those at the top know better than we do" and "Think offensive." The *vozhd* had always liked people like that.

On the night of June 21, Pavlov was 150 miles east of the border, watching a play at a theater in Minsk, the capital of Byelorussia. In spite of the buildup of German troops along the border and the German violations of Soviet airspace, Stalin had ordered his army not to worry, and Pavlov thought it was his duty to demonstrate sangfroid in spite of what was happening.

On the previous evening, six German aircraft had crossed the border, but Soviet fighters had escorted them back to German territory without opening fire. On the evening of June 21 itself, the commander of the Third Army, Lieutenant General Kuznetsov reported that the Germans had removed barbed wire barriers along their side of the border and that motors could be heard distinctly from the woods. When Pavlov learned of this, he fell back on his usual approach: "Believe me, Moscow knows the military and political situation and the state of our relations with Germany better than we do." When his chief of staff, Major General Klimovskikh, suggested increasing combat readiness, Pavlov was so annoyed that he swept a map off the table and barked, "War is possible, but not in the near future. Now we must prepare for the fall maneuvers and make sure that no alarmist answers German provocations with fire."

So now he was in the theater watching a patriotic musical, *The Wedding at Robin Village.* Shortly before midnight Pavlov's chief of intelligence visited his box and whispered that the Germans were bringing more troops to the border. Pavlov again dismissed the warning. "Nonsense," he said. "This simply cannot be."

At 1 A.M., Pavlov was told that the people's commissar of defense needed to reach him urgently.

"What's going on — everything quiet?" Timoshenko asked.

Pavlov said that he had been hearing reports of unusual movements on the part of the German troops.

"Stay calm and do not panic," Timoshenko advised. "Summon your staff in the morning. Something unpleasant might come about indeed, but make sure not to yield to German provocations. Call me if something happens."

▪ ▪ ▪

That same night, the commander of the Fourth Army, Major General A. A. Korobkov, was in the theater in Kobrin, watching a popular operetta, *The Gypsy Baron.* He knew that his boss, Pavlov, wanted everyone to remain calm, and Korobkov was a dutiful officer. If Pavlov went to see a musical, Korobkov had to follow suit. He was distracted, though, and paid little attention to the stage. In the early evening he had called Klimovskikh to report that the Germans had moved closer to the border and to ask permission to order his troops to the battle lines and aircraft to the airstrips. Klimovskikh said that that was impossible.

To Korobkov's immense relief, he was able to leave the theater early. At about 11 o'clock, Klimovskikh called and told him to go to headquarters immediately and remain alert throughout the night. Unlike their carefree and trusting boss, Klimovskikh had a sharp mind. Having smelled a rat, he was now taking his own quiet precautions.

Still forbidden to communicate anything to the troops, Korobkov sent for his staff officers. In the headquarters, the officers wandered from one room to another, discussing the situation in whispers and trying to determine whether the sudden summons meant war. All divisions stationed at the frontier as well as the border guards kept reporting abnormal activity on the German side of the Bug River.

At two o'clock in the morning, Korobkov got a call from the frontier city of Brest. The power was apparently out, and there was no running water. A few minutes later the town of Kobrin — the site of Korobkov's headquarters — went dark too. Half an hour after that the general realized that all communications with the military district headquarters and with the troops on the border had been severed.

Admiral Oktiabrsky, Sevastopol

The evening of June 21 was balmy. On the southwestern tip of the subtropical Crimean Peninsula, Sevastopol was bathed in a light breeze. The lights of the warships had been turned off, but the boulevards, parks, and streets of this Soviet Marseille were brightly lit and crowded with people taking a Saturday night stroll. The strong scent of white acacias in bloom reached even the ships in the middle of the harbor.

The officers on duty at Black Sea Fleet headquarters expected an uneventful night, but one thing did nag at them. Three German transport ships normally plied the Black Sea, making regular trips between Soviet ports and the harbors of Romania and Bulgaria. At least one of them was almost always in passage, but on the night of June 21 all three remained in Romanian and Bulgarian ports.

At 1:03 A.M. an urgent cable reached the headquarters. Sent by People's Commissar of the Navy Kuznetsov, it said, "Operational readiness #1 now." The message was devastatingly clear: war was at hand.

The fact that the navy had more warning than the army was, perversely, because of Stalin's neglect. On that critical night, Stalin had essentially forgotten about the navy, which left Kuznetsov largely to his own devices. While Zhukov's and Timoshenko's hands were tied by the dictator's confusing directive, Kuznetsov was left to act independently — and more decisively. Rightfully distrusting the telegraph network as slow, busy, and messy, the admiral had himself called Sevastopol, and also the headquarters of the Baltic and Northern Fleets. "Don't wait for the cable to arrive," he said. "Get ready now."

The duty officer in Sevastopol alerted the ships. Fleet Commander Vice Admiral Filip Oktiabrsky arrived at fleet headquarters, and at 1:55 A.M. the general alarm was sounded at the main base. Abandoning dates, meals, and movies, sailors hurried from all over the city to their ships to start loading ammunition, fuel, and supplies. The Sevastopol Party boss, Boris Borisov, reported to fleet headquarters too, looking slightly ridiculous with his pistol and gas mask.

The alarm didn't come as a surprise to Oktiabrsky, a vigorous and authoritarian man who regarded the whole city, and perhaps the rest of the Crimea, as a mere appendage to his fleet's base. A few weeks earlier he had warned his captains that war was imminent. In a way he had been looking forward to it. Oktiabrsky occupied one of the most conspicuous posts in the military establishment, as he was a successor to the legendary commanders of the Crimean War, Admiral Nakhimov and Admiral Kornilov, and he hoped to acquire glory on the job, as his predecessors had. Cultivating the connection, he worked not at an archetypal Soviet desk covered by dull green cloth but at an old-fashioned bureau of the kind that many great men of the past had used to record their history-making decisions. Now the conflict that could immortalize Oktiabrsky's name had arrived.

Although the city was plunged into darkness, the beacons remained brightly lit. In a few moments headquarters realized that communications with them had been cut, so motorcyclists were dispatched to turn them off immediately. Finally all the lights were extinguished, with the exception of Upper Inkerman Beacon, some distance away.

Aboard the ships, captains unsealed envelopes with battle orders from Kuznetsov. The instructions said to open fire on any enemy vessel or plane. At the airfields, machine guns roared as fighter pilots tested their ammunition. Shortly after 2 A.M., Sevastopol was ready for an attack.

About an hour later, two observation posts, one in Evpatoria, in the north, and the other at Cape Sarych, in the south, reported the sound of aircraft engines on a course toward Sevastopol. The dispatches were immediately transmitted to the commander of the fleet.

"Are some of our planes airborne?" Oktiabrsky asked.

"We have no planes in the air," the duty officer told him.

"Keep in mind that if there is a single Soviet aircraft aloft, tomorrow you will be shot," Oktiabrsky said.

Unabashed, the duty officer asked, "Comrade commander, are we allowed to open fire?"

Oktiabrsky replied, "Act according to the instructions."

When the duty officer transmitted the order to the commander of the air defense, the commander got scared. "Remember, you are fully responsible for this. I am writing this down in the log," he said.

"Write it down wherever you want," the exasperated officer yelled, "but for God's sake, open fire!"

At 3:13 searchlights were turned on. The gunmen could clearly see German bombers crawling toward the city at a low altitude. Oktiabrsky, still hesitant, phoned the only military leader he trusted, Zhukov. That was an outrageous breach of protocol, but he thought Zhukov was closer to Stalin than Kuznetsov. Oktiabrsky remembered only too well that just a few years earlier, eight out of nine senior admirals had been executed.

Instead of giving a no-nonsense command in his usual condescending manner, Zhukov replied with a question: "What are you going to do?"

"We are going to open fire."

"Go ahead and then report to the people's commissar of the navy," Zhukov said, and hung up.

At about that time the first German loads hit Sevastopol. The Soviet Union was under attack.

Both the ships and the ground batteries opened fire right away. However, that night the German planes were dropping not bombs but mines on parachutes, and in the beams of the searchlights they looked like a landing force of paratroopers. The chief of intelligence panicked. "They are going to seize the headquarters!" he cried.

Chief of Staff Rear Admiral I. D. Eliseev called for troops to surround the building, but he was told that no troops were available. Cursing, he sent a number of his officers outside, forcing them to abandon their stations.

Upper Inkerman Beacon still blazed with light. Obviously the motorcyclists hadn't reached it in time or had been killed by German commandos. The officers agitatedly argued over whether the beacon was now guiding the Luftwaffe.

Those officers who were still inside headquarters drew the blinds and looked out over the balcony. Searchlights feverishly brushed the sky, tracer bullets pierced clouds, and white bursts of exploding anti-aircraft shells flared here and there. "That was a good welcome!" someone said.

Meanwhile, Oktiabrsky had called Kuznetsov and was saying in a sharp voice, "Yes, yes, we are being bombed!" A strong explosion rattled the windowpanes. "There, a bomb fell just now, not far from the headquarters!" he added excitedly.

"Moscow does not believe that Sevastopol is being bombed," one of the officers whispered.

In a matter of minutes Lavrenty Beria called the police branch in Sevastopol to demand confirmation. Sevastopol was being pounded, but Moscow refused to acknowledge it.

Dawn

The war first reached people in sounds. Up and down the western border, people were woken at dawn by ferocious, deafening blasts that went on and on, making the ground and the buildings shake. Some thought it was an earthquake. The mistake was understandable — most men and women hastily putting on their clothes had never experienced an earthquake or, for that matter, war.

Other sounds followed — ones that definitely could not be caused by an earthquake. Buglers' horns trumpeted; officers yelled, "Alarm! Alarm!" and "Out! Quick!"; and an occasional hysterical voice wailed, "It's war!"

The soldiers were met with a different kind of sound as soon as they left their barracks or tents and ran outside. The noise was very close, very difficult to describe, but unmistakably deadly: the humming of shrapnel whizzing by. The invisible pieces of steel sounded almost alive, like a swarm of locusts, perhaps. "Something buzzing flew by," a young lieutenant wrote, "and, having hit the sand, went quiet."

After the soldiers adjusted to the sounds, they noticed the fires. In the dim light, flames dotted the horizon, leaping, flaring, blinking, and spreading. They looked particularly sinister in the woods, though in the cities they did more damage.

The German planes were faintly visible in the dawn air. Tight black packages — the bombs, or "lead hail," as many on the ground put it — separated from their fuselages. Boys climbed the trees to see the assaulting aircraft more clearly, but that didn't make the sight more realistic; it was "like watching a movie," one recalled.

When the sun rose, it subdued the glare of the fires, and pitch-black plumes of thick smoke dominated the landscape. The sun unveiled the devastation: corpses lying on the ground, buildings turned into smoking piles of rubble, burned-out cars littering the streets, craters bored by bombs. Parents hastily escorting their children out of town shielded their eyes, wanting to protect them from seeing the carnage. Most of the frontier ran near a river, and some people felt as if the water had turned brown with blood, although this might have been just their imagination.

Almost everyone noticed a strange byproduct of the shock: many people were worrying about a trivial loss or an insignificant problem. A border guard who had been showered by German shrapnel as he crossed the Bug River loudly lamented the loss of his service cap. Another soldier, trapped in a fort on the border, suddenly reached for his Komsomol membership card and complained that it had no stamp indicating that he had paid his dues in June. Often people found themselves absorbed by something totally irrelevant to their own survival, like a flock of rooks circling some felled trees that had once contained their nests.

▪ ▪ ▪

The Fourth Army headquarters at Kobrin remained ignorant, as the communication lines were dead. The soldiers who had been sent to fix them reported that hundreds of feet of telegraph wire had been cut. At last, at 3:30 in the morning, Korobkov connected with Minsk. Only then did he obtain instructions to put the troops on combat alert.

Almost all staff officers of the Fourth Army had assembled in the headquarters' basement, which contained the communications center. In the dim light of kerosene lamps, Korobkov was attempting to contact his units to send them to battle stations. Before he could do so, the Forty-second Rifle Division reported that the Germans had opened fire at Brest.

Fifteen minutes later, at 4:30, the commander of an air force division, Colonel Belov, ran into the headquarters yelling that German bombers were flattening the airfields. Before he could give details, an explosion shook the building. It was followed by the drone of aircraft engines. Those officers who had fought with Pavlov in Spain immediately recognized the sound as the unmistakable rumble of Junkers bombers. The officers dashed into the street. The German aircraft were right over their heads, and bombs were swiftly detaching from their dark bellies, cutting through the air with piercing shrieks.

After the planes were gone, Korobkov ordered immediate evacuation of the headquarters. The doors to the office safes opened and shut with a bang as the officers hastily rescued the most important documents. Nobody had bothered to sort out the files earlier.

Before they were finished, the Luftwaffe returned. A few seconds later the Fourth Army headquarters was shrouded in smoke and dust and the squadron of Junkers was confidently diving low to finish it off. After the Junkers left, the smell of fire filled the air, silence descended once again, and all that the surviving officers, now hiding in ditches, could hear was a high-pitched female voice crying out a hysterical "Ahh!"

■ ■ ■

Right before the Junkers unleashed their fury on Kobrin, Pavlov, in Minsk, got a shocking call from the commander of the Third Army, General Kuznetsov. The Germans were bombing Grodno, a major city at the northern corner of the Belostok salient. The Third Army's communications had been destroyed, and Kuznetsov couldn't reach his troops. Pavlov's response was "I don't understand what's going on."

While he was pondering what to do, the people's commissar of defense called from Moscow. Pavlov reported the situation, but Timoshenko had no advice to offer. Zhukov had contacted Stalin about half an hour earlier, and Timoshenko was still waiting for the conference in the Kremlin to start.

Soon Kuznetsov called Pavlov again — the Germans were intensifying the bombing. Other commanders reported similar air raids at Belostok, Lida, Tsekhanovets, Volkovyisk, Kobrin, Brest, and Slonim. At dawn the Wehrmacht smashed the weak border defenses and entered Soviet territory. Some frontier units resisted on their own initiative, some didn't, but all the commanders reported uncontrolled retreat, broken communications, and heavy losses of aircraft on the ground.

Pavlov sent for his staff. The officers listened to his stumbling remarks in disbelief.

"This can't be," someone said. "This is a gross provocation or a mistake. We have a nonaggression pact with Germany."

While Pavlov was away from his desk, Timoshenko called once more and spoke to Pavlov's deputy, General Boldin. "No actions are to be taken against the Germans without our consent," Timoshenko said.

"What?" Boldin shouted into the receiver. "Our troops are forced to retreat, cities are burning, people are dying —"

"Iosif Vissarionovich thinks that these may be provocations on the part of some German generals," Timoshenko replied dryly.

■ ■ ■

At 6 A.M., while the evacuation of the Fourth Army headquarters was still under way, the round black loudspeaker on Kobrin's main square rasped and came to life and the familiar Moscow signal rang out. Everyone in the square stopped and looked up hopefully.

"It is six o'clock Moscow time," the loudspeaker croaked. "We begin our broadcast of the latest news." Taking turns, the announcers praised the superb harvest and the amazing achievements of Soviet factories. They reported German air raids on Britain and the sinking of British ships, mentioned hostilities in Syria, and concluded with the weather forecast. Then the black loudspeaker fell silent.

"A special announcement is on its way," an officer in the square said uncertainly.

As if to confirm his doubts, the loudspeaker came back to life and cheerfully sang: "Time for exercise. Stretch your arms out, bend! Livelier! Up, down. Livelier! That's it. Very good."

The people gathered in Kobrin's main square did not hear the rest of the Sunday morning broadcast, as the roar of another squadron of Junkers overwhelmed it.

▪ ▪ ▪

The bulk of the Fourth Army was dying thirty miles west, in and around Brest.

With the early-morning light accentuating the explosions, it was obvious that German fire was concentrated on the Brest fortress and the military barracks. The area was flat and it was easy for the German artillerists to take aim. Both the barracks and the fortress were overcrowded, with men sleeping on bunk beds stacked three or four high, and each hit killed dozens.

The streets of Brest were hellish. German snipers placed strategically in attics and on balconies kept the panicking troops under fire. Felons from the local jail had forced the gates and were now roaming the streets, looting. The railway station was the scene of one big stampede. A hastily composed train took a number of women and children east, but it was the only one to escape the burning city.

At five o'clock German tanks started crossing the Bug River. They did so easily. Six bridges traversed the river in the Fourth Army sector, and none had been prepared for demolition.

▪ ▪ ▪

Six-year-old Lenia Bobkov was running down the stairs clutching his father's hand. In the Brest fortress, where they lived together with hundreds of other officers' families, everything was roaring and shaking around him, and his father said war had begun. Now his father was taking the boy, his mother, and his sister to the nearest basement. When they reached it, Lenia didn't like what he saw. The room was tightly packed with people, and he heard bullets whizzing by and something growling, something that he was as yet unable to name. The sounds were disturbing, but his father was holding his hand and he felt secure. Then suddenly his father let go.

Lenia didn't understand why. In the commotion he lost his father and, very scared, crawled into a corner. All of a sudden he felt two painful stings and realized that something hot was running down his body. The son of an officer, he knew that he had been hit by a bullet or shrapnel. When the shock receded and he was able to concentrate again, he discovered that his mother and sister were dead and his father was badly wounded.

Together with the other survivors and corpses, the Bobkov family remained in the basement for what seemed an eternity. The boy was in pain and incredibly thirsty. Eventually he heard the tramping of boots and people speaking in a language he could not understand. A few soldiers in weird uniforms rushed in and started yelling and gesticulating. It looked like they were ordering everyone out.

Those who could walk hesitantly rose and headed for the exit, but the Germans left as quickly as they had appeared. They didn't return, and the Russians went back to their basement, unsure about what to do next. As soon as they settled down again, a hand grenade hit the floor. It was hissing loudly. Perhaps it had been thrown by a German who thought there were Soviet soldiers in the basement, or perhaps by a Soviet hoping to reach the Germans there.

"Get it out! Get it out!" the women shrieked, prodding the older boys, but the boys were too scared to move.

At that moment Lenia's father whispered, "Lie close to me and cover your head."

The boy did as he was told, pressing his body against the hard, cold cement floor. Then he heard an explosion and felt a sharp pain, and after that everything went blank.

When he came around, he knew that his father was dead, and so was everybody else in the basement.

He was unable to say how long he had been there alone when a German soldier found him by flashlight. The man muttered something, bent over, lifted him, and took him outside. The sun blinded him. He didn't know where the soldier was taking him, but the German must have carried him to a field doctor. The doctor started bandaging his wounds, which was very painful, and soon all of his body was covered except his head and his right arm.

Before putting him into a car headed for the hospital, the upset soldier gave him a bag of candy.

Morning

While the Red Army was abandoning Brest, five men — Molotov, Beria, Mekhlis, Timoshenko, and Zhukov — were sitting in Stalin's office in the Kremlin, waiting for him to speak. But Stalin remained silent.

Zhukov had always found Stalin's pauses unbearable. "We should order the troops to stop the Germans," he said.

"Not stop them but destroy them," Timoshenko barked.

"Transmit the order," Stalin said. "But make sure that, with the exception of the air force, our troops do not cross the border."

Clearly the dictator still hoped he would be able to prevent an all-out war. If Hitler saw that the Red Army was measured in its response, Stalin argued, he might halt the onslaught and offer a diplomatic compromise.

At 7:15 A.M. the Soviet armies in the west were told to "destroy the enemy forces" at once. The order was christened directive #2, to distinguish it from the infamous edict of the night before, now referred to as directive #1.

No new defensive line was envisaged that morning. Overwhelmed and frightened, Stalin was still thinking offensively. He couldn't imagine that by the time directive #2 was issued, the Germans would have already advanced at least three miles east. The Soviets were losing roughly 600 square miles of territory per hour.

■ ■ ■

After Zhukov and Timoshenko left, Stalin called the Party chief of Byelorussia, Panteleimon Ponomarenko, and told him angrily that General

Pavlov did not understand the situation on the front. He ordered Ponomarenko to move to the military district headquarters immediately. This was his usual — though almost invariably counterproductive — custom: to send supervisors to local leaders or commanders to make sure treason and abuse of power did not take place.

Ponomarenko was not pleased with the mission. Only three of the one hundred top Party apparatchiks in Byelorussia had survived the recent purge, and he was worried that Stalin would hold him responsible for Pavlov's mistakes. Of course, he didn't dare to argue.

For some reason, even in the first hours of war, the dictator's mind, always looking for treachery, fastened on one name: Pavlov.

▪ ▪ ▪

By the time Zhukov and Timoshenko returned to the People's Commissariat of Defense, initial damage reports were on their desks. They were quite incomplete, as it was virtually impossible to get any accurate information from the front line. Yet even the limited information that had found its way to Moscow was awful. No commander had a clear idea of what was happening on his terrain, since almost all cable communications had been disrupted and messengers had been attacked by saboteurs. Many generals had left their headquarters for the combat zone and were now unavailable, which only made things worse. All major cities and railway junctions along the western frontier had been severely damaged. Almost all the army units were quickly yielding to the German offensive.

The worst news by far was that Hitler's commandos had managed to break the Red Army communication lines. An army deprived of communications in the first minutes of a foreign invasion is virtually disabled. As with many of that morning's mishaps, this one could have been prevented.

As mentioned, the officer corps did not trust wireless communications, which seemed to them too vulnerable in a society obsessed with control. As a result of that distrust, the military districts were acquiring radios slowly and were hesitant to put them to use. Of course each radio network was to have specific operational and reserve airwaves, each radio its own call sign. The wartime airwaves and call signs were different from the ones normally used, and military staff knew that it would take about a week to introduce them to every army unit down to the battalion level. It was decided that, for "security reasons," the call signs couldn't be communicated to the troops earlier, which meant that on June 22 the Red Army radios were not used.

Cable communications were mistakenly believed to be more reliable. In fact, only the last few miles of cable, in the immediate vicinity of front headquarters, ran underground. Most of the hundreds of miles of telegraph wires hung on poles lining the country's highways and railroads — an obvious and easy target for Hitler's commandos. All a saboteur had to do to disable a division was to cut out 100 feet of cable at the highway nearest its headquarters.

In something approaching criminal negligence, the telegraph lines had been left unprotected on the night of June 21. Neither the army nor the police, Zhukov nor Beria, the local field commanders nor the police chiefs had bothered to take the most obvious precaution. The army struggled with Stalin's first directive while the police force on the border — 10,000 men, not counting the border guards — busied themselves with imaginary "enemies of the people." These men could have been a formidable force: there was one policeman for every 10 square miles in the strip of land separating front headquarters from the frontier. This was not a bad ratio at all, given the fact that most telegraph lines were concentrated along highways and railroads.

The Soviet air force in the west had been devastated in what was surely one of the easiest missions of the Luftwaffe pilots' careers. In preparation for the preemptive strike, Stalin had placed his aircraft right on the border, and it took the Junkers only minutes to find and destroy them. Since the new airfields were still under construction, the existing ones were overcrowded and easy to pulverize. Stalin's directive #1 hadn't reached the air force commanders in time, and they were too terrified by the unfolding purge of their senior officers to display any initiative. In the end, with few exceptions, the Red air fleets were caught unaware on the ground.

Of the planes that did manage to take off, few had a chance of returning. Not every plane had a radio, and those that did often had just a receiver, so the crew couldn't transmit any message back to headquarters. Static was terrible and frequently made any exchange or even one-way guidance impossible. That made air reconnaissance virtually impossible too. In order to report on the progress of German troops, the plane had to land and the pilot had to report in person.

There was no good news that morning. Marshal Voroshilov summoned the person in charge of Moscow Air Defense, General Tiulenev, and asked, "What's the location of the high command post?"

The general was taken aback. "Excuse me, but no one has ever instructed me to prepare a high command post," he finally replied.

After an awkward pause, Voroshilov informed Tiulenev that he had been appointed commander of the Southern Front the day before and had to leave for Odessa immediately. Of course the whole concept of the preemptive strike had now been rendered ludicrous. Forestalled by Hitler, the Red Army was trapped in confusion and pain. Yet the bureaucracy was such that the previous day's appointments had to be acted upon.

Meanwhile, Zhukov and Timoshenko were impatiently awaiting Stalin's further instructions. Zhukov felt particularly nervous. Several hours earlier, at dawn, it had been he, not the Red Army's top commander, Timoshenko, who had delivered the bad news to the dictator, and he had even prodded Stalin to act. The telephone call had demanded a lot of courage. Zhukov procrastinated for about thirty-five minutes after hearing the first report of attack before he contacted the *vozhd*. Now he wasn't sure that had been a wise move. Stalin didn't like bad news any more than the next person. This time he could decide to shoot the messenger.

The high-frequency phone on Timoshenko's desk remained silent, and finally the generals decided to call the *vozhd* themselves. They asked him whether they could come to the Kremlin right away. They had two documents they wanted him to sign, a mobilization decree and an order creating a general headquarters with Stalin as commander in chief.

Stalin said he would be unable to see them until the afternoon, since he was busy at a Politburo meeting. That was a bald-faced lie. Nothing of the kind was taking place in the dictator's office. The tightly organized Kremlin routine had collapsed. Visitors saw Stalin together, were told to come back later, or were dismissed. One person followed another as the *vozhd* conferred with the police, the Party apparatus, and the Comintern.

Stalin acknowledged that he didn't have the courage to address the nation. He decided that Molotov should speak instead. Until very recently Molotov had been the head of government, and everybody knew that he was the *vozhd*'s undesignated yet obvious successor. But he was as dry as dust, humorless and unimposing, and he was an uninspiring speaker. Worse, he stuttered and therefore avoided giving public speeches. On the morning of June 22 he wasn't given a choice, though, and he started working on a draft of the speech. Stalin supervised.

▪ ▪ ▪

June 22 was a Sunday, sunny and warm all across European Russia. The western borderlands were bombed and shelled, but for the rest of the USSR it was just another fine summer morning. Often as close as 50 miles away people were dying under crumbling buildings, but their compatriots had no way of knowing. Students were almost done with their final exams, the season of vacations and summer camps had begun, and families assembled around their kitchen tables for a late Sunday breakfast.

Throughout the morning the radio kept broadcasting the previous day's news and the weather forecasts. Even some of the cities already hit by the Luftwaffe were still in doubt. In bread lines in Sevastopol, a natural daily social club in a society of constant shortages, some people explained away the night's shooting as a mistake, claiming that air defense personnel had fired at friendly forces.

▪ ▪ ▪

Shortly after eleven o'clock, Molotov's speech was ready, and at noon it was broadcast live on the radio. Fighting his stutter, Molotov spoke haltingly, as if out of breath.

"Citizens of the Soviet Union! The Soviet government and its head, Comrade Stalin, have entrusted me with the following statement.

"Today, at four o'clock in the morning, having lodged no claims against the Soviet Union at all and without having declared war, German troops attacked our country . . ."

He called the German attack "treacherous" and emphasized that the Soviet Union had done nothing to warrant it, subconsciously echoing his pitiful question to the German ambassador six hours earlier. "Now that the attack on the Soviet Union has become a fact," he said, "the Soviet government has ordered our troops to beat off the pillaging assault and expel the German troops from the territory of our motherland." The figure he gave for Soviet losses was completely fabricated — merely two hundred people. By noon it was at least one hundred times that many.

Despite the lies and understatements, the final three sentences of the address read quite well: "Our cause is just. The enemy will be crushed. Victory will be ours." In all likelihood, those lines had been written by Stalin.

▪ ▪ ▪

When the brief broadcast was over, some Soviet citizens sat paralyzed in front of their radios; some went to the already depleted stores for bread, salt, and matches, among other things; some headed to their local universities for spontaneous patriotic rallies; some roamed the streets aimlessly; and some headed for the draft office — where women were told that the army would not take them and angrily responded that they had been raised to believe that women were equal to men. Others rushed to the bank to withdraw their savings, although many banks, having run out of cash, had already closed. "The June day blazed on with unbearable heat," a witness wrote.

A Moscow student named Antonina Khokhlova, the coxswain of a men's rowing crew, was at the rudder when she heard the declaration of war. The crew landed, put the boat away, and went to the draft office — Antonina and eight boys. Antonina remarked to her friends that she was willing to fight for the country but not for Stalin. "He's a man," she said. "Let him fight for himself!" Remarkably, none of the boys reported her to the police.

In the Far East, gulag prisoners were preparing to meet death. They suspected that there would be no place for them, even behind barbed wire, in a country that had been invaded. They would either starve to death because there wouldn't be enough food to share with them, or they would be shot as Hitler's fifth column. "It's all over for us now," a prisoner in Norilsk said.

In western Ukraine, sixteen-year-old Maria Pyskir and her friends were standing at a train station when they saw the stationmaster hurrying toward them. "From the expression on his face, we could tell that something was very wrong.

"'Don't you know a war has broken out?' he asked us. 'With Germany.'

"'What?' we chorused in disbelief.

"Secretly, I was glad, and I think my companions and other passengers on the platform were too. I was saying to myself, 'Thank the Lord. This means that the Russians will soon be gone.'"

In the nearby city of Lvov, sirens howled an air raid warning. Policemen nervously shepherded pedestrians into the courtyards of apartment buildings. Red Army soldiers were dragging antiaircraft artillery up the hills. Many Lvov residents were already leaving the city to seek shelter in the countryside.

▪ ▪ ▪

Impressed and grateful, Stalin dropped by Molotov's office and congratulated him. "You sounded too nervous, but you spoke well," he said.

"I don't think so," Molotov replied.

Amazingly enough, although Stalin found time to encourage his proxy, he had no time for the Red Army leaders. The only general he received between 8:30 A.M. and 1:15 P.M. was the semiretired cavalryman Klim Voroshilov, whom he had sent for three times. At 1:15, Stalin decided to see Shaposhnikov. As for Timoshenko and Zhukov, they were in the doghouse. Concerned about the developments in Byelorussia, Stalin called not them but Ponomarenko, in Minsk, to ask, "What do you know about the situation on the front? How is Pavlov doing?"

Ponomarenko, who had already paid a visit to Pavlov, said exactly what was expected of him. The general, he reported, felt disoriented and could not command the troops properly. "I want to ask you, Comrade Stalin, to send an authoritative marshal to advise the commander of the front."

That was a smart request. If Stalin sent a military professional to Pavlov's headquarters, Ponomarenko could go back to the role he knew best, that of a political watchdog, and would have nothing more to do with arcane strategic options.

Obviously he had read Stalin's mind, because the *vozhd* replied, "I have already taken care of that. Marshal Boris Mikhailovich Shaposhnikov is leaving today. Remember, he is a very experienced military leader trusted by the Central Committee . . . Stay close to him and listen to his advice."

▪ ▪ ▪

It was 2 P.M. by the time the inscrutable Poskrebyshev ushered Timoshenko, Zhukov, and Vatutin into Stalin's study. The generals didn't like the group of people they found there. Only one was a friend — the timid but kind Shaposhnikov. All the others were potential enemies.

Stalin was pacing the room, holding an unlit pipe in his hand. An unlit pipe always signaled his irritation. He maintained a silence for as long as he possibly could, then finally growled, "All right, what have you got?"

Sullenly he read the drafts of the two decrees. He signed the one that mobilized the reservists. The next day, males between twenty-three and thirty-six were to report to local military authorities. He agreed with a proposal to impose martial law on the European part of the country; from now on, the local military command, not the Party committees, would be in charge (though the role of Beria's squads remained unclear).

However, he plainly refused to create a general headquarters, let alone assume the post of commander in chief. He said he needed more time to think. It was clear to everyone why he wouldn't want to lead the army now: he wouldn't accept responsibility for any blunders. At the same time, his refusal to create a central command was nearly inexplicable. The only explanation was his delusional belief that Hitler might still stop his troops and start bargaining.

Zhukov and Timoshenko did not dare to argue. They knew that they had reached an impasse. Technically, Timoshenko, as people's commissar of defense, commanded the army. The people's commissar of the navy, Admiral Kuznetsov, commanded the fleet. Yet neither could do anything without Stalin's approval, and Stalin bluntly refused to assume responsibility for military decisions. That augured just one thing for the foreseeable future: total chaos.

But this was not the final surprise that afternoon. Addressing Zhukov, Stalin said, "Our front commanders are inexperienced. It appears that they feel disoriented. The Politburo has decided to send you to the Southwestern Front as our representative. You are to fly to Kiev at once." He also told the army leaders that he was sending Marshal Shaposhnikov and Marshal Kulik to the Western Front and General Meretskov to the Northern Front.

Zhukov's assignment might seem an appealing one, yet it wasn't. The general would have been glad to lead the Southwestern Front in a preemptive strike, as Stalin had ordered the day before, but that was a far cry from salvaging a collapsing front line. Stalin's decision to send the chief of general staff away in the first few hours after the attack might also demonstrate his intention to fire Zhukov — or maybe even purge him.

Beyond these selfish reasons for Zhukov's reluctance, Stalin's order looked foolish to him in principle. "Who will lead the General Staff at such a difficult time?" he asked. "The military leadership will become disorganized."

"What do you know about military leadership anyway?" Stalin hissed. "Leave Vatutin in charge. Go — we will somehow manage without you."

At 4 P.M., Zhukov, Timoshenko, Shaposhnikov, Kulik, and Vatutin left Stalin's office. They did not know that the *vozhd* had already instructed his head of staff to start moving all the western provinces' industrial plants inland.

▪ ▪ ▪

The cable announcing nationwide mobilization wasn't transmitted by Central Telegraph dispatchers until five o'clock in the afternoon, which meant that draft offices wouldn't be able to process it until the next morning — more than twenty-four hours after the start of the war.

The only institution that functioned properly in the capital was the police. As soon as news about the German attack reached Moscow headquarters, a special order was issued to secure the capital and the suburbs. All officers were summoned to the barracks; 3,500 agents were to patrol Moscow, 15,000 the suburbs. All German citizens were to be immediately arrested, and all police files were to be reexamined to identify potential saboteurs and spies. The mood of the population had to be closely monitored and reported on regularly.

At 4:25 P.M. Beria walked into Stalin's office. He had already spent four hours with the *vozhd* that day, and he was the last person Stalin saw on June 22.

German Field Marshals and Soviet Generals

By the afternoon of June 22 the Germans were entering Soviet territory by the hundreds of thousands all along the immense border, from the muddy lagoons of the Danube delta to the tidy sand dunes of the Baltics. Some waded, some rowed, some ran, some walked, some rode in tanks or trucks. They looked the part of invincible conquerors, and perhaps they truly were, since they had subdued almost all of Europe.

An Italian author, Curzio Malaparte, watched in awe as a German soldier crossed the border with an owl perched on his fist. This was the sacred bird of the goddess Athena, and the man had stolen it from the Acropolis in Greece a few weeks earlier. The soldier looked triumphant and calm. Around him tanks, automobiles, and motorcycles exhaled blue tongues of smoke, filling the air with a pungent smell, and planes passed overhead with a swift hissing roar. Everything was going as scheduled.

That afternoon nobody in the Soviet Union, Stalin included, fully appreciated what was happening on the western frontier. The field commanders were too preoccupied with the survival of their units to try to see the larger picture. Moscow tried but failed. It received only random pieces of the strategic puzzle, and Stalin still thought a counteroffensive was possible. The Germans, however, knew very well what they were doing. They also knew that the Red Army had been completely overwhelmed.

▪ ▪ ▪

Adolf Hitler thought of himself as a great warrior. That was not wholly accurate, since his strongest talent lay in diplomacy. He occupied the Rhineland without a fight in 1936 and annexed Austria smoothly in 1938. Having fooled Britain and France in Munich, he grabbed Czechoslovakia. He recruited Stalin as an ally in 1939 and thus secured for himself an easy campaign in Poland. Although a pan-European war was technically a reality as of September 1, 1939, France and Britain had remained passive, thanks to Hitler's clever hints that he would prefer to settle the conflict by diplomatic means.

It is doubtful whether Joseph Stalin still believed in Communism in 1941. Hitler, though, was as fanatical about National Socialism as he had been twenty years earlier, when he had started rallying the Brown Shirts. For him, the conquest of Russia was not just a strategic necessity but a continuation of the long-standing crusade of the civilized Teutons against the crude Slavs. As early as July 1940, a few weeks after the dazzling blitzkrieg in the West, he started talking about a possible Russian campaign.

Yet it took him a while to make up his mind to strike at the east. At that time the alliance with Stalin was still yielding benefits. It even seemed that Stalin could be persuaded to attack the British colonies in the Middle East. Of course, that would have given the Kremlin too much power, and the Führer didn't want any competitors. Still undecided in November 1940, he received Molotov in Berlin and probed him on this matter. One of his closest associates, Minister of Propaganda Goebbels, wrote in his dairy: "Everything else depends on Stalin. We shall have to wait for his decision." But when Stalin reaffirmed the partnership, he demanded too much, not just in the Middle East but also in Europe. Hitler soured on the arrangement, concluding that the *vozhd* intended to keep out of the war until Europe was totally exhausted and "bled white. Then Stalin will move to bolshevize Europe and impose his own rule." This assessment was correct.

Hitler decided to upset Stalin's calculations "with one stroke." On December 18 he ordered the creation of a war plan. The operation was christened Barbarossa, after the red-bearded medieval German emperor-crusader. Goebbels referred to the forthcoming war as a "pre-emptive strike."

Hitler knew that the vast size of the USSR, its inhumane climate, the marshy and wooded terrain, and the sheer numbers of the Red Army made the task difficult. Of all these challenges, the country's size was the greatest. In principle the Soviets could engage the German army in a virtually unlimited chase, retreating as far as the Urals and then beyond, to Siberia or Central Asia. That was the strategy used successfully by a sly genius, Field Marshal Mikhail Kutuzov, in 1812. Knowing that he could not defeat Napoleon in a battle, he lured him into the harsh hinterland, sacrificing the heart of Russia, Moscow, for precisely that purpose. The ruthless winter reached Napoleon at the Kremlin, and that was the end of him and *la Grande Armée.* Exhausted, the French started a slow retreat westward, with the frost-proof Russians biting at their heels. By the time Napoleon reached the borders of Poland, his army had been all but destroyed.

Hitler was not sure about where to position his main thrust. Initially he intended to put the strongest forces on the flanks, in Ukraine and the Baltics, and to encircle the Red Army. His generals persuaded him to concentrate the main force in the center, in Byelorussia, as a lance. The spearhead was made up of two panzer groups, commanded by Heinz Guderian and Hermann Hoth. Put on either side of the Belostok salient, they were to squash the Reds there and then strike at Minsk. After that they would rush toward Moscow.

Hitler made it clear to his commanders that the eastern campaign wasn't meant to end in a peace treaty — the goal was to annihilate Russia once and for all and secure the vast east for German settlers. Meanwhile, people in the occupied territories were to be treated as subhuman. Their industries were to be destroyed and their grain was to be taken away, even at the cost of "severest famine." Any village that harbored a resistance group was to be totally exterminated, and all Communist Party officials and Red Army commissars were to be shot on the spot.

Troops were dispatched to the east. A special group of aircraft called Squadron Rowehl started dipping into Soviet territory for reconnaissance purposes — the planes that so alarmed Zhukov and Timoshenko between April and June. The Führer's new headquarters, the Wolfschanze, or "Wolf's Den," was built near Rastenburg, in eastern Prussia, close to the future battle line.

Originally Hitler planned to strike on May 15, to give the Wehrmacht plenty of time before bad weather arrived. After the invasion of Yugoslavia and Greece, Barbarossa was rescheduled for June 22.

On June 21, Hitler looked exhausted and very nervous. But a few hours before the strike he relaxed: now he was sure that the USSR would fall.

▪ ▪ ▪

The first reports Hitler received on the morning of June 22 trumpeted swift success. Hundreds of Red Army aircraft had been destroyed, Soviet generals were "in complete confusion," the resistance was "weak and disorganized," and the Soviet high command "could not be expected in the first few days to form a clear enough picture of the situation."

The chief of the German General Staff, Franz Halder, wrote in his journal: "Tactical *surprise* of the enemy has apparently been achieved along the entire line. All bridges across the Bug River, as on the entire river frontier, were undefended and are in our hands intact. That the enemy was taken by surprise is evident from the facts that troops were caught in their quarters, that planes on the airfields were covered up, and that enemy groups faced with the unexpected development at the front inquired at their Hq. in the rear what they should do."

Over 3.2 million German soldiers, 2,000 aircraft, 3,350 tanks, and 7,184 pieces of artillery, divided into three army groups — the central one being the strongest — were easily crushing the Soviet defenses. Army Group North, led by Field Marshal Wilhelm Ritter von Leeb, aimed at the Baltics and then Leningrad. Army Group Center, under

Field Marshal Fedor von Bock, was charged with flattening Byelorussia and then reaching Moscow. Field Marshal Karl Rudolf Gerd von Rundstedt's Army Group South dealt with Ukraine. Leeb and Bock were advancing very quickly, having covered 35 to 40 miles on the first day of war; Rundstedt was moving more slowly, at 10 to 15 miles. But the southern field marshal could not be held responsible for his relatively slow progress, because the strongest concentration of Soviet troops was in Ukraine.

If the three German army commanders lacked anything, it was not self-confidence. They all belonged to the Prussian military elite, sharing aristocratic origins, excellent military training, cold contempt for Nazi upstarts, and an overwhelming desire to avenge Germany's defeat in World War I, of which they were all veterans. In 1941 the field marshals were in their early to mid-sixties and still full of vigor. Each had a dazzling record from the previous two years of fighting. Field Marshal Rundstedt had led more than half a million men of Army Group South in the victorious Polish campaign of 1939. Even more impressively, in 1940 he smashed the French and the British in northern France. Bock had commanded Army Group North during the invasion of Poland, and in 1940 his Army Group B had conquered Paris. Leeb was commander in chief on the western front in 1939 and the following year led Army Group C into central France.

Unlike the Soviet generals, who had learned from the Great Terror to flee from initiative and responsibility, the field marshals cultivated political independence and strategic ingenuity. Knowing how suspicious Stalin was, the Soviet commanders didn't have the nerve to act as a group, but Rundstedt, Bock, and Leeb proudly belonged to one caste. Whereas chaotic change in high command during the purges had prevented the Soviet generals from getting to know one another's strategic habits and preferences, the three German field marshals had fought side by side in France, and Rundstedt and Bock in Poland. Finally, their previous victories had ensured the field marshals' high standing with the troops, but neither of the Soviet field commanders was distinguished enough to inspire trust. The generals who would have been capable of that were either victims of the purge, like Bliukher and Tukhachevsky, or had become little more than court jesters, like Voroshilov and Budenny.

▪ ▪ ▪

Every soldier in Hitler's army soon realized that the Soviets had been completely overpowered by the attack. It was particularly gratifying that German superiority in the air was now indisputable. For the most part, the Soviet air force had been destroyed on the ground. When obsolete Soviet planes did appear in the air, a German officer wrote, "we hardly bothered to take cover. We often had to smile, in fact, when, for want of bombs, thousands of nails rained down on us from their bomb bays."

The only piece of weaponry that gave the Germans trouble was the T-34 tank, which shelled at an awe-inspiring range and possessed impressive armor. The Germans also admired the fact that it was "an uncomplicated construction. Its armor plates were welded crudely together, its transmission was simple, everything without any great frills or finesse. Damage was easy to repair." Fortunately for them, the T-34s were scarce.

Western Front Headquarters

Pavlov faced off against Bock, whose Army Group Center included 750,000 men, among them the First Cavalry Division, which was designated to operate in the Pripet Marshes. Bock's friend Field Marshal Albert Kesselring led the grand Second Air Fleet. However, Bock's strongest asset was the Second and Third Panzer Groups, under General Guderian and General Hoth.

Heinz Guderian was the brightest star of the German panzer corps. Present when the armored armada was created, Guderian quickly became its most notable leader. His motto was "Not driblets but mass." A firm believer in the blitz approach, he demonstrated his genius in France during his amazing dash to the English Channel. Tough, paternalistic, and risk-taking, he was very popular with his troops. Hermann Hoth was less of a celebrity, but his performance in Poland and France had also been very impressive, and he too commanded the unwavering loyalty of his troops. Now Guderian's and Hoth's tanks were cutting the Western Front like a hot knife cuts butter.

In theory this shouldn't have been the case. The Western Front had 672,000 soldiers, 10,087 artillery guns and mortars, 2,201 tanks (including 383 KVs and T-34s), and 1,909 aircraft (424 of them new). That section of the border was guarded by 19,519 of Beria's men. Police troops were also stationed in the rear, along the old frontier, effectively quarantining the new Soviets, until 1939 the citizens of Poland.

In the preemptive strike plan, the Western Front played an important role, supporting the main assault in the south and occupying eastern Prussia and northern Poland. However, a defensive scenario hadn't really been developed, which was a huge problem, given that the terrain it protected was very challenging. The front stretched for just 175 miles from north to south, but the ground was difficult to hold. With the exception of a few hills near Minsk, Byelorussia was flat — a blessing for the attacker, a curse for the attacked. The only two significant rivers, the Neman and the Pripet, flowed parallel to the direction of the German invasion, the Neman westward, the Pripet eastward, neither blocking the way to Minsk.

Three rivers farther to the east, beyond Minsk, did help the Soviet cause, however. The West Dvina flowed northwest, the Berezina southeast, and the Dnieper south, and the Germans had to cross all three. Moscow lay only 300 miles beyond the Dnieper, though, and between them there wasn't a single major river to impede the German advance.

Byelorussia consisted largely of woods and swamps. Its muddy jewel, the Pripet Marshes, was an oval 125 miles long and 100 miles wide, containing very few settlements and even fewer roads. No attacker could ever hope to control it. But it wouldn't protect the defenders, either, since the swamp could not support tanks, cars, or artillery guns. As for soldiers, any unit bigger than a platoon could easily be spotted by a reconnaissance plane.

▪ ▪ ▪

The Soviets had four armies in the Western Front — the Third, Fourth, Tenth, and Thirteenth. The most important, the Tenth, occupied the Belostok salient.

Among the strongest units in the Red Army, this army had been envisioned in the preemptive strike plan as the driving force of an attack on Warsaw. But Pavlov and its commander, Konstantin Golubev, hadn't realized that because of the limited size of the salient, the Tenth had to be exceptionally vigilant. During World War I, enemy infantry or cavalry could not have advanced quickly enough to prevent the Tenth from mobilizing its rear units and getting ready for battle. Thanks to new technologies, however, tanks and trucks could cross the 75-mile-wide salient in a matter of hours.

The Third Army, commanded by V. I. Kuznetsov, was the northernmost; the Fourth Army, led by A. A. Korobkov, sat in the south. P. M. Filatov's semifictional Thirteenth, still in the making, was deployed in the rear. As soon as the German panzer groups started enveloping the Tenth at Belostok, the Third and Fourth knew they were in trouble — they were now separated by a messy 75-mile-wide gap.

▪ ▪ ▪

General Pavlov was not blessed with strategic foresight. He had no idea what Bock planned to do at Belostok and spent the day of June 22 in anguish, shuttling between different units and vainly trying to figure out what was going on. Because German saboteurs had competently interrupted communications in the Soviet rear, he could not reach most of his generals.

To make things worse, on June 22 the front was one big construction site. Fortifications, telephone and telegraph lines, roads, airfields, railroads, bridges, highways, fuel depots, and warehouses — everything was half finished. It was as hopeless to call such a front to order as it would be to transform a foundation into a fortress overnight.

Yet in this chaos, one thing was clear: the air force was all but gone. Most of the aircraft, including the newer MiG-3s, had been devastated on the cramped airfields. In the first minutes of war the Western Front had lost 738 aircraft, and now the Germans had full control of the sky.

The commander of the Western Front's air force, Major General I. I. Kopets, was gone too. A week earlier Deputy People's Commissar of Defense Kirill Meretskov, inspecting the troops and shocked by their total lack of preparedness, had asked him angrily, "For God's sake, what are you going to do if war starts and you lose your air force?" Impudently looking at Meretskov, whom he considered an old worrier and a loser, Kopets had haughtily answered, "I will shoot myself."

Like many other young pilots, whom Stalin doted on, Kopets thought himself invincible. A fearless fighter pilot and a veteran of the civil war in Spain, he had been propelled to his high position by the purge. Three years earlier he had been a simple captain, but now, at the age of twenty-nine, he held one of the most important military jobs in the country. On May 24, Stalin had brought him to the top-secret meeting in the Kremlin to discuss the future war, a meeting that even Meretskov had not attended.

On the evening of June 22, he did shoot himself.

The ground troops did not fare much better than the air force. The commander of the Third Army, Kuznetsov, reported to Pavlov "in a trembling voice" that all that was left of his Fifty-sixth Division was its name. He characterized the situation on the front as "catastrophic," and rightly so. The Third Army could not hold the front. Its units started a chaotic retreat toward the southeast. Fleeing with his troops, Kuznetsov changed locations three times in twelve hours.

Meanwhile, his northern neighbor, the Eleventh Army of the Northwestern Front, was retreating toward the northeast. Backing away in diverging directions, the two armies were leaving a frightening gap in the middle. That was exactly what the Germans had hoped to achieve, as the gap opened the road to Minsk. General Hoth immediately sent more tanks into the breach. Facing no organized resistance, he soon captured important crossings near Olita and Merkine.

The Third Army reported a catastrophe, the Fourth Army reported uncontrollable retreat, but the Tenth reported nothing, as all communications with it had been cut off. Pavlov ignored the plight of the Third and Fourth and said he was flying to Belostok to find out what was happening to the Tenth.

That was the worst choice he could have made. Instead of dealing with the damage done by Guderian and Hoth, he was rushing to the rescue of a missing unit as if he were a father looking for a lost child.

His deputy, General Ivan Boldin, was horrified at the idea that the front commander was abandoning headquarters to find an army that was probably doomed anyway. He tried to persuade Pavlov to stay, and volunteered to make the trip instead. Pavlov didn't listen. Ashamed, confused, and frightened, he sought action, and perhaps even martyrdom, on the battlefield.

Yet when Timoshenko called in Pavlov's absence, Boldin quickly asked for permission to fly to Belostok himself. When Pavlov returned, he faced a fait accompli. Having been denied making this heroic exit himself, he instead had to face the task he hated most: decision-making.

Stalin

Tired and overwhelmed, Stalin attempted to finish the first day of war early. Always careful to nourish himself with undisturbed sleep, he spent just three hours in bed that night. He dismissed the last visitor, Beria, at 4:45 P.M., but his mind kept working. The troops needed guidance. The second directive issued that morning had been vague, telling the Red Army to "destroy" enemy forces. He knew that wars were not fought that way. Troops needed specific instructions and a precise timetable to achieve their goals. In the evening he decided to issue another order, directive #3.

By that time Timoshenko was the only top military commander left in Moscow except Voroshilov and Budenny, who were useless. To his credit, and notwithstanding incomplete intelligence, he identified the exact area of greatest peril correctly: the northern side of the Belostok salient, where the Germans had attacked from Suwalki. That was where the Third Army was retreating, creating the gap between itself and the Eleventh in the north and abandoning the Tenth in the south. Timoshenko was also concerned about the German advance in Ukraine, at Vladimir Volynsky.

However, Stalin still hadn't grasped the proportions of the catastrophe. Firm resistance wasn't good enough for him. He told Timoshenko to order a massive counterattack.

Directive #3 ordered the Northwestern and Western Fronts to "encircle and destroy" the enemy and to take Suwalki by the evening of June 24. The Southwestern Front received a similar order: to "encircle and destroy" the Germans at Vladimir Volynsky and to take the Polish city of Lublin within forty-eight hours.

At that point the Northwestern and Western Front troops were about 75 miles away from Suwalki, and 75 miles also separated the Southwestern Front soldiers from Lublin. Stalin couldn't believe that such a small distance couldn't be covered in forty-eight hours, as long as the retreat stopped at once. A few hours earlier he had dispatched his personal representatives to the fronts, and it was their job to deal with panic-mongers, inept leaders, and cowards.

Intriguingly, the two towns he was targeting in this counterattack were precisely where the Red Army was supposed to strike according to the preemptive war plan. On the evening of June 22, Stalin clearly still hoped that when he had restored order on the front line, he would be able to conquer eastern Prussia and Poland.

Nonetheless, his instincts must have told him that the situation was still too risky for him to assume personal responsibility. The directive was signed not by him but by Timoshenko, Zhukov, and Malenkov, as the Party representative. It was sent to the fronts' headquarters at 9:15 P.M., putting an end to what was surely the longest day of Joseph Stalin's life.

4

DISASTER IN THE WEST

Western Front Headquarters, June 23

In the Baltics, the Soviet army lost roughly 5,000 men per day. In Ukraine it was 16,000, in Byelorussia 23,000. On average, a soldier died every two seconds.

Thanks to Stalin's almost yearlong equivocation, the troops found themselves prepared neither to attack Germany nor to defend the motherland. The results were catastrophic. The troops on the border were being decimated, and by the time the reserves reached the battlefield, the main force would be battered, if not destroyed.

There was just one sound strategic option — retreat. Lose territory but save the army. To Stalin and his generals, this was completely unacceptable. All military units, whether platoons or fronts, were ordered to assault until the last drop of blood or the last bullet was spent.

■ ■ ■

Finally it dawned on the officers at the Western Front headquarters that the situation was disastrous. Nobody knew what was happening to the Tenth Army at Belostok, but everybody understood what it meant when a unit of thousands simply disappeared into thin air. The Fourth

Army, in the south, was retreating, fighting local battles. The Third, in the north, was on the run. Meanwhile, Stalin's explicit order was that no matter what, Minsk — now barely 100 miles from the front line, where the ominous gap was widening — must not fall.

Stalin was thinking in terms of symbols, not strategy. Minsk ranked fourth among Soviet cities, after Moscow, Leningrad, and Kiev. If the USSR surrendered it to the Germans, that would be a frightening shock for the nation. But Minsk had no tangible strategic importance whatsoever — it didn't secure any transportation artery, it didn't sit on a major river, and its industries weren't particularly developed. A slow-paced city of 240,000 people, it was deemed significant only as the capital of a western Soviet republic. The Western Front would have been much better off if it had been allowed to pull its troops away from Minsk and arrange them in a straight line farther east. Instead the troops were ordered to stay where they were. Even being surrounded by the Germans would be better than abandoning Minsk, Stalin said.

General Pavlov, a yes man, didn't object to Stalin's obsession with symbols. As soon as directive #3 reached him, late in the evening of June 22, he contacted all the commanders he could reach and instructed them to counterattack the next morning. He sounded as if he believed it was feasible. In the meantime, Minsk was being heavily bombed, and Pavlov's headquarters were forced into the basement. Pavlov himself didn't hide in the security of the bunker; whatever else he was, he was not a coward, and he spent most of his time at the front line — not that it helped. With Pavlov hopping from one unit to another and Boldin lost along with the Tenth Army, there was no one of any real authority in the headquarters.

Meanwhile, Stalin's envoys, Shaposhnikov and Kulik, had reached Minsk and were making Pavlov's life even more difficult. Marshal Shaposhnikov was one of the best theoreticians the Red Army had, but he hadn't been to a battlefield in twenty-four years. He felt totally lost in the epicenter of the storm and sadly regarded himself as a nuisance. He wandered around aimlessly at the Western Front headquarters, browsing among the confusing reports.

Marshal Kulik was worse than useless. He was an unkind and stupid hanger-on, concerned with nothing but saving his skin. A few days earlier he had been fired from the position of artillery czar. His chief opponent, People's Commissar of Armaments Vannikov, was still in jail, yet Kulik couldn't be certain about his own future. He thought he had to do something heroic to win back Stalin's trust, so he decided to fly to the Tenth Army and secure the salient. It sounded like a suicide mission, and perhaps that's why nobody argued. Kulik was a dangerous man, and everybody was happy to see him go. Since he had left for Belostok, no one had heard from him.

One more of Stalin's representatives was at Pavlov's headquarters: the Communist leader of Byelorussia, Ponomarenko. If Shaposhnikov and Kulik had to watch Pavlov, Ponomarenko had to watch all three. Still, he had enough sense to call Stalin on the afternoon of June 23 to say that Byelorussia should be evacuated.

Stalin had ordered his Kremlin staff to start preparing for that eventuality just the day before, yet he now chose to feign astonishment. "Really?" he asked. "Don't you think it is too early?"

"It is already too late to start real evacuation in the western provinces," Ponomarenko replied bluntly. "I believe we should think about Minsk and the eastern areas before it is again too late."

"All right," Stalin said. He instructed Ponomarenko to make sure that all important state and Party archives were properly salvaged. The last thing he wanted was for his secrets to fall into enemy hands.

Most generals knew nothing about the evacuation sanctioned by the *vozhd* and believed that he was fully determined and upbeat, as his third directive, ordering the capture of Lublin and Suwalki, very much suggested.

Fourth Army, Western Front, June 23–26

The commander of the Fourth Army, General Korobkov, was as yet unaware of Stalin's directive #3. He was still struggling with #2, issued the morning of June 22 and received at the Fourth Army headquarters eleven hours later. It instructed the troops to destroy the enemy immediately. By then the Germans had already advanced at least 20 miles east. Pavlov's order, received about the same time and intended as a detailed supplement to directive #2, announced the specifics: counterattack at Brest and regain the prewar border.

"It's simply not doable," the army commissar moaned. "We should ask headquarters to let us shift to a defensive posture instead."

Korobkov lost his patience. He felt crushed by the retreat, and he didn't know where his wife and daughter were. When the headquarters had abandoned Kobrin, he had rushed to his apartment and found it empty; his family had fled in haste, leaving all their possessions behind — "as if they had gone for a walk," Korobkov thought. Now he wasn't sure whether they were still alive. He had seen German planes dropping bombs on columns of refugees too many times that day to feel hopeful.

"Do you want them to call us cowards and do away with us?" he asked, irritated by the commissar's naive suggestion. "You can approach them on your own — be my guest!"

Grimly, he cabled the front headquarters and confirmed that the counterstrike was on its way. As for the troops, he ordered them to "destroy the enemy" at dawn on June 23.

Korobkov wasn't a bad man. Any army is built on the assumption that orders will be carried out. A junior commander may voice his concerns, but he is not supposed to argue with his superiors, or the whole hierarchy will collapse. In the Red Army, even voicing concerns was dangerous, particularly when the country was losing a war. Korobkov hoped against hope that he still had a family, and he wanted to live.

Also, although he held a very high position — he was one of just nine army commanders involved in the fighting — there were at least two dozen other men more important than he was: front commanders, their chiefs of staff and commissars, and the deputies of the people's commissar of defense, not to mention Timoshenko and Zhukov. No one had dared to tell the *vozhd* that the very idea of a counterstrike was absurd.

▪ ▪ ▪

During the night Korobkov grew restless. He was haunted by guilt. In the morning his units would do his bidding and march toward the

German lines in a self-destructive attack. Meanwhile, he, their commander, had no idea where most of them were camped.

He started cruising the area in a car, looking for his men. He could find only a few detachments, but what stunned him was that almost all the military men he saw, whether soldiers or officers, were asleep. Granted, their sleep didn't look restful; the postures of the men spread out on the ground suggested a stony blackout. But the civilians he saw were not asleep. The roads that Korobkov traveled that night were crowded with women and children fleeing from the Germans. Perhaps his wife and daughter had passed him in the dark, unrecognized. Grim, exhausted, and scared, the refugees stubbornly plodded eastward. Some, like Korobkov's family, were fleeing because they feared that the Germans would hold them accountable for the actions of their fathers and husbands. Some were leaving because they were Jewish, and some were simply running away from the German bombardment. Some had abandoned homes already engulfed in fire and smoke, but others had had time to water the houseplants, lock the door, and even make sure to leave a window open so the cat could use it to get in and out.

No official had bothered to prepare evacuation plans, because no one was allowed to doubt the Red Army's invincibility, so the refugees were left to their own devices. Korobkov's soldiers could at least expect their superiors to provide them with food, medical care, and guidance, but the refugees had to be their own quartermasters, nurses, and navigators. A sympathetic officer or peasant might give them a piece of bread; a military ambulance might offer a bandage for a child hit by German shrapnel; a platoon might bury a corpse; and an old man might advise them about which direction to take, though that was largely meaningless, as the refugees rarely had a destination in mind. They had left their homes hoping that at some point the army or the authorities would take care of them. So far nobody had, and the majority of the people on the roads had no idea where they were going. In most cases, relatives who might give them shelter were many miles away — sometimes thousands of miles away — and they couldn't hope to stop at a farm and wait out the war: the farmers they passed, whether sympathetic to their plight or not, regarded them as dangerous guests who would be a burden. Those who had fled shrapnel and bullets already regretted their decision to leave, since the fighting in their hometowns was probably already over, and instead of finding themselves in the security of the rear, they had gotten mired in a war zone as the front line chased them eastward.

During air raids, mothers put buckets on their children's heads to protect them from shrapnel, and some, in desperation, used their purses for the same purpose. As soon as the Luftwaffe came in sight, people covered up girls wearing bright colors with coats and jackets, fearing that a red dress would certainly catch the eye of a German pilot.

Mothers stuffed birth certificates and home addresses in little bags and tied them around the necks of younger children so they would have some chance of being identified if the mothers were killed — and many were, particularly during the air raids. One witness saw an infant sucking a dead mother's breast, another a group of children begging soldiers not to bury their mother and pleading with the dead woman to open her eyes. In a macabre twist, many highways were covered with scores of dolls that young girls had snatched up before fleeing and then lost to stampedes and death.

Not just Korobkov, whose own family was probably traveling along one of the clogged roads, but practically every other Red Army soldier found the sight of the endless, impersonal, and desperate human stream virtually unbearable. However, there was nothing even the most conscientious person could do for the fleeing civilians. The two worlds rarely mixed, and their alienation filled the dark with tension and anger.

At 6 A.M. the Fourth Army tried to strike. Confronted by German armor, Korobkov sent the Thirtieth Panzer Division in to fight. The adversaries crawled toward each other, spitting fire. The Germans hadn't expected any resistance at all, so, surprised, they withdrew a few miles, unwilling to take unnecessary losses, and called in the air force. With a terrifying screech, the U-88 bombers dived at the Thirtieth almost vertically, delivered their load, and climbed back into the sky with a victorious roar. No Red air force fighters were there to stop them.

Soon the battlefield was studded with the carcasses of Soviet tanks. Like torches, they flared up one after another. The Thirtieth didn't stand a chance. After the Luftwaffe assault, Guderian's tanks moved into position and smashed the division, kicking its remnants back to the east.

The division lost 60 tanks out of 120. Another panzer division, the Twenty-second, had just 40 tanks left, and its commander, Major General Puganov, had been killed. Guderian's progress had been checked for a few hours, but the Soviets had paid too heavy a price.

Korobkov looked gloomy and exhausted. When he was told that by some miracle communications with Pavlov had been restored, he immediately contacted him. He asked Pavlov to send planes, fuel, and ammunition. Both knew that it was an unrealistic request, since the air force had been destroyed and the fuel and ammunition annihilated, but Korobkov felt obliged to ask, and Pavlov felt compelled to promise.

The June sun allowed Guderian to continue his thrust, and the fighting didn't stop until late at night. By 8 P.M. the Fourth was forced into an unmanageable retreat.

The army yielded 60 miles that day. The Germans were pushing it into a natural trap, the Pripet Marshes. Also, having dealt with the Fourth, they were making a sharp turn northeast, around its northern flank. It was obvious that they were going to strike the rear of the Tenth to strangle it in Belostok. Not only had Korobkov lost a fight, but the abortive counteroffensive had made the extermination of the Tenth Army a near certainty.

▪ ▪ ▪

At about 10 P.M., Korobkov again spoke with Pavlov, who told him to maintain the defensive line "at all costs." He promised two fresh rifle divisions in the morning. There was little doubt that this promise held nothing but Pavlov's usual bravado.

In the dark, the shooting all but stopped. The night turned balmy and quiet. All Korobkov could hear were short bursts of machine-gun fire. Occasionally a German rocket penetrated the night sky, but otherwise everything was silent and black.

That night all the staff officers had to fit into the only tent they had left. A Morse code machine and two candles stood on the table. The head of communications was trying to reach Minsk. The only way to contact the Fourth's units now was by messenger.

When Pavlov finally replied, Korobkov wished he hadn't. Not only did Pavlov repeat his demand to hold the defenses, he ordered another counterstrike in the morning. By that time Pavlov had received Stalin's directive #3, ordering the conquest of eastern Prussia and Poland — although Korobkov didn't know that.

"Another counterattack?" one of the staff officers asked helplessly. "Today we have already seen what happens when the Germans have more tanks and aircraft than we do."

Korobkov didn't respond, as he hadn't responded to other criticisms. He let his officers talk and then told them to leave for another, safer location, Milovidy, right away. The Fourth would strike in the morning as ordered.

▪ ▪ ▪

The staff reached Milovidy shortly after four o'clock in the morning of June 24, having had no sleep. On the road, away from all communication lines and unreachable by messenger, Korobkov was unable to monitor developments on the front. Approaching towns that had been designated only a few hours earlier as ad hoc headquarters, he never knew what news would be waiting for him. What they heard that morning in Milovidy was discouraging. The Fourth's lines had been smashed by a powerful Luftwaffe raid half an hour earlier, at dawn, and now the German panzers were pushing forward again. The Tenth Army remained blockaded in Belostok, and the Third was pulling back chaotically.

In comparison, the Fourth Army was doing fine — yielding, true, but slowly, while keeping an uninterrupted front line, a military virtue. Yet Korobkov didn't find that uplifting. He remained sullen and ignored all inquiries from the staff.

The new counterattack started as ordered, and throughout the day of June 24 the Fourth tried to repel Guderian's troops, pulling away and pushing forward at random. They hadn't gained any territory, but they could be proud of their slow withdrawal. Now they were clinging to the

Shchara River. Again Pavlov ordered them to stay at all costs. As frustrating as this was, at least he didn't insist on another counterstrike.

At one point a Soviet tank column met a stray German automobile, closed the ranks in gleeful anticipation, and opened fire. But the German driver hit the gas and took the vehicle out of shooting range of the slow Soviet panzers. Later in the day a captured German officer revealed that the car had been carrying Guderian himself.

The near capture of the German panzer genius tormented Korobkov. If he had delivered Guderian to Pavlov's headquarters, he and his army would have been forgiven everything. They had missed their chance.

He spent that night visiting various units, making sure they would be able to hold on to the Shchara in the morning. But things looked grim. Many trucks and cars had been lost. The commanders had stolen horses from local farmers, but the majority of the soldiers, it turned out, didn't know how to ride. What they had was not cavalry but mounted infantry.

The next day, June 25, the Fourth started losing its grip on the Shchara. Korobkov agonized over whether to withdraw the troops or to keep expending them on this insignificant waterway. He tried to get in touch with Pavlov and couldn't. Unexpectedly, one of his officers, just back from a reconnaissance trip, reported that two hours earlier he had met Pavlov not far from Baranovichi, about 25 miles away. The officer's automobile had been stopped by three armored cars. The commander of the Western Front had jumped out of the middle one and promptly asked about the state of affairs, industriously putting new marks on his map as the officer replied. Pavlov had said that the Fourth had to keep the Shchara, at least for a while, but that it should also start preparing a new defensive line in the rear, around Slutsk, 50 miles south of Minsk. When the officer asked about the fate of the Tenth Army at Belostok, Pavlov admitted that he did not know.

Korobkov felt encouraged. They were now entering the area of the original border between the Soviet Union and Poland, and Slutsk was part of the old defensive line. As far as Korobkov knew, the Slutsk district had good fortifications and powerful artillery. There was hope.

Since Slutsk was fairly close, he was soon able to send for the commander of the defense district to discuss logistics. What he heard was devastating.

"Please keep in mind," the man said calmly, "that all fortifications were abandoned in the beginning of the spring and none has guns now. All our guns were shipped to you at Brest. Now all I have is just one battalion guarding the forts."

"And we thought Slutsk would be a good armored shield," Korobkov muttered bitterly.

In the evening the headquarters started moving to Slutsk anyway. When they reached the old border, the column suddenly stopped. A few hours earlier it had started raining, and the roads had turned messy. Korobkov could see quite a few trucks stuck in the mud and at first thought that was the reason for the jam. But when he walked to the head of the column, he discovered that the cars were being stopped and checked by Beria's men. The commanding officer told Korobkov that he had been instructed to set up roadblocks all around Slutsk to catch spies and saboteurs.

Using his authority as a senior officer, Korobkov disbanded the checkpoint then and there. "You are only creating traffic jams and make people angry," he explained dourly.

By two o'clock in the morning of June 26, the Fourth Army staff had reached their new destination. At seven they heard cannon fire in the west. The Fourth's lines had been shattered again, and the Germans were quickly advancing along the highway toward Slutsk. One hour later German tanks hit the hastily constructed headquarters. Having no time to send orders to the fighting units, the commander left the insecure location.

Slutsk was on fire. Riding through the narrow streets, Korobkov's column saw thousands of people, cars, trucks, and cattle. German snipers shot from rooftops. One even threw a hand grenade, but the general was too frustrated to investigate or pursue.

Still, he decided to defend Slutsk, as Pavlov had ordered. He told his troops to stop. The German panzer divisions attacked a few times but couldn't get through the barricades that Korobkov's soldiers had built on the streets. Nonetheless, before dark fell, Guderian managed to fight his way into the city center.

Minsk Area, June 24–26

The counteroffensives ordered by Stalin and supported by his yes men were not simply a failure, they were an utter catastrophe. The Tenth Army was now surrounded at Belostok, the Third had virtually disappeared, and the Fourth had suffered staggering casualties and had been forced to withdraw. The gap between the Western and Northwestern Fronts had grown to 60 miles. The opening contained the highway to Minsk, and German tanks were now rolling speedily along it, approaching the Byelorussian capital. The frontier battle had been lost.

The bombing of Minsk was hellish. The Luftwaffe dominated, and although Soviet pilots shot down twenty-one German aircraft on June 24, that was not nearly enough to stem the tide. The pilots felt deeply betrayed by central command and still mourned the fighters and bombers that had been swept away like a bunch of toy planes while parked in neat rows on the airfields, but they refused to give up. As early as June 22, fifteen of them had rammed Luftwaffe planes in the air. The first to risk his life was Senior Lieutenant I. I. Ivanov, who ran out of ammunition in midair and put his plane in the way of a German bomber. In all, 358 of the 636 rams by the Soviets during World War II took place in the first weeks of war. Because fighter aircraft were light and slow, a ram wasn't necessarily fatal for the desperate crew if they had their parachutes ready; if they didn't damage the fuel tank, they could leap from the flaming plane. Nonetheless, instant death was probable.

On June 24 the evacuation of Minsk began. The railway junction became clogged as trains transported anything of value to the east: currency, gold, factory equipment, grain. Cows were slowly herded along the jammed roads. But if cattle were important enough for bureaucrats to count and track, refugees were not. Nobody took care of them, and they fled at their own risk.

To many, the decision to leave was made suddenly, provoked by a particularly severe air raid. In the morning a plant accountant might be handing out paychecks to workers. Seven hours later she would be gathering up her children and belongings and joining the stream of refugees. Panicky or numb, people walked through neighborhood after neighborhood, struck by the surreal nature of the carnage brought on by the Luftwaffe. One witness noticed three windowsills with spectacular cactuses in lush red bloom; the rest of the building was on fire, but both the cacti and the white curtains that framed them remained as yet unharmed. At the railway station, thousands of civilians begged the authorities to let them onto the trains. Most of these pleas were ignored.

On the night of June 25, state and Party officials fled Minsk. The day before, unable to function in the burning city, Pavlov had moved his headquarters to the nearby village of Borovoi. Borovoi had no communications center, so the general started communicating with his commanders by messenger. That proved disastrous, since it was so slow that the headquarters had no idea what was happening only a few miles away, while the troops were left to their own devices.

On June 25 pilots of the Forty-second Air Force Division accidentally discovered German troops just 15 miles west of Minsk. This should not have come as a surprise, given that there were no lines of organized resistance north of the Fourth's Army positions. Minsk was left with virtually no defenders except a few random units that had retreated from the border but been stopped at the city.

The Fourth Army, now at Slutsk, was protecting Minsk's southern flank and couldn't be brought closer. Of course, pieces of the decimated Tenth and Third Armies were dying to the west, and in principle some of their units could help defend the city. But that was problematic for a number of reasons. First, very few units could break through German positions to get back to the Soviet territory. Second, they were not supposed to — their orders said to stay where they were, even if it meant total devastation. Third, there was no way to communicate with the troops. The Third Army had completely disintegrated, its units were mixed up, and its headquarters were constantly on the move. Nothing had been heard from the Tenth Army for seventy-two hours. The fact that it still existed on the General Staff maps meant nothing. The only solution for the Western Front now was to abandon Minsk and take its sole fighting army, the Fourth, east of the city to create a realistic line of defense.

Nobody had the courage to suggest such a plan, but Marshal Shaposhnikov finally warned Moscow about the pending fall of Minsk and asked for permission to move troops from Belostok to Minsk and Slutsk. Although making this suggestion appeared to demand a lot of bravery, the idea was in fact rather delusional. What sort of evacuation was possible for the Third Army, now dispersed all over central Byelorussia, and the Tenth, firmly locked in the Belostok pocket?

Moscow's response was equally farcical. Timoshenko magnanimously allowed Pavlov to evacuate the units, but the troops were to relocate not to Minsk but to the Lida-Slonim-Pinsk line, 80 miles *west* of the city. Obviously, Timoshenko didn't know that on June 25 the Red Army was already leaving Slonim, having been overwhelmed by the pincer strike of Guderian and Hoth. However, he should have admitted that the Third and the Tenth had by then practically ceased to exist. Instead, the people's commissar of defense was sending ghost armies to nonexistent trenches.

The Western Front had just one army unscathed by fighting — the Thirteenth, located in the rear, at Moghilev. The defenders of Minsk eagerly awaited its arrival.

▪ ▪ ▪

The Thirteenth Army, commanded by General Peter Filatov, was barely six weeks old. When the war started, it was still being formed. It remained heavily understaffed and most of its units existed only on paper.

Twenty-four hours after the German attack, early in the morning of June 23, Filatov was instructed to move to Molodechno, one of the biggest railway junctions on the right flank of the Western Front, still some distance from the front line but just 45 miles from Minsk. Filatov and his staff left immediately, but only a few units were ready to accompany them. When Filatov reached Molodechno the next day, he learned that the Germans were already approaching the town. The information came from refugees; his own scouts had not returned yet.

The Party leader of Molodechno asked Filatov whether the Red Army would be able to hold the city.

"We have no troops and no orders from the front headquarters," Filatov replied. "If you ask me, I think you should start evacuating people now."

Meanwhile, a number of retreating units started to reach Molodechno from the west, and Filatov claimed them as his own. Their commanders reported the gap between the Western and Northwestern Fronts. Filatov knew that the gap led straight to Molodechno and from there to Minsk, and all he had was a group of already battered units. One of them, the Fifth Panzer Division, which had fled the front, had just fifteen tanks, twenty armored vehicles, and nine artillery guns left.

At nine o'clock on the night of June 24, Filatov finally got a directive from Pavlov, which commanded him to absorb the retreating units and organize them (which he had already done) and — this was the unbelievable part — counterattack. Filatov obediently instructed his nonexistent army to counterstrike, then, in the night, abandoned Molodechno and retreated to the suburbs. Amazingly, a number of his units held their positions against the Germans for several hours. Still, Molodechno fell on June 25. Barely 300 yards away from Filatov's headquarters, German tanks opened fire. They were so close that Filatov could see the smoke rising from their gun barrels after each salvo. Pursued by the German panzers, the staff of the headquarters fled.

The area was in total disarray. Retreating Soviet units, attacking Soviet units, German motorcyclists, refugees, German panzers, Soviet panzers — everything intermingled in an unending nightmare. At midnight Filatov's column ran into a bunch of naked German officers, who, certain that the battle was over for the day, had decided to spend the night in a grove beside a brook. While the soldiers were putting up tents, the officers had stripped and begun splashing in the stream. The Soviet scouts found them there. Fifty bathers were killed and five captured, and their cars were either destroyed or taken. Among the trophies were four briefcases, one containing the Army Group Center battle map.

When Filatov and his staff saw this, they shuddered. The map made it clear that they were facing two mighty panzer armies, one led by Guderian, the other by Hoth. Both were homing in on Minsk. As far as the officers could tell, the attack had gone as scheduled.

At the nearby headquarters of the Sixty-fourth Rifle Division, another directive from Pavlov awaited Filatov. It ordered him to hold Molodechno, which he had abandoned twenty-four hours earlier. Filatov decided to ignore Pavlov and his meaningless orders and assume command over the scattered units north of Minsk. He knew that the map he had sent by messenger to the front headquarters would make a stronger case than he ever could.

▪ ▪ ▪

When Filatov and his officers reached Minsk on June 26, they saw not a city but a bonfire. Even the parks were in flames. The capital of Byelorussia was shrouded in smoke, and blasts shook the air. One wave of German bombers after another rolled over the city, turning it into rubble. Thousands of refugees streamed east, only to be massacred by German pilots on blocked roads.

Coincidentally, June 26 was the day that Captain Nikolai Gastello and his crew became a legend. Over Molodechno, a German shell hit their aircraft's fuel tank. Instead of parachuting, Gastello sent the blazing plane into a convoy of German trucks and tanks on the ground — or at least that's how the careening course of his plane was interpreted by observers, who wished to see moral strength in the morass of defeat and failure.

But Captain Gastello's courage went unnoticed in Minsk. The situation had become so desperate that the Western Front headquarters decided to abandon the suburbs of the doomed city, knowing only too well that the Thirteenth Army was incapable of saving them. In small groups, staff officers started moving toward Bobruisk. Pavlov sanctioned General Filatov's plan and officially left him in charge of the "defense" of Minsk. The Western Front commander didn't dare admit that the city had been lost.

When the command reached Bobruisk, the staff was informed that the town was deemed unsafe and they had to continue farther east, to

Moghilev. As a result, Pavlov and his officers spent June 26 and the night of June 27 on the road, unable to advise the troops.

■ ■ ■

In Minsk the war was particularly brutal. Only four days earlier the people of the city had been vibrant — not happy, perhaps, but steady, uncomplaining, and resilient. The town had been the home of Colonel General Pavlov, a drama company, Byelorussians and Jews, Ukrainians and Russians, police stations and schools. Life in Minsk, like the rest of Stalin's empire, had been hard, yet now life itself was threatened.

German pilots looked at Minsk as one huge target and dropped bombs indiscriminately, making no distinction between Western Front headquarters and a grocery store. Many citizens of Minsk had lived through the devastation of the revolution and the civil war, but no one had ever before seen a blazing park or a city block turned into dust, and no one had thought that such destruction was in the power of humans.

About 40,000 people left their homes, but no one knows how many died on the way to supposed safety, killed by collapsing walls or friendly fire or mowed down by a machine-gun burst from a Messerschmitt. What is known is that about 200,000 stayed. Some had already heard the horrifying accounts of the first wave of refugees that had descended on Minsk from Brest, Baranovichi, and Molodechno, reporting clogged roads, indifferent army officers, deserters in the woods, and ferocious Luftwaffe strikes. Some people believed that Minsk would be miraculously saved by the Red Army, and others thought that life would be better under German occupation. But the majority, in all likelihood, just lingered in the ruins of their neighborhoods because they were too scared to attempt anything heroic.

Some Red Army units stubbornly remained in the city too, inspiring hope and unwittingly encouraging civilians to stay. But the soldiers themselves were desperate. Every unit was running out of ammunition. The commander of the One Hundredth Rifle Division, Ivan Russiyanov, who had used bottles with gasoline against Franco's troops in Spain, now grabbed twelve trucks with bottles from a glass-making plant and set his men to work. Of course the improvised hand grenades — later called Molotov cocktails — were a pathetic counter to German tanks.

One of the units ordered to fight in Minsk, the Seventeenth Mechanized Corps, had just 10,000 rifles for 30,000 men. By June 26 the Seventeenth had ceased to exist; the surviving soldiers dispersed in the woods, but thousands had died, defenseless, under the fire of General Guderian's tanks.

Filatov felt helpless. His army, though marked on General Staff maps and treated as an intact unit, remained illusory. He was getting reports not from divisions or corps but from ninety-man companies.

From his new headquarters, Pavlov ordered the Thirteenth to stay in Minsk even if the city turned into a flaming trap. To boost Filatov's morale, Pavlov lied again, saying that the defenders of Minsk would soon get reinforcements — the units of the Third Army retreating from the front. Nobody believed him.

Northwestern Front

One of the most shocking things about the first week of war was that no one in Moscow was paying much attention to the Northwestern Front, which originally covered 175 miles of the Baltics' southern area in Lithuania. Stalin was obsessed with the loss of Byelorussia, and therefore so were Zhukov and Timoshenko. The Northwestern was the only front to have no high command representative and no Party envoy at its headquarters. But the northwestern army group was rolling back almost as fast as the one in the west, and Leningrad sat in its rear.

Like almost everyone else in the armed forces, the commander of the front, Colonel General Fedor Kuznetsov, was a new appointee. A boorish person with an undistinguished pedigree, he was supposed to manage three armies — the Twenty-seventh, under Major General N. E. Berzarin, stationed on the coast of Estonia, far from the frontier; the Eighth, under Colonel General P. P. Sobennikov, in Lithuania's north; and the Eleventh, under Lieutenant General V. I. Morozov, in the south. According to Stalin's preemptive strike plan, the Northwestern Front was to remain passive during the opening phase of war, meaning that its role was to defend the Baltics regardless of who struck first.

In that, it failed. Field Marshal Leeb's Army Group North swept away its defenses at the Neman River and thrust deep into Lithuania.

■ ■ ■

Peter Kurochkin was a hardworking and conscientious man. But in June 1941, this veteran of four wars, now chief of communications of the Northwestern Front, was dismayed. He cursed the formerly independent Baltic states because they supplied a communications professional with almost insurmountable difficulties. He had to deal with three separate communications networks, and there was no time to tie them together. The Baltic nations were too developed for Kurochkin's taste, as all major wires followed highways and railroads and all main communication centers were located in big towns or railway junctions — the natural targets for air strikes. Kurochkin would have preferred something more out of the way.

In addition, being a Russian in the Baltics meant being an enemy. Contested by Russia, Poland, Sweden, and Germany for half a millennium, the Baltics had fallen under Russian rule in the eighteenth century. During the civil war of 1918–1920, the Communists had lost Lithuania, Latvia, and Estonia to local nationalist movements, and the three nations had finally acquired their long-sought sovereignty. The deal between Stalin and Hitler deprived them of that, and in 1940 the Red Army "liberated" them. The area had a remarkably low number of willing collaborators, and Red Army troops stationed there felt extremely insecure.

The military authorities in Moscow were another source of anxiety for Kurochkin. Reserve command posts in the rear remained nonexistent. He bombarded the General Staff with demands for more telegraph wire, but by June 22 he had received less than one twentieth of what he needed. Communication units had just 10 percent of their allotted wartime personnel.

After the situation had become especially tense, in mid-June, the Baltic Military District headquarters selected a special code word for German invasion of their region, "Elephant." In the atmosphere of nervousness and uncertainty, nobody knew what sort of conflict to expect, and the code word was expanded. "Little Elephant" would mean that a German company had crossed the border; only a larger unit would warrant the name "Big Elephant." However, at 0:20 A.M. on June 22, before either a "Little Elephant" or a "Big Elephant" had sounded, the Bodo telegraph machine at the headquarters clattered: "Chief of Staff go on line immediately to receive very urgent." That was Stalin's directive #1 coming.

It took General Kuznetsov about two hours to transmit his own order to the troops. Shortly thereafter German bombers appeared in the sky. The Junkers didn't notice the headquarters skillfully hidden in the thick woods 12 miles east of the town of Panevezys and proceeded east to flatten something else. Soon Kurochkin knew what — the Red air force front headquarters and the cities of Siauliai, Ukmerge, Kaunas, Vilnius, and Liepaja, as well as numerous smaller towns.

A short while later, to Kurochkin's horror, all communications went dead. The headquarters at Panevezys found itself isolated in the mocking safety of the woods.

▪ ▪ ▪

When Leeb struck in the early hours of June 22, he mainly aimed at the Eleventh Army, bordering Byelorussia, and the southern flank of the Eighth Army. He knew he could deal later with Lithuania's northern corner, where the bulk of the Eighth was situated. In the meantime he had to capture a number of important cities and break open the road to Riga and Leningrad.

Only a quarter of the Eleventh Army was on its defensive line that morning, while the rest lingered in barracks and training camps. On the night of June 21, concerned about possible mishaps, some officers had ordered the soldiers to deposit all the ammunition. Others had felt secure enough to plan a fishing trip for the following morning. The roar of the German aircraft reached them before they could get their rods.

The Eleventh was supposed to shield two main Lithuanian cities, Vilnius and Kaunas, the seat of Lithuania's Soviet government. Leaders of a Soviet republic had to be local men, but Stalin did not trust any Lithuanians and had dispatched a number of Russian emissaries to Kaunas to keep an eye on the native cadres. The Lithuanian Communists were annoyed by this, and when war started they didn't hesitate to stab their Muscovite brethren in the back.

At 9 A.M. on June 22, Stalin's appointees were invited to Party headquarters, where they were dryly informed about the disaster and told to wait. Grudgingly, they acknowledged that they didn't have much choice: they didn't speak the language, and it was not safe to go outside. In general there was no love lost between Russians and Lithuanians, and mass arrests a week earlier had angered the locals. So, frightened and angry, the envoys spent the whole day in the Party's head office. Meanwhile, the Lithuanian Communists completely ignored them. The only briefing the Moscow bureaucrats got during the day was Molotov's live broadcast at noon. After that they just loitered, too nervous to leave the building. Fuming with impotent rage, they tried to reach the Lithuanian leaders by phone, but the Lithuanians did not answer, since they were busy evacuating their families to Moscow.

Pragmatic Westerners, the Lithuanians had little faith in the Red Army, and they knew that their bitter compatriots would be only too ready to hand them over as soon as Hitler's troops marched into the capital. By 3 P.M. they had a special train ready. Kaunas was a small town, and in a few minutes everyone knew that Stalin's puppets were fleeing. The train departed at four, and the Party bosses wistfully said goodbye to their families at the platform, promising to join them soon. Indeed, they left Kaunas just three hours later, at seven at night. (An hour after that, the police fled. Not expecting to return anytime soon, they took all their belongings with them, including bed frames and mattresses.)

Shortly before midnight, someone remembered the Moscow emissaries still sitting in the Party building like chickens on a perch. They were politely advised to leave the city as soon as they could. Most of them had no means of transport beyond their own feet. As they set out eastward, toward home, they cursed the treacherous Lithuanians and vowed to lodge a complaint with the Central Committee.

■ ■ ■

Kaunas was abandoned with its power plants, radio station, post office, telegraph, archives, and warehouses all intact. The Lithuanian leaders even forgot to disable the high-frequency phone line to the Kremlin.

But that was of little consequence to the commander of the Northwestern Front, General Kuznetsov. He had more important concerns. For one, he didn't know where his armies were. Over the next two days, virtually blindfolded since his communications lines were down, yet determined to follow Stalin's directives #2 and #3, he kept ordering his troops to counterattack. By June 25 Leeb had advanced 80 miles east. Nobody in the Northwestern Front headquarters knew that Hitler himself was only 125 miles west of them, in his new command center in eastern Prussia. In one of the war's many ironies, a well-planned raid by Soviet bombers could have blown him to pieces and brought the war to an end.

In comparison with the disaster in Byelorussia, the Baltics were sitting pretty. The Northwestern Front's Eighth and Eleventh Armies drew back, but they did not let Leeb encircle them. Fortunately for Kuznetsov, the gap between the Eleventh and the Western Front, which the Germans had used to reach Minsk, would be blamed on the Western Front command.

On June 25, realizing that Leeb had moved too close, Kuznetsov ordered the evacuation of the headquarters from Panevezys to Daugavpils. Kurochkin was crestfallen. He knew that the reserve command post at Daugavpils existed solely on paper.

The staff left Panevezys the following morning. They moved in a caravan of one hundred vehicles, which Kurochkin felt was asking for trouble. Indeed, a German reconnaissance plane soon spotted them and immediately sent for Junkers. Soon cars were burning and officers were ducking into the woods.

Several hours later, having reached Daugavpils despite heavy losses, the staff discovered that no military communications were available there, just as Kurochkin had warned. Led by an infuriated Kuznetsov, they walked to the town's telegraph office, but one of the first cables they received said that the Germans were already approaching Daugavpils. At precisely that moment they heard loud blasts.

"Into the cars!" Kuznetsov yelled.

"But where are we going?" an indignant Kurochkin asked.

"Follow me!" was all the front commander said.

A Russian trench during World War I. Almost all of Stalin's generals fought in that war as privates or noncommissioned officers. *Courtesy of the author*

Joseph Stalin, the *vozhd* of the Soviet people, with his famous pipe, 1936. *AKG-Images*

Stalin presiding over a May Day parade in Red Square in 1935. Klim Voroshilov, his pet "cavalryman," is on the left. *AKG-Images*

Stalin and Voroshilov in 1936. Despite the informal setting, Voroshilov stands at attention in the presence of the *vozhd*. *AKG-Images*

The five marshals who survived the purge of 1937–1939. *From top left, counterclockwise:* Klim Voroshilov, Semen Budenny, Grigory Kulik (the three "cavalrymen"), Boris Shaposhnikov (the "classicist"), and Semen Timoshenko. *AKG-Images*

Young engineers conferring on one of the coal mines in the industrial heart of the Soviet Union, the Donbass. In the late 1930s, with war looming in Europe, the Soviet Union sped up industrialization. *Courtesy of the author*

Soviet officers talking with Heinz Guderian's commanders east of Brest, Poland, on September 20, 1939. Poland was partitioned under the secret agreement between Hitler and Stalin a month earlier. *AKG-Images*

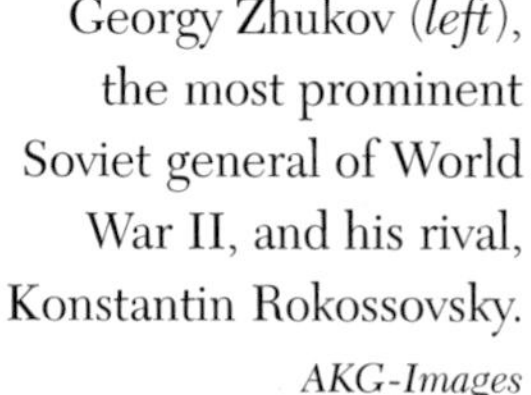

Georgy Zhukov (*left*), the most prominent Soviet general of World War II, and his rival, Konstantin Rokossovsky. *AKG-Images*

Rokossovsky in an iconographic portrait of 1946. Purged in 1938, he was one of the few military leaders rehabilitated on the eve of the war.
AKG-Images

A Black Sea Fleet pilot, Alexander Zhilenko, with his wife, Nadezhda, in November 1940. Alexander died on June 22, 1941, in the first hours of the war, when his plane was shot down off the Romanian coast. Nadezhda joined the Red Army as a nurse.
Courtesy of the author

Wehrmacht soldiers crossing the Soviet border on June 22, 1941.
AKG-Images

Wehrmacht soldiers in 1941. *Courtesy of the author*

German officers in an occupied town, apparently writing letters home.
Courtesy of the author

SS troops at the first fortification line in the USSR, known as Stalin's Line, in July 1941. *AKG-Images*

German officers being friendly to the locals in the occupied Crimea. The man on the right later tried to shoot the young woman in the picture, Anna Zimina, when she refused to go to Germany as slave labor.
Courtesy of the author

One of the "Uncle Vanyas" who eventually won the war, Ivan Kolyadin, a former White Army officer. A gulag prisoner, he was allowed to go to the front "to wash the crime away with blood."
Courtesy of the author

Night had fallen. Daugavpils was pitch black as the caravan crawled through it. The drivers were not allowed to use headlights, so the automobiles moved very slowly. Kuznetsov's car led the way, as the general scouted for a place to bivouac. Twenty-five miles out of Daugavpils, they stopped. Kuznetsov announced that they would spend the night there, in the woods. When Kurochkin protested, saying that the forest offered no means of communication, Kuznetsov ignored him.

While the general was deciding where to put the tents, Kurochkin explored the grounds. To his delight, he suddenly saw a telegraph wire, which turned out to connect the house of the local forest ranger with the village of Borovaya. Kurochkin at once guessed that he could call the town of Rezekne and then connect with Moscow.

Nervous and agitated, he started working on the connections. In a while he reached General Zhukov's duty officer at the General Staff. Not believing his luck, he rushed to Kuznetsov, but his unsolicited zeal made the front commander very angry.

"What's the point of talking to Moscow?" Kuznetsov snarled. "They will ask me about the situation, and I know nothing about it. We are not in touch with the armies, we have no idea what the troops are doing . . . Go, talk to Moscow yourself. My armies — that's who I want to talk to," he added pompously.

Kurochkin patiently explained that there was no way to communicate with the Eighth or the Eleventh, or with the Twenty-seventh, from the middle of nowhere. He suggested moving to Rezekne the following day. Kuznetsov agreed.

The next morning, in that sleepy Latvian town, Kuznetsov was finally able to talk to the Eighth, the Eleventh, and the Twenty-seventh. The armies reported uncontrolled retreat. The Germans were closing in again, and Kuznetsov took his staff to Pskov, 300 miles east of the border.

▪ ▪ ▪

The last week of June was so hot in the normally brisk Baltic states that soldiers were felled by heat stroke. Exhausted, they crawled to the rivers to quench their thirst and, if there was time, to take a quick plunge in the water. However, many walked into the woods and didn't return. They tore off their insignia, dumped their weapons, and disappeared into the thicket.

Kuznetsov had sunk into angry passivity. While his neighbor to the south, Pavlov, shuttled haphazardly between units, trying to figure out what to do, Kuznetsov remained with his staff, regally contemplating his misery. German troops were already in the suburbs of Minsk, and although that city's fate was as much Kuznetsov's responsibility as Pavlov's — after all, the flight of the Eleventh Army had opened the fateful gap for the German panzers — Kuznetsov didn't do anything to alleviate its plight. He quickly figured out that Stalin's anger was directed at the hapless Pavlov and wisely took on the role of innocent martyr.

From Pskov he could communicate with the retreating armies. Unable to provide guidance, he decided that he could supply vigilance.

"Read this," he said to Kurochkin one day. A number of cables had arrived from the commander of the Eleventh Army, Lieutenant General V. I. Morozov. They grew angrier and angrier with each transmission, as Morozov demanded reinforcements. In the last, sent from the lethal pocket, Morozov energetically reproached Kuznetsov for having failed the dying troops.

"What do you think?" Kuznetsov asked.

"The army is in a tough situation," Kurochkin muttered. "They are encircled . . ."

"You haven't understood a thing!" Kuznetsov exploded. "I have told you many times that you are not a genuine military professional, you cannot analyze facts! Do you know General Morozov?"

"Yes, I do."

"Can a disciplined and tactful person like Morozov be sending me rude cables like that?"

"He might, if the circumstances forced him," Kurochkin replied diplomatically. "It looks like he is very upset."

"I knew you would say that. This is not the response of a military professional. Morozov would not write this way. These cables are from the Germans. The Eleventh's staff must have been captured, together with the codes. The radio transmitter too. Now the Fascists are trying to trap us."

"If I may say so, radio operators know each other's hallmarks. Nobody has reported anything fishy about communications from the Eleventh."

"The hallmark wouldn't have to change. The Eleventh's radio operators could have been forced to work for the Germans . . . Discontinue all exchanges with them immediately."

Terrified, Kurochkin realized that the surrounded Eleventh Army was now doomed. He decided to talk to the front commissar, P. A. Dibrova.

The commissar listened to Kurochkin's agitated report attentively and then ordered him to contact the Eleventh by radio. "I will talk with them myself," he said.

Soon the operator was calling the Eleventh in the open. At first the Eleventh enthusiastically responded, but then they put Dibrova on hold. The army remained on the air for an hour or so and then abruptly cut off communications. Kurochkin monitored the line for the next two days, to no avail. Ashamed, he decided that Kuznetsov might have been right.

Only after Morozov and the meager remains of his army had escaped from the pocket did Kurochkin learn why the army had stopped responding. Having been told that Dibrova was calling them in the open, Morozov grew suspicious in turn; now *he* thought that Kuznetsov and his staff had been captured and that the Germans were trying to trick him.

This communications error cost the Eleventh thousands of lives. Believing the unit already lost, front headquarters abandoned every attempt to ease its predicament.

▪ ▪ ▪

The only army that attempted to stop the Germans in the Baltics was the Twenty-seventh, at the Daugava River, but its defenses crumbled within a few days. In the course of the fighting the Germans were again allowed to capture critical bridges and thereby gain a toehold on the eastern shore. After this debacle, nobody bothered to defend Pskov, and the Germans occupied it almost instantly. Lithuania and Latvia were now lost, and Leningrad was just 150 miles away from the German tanks.

5

HOPE IN THE SOUTH

The Kremlin, June 23–25

From the vantage point of Moscow, the devastation of the western part of the country seemed unreal. Despite the initial shock, most people still believed the war would be over soon, and life continued much as it had. There were no German aircraft in sight, and as for the horrifying losses at the border, they were grossly understated by radio and newspapers.

A full twenty-four hours after the war had started, on June 23, the General Headquarters, or Stavka, was finally set up. It was chaired by Timoshenko and included Stalin, Zhukov, Molotov, Voroshilov, Budenny, and Kuznetsov. A number of political and military leaders were listed as its permanent advisers.

The new high command was odd, if not laughable. How could Timoshenko possibly chair a committee of which Stalin was a mere member? What did Molotov know about military affairs? How was it that two of five generals on the committee were old-school cavalrymen?

Still refusing to accept the post of commander in chief, the *vozhd* browsed through the chaotic reports arriving from the west. The counterstrike he had ordered the day before was failing, and he couldn't understand why. Perplexed and angry, he decided to hold a late-night meeting with Timoshenko, Kuznetsov, and others. While they were sitting in his office discussing the situation, Stalin received a disturbing report: German planes were approaching Moscow.

The men jumped from their seats. They had assumed that the front line was still 500 miles away, but perhaps the Germans had secretly developed new, surprisingly long-range planes. "We will have to interrupt our session" was all that Stalin could say.

The group rushed by car to the Kirovskaya subway station, a mile northeast of the Kremlin. The Moscow subway system lay deep underground, having been designed not just to showcase triumphant Communism and transport its faithful foot soldiers but to serve as an enormous air shelter. However, like everything else in the country, it was wholly unprepared for war, and only at this point was Kirovskaya station, one of the deepest in the world, designated as the underground post for the high command. Construction was still in progress, but at least at Kirovskaya no German bomb would reach the *vozhd.*

Meanwhile, rank-and-file Muscovites were woken by howling sirens. Taking their children into the basements, they anxiously scanned the skies. There were no signs of an air raid.

At Kirovskaya, Stalin and his lieutenants were briefed by phone by the commander of Moscow Air Defense. One hundred and seventy-eight fighters were already in the air, at altitudes ranging from 6,000 to 21,000 feet, over the capital. In the meantime, the enemy aircraft kept getting closer. But suddenly the general called again and blurted out that the suspicious planes actually belonged to the Soviet air force.

Stalin was so relieved that he did not punish the man. The next day the newspapers reported that the alarm had been a drill.

The general was extremely fortunate, as the *vozhd* was becoming increasingly difficult to deal with. Invariably suspicious and untrusting, he had at least always been there to take the lead, to criticize, to rewrite, to decide, to mold. Now, unable to come to terms with the staggering retreat in the west, he sank into depression, which was occasionally interrupted by fits of uncontrollable rage.

His associates were accustomed to his anger; what unnerved them was his strange new passivity. He saw fewer people, issued seemingly random orders, and consulted with Timoshenko, Vatutin, and commanders at the front only sporadically. He wasn't completely absent from the Kremlin, but he didn't spend much time there either, lingering at his suburban dacha instead. Most troubling, he maintained his normal routine, which was to rest during the day and work from the late afternoon deep into the night. Of course, fighting generally stops during the night and resumes at dawn. When the first reports of new German strikes reached Moscow, Stalin was fast asleep, and Timoshenko had to wait another eight or ten hours before he could take action. By keeping to his usual schedule, Stalin was essentially abandoning the army.

Between June 23 and June 25, Molotov spent twenty-four hours and thirty-five minutes in Stalin's office — far more than anyone else. He was incapable of giving strategic advice and was there only because he was the closest thing the *vozhd* had to a friend. The cavalryman Voroshilov spent seventeen hours and forty-five minutes with Stalin. Despite his blunders during the Finnish campaign, Stalin kept him on as a private military adviser. The top Red Army leader, Timoshenko, came in third, with sixteen hours and forty-one minutes. Beria had fourteen hours.

The general who inspired both reluctant respect and unmistakable irritation in Stalin — Zhukov — was still with the Southwestern Front, so the only other military leaders the *vozhd* saw were People's Commissar of the Navy Kuznetsov, Zhukov's deputy, Vatutin, and the commander of the air force, Zhigharev. Stalin also received Beria's and Molotov's deputies; the people's commissar of tank industry, Malyshev; the people's commissar of aviation industry, Shakhurin; the head of Red Army intelligence, Golikov; the Leningrad Party leader, Zhdanov; the people's commissar of foreign trade, Mikoyan; and a handful of other dignitaries. Obviously his mind was consumed by frustration, urgent military decisions, worry about a popular revolt or a military coup, the defense of Moscow and Leningrad, and the production of tanks and aircraft. But after issuing his ill-fated directive #3 on June 22, he didn't send out a single meaningful military edict and sought no strategic solution to the retreat.

Stalin's attitude toward the progress of the war was hardly rational. No master plan could turn the tables on Hitler, but surely the Red Army needed more guidance than Timoshenko's pep talks over the phone. The *vozhd* was not ready to use the drastic maneuver that had saved Russia in 1812—withdrawing the troops inland, organizing viable defenses there, and luring Hitler's army to an exhausting pursuit. Neither was he ready for compromise measures, like building a second line of defense between the western border and Moscow. Instead he relied on a familiar tool: purge. Grand failures demanded high-profile scapegoats. On June 23, Kirill Meretskov, the former chief of the general staff, was arrested, and soon Beria's butchers were beating him and asking for a confession.

On the eve of war Stalin had sent Meretskov to scrutinize all the frontier military districts, and he had been satisfied enough with his report to entrust him, on the evening of June 21, with supervising two northern fronts and two northern fleets. That made Meretskov one of the most powerful men in the country, let alone the armed forces. Less than forty-eight hours later, however, the *vozhd* changed his mind. Looking for evidence of treason, he may have thought that Meretskov had been involved in some grandiose act of sabotage during his travels.

Hitler was now only 125 miles away from the front line, in the new headquarters in eastern Prussia, well hidden in the dense woods and exceedingly well fortified and guarded. Nonetheless, the Führer's headquarters were within reach of the Soviet air force. No matter how many Soviet planes had been pulverized on the first day of war, the Red Army still had more than enough to strike Hitler's lair, if its location had been betrayed. But the idea of reconnoitering the war zone never crossed Stalin's mind. He preferred to stay in Moscow, conferring with Beria and scowling at Timoshenko. He knew that he still owed the nation a personal address, but he couldn't rise to the challenge.

Instead of going to the front or preparing a radio broadcast, he spent much of his time at his dacha. The airy house had been custom-built in a pleasant woodland, and it was the only place in the world that Stalin considered home. He occupied just one room, where he slept on the sofa and took his meals surrounded by telephones, papers, and books. It was a solitary existence — the only people around were police officers, who had to secure the premises inconspicuously, so as not to disturb the misanthropic *vozhd,* and a few servants, including a kindly maid, Valentina Istomina, known as Valechka to Stalin. Nobody knew whether she shared his bed, but most, including Molotov, believed she did.

Before June 22, the *vozhd* had invited Molotov, Beria, Voroshilov, and sometimes other leaders to the dacha for late-night feasts where they enjoyed good food, plenty of alcohol, and no women. But he was not feasting now. Getting up very late, often in the afternoon, he ate his breakfast alone and then sat on his terrace overlooking the garden and woods. He never bothered to pick up a shovel, although he did prune a twig or two with a pair of shears, but his gardeners knew that he liked abundant blossoms and plenty of cherries, apples, and tomatoes. The greenhouses held lemon trees and grapevines as well as cages containing parrots and canaries. Little gazebos were scattered around the property. Stalin spent hours roaming the estate, restlessly moving from one to another. Normally the paperwork followed him, but nobody knew whether he was actually working.

His elder son, the independent, proud, and soft-spoken Yakov, whom he didn't like, had left for the front on June 23. Yakov's artillery battery had been thrust into the thick of the war in the burning woods of Byelorussia. Stalin's parting words to his son had been "Go and fight!" He hesitated over whether to let his favorite, the younger Vassily, a hard-drinking, promiscuous brat sporting an air force uniform, leave too. Vassily was everything Stalin was not: he drove cars, rode racehorses, and flew planes while drunk, and that caused his father secretly to admire him while occasionally admonishing him. He had sent his daughter, his granddaughter, and a number of in-laws to a resort on the Black Sea, Sochi, where he normally spent his own vacations. Although he had distanced himself from them years before, he still wanted his family to be in a safe place.

By June 25 the Soviet Union had lost a piece of territory the size of Britain. It was clear that more would be lost in the coming weeks.

The Southwestern Front, in Ukraine, kept sending hopeful reports, however.

Southwestern Front Headquarters, June 22

The commander of the Southwestern Front, Colonel General Mikhail Kirponos, was new on the job. He had succeeded Zhukov in the Kiev Military District only six months earlier, having attracted Stalin's attention during the Finnish campaign, when his division had boldly crossed a frozen bay under strafing fire.

Kirponos quickly found out that it was much more difficult to exercise bravery at headquarters. He had recklessly ignored Finnish bullets, but he felt intimidated by his own commissar. Every Red Army unit had a political officer, but few were as daunting as Nikolai Vashugin.

Vashugin was handsome and stylish, with a fashionable haircut and a neat mustache. His dark eyebrows looked as if they had been painted on, and his nose was aristocratically aquiline. But there was something about him that made people uneasy. Perhaps it was the unnerving dark eyes set deeply in a very pale and slender face. The lid of his right eye jerked whenever he was nervous.

Vashugin had spent twenty-two years in the army and had seen two wars, the civil war and then the Finnish conflict, just like Kirponos. Everybody knew that he had made a brilliant career for himself during the Great Purge, jumping several steps up the promotion ladder, and people also assumed he had dispatched quite a few rivals to their graves. He was fanatical, ambitious, and vain. Those who had served under him during the Finnish campaign remembered that he had personally led the infantry attack through heavy snow, his boots shining, his sheepskin coat immaculately white and well tailored. He was distrustful and hot-tempered with subordinates, known as a tough disciplinarian and a controller. Colleagues euphemistically referred to him as "an upfront man of principles."

On the evening of June 21, Kirponos sent on a last warning of war to Moscow, after a German defector reported that hostilities would start at four o'clock in the morning. Stalin wasn't particularly alarmed and went to bed. His confusing directive #1 didn't reach the Southwestern headquarters in Ternopol until 2:30 A.M.

▪ ▪ ▪

In the south, the Germans were led by Field Marshal Karl Rudolf Gerd von Rundstedt, second to none except possibly Rommel. A tireless leader, he had more or less single-handedly created the new German infantry several years earlier. No matter how important tanks and aircraft were, Rundstedt knew that it was still the infantry that eventually conquered continents.

A flawless strategist, he laid claim to a number of brilliant victories in 1939–1940 that had made his reputation. He also knew the Eastern European terrain fairly well; he had fought there during World War I, and in 1939 his troops had conquered southern Poland. The attack on Ukraine was his third campaign in the area in twenty-five years.

The southwestern front stretched for 250 miles. Unlike the western front, it had geography on its side. Hills that started at Vladimir Volynsky in the north grew into the Carpathian Mountains in the south. A major river, the Dniester, a strong tributary of the Danube, crossed the region from northwest to southeast, barring the way to the Germans. After the Dniester, though, there was no major river for 250 miles, until one came to the Dnieper, where Ukraine's capital, Kiev, was situated. Beyond Kiev lay the industrial heart of the Soviet Union, the Donbass.

Just like the Western Front, the troops of the Southwestern Front had their own salient, at Lvov, but this posed no immediate danger to the Soviet troops. It was bigger than the one at Belostok and 200 miles wide, protruding 100 miles into territory belonging to Germany and its allies Hungary and Romania. It was an ideal springboard for a Soviet attack on Europe, and a challenge for the Wehrmacht. Even with tanks, it would be difficult to surround and destroy the Soviet forces there.

Like Pavlov, Kirponos operated on territory that had been occupied only recently, during the Polish campaign. However, the outspoken and short-tempered people of western Ukraine made the western Byelorussians seem docile by comparison. Tossed back and forth between Russia and Poland for centuries, Ukraine as a whole had failed to develop a strong identity, but this wasn't true of its western edge, which was geographically compact and culturally rich. In the rest of the land, even Kiev, many people felt comfortable with Russian rule: the two languages were close, and Stalin regarded Ukrainians as part of the Slavic core of the country — unlike Jews, Estonians, and Chechens. But western Ukraine, occupied during the dismemberment of Poland in 1939, craved independence. Now local Ukrainians gleefully told the wives of Soviet officers, "You just wait — the war will begin soon. The Germans will show you!" The resilient terrorist underground, the famous Organization of Ukrainian Nationalists (OUN), established a decade earlier, had been responsible for hundreds of assassinations and acts of sabotage, first against the Poles and then against the Soviets. By the summer of 1941, the OUN's aggressive symbol, the trident, was very well known to the Red Army.

Among the Red Army fronts, the Southwestern was the strongest. Intended by Stalin to launch the preemptive war, it had fifty-nine divisions organized into four armies — the Fifth, Sixth, Twenty-sixth, and Twelfth. The Fifth, commanded by Major General Mikhail Potapov, was the northernmost. It covered 100 miles and pushed up against the Western Front. The Sixth Army, under Lieutenant General Ivan Muzychenko, protected Lvov. Lieutenant General Fedor Kostenko's Twenty-sixth Army was stationed on the border with Hungary. The Twelfth Army, under Major General Pavel Ponedelin, touched Romania.

Farther south, the Southwestern had a neighbor, the Southern Front, which had twenty-one divisions, to be used against Romania in the event of a preemptive strike. Combined, the two fronts had 1,412,200 soldiers, 26,580 artillery guns and mortars, 8,069 tanks, and 4,696 aircraft. Rundstedt's Army Group South didn't have nearly that many.

For Kirponos, preparations for the preemptive strike had begun in May, when he started mobilizing two armies, the Sixteenth and the Nineteenth. Both Kirponos and Vashugin attended the top-secret meeting in Stalin's study on May 24 at which the preemptive strike was probably discussed. On June 15, Kirponos was instructed to move five rifle corps closer to the frontier. The first one was to reach it by June 25.

On June 19, Zhukov ordered the military district to be prepared to act as a front and move its headquarters to Ternopol by June 22. The order was marked "Top Secret" and indicated that war was imminent: Ternopol was just 100 miles from the German lines.

Kirponos ordered immediate relocation, but most officers were unable to leave until the evening of June 21. The staff's automobile column was still on the road when it was attacked at dawn by speedy aircraft with black crosses on their wings.

▪ ▪ ▪

Hitler longed for Ukraine. Its grain, coal, iron, and pork promised an easy life for the Third Reich. Once the Wehrmacht had swept through Ukraine, it would reach the oil-rich Caucasus, gateway to the Middle East.

On June 22 the Luftwaffe bombed Kiev, Sevastopol, Rovno, Lvov, Zhitomir, a number of smaller cities, and all the important airfields in the region. On that day alone, the front lost 250 aircraft. German bombers arrived in combat groups of twenty to thirty planes. Escorted by fighters, they reached their targets in waves and drowned them in fire, smoke, and dust. Yet the Southwestern Front did not yield much territory that day. It was in the evening that the southern flank of the Fifth Army collapsed.

Of all possible developments, this was the worst. The Fifth was located to the north of the Lvov salient, and Rundstedt knew that if he could create a breach between it and its neighbor in the south, the Sixth, the salient would turn into a gigantic pocket, like the smaller one at Belostok.

Kirponos couldn't get detailed reports from the Fifth because, as everywhere else, German commandos had cut miles of unprotected telegraph wire hanging conspicuously on poles. With some effort he could reach Moscow, but not his units on the battlefield. "I cannot command the troops," he said angrily.

At about eleven o'clock at night, Stalin's directive #3 arrived. It sounded totally nonsensical, as if Moscow had no clue about what was happening on the border: "While maintaining a solid hold on the state boundary adjoining Hungary, concentrate attacks by the forces of the

Fifth and Sixth Armies in the general direction of Lublin, and with at least five mechanized corps and all the front's air force surround and destroy the enemy group attacking on the Vladimir Volynsky–Krystynopol line. Capture Lublin by the end of the day on June 24. Protect yourself well from the direction of Krakow."

Kirponos read and reread the directive in amazement. Stalin was attempting to implement the preemptive war plan. It had envisaged the strike at Lublin in exactly this way. However, the Fifth and Sixth Armies were currently being crushed by Rundstedt's juggernaut, and no joint counterstrike was possible.

"What are we to do, Mikhail Petrovich?" Kirponos's chief of staff asked indignantly. "We would be lucky if we could stop the enemy and disrupt him in defensive battle, but they are demanding that we take Lublin the day after tomorrow!"

Kirponos knew that the task was impossible. If he cried uncle, though, Vashugin would call Moscow to report high treason in the headquarters. Keeping silent, he let his chief of staff give Vashugin the obvious strategic objections. German ground troops in the border area had clear numerical superiority, the Luftwaffe controlled the sky, and the Red Army had been caught off-guard by the attack.

Just as Kirponos anticipated, Vashugin exploded. "Have you thought of the moral damage? We, who have trained the Red Army to think offensively, would shift to passive defense in the first days of war and, unresisting, leave the initiative in the hands of the aggressor! If I didn't know you for a good Bolshevik, I would say that you have panicked!"

Sensing that the situation was getting out of hand, Kirponos reluctantly stepped in. "An order is an order," he said. "It has to be carried out."

He commanded a limited counterblow by the forces of a few mechanized corps. In principle, mechanized corps were the strongest among the Red Army ground troops, since each had 30,000 men and 1,000 tanks. However, they were an awkward combination of panzer force and infantry, and they remained untested. Kirponos also knew that the district's mechanized corps were still being formed and lacked tanks, trucks, and skilled personnel. At that point, though, he felt he didn't have a choice.

Vashugin approved; the other officers present didn't. As military men, they knew that the mechanized corps were being sent to their deaths.

Shortly after the decision was taken, headquarters got two exceedingly important visitors: Chief of General Staff Georgy Zhukov and the viceroy of Ukraine, Nikita Khrushchev.

General Zhukov, Southwestern Front, June 22–24

When Stalin was looking for a commander in chief in Mongolia in 1939, he informed his staff that he needed someone who would not just defeat the Japanese but "shred them into pieces, so that they would lose any desire to expand northward." Georgy Zhukov proudly believed that he had done exactly that. The victory in Mongolia had been the highlight of his career. He savored it, but he definitely craved more — he thought he was the best general the Red Army had. Obviously Stalin agreed, because he had dispatched Zhukov to the Southwestern Front in the hope that he would successfully shake up the strongest army group in the country and turn the tide.

Zhukov's strength of character and firm opinions were also his weaknesses. Owing to his remarkable arrogance, relations with quite a few of his colleagues were strained. Admiral Kuznetsov complained that Zhukov was impossible to work with. That was probably true, as one of Zhukov's idiosyncrasies was his intense dislike of the navy. When asked why he despised the fleet so much, he reframed the question: "Tell me, what does Russia do first when attacked?"

"A czar's manifesto or a government statement is issued . . ."

"Wrong."

"Mobilization starts."

"No. It sinks its navy."

Zhukov had a point. Over the previous hundred years, the Russian navy had scuttled its ships three times.

He was also extraordinarily vain. When his photo was to be published in the military daily, *Red Star,* in 1940, he called up the editor and said, "You have my picture, but I don't like it. I look as if I were bald. You have plenty of artists, don't you? Can't they fix it?"

"Yes, comrade army general," the editor replied, and the picture finally published in *Red Star* shows Zhukov's hair as appropriately virile.

The general had a well-deserved reputation for rudeness, and it was not uncommon for him to tell a subordinate commander, "You are not a general but a bag of shit!" People remembered comments like that as long as they lived, but Zhukov didn't care.

However, on the afternoon of June 22, on a plane heading for Kiev, he showed no sign of his characteristic arrogance, malice, and conceit. He was simply a man alone in a small plane, flying across unfriendly skies on a difficult mission. He still mourned the victims of the 1937 purge — Uborevich, Yegorov, Bliukher, and of course the brightest star of them all, Tukhachevsky — and no doubt that afternoon he felt their absence acutely. Modesty wasn't one of his virtues, but he always recognized talent when he encountered it. And he didn't think he had seen much of it recently.

He had been elevated to his post just five months earlier, but his short tenure had already allowed him a close look at Stalin. The father of the nation had proved erratic, suspicious, unfair, and vengeful. The people he patronized were unworthy. Indeed, wouldn't it have been far better if the military virtuoso Tukhachevsky and not the colorless Timoshenko had been people's commissar of defense? And if the thoughtful Uborevich had commanded the Southwestern Front instead of the dull Kirponos?

In his nostalgia for the great warriors, however, Zhukov inadvertently romanticized them, endowing them with qualities they had never had. Tukhachevsky, Uborevich, and others had been infinitely more talented and experienced than the men who replaced them, but it was unclear whether they would have made a real difference if they had been spared. They too would have had to persuade Stalin to start serious military deployment, whether defensive or offensive, a few months earlier — in February 1941, not May. But nothing in their careers indicated that one day they would have defied Stalin, so they probably would have been just as helpless as Timoshenko or Kirponos — or, for that matter,

Zhukov. If they *had* managed to stand up to Stalin and persuade him that his equivocation was dangerous, they would have been shot instantly, changing the date of the purge but not the final outcome.

Nonetheless, Zhukov's nostalgia was not totally misplaced. The generals would definitely have done things differently on a local level, as commanders of military districts, armies, and corps. Powerless to educate Stalin in the basics of military strategy, they could have kept their units fit and prepared to face the ultimate challenge, even if the strategy was wrong.

They could not have pulled their aircraft or fuel depots from the border areas or their troops from the treacherous salient. They could not have supplied their units with better tanks or rifles or put them on combat alert against the dictator's wish. But there were things they could have done discreetly. They could have forced conservative junior officers to use radios, had cable lines patrolled, kept field commanders alert, trained staffs better, camouflaged aircraft, taught officers to read a map correctly.

After all, not every unit in the west was taken by surprise in the small hours of June 22. The commander of the Western Front, General Pavlov, learned about the attack fifteen minutes after it occurred, and his reaction was "I can't make this out." But the commander of the Black Sea Fleet, Admiral Oktiabrsky, knew about the attack fifteen minutes *before* it happened, and his ships met the Junkers with an effective firewall.

Even after the invasion started, there was a place for determination and professional decency, if not initiative and wisdom. The commander of the Third Army, Kuznetsov, just rode the wave of retreat, while the commander of the Fourth, Korobkov, notwithstanding his remarkable weaknesses, fled fighting. If the armed forces had not been drained in 1937, there would have been dozens, if not hundreds, of generals and admirals like Oktiabrsky and Korobkov.

■ ■ ■

Zhukov didn't reach Kiev until the end of the day on June 22. He was exhausted, and he hadn't eaten anything except for a couple of sandwiches for twenty-four hours. The person meeting him was someone he had never liked: Nikita Khrushchev, Moscow's viceroy in Ukraine, or, in the new language, the first secretary of the Communist Party of the republic. Zhukov found him stupid and sycophantic. He had spent plenty of time with the plump and enthusiastic fellow when he had been commander of the Kiev Military District. Now they were supposed to travel to the front headquarters together.

Khrushchev said it was too dangerous to fly and they would have to drive. Zhukov didn't argue. The journey proved an ordeal. Khrushchev was loud and importunate. He said the thing that concerned him most about Hitler was that Hitler never touched alcohol. Khrushchev had never concealed that he preferred Timoshenko to Zhukov, because Zhukov hated binges, while Timoshenko drank like a fish.

The Party secretary was agitated. The Germans had bombed the airfield in Kiev and set the hangars on fire. Stalin hadn't addressed the nation, and that was confusing. He was also apprehensive about his own safety. After choosing to drive instead of fly, he had second thoughts: the countryside, he said, was swarming with German commandos. The wheat and rye were quite tall that year, and Khrushchev thought that German agents might be hiding in the fields. Each time the car stopped, he panicked.

They reached the Southwestern Front headquarters late that night. Located in a village northwest of Ternopol, the headquarters weren't yet constructed, and officers were being housed in peasants' huts. Zhukov was very angry. As soon as he could get to a phone in one of the huts, he called Vatutin.

The news was dire. No matter how hard the General Staff tried, it was unable to get accurate reports from the front line, as communications in the west hadn't yet been repaired. As far as Vatutin could tell, the Germans had advanced 10 to 15 miles east. He confirmed that the Western Front's air force had been decimated, but he had no idea where General Pavlov was. The commander of the Northwestern Front, General Kuznetsov, was also unreachable.

Embarrassed, Vatutin told Zhukov that Stalin had issued directive #3 in Zhukov's name, among others.

"What does the directive say?" Zhukov asked.

"It orders the troops to counterattack, to smash the enemy and then enter his territory."

"But we still have no idea what is taking place on the front!" Zhukov exclaimed. "Wouldn't it be better to figure this out first and then decide?"

"I agree, but the orders have already been issued," Vatutin answered timidly.

To Zhukov's immense displeasure, he now had to discuss the absurd directive with Kirponos. Putting on an approving face, he confirmed Kirponos's decision to send the mechanized corps into battle. It simply had to be done if the generals were to escape Stalin's wrath. As if to remind them of what was at stake, one of those corps, the Ninth, was led by Konstantin Rokossovsky, a classmate of Zhukov's at the High Cavalry School, who had been released from the gulag only the previous year, after thirty months in the house of the dead.

Kirponos was relieved to have the chief of general staff at his headquarters. Now he could argue that the ultimate responsibility lay with Zhukov. Even if Zhukov wanted to shed that burden, he couldn't. He wasn't able to resist the limelight, regardless of how dangerous the exposure was.

He started visiting different units, trying to get firsthand reports and also to boost morale. On the evening of June 24, east of Lvov, he ran into the commander of the Eighth Mechanized Corps, Dmitry Riabyshev. The Eighth was one of the corps designated for the counterstrike.

General Riabyshev, Eighth Mechanized Corps, June 22–26

An avowed cavalryman, Lieutenant General Riabyshev had always trusted horses more than tanks. Only a year earlier he had been in charge of a cavalry corps. He now tried hard to like the steel monsters that he commanded.

He spent the morning of June 22 in the corps' compound in Drogobych, waiting for orders from the Sixth Army commander, his immediate superior. Meanwhile, the Germans kept up their ferocious bombing of the Eighth. At ten o'clock a messenger arrived: by the end of the day Riabyshev's men were to relocate to the woods west of Sambor. Sambor lay very close to the border, which meant that they would soon be in contact with German tanks. No evacuation of civilians had been ordered, so the officers were forced to leave their families in the compound, which was now blazing but only a few hours earlier had been a secure base and a comfortable home.

The 50-mile march to Sambor proved stressful. The corps, with 30,000 men and an awkward assortment of 932 tanks, proceeded slowly. Only 169 of the eight kinds of tanks were the new KVs and T-34s. The older tanks couldn't go more than 300 miles without needing repairs, and 197 of them already had serious mechanical problems. Most of the tanks used gasoline — three different kinds of gasoline — but 171 had to have diesel fuel. The tanks' guns were equally diverse: there were five models, demanding five different kinds of shells. Difficult even in peacetime, logistics were now a nightmare.

To boost morale, the commissars painted bellicose slogans on the sides of the tanks, ranging from the uninspired ("Long Live Communism!") to the audacious ("To Berlin!"). Soldiers who had fallen for the propaganda now asked whether the German working class had already risen against Hitler. Many said that the war would be over in a few months. Riabyshev wasn't so sure.

The Eighth soon met the first refugees. Women and children sitting on bags and bundles in the open trucks looked frightened, but at least they didn't have to flee on foot — some kind army commander had provided them with transportation. Riabyshev's officers thought about their own families, abandoned at Drogobych, and their hearts ached. Almost every truck carried scores of wounded too. Many houses along the road had been blasted by German bombs, and several times the soldiers saw dead children lying in the rubble.

Someone in army headquarters had made a mistake, and Riabyshev soon discovered that while the Eighth was marching from Drogobych to Sambor, General N. K. Kirillov's Thirteenth Rifle Corps was moving from Sambor to Drogobych along the same highway. The road was narrow, and the two corps had to sidle past each other. Riabyshev's tank crews had a harder time than Kirillov's infantrymen, because bridges

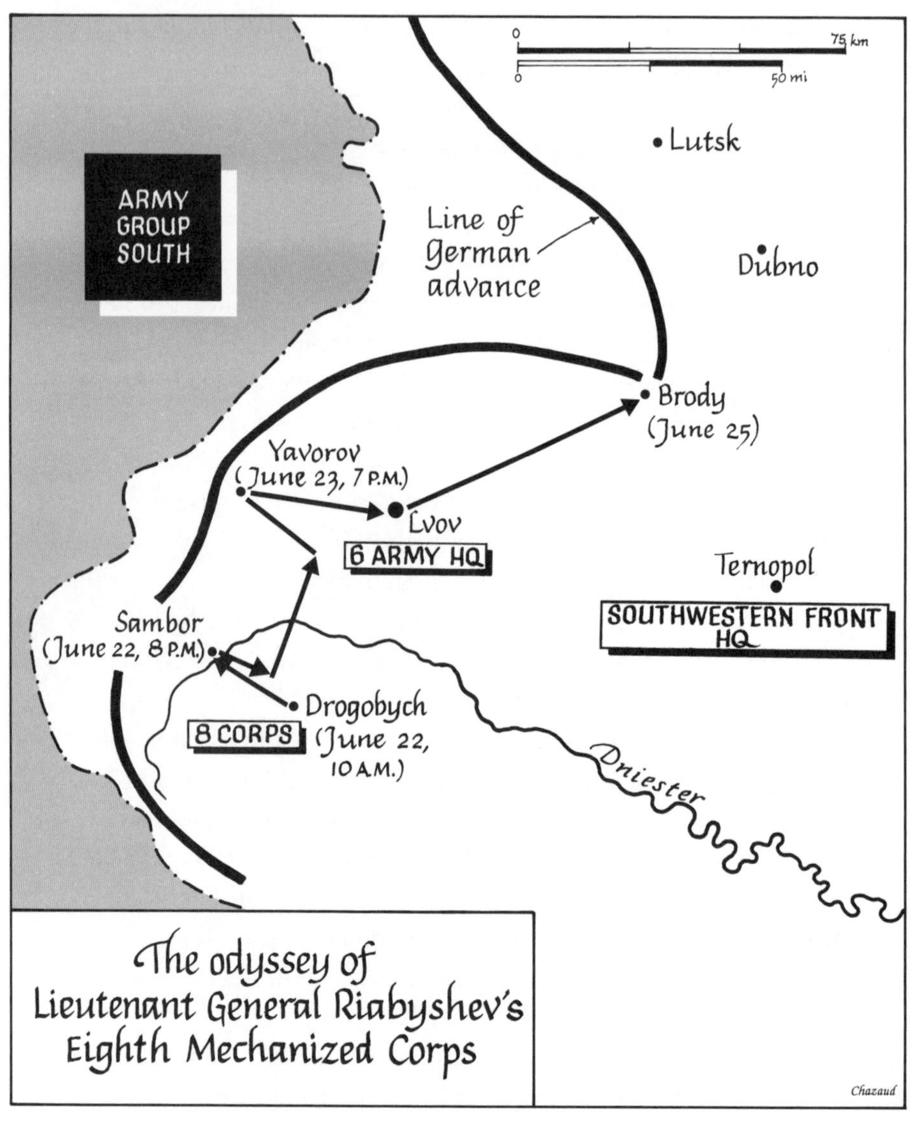
0
75 km
0
50 mi
Lutsk
ARMY GROUP SOUTH
Line of German advance
Dubno
Brody (June 25)
Yavorov (June 23, 7 P.M.)
Lvov
6 ARMY HQ
Ternopol
SOUTHWESTERN FRONT HQ
Sambor (June 22, 8 P.M.)
Drogobych (June 22, 10 A.M.)
8 CORPS
Dniester
The odyssey of Lieutenant General Riabyshev's Eighth Mechanized Corps
Chazaud

collapsed under the weight of their vehicles and the heat caused the tank wheels to tear up the road, making it almost impassable for those in the rear.

When they finally reached the woods at Sambor, they stopped and stared. The trees looked as if they had been hit by a monster thunderstorm and were burned, bruised, and felled. Obviously the Luftwaffe had been looking for Soviet troops there. The devastatation frightened Riabyshev's men. "A hurricane of steel," somebody muttered.

But Riabyshev didn't have time to contemplate the destruction. He had received a report saying that only 700 of his tanks were ready for battle, since nearly 200 had been lost during the march.

A messenger from Kirponos then showed up unexpectedly, with an order that made no sense at all. It instructed Riabyshev to go back to Drogobych and on to the capital of western Ukraine, Lvov, immediately. The exhausting march of June 22 had been just a warm-up exercise. Now the corps had to cover another 75 miles.

As the order dictated, the Eighth turned back. Soon German bombers discovered them. Unaware of Stalin's preemptive strike plan, Riabyshev had been complaining that the new airfields had been built right at the frontier, apparently for no purpose. Of course there *had* been a purpose, but the grand design had gone up in flames and the Red Air Force had been crippled. The soldiers sought refuge in the fields of wheat. It took ages to summon them back, particularly after they saw their brothers in arms lying dead on the ground.

Riabyshev decided to keep the troops moving throughout the night. It wasn't long before some of the sleepy drivers began bumping into the cars and tanks in front of them. The corps stopped and painted white circles on the backs of the vehicles, but that didn't seem to help.

When they reached their compound in Drogobych, the officers' families were still there, though the town was now on fire. The women asked why they could not leave, and their husbands didn't know what to say. Some of the women learned that they had already become widows; some officers found their families dead in the ruins. Tears and angry words took time, and Riabyshev was getting nervous. He didn't want to be late arriving in Lvov.

In the morning the troops finally reached the Sixth Army headquarters, northwest of Lvov. There its commander, Lieutenant General I. N. Muzychenko, informed Riabyshev that his corps again had to change course. Muzychenko sounded apologetic; he said he had sent a messenger a few hours earlier, but the officer had probably gotten lost, or maybe been killed.

For the second time in forty-eight hours the Eighth was ordered to make a 180-degree turn, and the men now headed for Yavorov. When they reached that town, a messenger from the front headquarters intercepted them. Kirponos ordered them to travel 75 miles farther, to Brody, where on the morning of June 25 they were finally to attack the Germans.

The tired and dispirited soldiers couldn't be sure they wouldn't be herded to a new location once again. As it was, the progress of the Eighth marked on the officers' maps looked like a big Z, with its upper line crossing Lvov.

At eight o'clock in the morning on June 24, the Eighth Mechanized Corps marched into that city. Lvov looked ancient and quiet, the spires and rooftops looming against the bright sky but its dark alleys abandoned. If ever there was a place where Russians were abhorred, it was in the capital of western Ukraine. Beria tried hard, but his henchmen could do nothing about the determined urban guerrillas of the OUN, and on the morning of June 24 its fighters ambushed the Eighth.

The guerrillas had climbed into attics and now rained bullets onto Riabyshev's men. On a narrow street, a skillful sniper could easily impede the progress of a whole regiment, and the officers, cursing, rushed their men upstairs to catch the guerrillas. Outnumbered, the snipers retreated to the roofs, and the soldiers could see that many of them were wearing Red Army uniforms. The disguise couldn't save the freedom fighters, however, and they were forced to flee. One of them slipped at the roof's edge and fell five stories. When the soldiers reached him, he was convulsing, with blood all over his body. Looking for proof of his identity, they unbuttoned his shirt. The chest of the dying man carried a blue tattoo — a sharp trident, the symbol of the Ukrainian resistance.

For the soldiers, Lvov was just one more hostile city on their roundabout route. They didn't realize that they had walked into a nationalist uprising. On the first day of war, the authorities had panicked, and the police had started shooting the inmates of the city prison. Before they could finish everyone off, the OUN retaliated, and Beria's men had to run for their lives. However, they soon returned, reinforced by border guards fleeing from the frontier. By June 24 skirmishes were erupting all over the city, and it was impossible to say who actually controlled Lvov.

But the Eighth Mechanized Corps wasn't there to introduce order. Having dealt with the snipers, it sullenly marched through the city, heading east, as its orders dictated.

In the suburbs the convoy stopped. Somebody had told the commissar, Nikolai Popel, that German motorcyclists had been spotted in the area. But instead of Germans, Popel saw a Russian woman hurrying toward the tanks, carrying two infants. Two older girls were running after her, out of breath.

"For God's sake, don't leave me here," the woman cried. "If you do, I will throw myself under your tank."

The woman was barefoot, disheveled, and haggard. She was an officer's wife, and the infants were her newborn twins. Her husband had left for the front, but no one had bothered to evacuate his family.

Popel promised to send a car, but the woman didn't believe him. "Take me now," she said. "If you don't, I will put all my children under your wheels."

Commissar Popel wasn't an unfeeling man. He sighed, shrugged his shoulders, and helped the family into the tank.

After the vehicles had started their engines again, three more civilians suddenly appeared, filmmakers from Moscow who had been trapped in the combat zone. Unaware of what was going on, they asked for permission to film the Eighth. One of them boastfully added that he was a Stalin Prize laureate. Very annoyed, Popel advised the men to make themselves scarce.

But that was not the end of Commissar Popel's troubles that morning. A short while later he spotted a lieutenant and two soldiers escorting a middle-aged man who was holding his trembling arms high up in the air.

"Who is that?" Popel yelled.

"A spy, comrade commissar. Gonna shoot him."

"Nikolai Kirillych, dear . . ." the man whined.

Popel moved closer and in horror recognized the commander of the Eighth's artillery, Colonel Chistyakov.

"Why have you arrested him?" he asked the lieutenant.

"He had no ID and no car. Was asking for the location of a regiment. Also, the guy has a colonel's insignia but a capitalist's paunch."

Later, when the redeemed Colonel Chistyakov calmed down, he told Popel that he had lost both his car and his ID during an OUN attack.

. . .

At dusk Riabyshev told his driver to stop. The corps had had nothing to eat since the morning, and Riabyshev felt that the soldiers couldn't go any farther without food. While they were making tea and sandwiches, a conspicuous car, a ZIS, stopped in front of them. ZISes carried dignitaries, and indeed, a moment later the distressed Riabyshev saw Chief of General Staff Army General Zhukov climb out of the vehicle.

Riabyshev didn't have much to report except the story of his outrageous odyssey, but Zhukov wasn't particularly sympathetic to the plight of the Eighth. He was growing progressively nervous about the forthcoming counterstrike. All he cared about was the fact that the Eighth would need another twenty-four hours, at least, to reach the front line. The Germans could easily improve their position in that time. He also knew that other mechanized corps would reach the Germans even later. Meanwhile, the Eighth wouldn't be able to do much, if anything, on its own.

He was still listening to Riabyshev when a squadron of Junkers arrived.

"Oh, my," Riabyshev said, feigning calm. "We've had no time to dig air shelters. Well, comrade army general, we'll just have to pretend we are in one."

Zhukov was delighted by the general's sangfroid and smiled back happily. Encouraged, Riabyshev suggested having a snack as they were bombed. Zhukov ate sandwiches while listening to the Junkers' wail and felt very proud. After the air raid was over, he chatted with the brave commander for a few minutes more and then left. For some reason, eating a snack during an air raid had cheered him significantly. He thought more highly of Riabyshev as well, and said to himself that the Eighth was in a "sanguine" mood. "Good guys," Zhukov thought, getting into the car. "One cannot lose a war with people like that."

Soon after the ZIS carried Zhukov away, the column moved on, expecting to meet the enemy in the morning. At the end of the day General Riabyshev told his orderly to give him a clean uniform. This was the way a Russian military man prepared for death.

■ ■ ■

On June 25 the Eighth found itself in a pine forest close to the town of Brody. No Germans were there, but no friendly units were there either. Riabyshev sent the scouts out. The area where he was supposed to attack was a woody swamp. If his tanks didn't sink to the bottom of the bog, they could easily get stuck on the shores of the four marshy rivers they had to ford.

In a while the scouts returned and reported that they did have a neighbor after all — the Fifteenth Mechanized Corps, commanded by General Karpezo. According to the initial plan, the Fifteenth Corps was to strike at the same time as the Eighth, but Karpezo now told Riabyshev that his men were too exhausted and only one of the corps' three divisions would be joining the Eighth.

Riabyshev knew what that meant. For a while he even considered hiding the truth from his officers, but shame compelled him to tell the commanders that in the morning they would have only themselves to count on.

He sent the scouts out again, but when they came back, they reported that although they had found the Germans, they had failed to penetrate their lines and thus knew nothing about their numbers. By that time Riabyshev had learned that he would receive no air support either.

Nonetheless, the offensive started the next morning. The swamp proved just as treacherous as Riabyshev had thought it would. While the tanks were struggling along the boggy ground, the German artillery opened fire. One tank after another was enveloped first in black smoke, then in scarlet flames. In despair, the officers looked at the sky. It remained brilliant and empty — the air force had indeed failed them.

Only after they had lost a number of tanks to artillery fire did Riabyshev's troops see the German panzers. Moving in and out of the wheat fields, sometimes disappearing completely but always reappearing, the tanks proudly displayed their black-and-white crosses, their guns pointed at the Soviets. When the distance shortened to less than 800 yards, the Eighth opened fire.

No tank crew knew exactly what was happening around their vehicle. They fired at the Germans and the Germans fired at them, but the bigger picture of the battle was blocked by the tall wheat. All a soldier could see was plumes of black smoke calmly drifting above the golden fields.

Riabyshev's men stubbornly pushed forward yard by yard, despite the enemy fire. Occasionally a tank drove over a German soldier. Still unaccustomed to the brutality of panzer combat, the Russian driver would close his eyes as the man disappeared under the wheels of his tank. He would feel a soft bump and then the familiar pits and grooves of the terrain.

Men were deafened by the roaring blasts of the guns and sickened by the smell of burning explosives. Their faces were covered in blood, since each time a German shell hit a tank's armor, tiny pieces of steel shot from the cabin's walls and penetrated their cheeks, foreheads, and jaws.

That day the Eighth Mechanized Corps liberated the town of Leshnev, which had been occupied by the Germans just the day before. Riabyshev himself barely made it: his KV's wheels jammed and spun for what seemed an eternity in front of the bridge. Miraculously, the tank was not hit.

Exploring the liberated town, officers and soldiers searched for something that would explain the Germans' military superiority. Everything the Germans had left behind looked alien but impressive to them. The horses were huge and well fed, their tails luxuriously long and thick; the carts were unusually tall; the magazines were glossy.

A damaged Opel Admiral stood in front of the church. Its engine had been destroyed and its passengers had fled, but the driver lay lifeless on the bright orange seat, the wind playing with his blond hair.

▪ ▪ ▪

Driving back to headquarters in a KV, Riabyshev contemplated the devastation around him. Standing in the open gun tower and smoking a cigarette, he suddenly said to Popel, "This is a war of iron. A cavalryman cannot do much any longer. I will give my Damascus saber to my grandchildren as a toy. They won't believe it used to be possible to sever a head with it. No, they won't believe that."

Close to the headquarters they smelled burning wood. The smell grew stronger, and soon they could see clouds of blue smoke and steaming trees. The headquarters had been bombed, but they were still standing. While Riabyshev tried to get in touch with the units still fighting the Germans, the bombers unexpectedly returned. This time they sent their load into the midst of the staff cars. When the smoke cleared, the officers realized that Riabyshev had disappeared. They found him under a tank, thrown there by the explosion and covered in dirt, unconscious but alive.

When the general came to, he saw that the woods around him were on fire. The flames were spreading and the torchlike trees kept falling, enveloping tents, trucks, cars, and corpses in the blaze. The interminable day of June 26 was finally coming to an end.

General Rokossovsky, Ninth Mechanized Corps

The Eighth was not the only corps that participated in the counterstrike. Among other units involved in the suicidal mission was the Ninth, under the command of General Rokossovsky, who had been released from Beria's underworld just fifteen months earlier.

Throughout Konstantin Rokossovsky's life, luck had played tricks on him. At fifteen he was a working-class boy laboring at a quarry in Warsaw, at nineteen a distinguished soldier with the Russian Imperial Army, at twenty-four a cavalry regiment commander in the Red Army, at forty one of the most promising young generals in the country, at forty-one mere fodder for the torture mill.

Very tall, dazzlingly handsome, and, according to many people, built like a Greek god, Rokossovsky lost nine teeth, had three broken ribs, and had his toes smashed with a hammer under torture. But he stubbornly refused to admit that he was a Polish spy, and it took two interrogators to hold him while a third was beating him. Twice his torturers took him out for a mock execution, during which people around him were shot dead but he was spared for more pain. In the end he was shipped to the gulag. By the time he reached one of the most dreaded camps in Vorkuta, he was so weak that the authorities deemed him unfit for the coal mines, so he became the orderly for a loutish warden.

Exhausted but not broken, he was released on March 22, 1940, after thirty months in hell. He never figured out why he was released. It was probably just a fluke — he had held out long enough to see a brief thaw announced in the purges, and his name had slipped onto a list of rehabilitated military personnel. Almost straight from the camp he was sent to the Romanian border, where, under Zhukov's command, he participated in the occupation of Bessarabia. At the end of that year he was appointed commander of the Ninth Mechanized Corps.

If Rokossovsky harbored any ill feelings toward Stalin, he never shared them with anyone. After all, 35,000 officers had been killed, and he was one of the lucky few to make a most improbable comeback. His case seemed to support the theory that Stalin had had nothing to do with the massacre and, having finally grasped the extent of the injustice, had magnanimously brought the slaughter to an end.

He felt differently about the generals he served with. He suspected that many had been supplying the authorities with phony evidence about "enemies of the people," and those who were too decent to do that, like Zhukov, had still benefited from the purge. Until 1937, Rokossovsky and Zhukov had been like twins, being the same age and with nearly identical careers. They were good friends too, though at the same time rivals. People who knew both said Zhukov was tougher, Rokossovsky smarter. For a while Rokossovsky had the upper hand, commanding a cavalry division in which Zhukov served as an ordinary regiment commander. Yet now, in 1941, Zhukov was the Red Army's number-two man, while Rokossovsky languished in the second hundred of its generals.

Hurt and angry about his fate, Rokossovsky was put off by Zhukov's roughness — his barnyard language, his stormy rebukes, his superior airs, his lack of learning. Like Zhukov, Rokossovsky came from the lower classes, but unlike Zhukov, he was a confirmed reader, and unlike most military men, he didn't limit himself to books required by the academy or praised by popular culture. In spite of this, Zhukov now had Stalin's ear, and Rokossovsky was an armchair strategist in a provincial garrison.

He spent much of the spring trying to figure out what Moscow would do if the Germans attacked. Unlike other generals, Rokossovsky guessed that the *vozhd* was preparing an offensive maneuver, which he delicately called "a leap forward." For him, this was obvious from the deployment of the Red Army forces, particularly the positioning of airfields and warehouses right on the border. Yet Rokossovsky was sure that the "leap forward" would not occur in the near future, as the frontier still lacked enough ground troops to launch a successful attack. Meanwhile, he had read Hitler's *Mein Kampf,* which explicitly advocated eastward expansion, and he thought that after the defeat of France, a German assault on the Soviet Union would be imminent. He knew that if Hitler preempted Stalin, the consequences would be dire.

Rokossovsky was unhappy with his corps. The tank divisions consisted mostly of outmoded T-26s, BT-2s, BT-5s, and BT-7s. Even those vehicles were in short supply — the corps had just one third of its quota of tanks and trucks. One of the regiments had only 430 rifles and 5 revolvers for 1,835 soldiers, and 28 artillery guns instead of the requisite 80.

He also struggled with new recruits and young officers. Many of them didn't know how to handle tanks or trucks or even their own rifles properly. Nor could they correlate a map with the terrain. Since the purge, professionalism had been in short supply, and Rokossovsky knew that was going to have catastrophic effects in the event of war.

The Kiev Military District was mismanaged. He thought that its commander, Kirponos, was just a shallow upstart completely unfit to command larger units — a person of ego but with no knowledge or intuition. He was even more concerned that the military establishment in Moscow seemed totally unperturbed by what was happening on the western border. Technically, the area should be sealed, but German officers cruised along it, allegedly searching for World War I graves. Once a German aircraft performed an emergency landing in Soviet territory. When the Red Army officers searched it, they found sophisticated cameras storing images of bridges and railroads. The episode was reported to Moscow, but the officers were ordered to let the pilots go.

Rokossovsky thought that Zhukov and Timoshenko were guilty of criminal complacency. Of course he had no way of knowing that the two leaders were just as frustrated as he was and in fact had no real influence, choked as they were by the *vozhd*.

▪ ▪ ▪

At four o'clock on the morning of June 22, an officer on duty reported to Rokossovsky that army headquarters had called to instruct him to open the envelope with the top-secret operational plan. Rokossovsky was apprehensive. The document was highly sensitive. Only Stalin or Timoshenko could authorize its release.

Remembering the torture chamber only too well, he told his aide to verify the order as soon as possible. Meanwhile, he called for his chief of staff, his commissar, and, just in case, the police commissioner (every big military unit had one). Before they could reach any decision, the aide reported that all communications had been cut off. Rokossovsky could not get in touch with Moscow (the People's Commissariat of Defense), Ternopol (military district headquarters), or Lutsk (the Fifth Army headquarters). At his own risk, he unsealed the envelope.

The directive sent Rokossovsky's corps northwest, to Rovno, Lutsk, and then Kovel. Kovel lay just 85 miles from the Polish city of Lublin. That looked like the beginning of a major offensive, the audacious "leap forward" he had been anticipating. Nonetheless, Rokossovsky frowned. His corps was still being formed, but the plan treated it as a fully developed, well-equipped unit. That didn't sound right.

On the way home to say his goodbyes, he met his young daughter running toward the officers' common room, late for a Sunday matinee she was performing in. "Run back home right away," he said. "It's war, honey."

After his goodbyes were said, Rokossovsky had to figure out where to get more trucks, cars, fuel, and ammunition. He decided not to wait for an invitation to visit the warehouses and sent his officers there to take everything that was available. The quartermasters were indignant and demanded receipts signed by the general. "I have never signed so many receipts in my whole life," Rokossovsky remarked dryly. In an audacious move, he also took two hundred trucks from the front reserve and gave them to his men.

Finally, at 10 A.M., communications with the army headquarters were restored. Before they broke down again, an officer at Lutsk hastily reported that the town was being bombed, that communications with all units were very poor, and that he had no idea what was happening on the front line.

The corps didn't depart until two o'clock in the afternoon. On the move, they saw plenty of German aircraft but not a single Red Army plane. Soon they learned why: the airfields they passed were littered with the burned-out hulks of fighters and bombers.

By the end of the day Rokossovsky's mechanized corps was nothing but a tired infantry unit. They had covered 30 miles and were exhausted. Because of the lack of automobiles, the soldiers had to carry machine guns, ammunition, and even mortars on their backs. The day had been exceptionally hot, and every mile had been costly.

Still, in the morning they marched on. The Luftwaffe rarely left the roads unattended. Its planes indiscriminatingly attacked both Rokossovsky's troops and the endless columns of refugees streaming east. The roads zigzagged through the boundless fields of wheat. The harvest was abundant, and stalks stood taller than people. Soon Rokossovsky noticed that the fields were swarming with men — some in groups, some alone; some wearing worn peasant clothes, some wearing only Red Army underwear — discreetly moving east. Alarmed, he gave chase. When the men were captured, they proved to be not German saboteurs but Red Army deserters. To Rokossovsky's immense frustration, two of his own soldiers, who had been sent ahead to build a new command post for him, were among them.

Having noticed the commotion, other deserters wading through the wheat fled. Rokossovsky sent more patrols into the fields to introduce order. Knowing very well what that meant, a number of the deserters opened fire. Rokossovsky's men angrily responded, but no matter how many corpses ended up lying in the wheat, more fugitives disappeared into its gleaming protective blanket.

For those marching along the road, this was an unnerving sight. Soldiers grew increasingly anxious. Rumor had it that German paratroopers dressed as policemen and Red Army officers pervaded the rear. Rokossovsky got the first suicide reports — even before combat started, the strain was more than some servicemen could handle.

On the evening of June 23 the corps saw five German tanks and three trucks carrying infantrymen. Realizing that they were heavily outnumbered, the Germans quickly retreated into the woods. Fighting didn't start until the next day, June 24. It went badly, but that didn't come as a surprise to Rokossovsky. A counterstrike was absurd; his troops couldn't even hold the defensive line. Occasionally, from the top of a hill, he could see columns of German armor rolling through the wheat, and they looked unstoppable.

By the end of June 25, the commander of a tank division belonging to the Twenty-second Corps, Major General Semechenko, reached Rokossovsky's command post at Klevan, a small town near Lutsk. His right wrist was bandaged, and he looked utterly worn out. He told Rokossovsky that his division had been wiped out and that he had walked several miles on foot to reach safety.

The last thing Rokossovsky wanted people to say about him was that he encouraged defeatism and panic-mongering; he still felt as if he were on probation. Technically speaking, General Semechenko's misfortunes didn't concern him directly and should have been reported not to him but to the commander of the Twenty-second Corps, General Kondrusev. Rokossovsky chose to dismiss Semechenko with deliberate rudeness. "Stop talking about the devastation of your corps now!" he snarled. "It is still fighting. Go and try to find your units . . ."

At that moment, as if to test his resolve, a commissar from the Twenty-second arrived and reported that the entire corps had perished, including its commander, General Kondrusev. That was unambiguously bad news for Rokossovsky. First of all, it meant that the counterstrike was collapsing, just as he had thought it would. The defeat of the Twenty-second Corps jeopardized his own troops on the northern flank. On the southern flank, the Nineteenth Corps was retreating too. Riabyshev's Eighth, 25 miles to the south, had scored a victory, but that would have no immediate impact on Rokossovsky's men. However, given his past, Rokossovsky had to worry about the potential personal consequences of the Twenty-second's collapse. Taking responsibility for the retreat of his own troops was bad enough for a gulag survivor, but dealing with the annihilation of somebody else's unit was more than he could bear. He angrily ordered the general and the commissar to "stop lamenting" and start looking for their men.

However, the ghost of the perished Twenty-second wouldn't leave his side. More men reached Klevan in the evening, looking destitute. No matter the consequences, he realized he had to deal with the problem. Grudgingly, Rokossovsky put the men under his guard. To his dismay, he saw that the Twenty-second's officers had already torn their insignias off; very few carried guns. Beside himself with anger, he spotted an older man sitting under a pine tree next to a very young nurse. Rokossovsky immediately knew that this man was a senior officer. For some reason, the sight of him sitting calmly under a tree next to an attractive woman, as if the war were over for both of them, doubled Rokossovsky's rage, and he barked, "Officers, come here!"

Nobody moved.

"Officers, come here! Come here!" he yelled.

The group of a hundred or so men remained silent and still.

Rokossovsky walked to the older man. "Get up! What's your rank?" he said.

"Colonel," the man said indifferently, deliberately challenging Rokossovsky.

The general pulled his revolver out.

That was too much. The colonel slipped to his knees and muttered, "Don't shoot. I will do whatever you say."

Rokossovsky stared at him, disgusted but also a little remorseful. "Gather others like you," he said. "Form a unit. Report to me tomorrow."

The next day five hundred people assembled by the colonel during the night were sent back to the front.

To Rokossovsky's indignation, there were more desertions. Five thousand deserters from the Sixth Rifle Corps were caught and returned to the front, and another hundred were shot on the spot. In the Ninety-ninth Division, eighty Ukrainians refused to participate in combat and were executed in front of their peers.

Soon the general learned a new term, "the left-handed." It referred to soldiers and officers who shot their left hand, a relatively minor injury, in order to be sent to the rear. Sometimes, desperate to secure safe passage back home, the men shot a few of their fingers off. As soon as the strategy became common, everyone with an injury to the left hand was treated with suspicion, so those who were most frantic started shooting their right hands. Sometimes two friends would agree to maim each other's limbs. All this was referred to as "self-shot." People who were caught in the act were executed.

General Zhukov, Southwestern Front, June 25–26

The insane counteroffensive in the southwest failed. Its futility was obvious to Zhukov and Kirponos by the end of the first day, June 24, but they didn't dare to stop the mission.

Tank units got stuck in swamps. Most vehicles were obsolete, slow, and fragile. The new KVs could move at 15 miles per hour, which was a decent clip, but on a hot and dry day, with plenty of sand and dust around, their engines became clogged. Some units lost more than half their tanks before they even reached the enemy.

On the battlefield, a Soviet mechanized corps didn't stand a chance against the advancing Germans — the Soviets had no air support, too few modern tanks, inexperienced soldiers, and confused commanders. Soviet generals exposed to panzer duels in Ukraine couldn't help but marvel at the German attack technique, which was well practiced, well performed, and almost automatic in its precision.

The Germans advanced in a perfect wedge. Heavy T-IVs, shielded by thick armor, led the triangle, with lighter T-IIIs and T-IIs following at the flanks. Then came motorcyclists, with the infantry and the artillerymen, the most vulnerable and the slowest, in the rear. The wedge started unhurriedly, with the T-IVs sniffing out the Soviet artillery. If the Germans discovered that no heavy guns faced them, the T-IVs' drivers rushed forward at maximum speed, literally trampling everything in their path.

Nonetheless, compared to Bock in Byelorussia, Rundstedt was making slow progress. The counteroffensive in the southwest had failed, but units like Riabyshev's Eighth Corps did manage to impede the German advance. General Guderian's tanks didn't meet with serious resistance during their speedy race from the border to Minsk, but Guderian's peer in the south, another German panzer leader, General Kleist, moved in jerks, now capturing a town, now losing it, then capturing it again the next morning. The problem was that the effort cost the Soviet mechanized corps too much. The battle for the town of Leshnev, recaptured by the Eighth from Kleist, inflicted considerable losses on the Germans and forced them to retreat, but the Eighth was all but finished after it.

Unlike Rokossovsky, Zhukov refused to admit that the counterstrikes had so drained the Southwestern Front that it could no longer defend the industrial core of the Soviet Union. Like Stalin, Zhukov didn't see the wisdom in withdrawal, and like Stalin, he wasn't paying much attention to his underlings. He keenly missed the murdered generals like Tukhachevsky, but he had little time for generals like Riabyshev, to say nothing of the 30,000 foot soldiers who made up the Eighth Corps and who were now dying in a senseless "fighting retreat."

Sensing that the *vozhd* didn't want to be bothered and suspecting that he was already considerably irritated by Zhukov's unsolicited queries and advice, the general did not call the Kremlin during these days. Instead he went through his deputy, Vatutin, at the General Staff. Vatutin reported that the Western and Northwestern Fronts were doing much worse than the Southwestern. The Western Front troops had been pushed to the suburbs of Minsk, and the Northwestern had abandoned Lithuania. Vatutin said that Stalin was particularly nervous about the situation in Byelorussia and cursed not only General Pavlov but his own representatives in the west, particularly Marshal Kulik. This was good news, as Zhukov hated Kulik with a passion. Even better, Kulik had left for the Tenth Army at the Belostok pocket a few days earlier and had been missing ever since.

But another piece of information was chilling. The former chief of general staff, Zhukov's predecessor, Kirill Meretskov, had been arrested. Zhukov knew that at least two hundred senior officers and generals who had been rounded up on the eve of war were still sitting in the Lubyanka dungeons, and he decided that he could be next.

Of course, Zhukov didn't know that by that time Beria's men had already persuaded forty prisoners to turn against Meretskov. While German tanks were approaching Minsk, Meretskov was being tortured. At one point an interrogator arranged a confrontation between him and the former commander of the Baltic Military District, Loktionov. Both were in pain after their recent beatings. Meretskov's face was bleeding and his eyes were glazed. He had finally confessed that he and Loktionov had been involved in a conspiracy.

But General Loktionov hadn't given up. "Kirill Afanasyevich, these are just lies, lies, lies!" he said, appealing to Meretskov. But he was met with a blank stare.

In another cell the former people's commissar of armaments, Vannikov, wailed in pain, sure that he would suffer a cardiac arrest because of his inability to stand the torment.

Zhukov didn't know all this, but he suspected that the *vozhd* was launching another purge.

Early in the morning of June 26, Vatutin called. Byelorussia and the Baltics were slipping away. Minsk had not yet fallen, but the situation in the west was becoming catastrophic.

Later in the day, Stalin called.

The Kremlin, June 26

Flying back to Moscow after less than four days with the Southwestern Front, Zhukov couldn't be sure what awaited him. On the phone Stalin had sounded businesslike. "The situation on the western front has become difficult," he said. "The Germans are approaching Minsk. It is unclear what Pavlov intends to do. Nobody knows where Marshal Kulik is. Shaposhnikov has gotten sick," he added with irritation. "Can you return to Moscow right away?"

In principle, the exchange had been very flattering. The *vozhd* had admitted that no other leader looked as reliable to him as Zhukov did — not the nominal chief of the Red Army, Timoshenko; not the cavalrymen Voroshilov and Budenny; not the seminarian, Vasilevsky, or Zhukov's highly efficient and hardworking deputy, Vatutin. It looked as if he had invited Zhukov to return from quasi-exile to save the day. But with Stalin, one never knew.

When Zhukov reached the Kremlin at 3 P.M., he discovered that the *vozhd* was in a more typical mood — one of cold fury. Timoshenko and Vatutin, both pale and visibly frightened, stood at attention before him.

Stalin barely nodded to the general and threw the Western Front map on the table. "Discuss the situation and report what can be done," he barked.

"We will need about forty minutes to figure it out," Zhukov said.

"Well, then report in forty minutes," Stalin snarled.

Zhukov didn't like what he heard from Timoshenko and Vatutin. The Third and Tenth Armies were dying in pockets west of Minsk. The Fourth Army had withdrawn south. It was almost certain that the Germans would capture Minsk very soon and then proceed quickly to Moscow.

Acknowledging that they knew no real remedy for the situation, the generals suggested a palliative. They told Stalin that two parallel lines of defense had to be formed. The first was to be created from Polotsk to Vitebsk, Orsha, Moghilev, and Mozyr. Shaped like an arc approximately 200 miles long, it would protect Moscow, just 300 miles away. Zhukov placed the arc along two major rivers, the Western Dvina and the Dnieper, the only two natural obstacles beyond Minsk. The second, parallel arc was to be built only 50 miles farther east, on a line running from Selizharovo Lake to Smolensk, Roslavl, and Gomel. Clearly, Zhukov didn't expect the first line of defense to last long.

He knew he didn't have much manpower to use. On the first arc he would assemble the remnants of the Western Front and also the Nineteenth, Twentieth, Twenty-first, and Twenty-second Armies, which had originally been summoned for the preemptive strike and had been creeping west since late May. On the second arc he would place two other contingents of the aborted preemptive war, the Twenty-fourth and the Twenty-eighth. He realized he needed more people urgently, to form at least two more armies. For that he needed a new draft.

Stalin agreed to everything. Obviously, he was desperate. Like Zhukov, he understood that the main thing now was to slow Hitler's march to Moscow until reinforcements could be shipped from Siberia and the Far East.

For Zhukov it was a moment of triumph. For the first time his ambitions had been realized: he had devised a solid battle plan on the spot, and the *vozhd* had unequivocally approved it. Strategically, the arcs looked like a major coup, the stuff of military history textbooks. Conceived on the fly, they nonetheless made sense. Using the remnants of the Western Front troops as a human shield, he would place the reserves along a major natural obstacle and, he hoped, stall the unchecked progress of the enemy panzer corps.

Stalin was apparently glad finally to deal with someone of character. Paradoxically, it was Zhukov's willpower that now attracted him — exactly the trait that he had aimed to destroy in the purge just two years earlier. Zhukov wasn't an easy person to get along with, yet he seemed to be endowed with the combination the *vozhd* was looking for: talent and loyalty. The former had been displayed first in Mongolia, then during the strategic game in January, then in the preemptive strike planning in May, and finally now, on June 26, in Stalin's office. Stalin must have liked the fact that Zhukov had suggested not a withdrawal but rather a cold-blooded sacrifice of the surviving troops until reinforcements from the rear established the new arcs of defense.

As for loyalty, Zhukov had passed his test on the southwestern front. The only one of Stalin's envoys capable of fulfilling the *vozhd*'s gloomy prophecy about a Bonapartist revolt in the armed forces, he had behaved deferentially and obediently and hadn't inundated Stalin with telephone calls from Ternopol. Also, Zhukov owed everything to Stalin: his career, his benefits, his survival during the purge. He had no capital of his own, unlike Voroshilov, Budenny, and Shaposhnikov; even the pathetic Kulik could exploit his civil war heroics. Zhukov belonged to a new brand of military leader: he was a self-made man, yet one completely molded by the system.

However, that afternoon, despite Stalin's admiration for Zhukov, or maybe precisely because it made him insecure, the *vozhd* did not want to meet with the general alone, so a number of dignitaries were present during the conversation: Molotov, Malenkov, Kaganovich, Budenny, Voroshilov, and of course Beria. In the evening Stalin sent for Timoshenko, Zhukov, and Vatutin again, and again Beria was there. During the next few days the *vozhd* would see the military men only in the presence of the chief of political police.

Clutching at Zhukov's defense as his only hope, Stalin ignored the fact that the plan held out salvation just to the central part of the country, between Latvia and Kiev, and provided no protection for Leningrad or southern Ukraine. Zhukov was no doubt aware of that, but he kept silent about it. After all, he was only doing Stalin's will — saving Moscow at all costs, even if it meant abandoning the rest of European Russia.

▪ ▪ ▪

Lavrenty Beria may have been the only person who knew that around June 26, the day Zhukov's plan was conceived and adopted, Stalin panicked. Beria's secure convoys were ordered to take the Diamond Treasury, with its fabulous gems, gold, platinum, and the Romanovs' crown jewels, to the Urals for safekeeping. The Hermitage and other important museums were told to surrender all art made of precious metals and gems to Beria's representatives. More important, at about the same time Stalin ordered Beria to transmit a message to the Germans: he wanted peace at all costs.

Stalin was prepared to cede the Baltics and Ukraine and also the stolen areas of Romania and Finland. If that was not enough, he wanted to know what would satisfy the Führer. He also instructed Beria to ask the Germans why they had attacked.

Beria decided that the message could be delivered through the Bulgarian ambassador in Moscow, Ivan Stamenov, who was known to be close to German intelligence. The person to meet with Stamenov was Pavel Sudoplatov, one of the best officers Beria had. A year earlier, at Stalin's direct order, Sudoplatov had arranged for the assassination of Leon Trotsky in Mexico, which had involved a young idealist and an ice pick.

Beria called Stamenov his agent, but that was not really the case. Stamenov had indeed agreed to cooperate with Soviet intelligence as far back as 1934, when he was a junior diplomat stationed in Rome, but that didn't mean that Moscow could tell him what to do now. An enthusiastic patriot, Stamenov thought that his risky relationship with the Soviets might win more influence for Bulgaria in European affairs. He exchanged information with the Soviets when necessary, but he didn't take orders from them.

Of course Beria knew that very well, but he liked the idea of having an ambassador as an agent. It looked good on the books. To enhance the impression, Sudoplatov was referred to as Stamenov's "case officer." Instructing Sudoplatov now, Beria emphasized that if he ever said a word about the mission to anybody other than Stamenov, he and his family would immediately be killed.

Sudoplatov met Stamenov in a restaurant called Aragvi in downtown Moscow. With its low ceilings, discreet alcoves, and fabulous Georgian food — which, as everybody knew, was Stalin's favorite — Aragvi had traditionally been the secret service's playground. Many shady deals had been successfully negotiated there, but this time, to Sudoplatov's disappointment, the operation failed. Stamenov remained noncommittal, and even expressed his belief that Germany would eventually be defeated, if not in Byelorussia, then at the Volga River. Stamenov was an experienced double-dealer, and he clearly had his own agenda: to maintain Bulgaria's sovereignty, whatever it took. To this end, he was probably interested in prolonging the Soviet-German war, hoping that the combatants would exhaust each other and by default leave Bulgaria alone. It remained unclear whether he would even deliver the *vozhd's* message to Berlin.

General Riabyshev, Eighth Mechanized Corps, June 27–July 2

General Riabyshev spent the night of June 27 checking in with different units. After liberating Leshnev the day before, he was facing another day of counterstrikes. What he saw and heard around him did not inspire much confidence. Peasant huts and haystacks were on fire, apparently attacked by German commandos. Here and there rifle shots sounded, suggesting the presence of German units. Occasionally he heard a bullet rustling past his face. In the dark, it was impossible to say who was shooting.

At four o'clock in the morning his plans collapsed. Kirponos sent an order telling Riabyshev to abandon the position won the day before and to withdraw to the east. The order deprived Riabyshev of his pricy achievement and transplanted the Eighth into the front's reserve. Very angry, Riabyshev realized that at such short notice he would be unable to stop the units that were supposed to strike at dawn. Indeed, the Thirty-fourth Tank Division had already attacked, and its withdrawal from the fight proved very costly; it took the division two and a half hours to disengage, shake off the Germans in pursuit, and start the march east.

Bad luck pursued the Eighth that day. At 6:40 in the morning a new order from Kirponos arrived, saying not to withdraw but to attack again and capture the town of Dubno by the end of the following day, June 28.

Cursing Kirponos and feeling betrayed by him, Riabyshev had no idea what was going on in the front headquarters. Almost immediately after Zhukov had left for Moscow, Kirponos had decided on the risky but wise move of taking his troops into the rear and letting them form a firm new defensive line there. As soon as he informed Moscow, however, the General Headquarters banned the retreat. "Continue with the counterstrike," its cable said.

The telegram reached Kirponos in bed. He swore, put his clothes on, and went to the communication center to talk with the General Staff personally. When he returned, he said nothing but silently signed the order canceling the lifesaving maneuver.

■ ■ ■

In the early morning Riabyshev learned that two divisions were still holding the combat line but that the third had withdrawn. It was a clear sign that his corps was not fit for an offensive. He decided he would need about twenty more hours to prepare the troops, do the reconnaissance, and establish contact with friendly forces before he could command any attack.

He was sitting in the woods with a map laid out on a stump, wondering how he could do that, when he heard the hum of automobile engines approaching. He looked up to see a line of cars crawling through the forest — the convoy of the Southwestern Front commissar, Nikolai Vashugin.

Vashugin's face was pale and his right eyelid fluttered in anger. Naturally, Riabyshev supposed that he carried an order from Kirponos, but to his enormous surprise, and in an outrageous breach of discipline, Vashugin was plotting something on his own. Riabyshev didn't know it, but the commissar was considering a major coup in the front headquarters, aspiring to get Kirponos dismissed and to take his place.

Now, without answering Riabyshev's greeting, Vashugin hissed, "How much have they paid you, Judas?"

"Let me report —" Riabyshev began nervously, not understanding what he was being accused of.

But Vashugin interrupted. "You will report to a court-martial, traitor. We will listen to you right now and shoot you right here."

Riabyshev stopped, petrified.

Fortunately, the Eighth's commissar, Nikolai Popel, was standing next to him. Popel was a starry-eyed Party man who fanatically believed in fairness and camaraderie, and now he interfered loudly and indignantly. "You can blame us for whatever you want," he told Vashugin, "but first you have to listen."

Vashugin swore.

Popel continued: "We don't know why you ordered us to abandon the territory wrested from the enemy."

Vashugin, unaware of Kirponos's vacillations the previous night, was unpleasantly surprised. "To abandon the territory? What are you talking about? General Riabyshev, report!"

Riabyshev haltingly recounted the contradictory orders he had been receiving. Vashugin listened, restlessly pacing around the clearing and providing no comment. Then he looked at his watch. "Report in twenty minutes what you plan to do."

When Riabyshev joined his staff, his hands were shaking and his eyes were moist.

The staff agreed that they could not act until the next morning. When Riabyshev told Vashugin that, the front commissar whispered, "You have twenty minutes to start the attack."

"This would be criminal," Riabyshev said. "This would mean killing our soldiers for nothing."

"I order you to start the offensive immediately. If you disobey, you will be court-martialed."

Riabyshev gave up. Crestfallen, he said that a number of units could be organized into a special task force and sent into combat right away. The rest of the Eighth would join them the next day.

"Right," Vashugin said, inspecting Riabyshev's face closely. "When a person wants to help his motherland, he can always find a way."

Riabyshev didn't respond. He stood at attention, looking at the sky.

Vashugin told the outspoken Commissar Popel to assume command of the special force. "If you take Dubno by tonight, you will get a medal. If not, you will be shot."

After Vashugin left, Riabyshev and Popel said a hasty goodbye. Riabyshev promised Popel that he would join him in the morning with reinforcements. Neither could be sure they would ever meet again.

■ ■ ■

Vashugin returned to the front headquarters anxious and agitated. He was ruthless and self-centered but not stupid. On the way back from

Riabyshev's clearing, he realized that the front was in total disarray, chaotically rolling east. He called on the Fifteenth Mechanized Corps headquarters, but this time even threats didn't get him anywhere. The commander of the Fifteenth outright refused to attack. The terrible truth finally dawned on Vashugin, although he hadn't believed it when Riabyshev had told him. He now understood that he had sent Riabyshev's corps to certain death.

At the front headquarters he asked about Riabyshev and was told that communications with the Eighth had been broken. The next day, however, Riabyshev reported that the Eighth had struck and had even captured Dubno, as it had been ordered. Vashugin cheered up, and so did Kirponos. Together they instructed the Eighth to hold on to Dubno.

Their euphoria proved fleeting. The attack of the Eighth had cost it all its strength. Now the corps was locked in Dubno. The front headquarters' messengers could not penetrate the German panzer ring, and a messenger sent by aircraft was never heard from.

On June 28, Kirponos got a shocking cable from Zhukov. A fresh army mobilizing in the Southwestern's rear, the Nineteenth, was to withdraw immediately to the Dnieper. Kirponos felt cheated, as he didn't know that Zhukov had started building his two defensive arcs and badly needed the Nineteenth. The rest of Zhukov's cable didn't sound right to Kirponos either: the units fighting in the pockets on the border were instructed to "bury" heavy equipment and "break through the woods" to Kovel, a town in northern Ukraine on the boundary of the Pripet Marshes.

Kirponos was edgy. It seemed that the General Headquarters had given up on him and his troops, but no general retreat had been ordered. What was he supposed to do now? The units surrounded at the border were as good as lost; by June 28 they found themselves in the deep rear of the German advance. Even Kovel had already been captured by the enemy. The rest of the troops were barely holding an uninterrupted front line and were slowly backing eastward.

While Kirponos was debating the situation with his officers, two messengers from the Twelfth Tank Division arrived. They reported that the Eighth had been completely surrounded at Dubno and by now was probably finished. When he heard this news, Vashugin grew terribly pale and left the room, forgetting about strategy, General Headquarters, and his personal high standing with Stalin. Jittery, he visited the bathroom every other minute, probably afflicted with what Russians call "bear's disease" — uncontrollable diarrhea caused by fear.

Vashugin's intestinal condition remains a mystery, but his words are on record. He told his staff that everything was lost and that the Soviet Union was going to fall in a matter of days, as France had. "We are destroyed!" he claimed.

Crippled by panic, he went to the top political officer of the Southwestern Front, Nikita Khrushchev, as another would have gone to see a priest, and told him that he had decided to shoot himself.

"Come on," Khrushchev said with a snort. "Why say silly things like that?"

"I am guilty of having given incorrect orders."

"What kind of incorrect orders?" Khrushchev asked. "You have delivered our orders to them, haven't you?"

"Yes, I have."

"Well, orders tell mechanized corps what to do. Why should you feel guilty about that?"

"Well . . . I gave them verbal orders that contradicted the written ones."

Subtlety had never been one of Nikita Khrushchev's virtues. "Stop talking nonsense," he snapped. "If you have decided to shoot yourself, then go ahead — why waste time?"

Khrushchev could barely blink before Vashugin took his pistol out, put it to his temple, and pulled the trigger. As his body fell to the floor, the flabbergasted viceroy of Ukraine rushed out of the room for help.

▪ ▪ ▪

By June 29, Riabyshev's men had almost given up hope. They were unsuccessfully trying to break through the German lines, and no other Red Army unit was in sight.

In the evening a Soviet plane hit the woods like a shooting star. The pilot, badly burned, still managed to parachute to safety. When

Riabyshev bent over him, the young man whispered, "Was carrying an order for you . . . Had to destroy it . . . The general offensive has been canceled." He couldn't say anything else and soon died.

Now Riabyshev could only guess what Kirponos and Vashugin expected from him. He doubted that the offensive had in fact been canceled, and that made him uneasy. He hadn't found Popel, and that made him feel guilty. In the end, he decided to retreat. But to do that he first had to break through the German ring.

On the night of June 29 the Eighth attacked, no longer doing somebody else's bidding but fighting for their lives. The Germans yielded, and the corps broke free and started the exhausting march east, with the Germans in pursuit.

At one point on the run, Riabyshev was told that Commissar Popel was trying to reach him by radio. Riabyshev didn't recognize the voice coming through the headphones. Suspicious, he asked, "Tell me, what is my dog's name and where is he now?" The person on the other end did not know that Riabyshev's dog was named Buddy or that he had been poisoned shortly before the war started, so he cut off the transmission. It had been a German, not Popel.

Soon Riabyshev ran across a regiment commander who had fought with Popel at Dubno. The man said that in all likelihood, Popel had been killed.

At about the same time, Riabyshev finally found Kirponos. The front leader had nothing to say to him. He listened to the general's report with his eyes closed, not interrupting and not asking questions. The campaign had been lost, and his own headquarters were also on the run. It was then that Riabyshev learned that Commissar Vashugin had killed himself. If he felt vindicated, he didn't show it.

The retreat was becoming chaotic, and Riabyshev soon lost Kirponos again. In Vinnitsa, 250 miles from the border, he accidentally met another senior general, the Southern Front commander Tiulenev. Tiulenev gazed at the unshaven and worn-out man in dirty, torn overalls. "You must be hungry as a wolf. Go get something to eat," he said.

■ ■ ■

The military leaders in Moscow were glad that Kirponos's troops had slowed German progress in the south. General Zhukov claimed that as his personal achievement. He bragged that the counterattack could have been even more effective if he had had more air support, at least one more rifle corps, and better intelligence. That was mere bluff, though.

Rundstedt's onslaught had indeed been impeded, but the price paid was high. The Southwestern Front had lost 2,648 tanks in suicidal attacks — about one fifth of the Red Army's panzer armada. Three armies, the Fifth, Sixth, and Twenty-sixth, had been destroyed, and at least 160,000 men had been killed. Very few troops were left to protect Kiev and the Donbass.

Ambitious and reckless, the counterstrike in the south was one of the worst blunders of the 1941 campaign. Instead of saving the strongest army group in the country by withdrawing and organizing viable defenses in the rear, the General Headquarters destroyed it by ordering one senseless attack after another.

6

THE LOSS OF BYELORUSSIA

Soldiers

The Red Army retreated up and down the gigantic, thousand-mile-wide isthmus between the Baltic Sea and the Black Sea, where the core of the Soviet Union sat. Yet nowhere was the flight as desperate as in Byelorussia.

Running, walking, or crawling east before the German juggernaut, the Soviet soldiers were shaken by the air of abandonment pervading the rear. The airfields, where hangars and planes were still ablaze, contained no servicemen, and the smoking Red Army compounds had been deserted, as had the homes of many local people, particularly Jews. Trenches — some vital, some precautionary, some totally unnecessary — crossed almost every field and many forests. Dug in hasty desperation and in many cases abandoned before they could be used, they spoke of fear and loss.

The roads abounded with surreal sights, like a downed but intact German Messerschmitt sitting on a highway, with three peasant boys busily looting cartridges from its machine gun (the wounded pilot had dropped his bloodied helmet on the road before disappearing into the woods). A hungry unarmed soldier stood at a crossroads, directing fleeing troops to a location that was already irrelevant; he had been placed there the day before, only to be abandoned by his superiors. There was a young female pilot who had left the hospital and was now walking east, feverish from pleurisy and looking for "an aircraft without a pilot" that she could "fly somewhere." A village cemetery had been hit by an air strike, and its dead, brought to the surface by the bombs, now lay on the ground in plain view. A deranged teenage infantryman told anybody who was willing to listen that they were all already in captivity and all the officers around them were German.

Virtually every witness took note of the hot, sunny weather and the immensely tall wheat and rye that summer.

▪ ▪ ▪

Fear gave rise to panic and loose trigger fingers. A military technician, unnerved by gunshots in the distance, yelled, "The motherland has been betrayed!" and fired randomly, killing two fellow Russians. His peers from the Twelfth Air Force Division had heard the sound of a tractor's engine, thought it was the German panzers, and fled. They drove for 40 miles before a patrol stopped them. A civilian, when detained by a patrol squad that asked for an ID, screamed hysterically, "You need my ID? Do you think you're gonna catch Hitler? No such luck!" He was shot point-blank.

More and more soldiers committed suicide. Officers started anesthetizing themselves with alcohol during the day, and many soldiers left their units while their commanders were watching and shot wildly at their pursuers when chased. A Commissar Grigorenko slipped away from his detachment, slid into the water under the Berezina River bridge, camouflaged himself with leaves and grass, and started firing at Beria's officers, cleverly using the roar of air raids as a cover. When he was eventually discovered, he fought stubbornly until he was shot dead.

The most dangerous threat came from the skies. Nothing could be worse than a Luftwaffe foray. Enjoying the unchallenged control of airspace, German pilots exterminated the retreating troops and refugees methodically and maliciously. They saved their bombs for tanks, trucks, and artillery pieces slowly moving along the clogged roads and killed people efficiently enough with machine-gun bursts. The Luftwaffe aces felt completely at ease. Sometimes, having run out of bullets and bombs, a pilot flew his plane so low to the ground that he could crush the Russians with its tires. Survivors of those attacks bore improbably wide blue bruises across their backs.

▪ ▪ ▪

No state official or army commander knew how many refugees had abandoned their homes for the roads and forests, but in Byelorussia the numbers were particularly high. Divided by Russia and Poland centuries before and still largely rural and undeveloped, Byelorussia had never had the chance to forge a strong national identity like its counterparts in the Baltics. More people identified with Moscow, and fewer hoped to benefit from German rule, so Byelorussians were more likely to flee east than Lithuanians were. Also, many Byelorussian towns had vibrant and populous Jewish communities, and although many Jews, distrusting Stalin's propaganda, didn't believe the stories about racial pogroms in Germany and chose to stay, tens of thousands joined the columns of refugees on the roads.

Refugees walked east, toward the army's more secure rear. So did the retreating Red Army soldiers, though some units, ordered to counterstrike, gloomily marched west, further congesting traffic on the narrow roads. Refugees and soldiers mixed on highways and dirt lanes, and the Luftwaffe shot at them indiscriminately. Very quickly the refugees realized that even if the German pilots didn't aim at them specifically, they were part of an enormous moving target. However, if they wanted to reach the rear, they had to use the roads. It was impossible to navigate in the woods, and no one could travel through the thickets burdened with children and luggage, no matter how few bags he or she carried.

Also, Byelorussia's forests were notorious for their dangerous marshes. The amazing Pripet Marshes stretched all the way along Byelorussia's southern ridge, and it was common knowledge that even the Red Army and the Werhmacht avoided them. Even if one could be sure that the terrain adjoining the road would be firm and safe, the woods swarmed with Red Army deserters, who posed a challenge that women with children didn't want to face.

Occasionally planes with red stars on their wings flew overhead. There were very few of them, and they were slow — a single German plane could easily shoot a couple of them down, approaching from the rear and hitting each with a short, precise burst. Sometimes the Red Air Force pilots, confused and panicky, gunned down friendly forces. If their attack was persistent, the outraged soldiers on the ground had no choice but to respond with fire, at times shooting their own planes down.

The retreat quickly taught people a number of survival skills that the soldiers had never learned in boot camp. One was never to seek shelter inside a building; when hit by bombs, a building collapsed like a house of cards, burying everybody under the rubble. The Germans could strike at any minute in any place — not only the air force but tanks too. The summer of 1941 was unusually dry and the rivers were at their lowest, so the German armor could find fords in unexpected places.

One could rarely hope to spend more than a single night at any given spot, so it wasn't worth the effort to prepare a proper bivouac. Also, quartermasters had vanished, together with all the good things they were supposed to keep, so now every soldier had to be responsible for his own meager stock of cigarettes, dried bread, and canned food — often just salty and spicy anchovies. The people who had prepared the rations apparently knew nothing about human physiology: anchovies provoked fierce thirst, and water was in short supply. In the villages, fairly deep wells were usually available, and their water was cold and tasty. But those fleeing through the woods depended on springs, and if there weren't any, they had to take water from rivers, ponds, and brooks. In the heat of summer, this water swarmed with bugs and had to be boiled before it was used. But there was almost never time for that. Acute cases of giardiasis were the result.

The roads had dried up since the muddy spring, and even dirt lanes had become usable again. But every thunderstorm brought the mud back, and in a matter of minutes a perfectly good road could turn into a trap for tanks. After the storm, while the mud was drying, drivers had to be careful not to tear up the roads; if they did, those who followed would get stuck in the hardened ruts.

Despite the water problem, a flight through the woods was the best possible option for soldiers, if not for civilians. The western borderland still contained a huge swath of the great Eurasian forest, with dense thickets of oak, pine, and birch. Lush foliage supplied cover. In the hot weather, many of the swamps had dried, providing soldiers with narrow paths and even firm islands amid the boggy mess. However, tanks stood no chance in the swampland, as their wheels destroyed the paths and stuck to the bogs' bottom.

The woods could be silent and empty or overcrowded with an improbable mixture of humans: retreating bands of soldiers, random deserters, officers just back from leave who were frantically trying to find their units, teenagers who had been drafted into the army just a few hours earlier, refugees. Most people looked so exhausted that it was hard to tell their age.

Once in the woods, people immediately headed for the thickets, since the Luftwaffe hung in the air, hunting for fugitives, and every open grove was a potential trap. The thickets teemed with mosquitoes, though, which made even the vicious midsummer flies look timid. Many people suffered from diarrhea caused by fly-borne disease and contaminated water, and some shivered with fever, because the mosquitoes carried malaria. But the worst was that one never knew what one would see when one emerged from the forest's eastern edge. One could spend days struggling to survive, only to find oneself on territory already occupied by the Germans or, worse, on the front line.

▪ ▪ ▪

While the remnants of the Western Front armies dragged eastward, another, much thinner flow of servicemen moved west. Few fresh divisions were available, but many higher-ranking officers were urgently dispatched to Byelorussia to address the situation. Special trains hastily assembled from shabby commuter cars took officers and generals west. The Moscow railway stations from which the trains departed were pitch black, the few blue lamps looming here and there only serving to accentuate the darkness. Crowds of refugees and officers mixed, and the steel barriers set up by the police to channel traffic only increased the confusion. Cursing, people jumped over them, searching for the right train. No train ran on schedule.

By June 26 Minsk had become unreachable. Nobody could make out exactly what was going on there, but all the trains now stopped in Orsha, 100 miles to the northeast. Tired and confused, the officers assembled at the Orsha railway station and discussed what to do next. That was when the Junkers hit them. At that point few could tell German planes from Soviet ones, and only when the air was filled with fireballs and smoke did the men realize that they had been attacked. Junction authorities had been warned about the raid in advance, and they had ordered the steam engines jamming the tracks to send a warning whistle. It sounded more like a roar, "monstrous, dreary, endless." The shaking engines were enveloped in thick white steam, and the people around them said that for some reason, that sight was even more unsettling than the air raid.

The roads west of Orsha were permanently clogged. Cars taking reinforcements west mixed with cars bringing the wounded east. Refugees flooded the lanes. Desperate and anguished, quite a few now showed open contempt for the Red Army, something totally unimaginable only a week earlier.

Children suffered the most. Many had already lost parents to air raids, and now Red Army officers put them on trucks heading for the hinterland and told the drivers to find a traveling orphanage for them. This task wasn't as difficult as it sounded: quite a few orphanages were moving along Byelorussia's roads now. The Great Purge of 1937 had orphaned hundreds of thousands of children, and the authorities were now evacuating the children of "enemies of the people," deeming them a security risk. Some newly orphaned children were too young to remember their family name, and not every mother had supplied her child with a birth certificate in a bag, so when they finally joined an orphanage, the director had to supply them with new names. As often as not, he used the name of the railway junction or the town where the child had been found.

Many summer campers had become refugees as well. The German attack had been so sudden that camp staff hadn't had time to send the children home, and now they were taking them away from the front line, with no particular destination in mind. A lot of camps had been attacked by the Luftwaffe. That was probably unintentional, because the campers' tents could be taken for soldiers' quarters from the air. Few camps had trucks, so the children often had to walk to the nearest railroad station in the hope of catching a train. Thinking that an engineer was more likely to stop for a group of frightened children than for adults, the camp staff placed the children beside the tracks, and there they stood, waving to passing trains with their scarlet scout kerchiefs. Sometimes the trains stopped and sometimes they didn't. Sometimes an engineer would just slow down, and the camp staff would toss the children onto flatbeds already full of people.

On the highways the traffic was aggressive and frenzied. The chassis of burned cars and bomb craters created an obstacle course for automobiles and trucks. At night drivers were not allowed to use their headlights, and there were many accidents. At daybreak the air raids inevitably began. Cars rushed into the woods like frightened sheep, in many cases getting stuck between tree trunks or in a hidden mire. The Germans seemed omnipotent and omnipresent, and people imagined that they saw them even miles away from the actual front line. The puffs of white smoke that resulted from firing antiaircraft guns were enough to make people believe that German paratroopers were descending from the sky.

The Commissariat of Defense urgently shipped troops and military equipment to the front, but the congested railroads were unable to accommodate all the trains. Broken communications made it impossible to follow the progress of the reinforcements. The Commissariat of Defense didn't know the whereabouts of ten out of twenty-six special trains sent west. Several trains had been rerouted to the wrong destination. In Orsha, two trains with tanks, #7/3016 and #7/3017, were pushed from one track to another for several days. Some of the tanks were no doubt intended for the Fourth Army, which was now engaged in a fighting retreat along the edge of the Pripet Marshes 100 miles to the southwest.

Fourth Army, Western Front, June 26–28

On the night of June 26, the commander of the Fourth Army, Major General Korobkov, experienced a weird feeling: schadenfreude. Chronically insecure, he had been thinking since the beginning of the war that he would have been better off commanding not the important Fourth Army in strategic central Byelorussia but his previous unit, an inconspicuous corps stationed near Vilnius, in marginal Lithuania. But that night his aide reported that Soviet troops near Vilnius had been badly battered and that their retreat had opened the road to Minsk for the Germans.

The terrible news had an unexpected effect on the commander. The fact that all frontier units were doing poorly significantly cheered him up. He became friendly and accessible to staff officers and reassured them that the Fourth would keep rolling back if it didn't get reinforcements right away. By this time the army had retreated to Warsaw Highway, a strategic artery leading first to Minsk and then to Moscow. Now Korobkov openly admitted that the Fourth alone would not be able to hold it.

His assessment proved correct. During the night of June 27, the Fourth's defenses were crushed and the headquarters had to move. It didn't stay long in its new location either — by midday Guderian's tanks unexpectedly showed up at the doorstep. Korobkov barely had time to jump into his car and start racing along Warsaw Highway. Guderian's guns spat fire, but Korobkov's driver managed to cross the bridge over the Ptich River and escape the pursuit. Right after they crossed, Korobkov stopped the car, got out, and ordered that the bridge be destroyed immediately. He grimly watched as soldiers sprinkled gasoline on it. But just as a soldier struck a match, Guderian's tanks reached the far side. Before the bridge could catch fire, the Germans pulverized the weak Soviet blockade and successfully crossed the Ptich.

▪ ▪ ▪

At the end of the day Korobkov found himself in Bobruisk, a city on the Berezina River where Napoleon's army had suffered a stunning defeat in 1812. Korobkov was sure the Fourth would fail to hold it, but he hoped that the army could cling to the eastern shore of the river, behind Bobruisk. Explosives were assembled to prepare the bridges for destruction, and the staff officers insisted that the bridges should be destroyed immediately in order to prevent another debacle like the one on the Ptich. But Korobkov hesitated.

"What about the troops still on the western bank — how will they cross?" he asked.

"There are ferries and boats."

"The bridges are very important and expensive," Korobkov said. "We should seek the approval of the front commander."

The silence of his officers spoke volumes, and Korobkov felt ashamed. "Well, communications with the front headquarters are broken anyway," he said uneasily, "and the enemy can seize the bridges at any moment . . . I authorize the destruction."

Visibly upset, he watched the bridges shatter and fall. It was a disheartening sight, no doubt, but at least for the time being Warsaw Highway was safe.

Before long, communication with Pavlov was restored. The front commander ordered the Fourth to stay on the Berezina. He said that the next line of defense, along the Dnieper, wasn't yet in place, so the Fourth had to hold out at any cost. He also instructed Korobkov to report to him in person the next day.

Korobkov grew nervous. He wasn't afraid of Guderian's tanks, but a potentially stormy interview with a superior was a terrifying thought. Distraught and angry at himself, he sought the advice of the staff. "Let's think about what I can say tomorrow," he suggested.

The officers were equally distressed. Guderian had captured the western leg of Warsaw Highway without any difficulty and had been stopped at the Berezina only by the timely destruction of the bridges. Some units of the Fourth were still fighting on the western bank, but Guderian was hardly fazed. The German panzer genius was no doubt pleased that he had been able to pierce the Russian defenses by a thin "skewer," as one officer put it. Without reinforcements, the Fourth would surely lose this battle. The staff thought Korobkov had to ask Pavlov for at least one rifle division.

"You don't have to persuade me," Korobkov grunted.

The next morning he saw Guderian's tanks on the western bank of the river. Bobruisk had fallen, and the units left behind had probably perished.

Korobkov admitted that he had no strength left to confront Pavlov in person. He summoned his chief of staff, Leonid Sandalov. "I am sick," Korobkov said. "You go."

Leonid Sandalov was a determined yet sensitive man. He was sorry for Korobkov and felt devastated by the retreat, but he hoped things would improve. Riding toward Pavlov's headquarters, he savored the quiet calm — he could no longer hear the disturbing cannonade — and he admired the meadows in lush bloom.

The driver was taking the car to Moghilev. To a military professional, the name had a sinister ring. In 1916, when Russia was losing another war against Germany, that had been where the czar had his headquarters.

Not far from Moghilev, Sandalov noticed two armored vehicles and an automobile. "Could it be Pavlov?" he thought incredulously.

Yes, it was the commander of the Western Front. Colonel General Pavlov was inspecting the defenses.

Sandalov was saddened to notice that in the few days of war Pavlov had aged considerably. His eyes were anxious, his voice muted, his body thin; he even stooped. Unable to suppress the unpleasant sensation that he was talking to a loser, Sandalov reported that Korobkov was asking for reinforcements.

Pavlov replied that Korobkov could have the retreating units that were moving to Bobruisk across the German rear. But to organize them, he continued, Korobkov would have to retake Bobruisk. "I am highly displeased by the easy way in which you have given up on Bobruisk," he concluded.

"We are weak," Sandalov said helplessly. "We can barely contain the enemy at the river."

Pavlov preferred not to respond. Instead he started talking about the bright future. "The Dnieper area is going to get a few armies from the high command reserve. They will be led by Budenny. One of them, the Twenty-first, will back you up. But I can't give you its units . . . Let's go to my headquarters and discuss the details," he said.

"Where are the headquarters?" Sandalov asked.

Pavlov smirked bitterly. "No, not at the czar's site . . . Follow my car."

■ ■ ■

General Pavlov's headquarters had had to move to Moghilev on June 27. Since nobody had bothered to prepare a backup command post before the war, everything had to be made from scratch. The new location in the hilly woods was chosen to protect the command from air raids; the front line was 50 miles away.

The trees were tall and old, and the air smelled of tar and hot pine needles. The forest buzzed with activity. Soldiers were digging underground shelters for generals and building covers for cars. Communications personnel were busy connecting numerous wires, making the woods look like an oversized cobweb. Tables and chairs had been placed under the trees, and maps and folders were spread haphazardly on them. Typists filled the air with clattering. In spite of the rumors about German paratroopers lurking in the woods and the fact that numerous checkpoints had been set up to deter them, anyone who cared to could get to the headquarters without being stopped. However, once there, officers spent precious hours looking for the tent they needed, since no one knew where this or that department could be found.

Pavlov took Sandalov to Marshal Shaposhnikov. The old classicist sadly listened to Sandalov's depressing report and then said that the Fourth had to cling to the eastern bank of the Berezina in order to give Budenny time to place fresh armies on the Dnieper. The Fourth also had to assemble the retreating units that turned up at Bobruisk. For that, it had to reestablish some presence on the western bank. The headquarters of the Fourth, however, could move to safety, farther east.

Very upset, Sandalov said his farewells and left. He knew that he had failed. Pavlov and Shaposhnikov hadn't given the Fourth a single battalion.

General Pavlov, Western Front, June 27–28

Sandalov felt betrayed by Pavlov. He thought that the front commander had just dismissed him without providing either material support or understanding. But few would have liked to be in General Pavlov's place that day.

The night before, Zhukov had cabled an order consisting of five points, each demanding immediate action. The first instructed Pavlov, five days after the start of hostilities, to get in touch with all the front's units. Second, he was to be sure not to abandon tanks and artillery pieces on the battlefield because they had run out of fuel; if necessary, he should airlift extra fuel to the troops. Third, he should evacuate the troops to Polotsk, Minsk, or Bobruisk. Both Polotsk and Bobruisk lay to the east of Minsk, so Zhukov obviously thought that the struggle for the capital was a waste of resources, though he didn't say so. Fourth, the advancing German armor had left a gap between itself and the slow-moving infantry, and Zhukov suggested sending the Red Army into the breach. However, he stressed, that would make sense only "if your commanders reassume control over their units." Fifth, Pavlov was to take the remaining cavalry into the Pripet Marshes to engage in guerrilla warfare.

None of the instructions were feasible. Communications remained interrupted, and Pavlov had trouble maintaining contact even with the Fourth Army, the only unit still fighting. The Tenth Army was silent in the pocket at Belostok, and the Third remained hopelessly dispersed and impossible to track. An airlift to send extra fuel to the front line was an absurd notion, since most of the Western Front air force had been destroyed in the first hours of war. Each day brought more losses; on June 26 alone the air force had lost eighty-nine planes.

The most crucial clauses of the directive, those concerning the relocation of troops, contradicted one another. What was Pavlov supposed to do — evacuate the troops or counterattack? Did Zhukov believe that cavalry left alone in the Pripet Marshes would last longer than a few days? Most important, was the front expected to defend Minsk?

Pavlov couldn't deal with the contradictions and was too frightened to ask for clarifications. Only half a year earlier he and Zhukov had been rivals competing for the *vozhd's* attention. Now Zhukov was at the pinnacle of power, presumably supported and liked by Stalin, while he had turned into a pariah commanding an illusory front.

That day, June 27, a very dubious reinforcement arrived at Western Front headquarters: Marshal Klim Voroshilov. Angry at virtually everybody there, Stalin had dispatched the Red Army's poster general to the struggling region. Armed with his newly coined motto, "The main thing now is to overcome the panzer phobia," Voroshilov drove up in a long black Packard heavily escorted by smaller cars, swearing and yelling at the top of his voice. His exuberance just exacerbated the general confusion and apprehension.

The third event to occur on June 27 was the delivery to Marshal Shaposhnikov of the map captured by General Filatov's scouts from the naked German bathers. As soon as he glanced at it, he realized that despite Stalin's expectations, the Germans were delivering the main blow not to Ukraine but to Byelorussia. He contacted Moscow right away. Two things had to be done urgently, he argued: a number of reserve armies currently moving to Ukraine should be rerouted, and all Western Front troops should be evacuated east, to the Dnieper. There was no immediate response from Moscow. Stalin probably thought that he was just being an alarmist.

One question simply had to be dealt with right away: what to do about Minsk. It was clear that Stalin wanted to hold it at all costs, but no reinforcements were available and the city would soon fall. Meanwhile, the troops that were senselessly dying there could have been better used farther east, along the Dnieper.

At 2 A.M. on June 28, Pavlov's chief of staff, General Klimovskikh, got a call from Zhukov. "Who controls Minsk?" Zhukov asked.

"We still do," Klimovskikh responded tiredly. He then acknowledged that the Western Front command had no idea what was happening to the Third and Tenth Armies and confirmed that the Fourth was experiencing severe fighting southeast of Minsk.

Throughout the conversation, both parties were at their worst, Zhukov rude and unforgiving, Klimovskikh uncertain and vague. Both wished that Pavlov had been on the phone instead of Klimovskikh, but the Western Front commander was avoiding Zhukov. He was becoming progressively more nervous, suspecting that Stalin would make him pay dearly for the loss of Byelorussia. Belatedly, he started worrying about the destruction of bridges and highways. Completely oblivious of the option only a few days earlier, he now cornered an expert saboteur, Colonel Ilia Starinov, whom he knew from Spain.

"Don't have enough explosives? Get more, Wolf!" Pavlov said, calling Starinov by his alias, as Spanish civil war veterans often did. "Tell Moscow you need them! We managed at Teruel and Ebro. Can't do worse at home!"

By that time the Western Front had just one army that was doing any real fighting — Korobkov's Fourth. Intending to boost its morale, Pavlov decided to go to Bobruisk himself, but when he met Sandalov on his way there, he decided on an easier path. Instead of continuing to Bobruisk, he accompanied Sandalov back to the front headquarters, equipped him with resolute instructions, and sent him back into battle.

He didn't do even that much for General Filatov at Minsk. The Thirteenth Army, which Filatov commanded, had found itself hostage to Stalin's make-believe world. Still being formed on June 22, it was nothing but a mishmash of troops, although it was being treated by superiors as a battle-worthy unit. Worse, it was expected to protect Minsk, though Filatov didn't have nearly enough soldiers to man the defensive lines around the city. Nobody at the Western Front headquarters dared confront the fact that there was no front line around Minsk, just isolated pockets of resistance. Pavlov kept promising Filatov that the retreating units of the Third and Tenth Armies would arrive soon and save the day, but he didn't really believe it.

General Filatov commanded a ghost army that was supposed to hold a real city. Exasperated, on June 28 he asked Pavlov for permission to withdraw east and abandon the hopeless cause. Pavlov repeated his previous instructions to stay in Minsk, even if surrounded, and wait for reinforcements. To Filatov's credit, he told Pavlov that that was folly. A number of soldiers from the Third and the Tenth had already reached Minsk, but there were only 3,000 of them, and they were scared, angry, and exhausted. Filatov had hastily organized them into two crippled regiments, but they wouldn't be able to make a difference. In response, Pavlov announced that he was sending a messenger with a written order not to abandon Minsk.

At his own risk, Filatov allowed the Second Rifle Corps, whose situation was particularly precarious, to withdraw; other units were ordered to fight. In the evening, his own headquarters were hit. The Germans informed the Soviets through a megaphone that Minsk had been captured and they had better surrender, saying, "You will keep your lives and your officers' insignia. You have demonstrated valor and deserve this. You have twenty minutes to decide and to finish off the commissars and the kikes."

The officers hopped into their cars and fled. Fortunately for them, the road going north was not blocked. As they left the blazing city, they noticed a few units still fighting behind the German lines. Meanwhile, General Guderian's tanks had gained access to the excellent Minsk Highway and were rapidly rolling toward Moscow.

Moscow, June 29–30

The first unconfirmed reports of the surrender of Minsk reached Moscow on the morning of June 29. Upon hearing the news, Stalin became flushed with rage. Minsk didn't amount to much strategically, but in a country of false pretenses it had been upgraded to a glorious metropolis, because it was the capital of a Slavic Soviet republic, Byelorussia. (Stalin promoted Slavs as the ethnic core of the empire, just as the czars had, though he himself was a Georgian.) No matter how cynical Stalin was, he had a dangerous habit for a dictator, which was believing his own propaganda. Now, instead of bemoaning the loss of Minsk as he had bemoaned the loss of Kaunas in Lithuania and Lvov in Ukraine, and instead of focusing on the new defensive arcs along the Dnieper River, he regarded the loss of Minsk as a major strategic setback and angrily called Timoshenko. "What's happening to Minsk?" he demanded.

"I am not ready to answer that question, Comrade Stalin," Timoshenko answered uneasily.

The equivocation was not Timoshenko's fault. Pavlov still hadn't verified the surrender.

"You should be able to," Stalin said, and hung up.

Molotov, Malenkov, Mikoyan, and Beria, present during the conversation, couldn't find anything clever to say. After being silent for a while, Stalin said, "I don't like this uncertainty. Let's go to the General Staff and check the reports from the front ourselves."

Several minutes later the five most powerful men in the country were entering the heavy brass-laden doors of the General Staff building. The sentry guarding the entrance was so stunned that he didn't say anything. Silently the mighty five passed him and walked up to the second floor, where Timoshenko's office was. When they walked in, Timoshenko and Zhukov, along with a group of officers and generals, were arguing over the war maps spread on the tables.

Everybody in the room stopped what he was doing. Timoshenko turned pale but marched over to Stalin and reported distinctly, "Comrade Stalin, the People's Commissariat of Defense and the General Staff command are examining the situation on the fronts and working on the directives."

Stalin didn't say a thing. He slowly walked by the tables, looking for the Western Front map. When he found it, he stared at it for quite a while, again not saying a word. Finally he faced the generals.

"Well, report. Tell us what the situation is."

"Comrade Stalin, we haven't had time to process the information yet. Many things still have to be confirmed. The accounts are ambiguous. I am still not ready to report."

Stalin exploded. "You are simply scared to tell us the truth! You have lost Byelorussia, and now you want to surprise us with new blunders! What's happening in Ukraine? In the Baltics? Are you leading the fronts or just registering losses?"

"Let us continue with our work," Zhukov said.

Beria asked ironically, "Perhaps we are a nuisance?"

"The situation on the fronts is critical, and they are expecting our orders," Zhukov snapped. "Maybe *you* could issue some."

"If the Party says so," Beria replied snootily.

"Yes, if it says so," Zhukov retorted. "Meanwhile, it's our job."

Then he addressed the *vozhd.* "Comrade Stalin, our duty is first of all to help the front commanders and only then to inform you — "

Stalin flared up again. "First, you are making a huge mistake by distancing yourself from us! Second, we should all think how to help the front commanders now."

After this outburst, he seemed to calm down. The generals were allowed to speak. Nonetheless, a bit later, when he was told that there was still no reliable communication with the commanders in Byelorussia, Stalin lost his temper again. This time he called Zhukov useless and lost.

Tears welled in Zhukov's eyes, and he hastily left the room. Molotov followed. When Zhukov returned, his eyes were still red.

Stalin fell silent and then told his escorts, "Let's go, comrades. It looks like we have come at the wrong time." Leaving the building, he gloomily pronounced, "Lenin left us a great legacy, and we have fucked it up."

▪ ▪ ▪

It had been just a few days since the war had started, but all familiar notions of authority in the armed forces had collapsed. The Red Army, modeled on a perfect pyramid with an impeccably straight line of command, had turned into something untidy, unpredictable, and unmanageable. Neither Stalin nor Timoshenko nor Zhukov could hold it together now, since their decrees and wisdom either entered a void, aimed as they were at destroyed armies and conquered cities, or were too late to have the intended effect. It would be wrong to say that the directives had no impact at all; directives #2 and #3, ordering forceful counterstrikes, did eventually thrust hundreds of thousands into battle. However, the result was the opposite of what Stalin, Timoshenko, and Zhukov had hoped to achieve. The troops perished, yielding more territory and leaving the hinterland unprotected. It couldn't have been otherwise, as the basic cycle of war — battle report, high command decision, implementation of the decision — had been completely disrupted. Normally it took just a few hours for all the communications to go through; in principle, with radio and telephone, it was feasible to squeeze the whole cycle into an hour or so. In reality the process often took days.

Granted, Stalin expected too much from his troops, thinking that discipline and purge could substitute for ammunition and fuel. If he had been given timely and comprehensive reports from the front line, though, he probably would have set lower standards for the field commanders. His general strategic outlook — that retreat was not a viable option — would not have changed, and he would never have authorized the abandonment of Byelorussia for the sake of stable defenses deeper inland. But his persistent instructions to keep Minsk at all costs could have been modified if he had known the real situation along the western border. Instead, he assumed that the Third and the Tenth Armies, though surrounded by the Germans, still existed as combat units and therefore could save the day after they broke through the Wehrmacht's lines.

For a person unschooled in the ways of modern warfare, it was hard to believe that 400,000 soldiers could be taken out of the equation in a matter of hours. The only way to persuade Stalin that such annihilation was indeed possible was to keep giving him regular reports from the commanders of the two armies, Lieutenant General Kuznetsov and Major General Golubev, registering the shocking losses. However, the units of the Third provided only scattered communications, and there had been no communication at all from the Tenth since June 22.

The failure of communications in June 1941 proved truly lethal and probably explained the scope of the defeat as well as its absolute, instantaneous, and unmanageable nature. It was totally unforgivable that the leaders of the Tenth Army at Belostok had not developed a radio network, which would have enabled them to stay in touch with the high command even from the pocket, and it was inexcusable that Stalin had not insisted on such a network before the war started.

With a carelessness that was remarkable for a regime otherwise obsessed with security issues, the Soviet leaders had failed to take proper care of the communications available to them: thousands of miles of telegraph wire in the western part of the country. Granted, radio was a novelty for the backward nation, and the technological conservatism of

Stalin, the officer corps, or both made introducing its use difficult. But would it have demanded exceptional foresight for Stalin, Beria, Timoshenko, Zhukov, and the military district commanders to realize that cables hanging on telegraph poles all over the western borderland would be a ridiculously easy target for Hitler's commandos? Admittedly, it was impossible to put a soldier or a policeman next to each pole, but surely they could have patrolled the cable arteries, particularly on the night of June 21, after the army had been alerted to possible German "provocations."

Even when communications had been interrupted, Soviet generals should have been able to assess the overall situation without hourly reports from the front line. That was especially true regarding the units that were surrounded and destroyed in the first days of war. Leaders like Pavlov could have firmly stated that the "vanished" units had actually been *lost.* Unlike Stalin, Pavlov saw the general disruption around Minsk firsthand, and it was his duty to tell Moscow that the Third and Tenth Armies couldn't be counted on. That assessment might have been premature on June 23, but by June 25 it was obvious. But Pavlov fed both Moscow and his own commanders lies about the inevitability of these armies' eventual arrival at Minsk. Those who were unfortunate enough to be his subordinates, like Korobkov and Filatov, didn't believe him, because they were part of the catastrophe in Byelorussia. Those who were unfortunate enough to be his superiors, like Stalin, Zhukov, and Timoshenko, did believe him — because they wanted to.

The two top Red Army commanders, Timoshenko and Zhukov, chose to keep themselves tangled in a web of false hopes and vain promises. Timoshenko had been exposed to modern warfare during the Finnish campaign, Zhukov at Khalkin Gol and more recently at the Southwestern Front. It is inconceivable that they failed to comprehend the true situation of the Third and Tenth Armies, yet they never confronted Stalin. Their fear of the *vozhd* silenced them, and in this respect the two gifted generals were the same as the ignorant Pavlov.

The catastrophe on the western border was the ultimate proof of the failure of the Soviet system. Maintained by terror and believed to be reliable, if inhumane, it proved frighteningly inefficient. Military commanders failed to introduce modern communications, railway dispatchers couldn't send a train to the right destination, staff officers made two corps elbow each other on a narrow highway, quartermasters supplied troops with anchovies instead of beef. Even the dreaded police, thought to be a perfect instrument of control and intimidation, failed to prevent German agents from cutting miles of cable all along the border.

It seems that Stalin finally began to realize what was happening on June 29. That afternoon he left the General Staff building in a mood of uncharacteristic self-loathing. Too dispirited to continue with his schedule that day, he told his bodyguards he was returning to his dacha.

▪ ▪ ▪

At 6:45 A.M. on June 30, still recovering from the shock of Stalin's visit, Zhukov called Pavlov.

"We cannot reach any decision without a clear understanding of what's going on around Minsk, Bobruisk, and Slutsk," he said. "I am waiting for the specifics."

As usual, Pavlov was at a loss. All he knew for sure was that the Forty-fourth Rifle Corps was retreating from Minsk, that the Germans had built a bridge across the Berezina River near Bobruisk to replace the one destroyed by Korobkov, and that twelve German tanks had already crossed it. His aircraft had also spotted the 210th Mechanized Division engaged in combat with the Wehrmacht.

The situation was laughable. The Forty-fourth Rifle Corps and 210th Division accounted for less than 10 percent of the Western Front's units. As for the twelve German tanks, they stood for just a tiny fraction of General Guderian's armor.

"German radio says that two Soviet armies have been encircled east of Belostok," Zhukov said, touching upon the delicate subject that neither he nor Pavlov really wanted to discuss. "That must be partially true. Why can't you send messengers to get in touch with the troops? Where are Kulik, Boldin, Kuznetsov? Where is the cavalry corps? It can't be that the pilots couldn't see the cavalry from the air."

"The [radio] reports sound rather accurate," Pavlov cheerfully agreed, as if he were happy for any solid information, and he admitted that he hadn't heard from the Tenth and Third Armies for several days. He added that the pilots couldn't find the cavalry corps or the mechanized corps, "as they are carefully guarded in the woods against enemy air raids."

Neglecting to ask Pavlov how he knew that the corps were "carefully guarded against enemy air raids" if he hadn't heard from them for days, Zhukov ordered him to collect the troops and move them to the Berezina, where Korobkov's army was desperately clinging to the eastern shore. Holding the Berezina was critical if the arcs protecting Moscow — conceived less than four days earlier — were to have any chance at all.

▪ ▪ ▪

The surrender of Minsk had a disproportionately devastating effect on Stalin. Even given the city's inflated stature in the Soviet propaganda machine and Stalin's own mind, he still seemed to overreact. In all likelihood, the surrender of the city was the last straw for him, completely shattering his fantasy world and tossing him into an abyss of despair. After he visited the General Staff on June 29 and unleashed his rage on Zhukov and Timoshenko, he headed for his dacha. He didn't show up in his office the next day either, and he refused to answer the phone.

June 30 could have marked the beginning of the end for Stalin. His abandonment of the helm coincided with a dramatic loss of land and lives, an absolutely unprecedented defeat in Russian history. The first Russian revolution, in 1904–1905, in which workers, peasants, intellectuals, and even liberal aristocrats pulled together to dismantle the czarist autocracy, was triggered by the loss of colonies in China that a majority of the rebels would have had trouble finding on a map. Twelve years later, the deprivations of World War I gave rise to the second revolution, which toppled Czar Nicholas II and his regime in a matter of forty-eight hours. Compared to Stalin's strategic blunders, Nicholas's had been relatively minor. It had taken the czar's headquarters two years to roll back to Moghilev, but the Western Front leaders made the same journey in five days.

Purges or no, in a country created by rifle and saber and ruled by the military caste, it would have been only natural for an army commander to stage a mutiny or for senior generals in Moscow to start plotting a coup d'état. Having left the Kremlin, Stalin became physically vulnerable, and it wouldn't have taken more than a few planes to turn his dacha into a pile of ruins. But leaders like Zhukov kept to their war rooms, waiting for instructions, paralyzed by habitual slavishness. It seemed to them that Stalin could get away with virtually anything: arresting their friends, scorning their expertise, even making them weep in public.

Nonetheless, slavishness and fear tend to fade without constant intimidation and pressure, and Kremlin insiders worried that if Stalin continued to stay away, his generals might recover from their hypnosis and do the one thing he had always feared: launch a coup. Stalin's henchmen grew concerned, although no general in particular could be suspected as yet.

Late in the afternoon of June 30, Molotov, Beria, Malenkov, Mikoyan, and Voznesensky, the *vozhd*'s inner circle, gathered in Molotov's office. They felt bound to act. Ultimately, they decided that Stalin had to be lured back to his duties. How they would do it was unclear. The four civilians present at the meeting felt lost, but Beria was full of ideas. After Stalin, he was the most dreaded man in the country, but without Stalin, his downfall was all but guaranteed. Having exterminated thousands of important people in the preceding three years, he had earned the undiluted hatred of those who had survived, including the four men with him in the office. If Stalin was toppled, Beria would die.

He insisted that they had to go to Stalin's dacha with a solid proposal. He suggested that they create an emergency government, the State Committee of Defense, with Stalin as chairman. Beria did not recommend that the *vozhd* be declared commander in chief, because he knew that nothing would make Stalin assume responsibility for the unstoppable retreat in the west.

Beria's compromise solution looked problematic to the cautious and pessimistic Molotov. Stalin was too depressed and confused, he said, and would be unlikely to agree.

Voznesensky, the least experienced of the four civilians, was on the verge of a nervous breakdown. He took Molotov's criticism for an explicit denunciation of Stalin and blurted, "Then you lead us, Vyacheslav — we will follow!"

That was the closest Stalin ever came to losing power. In principle, if the five men had wanted to, they could have rid themselves of him then and there, before nightfall. But nobody supported Voznesensky, and they hastily dismissed his comment as a slip of the tongue. Molotov, the only viable alternative to the *vozhd,* was doggedly loyal to him. Mikoyan was proverbially gutless, Malenkov stupid. As for Beria, he knew that with Molotov in charge he was a dead man.

Voznesensky's reckless remark did have an unexpected effect on Molotov and the others, however. Shocked by it, they quickly sided with Beria and agreed to go to Stalin's dacha immediately. Arriving at the estate, they found the *vozhd* sitting alone in his dining room. He hadn't expected visitors and stared at them with a strange expression on his face. He looked poised, but there was a flicker in his eyes that they couldn't quite read.

Pensively, he asked, "Why have you come?"

"We need you to concentrate all authority in your own hands," Molotov mumbled.

Suddenly the men realized that Stalin had been expecting something very different. He looked genuinely surprised and relieved. "All right," he said.

The State Committee of Defense was thus established, with Stalin as its head.

▪ ▪ ▪

The events of June 30 brought Stalin back to life. He never shared with anyone what he had felt in the previous twenty-four hours, but when the five men walked into his dining room, they clearly looked to him like enemies. However, as soon as they started talking they proved to be as frightened of him as ever, and to Stalin that must have been the ultimate victory. Even after he had publicly admitted that he had "fucked up" the war, nobody dared to hold him accountable.

No matter how horrendous the news from the front line, millions of Soviet men still signed up to fight. Women and teenagers besieged draft offices or headed for factories and plants to replace their fathers, brothers, husbands, and sons. Young pilots added hours to their totals in order to be accepted by the army, and in the first days of war the Young Communist League headquarters received so many letters from female pilots asking for permission to go to the front that they could have formed three air force regiments. Those who had been far away from home when the war started now traveled on the roofs of trains, desperate to reach draft offices in their home towns as quickly as possible.

Though Stalin had lost control over the armies dying in the west, the rest of the country still behaved as it was expected to. He must have credited himself for that. The Great Purge, which had struck people at random and which many said had been senseless, had in fact been the wisest thing Stalin had ever done for the regime. Incapacitated by fear, the nation and its elite didn't dare to speak up, let alone end his reign.

Of course, he couldn't be sure that loyalty and trust would last. Military defeats were certain to continue, and he had to keep a close eye on his people, particularly the generals. On the eve of war he had commanded a new purge of the military, and on the second day he had arrested Meretskov. Now the question was whether to proceed with the purge — to arrest, say, people like Zhukov and Timoshenko, drag them through Beria's torture chambers, and then put on a show trial in which they would admit they were German spies.

Still in doubt, having barely recovered from the shock of the day's events, he called Zhukov and ordered him to summon General Pavlov to Moscow.

Western Front, Change of Command, June 30–July 1

On that day, June 30, an important general reached the capital. His name was Andrei Yeremenko, and until recently he had been commanding the elite First Red Banner Army, stationed in the Far East in anticipation of a war against Japan. Now, after a weeklong journey through Siberia, he was finally standing in front of the people's commissar of defense, Marshal Timoshenko.

"I've been waiting for you," Timoshenko declared, and he started briefing the general on the situation in the west. The more Yeremenko heard, the more concerned he became. Now he knew that the reports that had been reaching him on the train were terribly incomplete. When Timoshenko took a map and showed him the territories that had already been lost, the general didn't believe his eyes.

Echoing the *vozhd*'s view, Timoshenko promptly explained that the defeats were a result of poor leadership on the ground. He pointedly said that the commander of the Western Front, Pavlov, was particularly incompetent, which was why his front was now in trouble. "Here we are, Comrade Yeremenko," the marshal concluded. "Now you know."

"Yes, it's a sad picture," Yeremenko mumbled.

Like many of Stalin's lieutenants, well versed in dramatic effects, Timoshenko held the silence for a while and then announced what Yeremenko might have already guessed anyway. "General Pavlov and his chief of staff have been relieved of their duties. The government has appointed you commander of the Western Front, with Lieutenant General Malandin as your chief of staff. You should both depart for the front immediately."

The promotion was hardly a thrilling one, but Yeremenko simulated enthusiasm and appreciation. "What's the mission of the front?" he asked.

"To stop the enemy's advance," replied the people's commissar of defense.

▪ ▪ ▪

If there was terrain General Yeremenko knew well, it was the western marshland. Two years earlier he had led the Sixth Cossack Cavalry Corps into Poland. When crossing the frontier, he had ordered marker post 777 uprooted and moved to the new border. He had no idea where that would be until his troops encountered the Wehrmacht at Belostok, in the friendly manner prescribed by the new accord between the USSR and Germany. Yeremenko put the border post on the Narew

River north of Brest. The name of the German commander in the area was General Guderian.

Nine months later the Sixth Corps rushed north into Lithuania, taking only forty-eight hours to reach Kaunas. In order to impress the foreign military attachés there, Yeremenko told his Cossacks to put on their fancy parade uniforms. Stalin liked that.

Now, driving toward Moghilev and Pavlov's headquarters, Yeremenko felt slightly hurt that Stalin had not granted him an audience. He currently held arguably the most crucial position in the Red Army, but for some reason the *vozhd* could not spare a minute to see him.

The journey lasted the whole night, and when Yeremenko and Malandin finally reached Western Front headquarters on the morning of July 1, Pavlov was having breakfast in his tent. Yeremenko sent Malandin to find the man he was replacing and entered Pavlov's tent alone.

Accustomed to the parade of annoying but generally innocuous envoys from Moscow, Pavlov didn't suspect trouble and greeted Yeremenko loudly and cheerfully. "How long it has been!" he cried. "What fate brings you to us? Are you staying long?"

Instead of answering, Yeremenko handed him Timoshenko's order. Pavlov scanned the document and could not conceal his fear. "And just where am I going?" he asked.

"The people's commissar has ordered you to Moscow," Yeremenko replied dryly.

Visibly shaken, Pavlov invited him to share the meal, but Yeremenko declined. He didn't feel the need to be gracious with a dead man. Instead he demanded a report on the state of the troops.

"What is there to say about the situation that has developed?" Pavlov sighed. "The stupefying strikes of the enemy caught our troops unawares. We were not prepared for battle." Knowing that he had nothing much to lose, he emphasized the enormous casualties in soldiers, aircraft, artillery, and tanks and also the horrendous loss of territory. Feeling somewhat liberated by his dismissal, or maybe already preparing an affidavit, he bitterly complained that the high command had failed to give him early warning of the German attack.

Yeremenko knew that this was undoubtedly true, but he neither confirmed nor denied it. He had nothing else to say to Pavlov and wrapped up the conversation quickly. Pavlov no longer mattered, but the three envoys lingering in the headquarters did, and the politically savvy Yeremenko chose to pay them each a visit.

Marshal Voroshilov sounded almost hysterical. Earlier in the day, panic-stricken at the loss of Minsk and apprehensive of Stalin's wrath, he had decided to act on his own and had ordered the long-suffering Thirteenth Army to counterattack and destroy the enemy forces. Yeremenko politely informed him that he was going to overrule this order. Voroshilov didn't argue. He had already switched to another project: Byelorussia would be saved by guerrilla warfare, he prophesied. He stopped every new visitor from Moscow, inquiring whether he knew how to train the partisans.

Marshal Shaposhnikov was crestfallen about the collapse of the front but specific in his advice. He told Yeremenko where to deploy reinforcements without delay. The problem was that Yeremenko hadn't brought any.

The third dignitary, the Byelorussian Party boss, Ponomarenko, didn't pretend to understand strategic matters and said only that Pavlov and his staff had commanded the troops poorly. Ponomarenko was the only person at the Western Front headquarters to report success, however. Notwithstanding the mayhem, the evacuation of Byelorussia had gone well: 13,000 machines, 4,000 tractors, 842 tons of rare metals, and 600,000 head of cattle had been sent east, as had all the currency and valuables from Minsk. Out of 150,000 tons of Byelorussian grain, 44,000 had been salvaged and 42,000 destroyed. The Party archive had been sent to Ufa, and the police had taken their own records to an undisclosed location in the rear as well. The Council of People's Commissars' papers had been left behind, but because they contained highly sensitive documents on the brutal collectivization, the 1937 purge, and the 1939 occupation of eastern Poland, Ponomarenko had dispatched a special group to Minsk to destroy them. Unfortunately, the men had failed to penetrate the German ring.

After interviewing all three men, Yeremenko headed for a staff meeting. The data presented to him there were disheartening. Bock's Army Group Center was clearly aiming at Moscow. Having taken Minsk, the Germans were now attacking in a fork, at Borisov in the northeast and Bobruisk in the southeast, intending to surround the rest of the Western Front troops.

▪ ▪ ▪

After Sandalov returned to the Fourth's headquarters and reported that Pavlov hadn't given them any reinforcements, Korobkov was dejected. The army's commissar reproached him: "You and I should have gone to the headquarters ourselves." Korobkov pretended not to hear.

Pavlov had sent three orders. The first, to cross the Berezina and take Bobruisk, could not be done. The second, to reassemble the retreating units, was already happening. Fragmented groups of soldiers kept pouring in from the west, having crossed the Berezina on rafts and boats. The third, to move the Fourth's headquarters to the rear, to Rogachev, was the easiest, and Korobkov eagerly ordered the relocation.

On the morning of June 29 he started preparing for a hopeless mission: crossing the Berezina. Never a man of character, by that time the commander of the Fourth had lost all resolve. He expected Guderian to materialize at the threshold of his headquarters any minute and, believing the rumor that a German panzer could roll 100 yards below the surface of water, suspected that German tanks were already crossing the river. The Berezina was only about twelve feet deep.

The next day, before dawn, Korobkov's men quietly ferried across the river. Landing on its western bank, they surprised the Germans by storming the old Bobruisk fortress. The troops had been promised that other units would soon join them, but as the landing force buckled under fierce German fire, no reinforcements came their way. Feeling betrayed and angry, they rafted back to the eastern shore at the end of the day. There they discovered that they had been abandoned for a reason. Shortly after they had left, Guderian's tanks had forded the Berezina, and now the remnants of the Fourth, personally led by Korobkov, were fighting them on Warsaw Highway.

The front headquarters rushed all remaining planes to Bobruisk, but the situation was hopeless. The Red Air Force lost eighty-eight aircraft to the Luftwaffe.

▪ ▪ ▪

Nothing could save Byelorussia now, and there was little to suggest that the Germans could be stopped at the Dnieper. After crossing the Berezina, Guderian was separated by less than 50 miles from the still unfinished arc of Soviet defenses. No matter how hard the Red Army soldiers and hastily drafted civilians tried, they wouldn't be able to build fortifications sturdy enough to halt the German panzers' blitz. The armies reaching the Dnieper from the rear looked to be a formidable force, but not a winning one. In the best scenario, the Dnieper ramparts would slow the German onslaught — not a trivial matter, as that would give Stalin time to move the Far Eastern army group to European Russia, if and when it became obvious that Japan would not abrogate its nonaggression pact.

Meanwhile, the Western Front troops had melted away. Yeremenko was a general without an army. He had spent about thirty-six hours in the headquarters, busy issuing detailed but otherwise meaningless directives, when Stalin suddenly called.

The beginning of the conversation was surprisingly civil. "Comrade Yeremenko," the *vozhd* said, "I am sorry I could not see you in Moscow. We were in a hurry to send you off."

When Yeremenko reported the lack of any tangible success resulting from his leadership, Stalin didn't seem to be particularly upset. However, his next remark had a chilling effect on the vain general. "To strengthen the Western Front command," Stalin said, "in a few days we will send People's Commissar of Defense Timoshenko to lead the troops. You will be his deputy."

Feeling undeservedly humiliated, Yeremenko vengefully asked for reinforcements.

"All right, we will do what we can," Stalin replied calmly. "Goodbye, Comrade Yeremenko, and good luck."

■ ■ ■

The former commander of the Western Front, General Pavlov, was not reassigned but instead was taken into custody by Beria's men. The arrest didn't come as a surprise to him, of course. A witness present when he was arrested believed that the unfortunate general, exhausted by fear and uncertainty, exhibited something close to relief.

On July 1 the commander of the Fourth Army, Korobkov, was informed that his remaining troops were to merge with the Twenty-first Army under Lieutenant General V. F. Gerasimenko. Gerasimenko, however, had his own idea about what the merger meant. When Korobkov reported to him in Gomel, a Byelorussian town just 25 miles from Russia, Gerasimenko told him to keep fighting so the Twenty-first could finish building its defenses. The Fourth had been a sacrificial lamb since the dawn of June 22, and now its few survivors were also expected to die uncomplainingly.

A few days later Korobkov was unexpectedly invited to the front headquarters. He never returned.

7

THEIR MASTER'S VOICE

The Conquered

In the first days of July, the German command was feeling good about the Russian campaign. According to General Guderian, the plan had been to break through the Red forces stationed near the border, encircle and destroy them, and then push deep enough into Soviet territory to prevent the enemy from forming new defensive fronts. By and large that goal had been achieved. Of course, not every Soviet army unit had been destroyed, but the Third, Fourth, and Tenth in Byelorussia, the Eighth and Eleventh in the Baltics, and the Fifth, Sixth, and Twenty-sixth in Ukraine had practically ceased to exist. No new defensive front had emerged either.

A week before the war had started, on June 14, in Berlin, Hitler had asked Guderian how long it would take him to reach Minsk. Guderian's answer was "Five to six days." Having pushed through the border defenses and either captured a number of bridges or forded rivers, sometimes crossing them underwater, his panzers had reached the suburbs of the Byelorussian capital on exactly the fifth day of war. His rival, General Hoth, had arrived in Minsk one day earlier.

A few Western Front units still held out in the Pripet Marshes, hampering the German rear, but the chief of the German General Staff,

Franz Halder, believed that though "there are enemy forces in this maze of swamps and forests . . . they certainly are not stronger than two or three divisions; there cannot be any doubt that they include some motorized elements and tanks. The attacks are conducted in a manner which plainly shows that their command is completely confused. Also, the tactics employed in these attacks are singularly poor. Riflemen on trucks abreast with tanks drive against our firing line, and the inevitable results are very heavy losses to the enemy."

Among other problems on Byelorussian terrain was General Korobkov's despairing Fourth Army at the Berezina River, where German commanders registered "stubborn enemy resistance." Guderian thought that the Fourth's "battle technique," particularly camouflage, was "excellent," but it was evident to him that the Soviets had not "reestablished a unified command yet."

In general, Army Group Center was doing well. The Belostok pocket — that is, the Tenth Army — had been all but liquidated. Between June 26 and June 30, just one German regiment, the Seventy-first Infantry, had captured as many as 36,000 Soviet soldiers. The Novogrudok pocket, where the Third Army was helpless, had been "further contracted and sealed." General Guderian had crossed the Berezina and General Hoth had reached the Dvina. Moscow was a mere 300 miles away.

The advance of Army Group North had slowed somewhat, owing to "very bad weather" and terrible road conditions. Still, the German troops were already at Pskov. There was every reason to believe that Leningrad would soon be surrounded.

General Riabyshev would have been utterly surprised to learn that the efforts of his Eighth Mechanized Corps, sent on its long, circuitous march by mistake, had become a matter of grave concern to Army Group South in Ukraine. The Eighth was one of the very few Soviet units mentioned in German memos as distinct from the general fleeing mass. Thanks to the Eighth, for a while the situation remained "tight" for Rundstedt. The counterattack that Riabyshev had found so senseless and deplorable had "caused a lot of confusion in the area between Brody and Dubno." In Halder's view, the Soviet command in Ukraine was "doing a pretty good job," and Army Group South was advancing "slowly, unfortunately with considerable losses." By the beginning of July, though, Army Group South had gathered steam, and the Red Army, exhausted by counterstrikes, had collapsed.

In the first days of the campaign, the German high command had been a bit nervous about Stalin's overall strategy. If he applied the 1812 solution, withdrawing into the depths of Russia and thus yielding territory but saving the army, the Wehrmacht could eventually run into difficulties. However, it soon became clear that Stalin didn't put much stock in the 1812 war. "The enemy's withdrawal and the crumbling of his front," Halder wrote in his diary with obvious satisfaction, "certainly cannot be interpreted as a disengaging movement planned by his command; it must be explained by the fact that his troops have been cut up and, for the most part, scattered by our unceasing massive blows . . .

"On the whole then," he summed up on July 3, "it may be said even now that the objective to shatter the bulk of the Russian army this side of the Dvina and Dnieper has been accomplished."

One of the issues German generals kept debating among themselves was whether Stalin had been planning a preemptive strike or not. Hitler answered the question in the affirmative. After entering Soviet territory, however, his generals were not sure. One of the leading tank commanders, General Manstein, thought that "the layout of the Soviet forces on 22nd June 1941 did not indicate any *immediate* intention of aggression on the part of the Soviet Union." He preferred to call the Soviet formations a "deployment against every contingency," a "latent threat."

■ ■ ■

With understandable pride, General Halder reported that "morale of our troops everywhere is described as very good, also where they had to go through hard fighting." Then he added, "Horses very tired."

Morale must have been very good indeed, but far from unbreakable. The Germans were intimidated by Russia's climate and topography — "vast forests and steppes, and roads that we would not even designate as country lanes. After brief downpours of rain, they turned into muddy tracks which were only passable in some places after engineers or off-loaded grenadiers had felled trees to make a wooden runway with the trunks. It was not so much our opponents that held up our advance as the catastrophic roads."

The fear of falling into Russian hands gnawed at many, as it was widely believed that Stalin's commissars tortured their captives. The wounded said, "Please take me with you or shoot me. I won't be able to stand Russian captivity." Having come across the "gruesomely mutilated" bodies of a German patrol captured by the Soviets, General Manstein and his adjutant agreed that they would never let the Reds catch them alive.

Sometimes, "after throwing up their hands as if to surrender," Soviet soldiers "reached for their arms as soon as our infantry came near enough." Occasionally "Soviet wounded feigned death and then fired on [the Germans] when their backs were turned." Such fierce and cunning resistance was different from what the Wehrmacht had encountered in the rest of Europe.

The "sparsely furnished" wooden rural homes made a deep impression on German soldiers. Each dwelling had a large clay oven in the center, which the whole family slept on in cold weather. Germans also remarked on the abundance of icons. It appeared that many people were still religious, despite the fact that almost all the churches had been converted into warehouses. To the Germans' surprise, they discovered that backward villages had saunas too.

But the German officers were squeamish about staying in villages. During the campaign in the West they had been spoiled, lodging in castles, manors, and nice hotels. Small wooden huts with bugs weren't quite as appealing. A Russian "sauna" more often than not turned out to be a dirty shack on a muddy riverbank, swarming with cockroaches and spiders. Officers preferred to stay in tents or on their command wagons. Some even slept in their cars. Normally they pitched camp in groves near a lake or a stream, so that they could "take a quick plunge before breakfast or whenever we came back caked with dust and grime from a trip to the front."

By early July, with rare exceptions, the soldiers were reduced to a diet of rye bread, smoked sausage, and margarine. They dreamed about Russian chickens and geese, but those "were very hard to come by." Many villages were so poor that there was absolutely nothing the Germans could steal, and some soldiers were so depressed by the miserable poverty that they offered the local people chocolate and cigarettes from their own rations.

▪ ▪ ▪

By July 1, more than 20 million Soviets already lived under German rule. Their predicament was horrendous, whether they loathed Stalin or adored him, whether they were Russian, Polish, Latvian, or Ukrainian. The war had reached them unexpectedly, just as it had reached everybody else in the vast country, but they had been given no time to adjust to it.

People in the villages fared better than those in cities, as the tiny settlements they inhabited were of little interest to the combatants. A city or a town looked important both to the Red Army, which wanted to keep it, and to the Wehrmacht, which wanted to seize it, as it often had warehouses, army barracks, a railway junction, or a major bridge. Yet even in the villages the war's toll was incredibly high. A single bomb occasionally took out a whole house, random gunfire killed dozens, and sometimes a burning plane crashed into a settlement, turning it into a blazing hell. The retreating Red Army drafted men and grabbed food and horses, thus condemning the inhabitants to starvation. The conquering Germans combed back yards for chickens and geese. For people living in isolated rural communities, seeing any stranger was unnerving, but it was particularly frightening to encounter people who spoke a foreign language and who from now on would govern the land.

Someone had to bury the tens of thousands of Soviet soldiers whose corpses now littered woods and fields all over Byelorussia, so the farmers started digging graves. There was no time to bury each man properly; the dead were dumped into pits. Sometimes the farmers kept their IDs in case they ever summoned the courage to write to their families, but sometimes they were too frightened to do even that, thus condemning the dead soldiers to remain missing in action forever.

The Germans herded thousands of prisoners of war along the rural lanes. The coagulated blood on their bandages turned black, as did their soiled faces and even their tears when they saw children in the street. The Germans didn't give them any food, so the prisoners scavenged in the woods. Where POW columns had passed, even the bark from the trees had disappeared.

As difficult as life in the villages had become, however, conditions were much worse in the cities. After a few hours or days of atrocious German bombing, the Red Army would abandon a city. If the place had a power station, it had to be disabled; if it had a food depot, it had to be burned down; if it had a factory, it had to be destroyed. Most of this destruction was carried out by the army, but civilians were frequently ordered to help. Engineers were told to calculate the amount and placement of explosives, and workers had to assemble the charges and put them in the designated areas. This caused immense frustration. Not only were men and women destroying their workplaces, they were also destroying their future, as their city would now lose electricity, food, and manufacturing capacity.

The retreating troops smashed shop windows, telling onlookers to help themselves to whatever caught their eye. The citizens were not looting but were doing the *vozhd*'s will, since everything had to be destroyed or hidden so the Germans would get nothing. The problem was that those left behind had to share the "scorched earth" with the Germans.

If there was time, Party and government executives and sometimes their families were invited to leave a city together with the army. Ordinary people were strongly encouraged to leave as well, but nobody guaranteed them a seat on a truck, and they would be left to their own devices on the road. The majority refused to go, especially because German pilots coldly and determinedly attacked everything that streamed along the roads, whether it was a panzer column or a cart full of children.

Minsk was subjected to air strikes on the first day of the war. Seven days later, when the Germans finally entered the city, 80 percent of its buildings had already gone up in flames. Meanwhile, 200,000 of Minsk's 240,000 inhabitants still remained in the city, so at least three quarters of them had nowhere to live. Many of those who had fled a few days earlier had returned, having failed to catch up with the rapidly retreating Red Army. They found their neighborhoods annihilated, with sand and ashes where buildings and gardens had been. For some the shock was so profound that it shattered their psyches. "I kept talking to myself for several days," one survivor recalled.

A frenzy started. Marauders attacked the few surviving shops, going for anything and everything; hooligans roamed the streets, harassing, abusing, and plundering. After a week of lead hail, a human deluge now covered the ruins. Quite a few people expected the Germans to introduce law and order and maybe, eventually, even justice. The line was that "Germany is a cultured nation." But when the Germans marched in, things got far worse.

Every soldier needed a place to stay, every one hoped to find fresh food, and many demanded sex. In principle, looting and raping were unacceptable in Hitler's army. After all, licentiousness endangered discipline. However, in times of war all armies operate in a huge gray area between what is forbidden and what is accepted. When Budenny's First Cavalry Army soldiers had entered the same cities twenty years earlier, they had raped, killed, and looted with abandon. Hitler's troops were supposed to serve a higher purpose, but no leader and no ideology could prevent the soldiers of a victorious army from taking an interest in the material fruits of their efforts, particularly when their leader had said that Eastern Europe was populated by despicable Jews and subhuman Slavs.

When a soldier was billeted in a Soviet home, he exercised the natural privilege of a conqueror, helping himself to all of the conquered's possessions. When he raked through a household in search of food, his justification was that he was seeking sustenance for the Reich's war effort. When he took off his clothes in front of a Soviet woman, as often as not he didn't force her to comply with his wishes and therefore didn't regard the resulting sex as rape. He sometimes even rewarded her afterward with a gift, or at least temporary protection.

Soldiers in the invading army held diverse moral attitudes and values, and some shared meals with their hosts, played with their children, and taught them German. Sometimes friendship or even a true love affair developed. Many German officers were bothered by the notorious "Commissar Order" sent out by the Supreme Command of the Armed Forces, O.K.W., a few days before the war started; it said that all commissars captured by the army were to be shot as exemplars of Bolshevik ideology. Those who didn't particularly care about the Nazi cause thought that the order violated one of the army's basic rules: do not shoot prisoners of war as long as they don't attack you. Such people said that the order was dishonorable, and they refused to carry it out. But many didn't mind. As soon as a Wehrmacht soldier left his bivouac, he was expected to do his duty as a member of the Aryan occupying force, and that included hunting down Communists and Jews.

Very few Communist Party members were fanatical about Stalin's enterprise. Many, if not most, had joined the Party because they wanted to go to college or be assigned a better apartment or job, or both. Now they had to pay for their opportunism. Pursuing not just commissars but rank-and-file Communists as well, the Germans carried out a variety of "safety measures." Many bookshelves contained volumes by Lenin and Stalin that were required reading in schools and political awareness groups — indeed, obligatory for nearly every enterprise — and now people hastily buried them in their gardens, fearful of German retribution.

In bigger cities, "safety measures" meant more detentions. In Minsk the Germans created a prison camp for all males between the ages of eighteen and forty-five. Thirty thousand men found themselves contained in an open field less than a square mile wide on the outskirts of the city. Soon they were joined by 100,000 POWs captured in the Minsk pocket. Every day the SS combed the camp for Jews, commissars, and Soviet officials. Prisoners were shot in the hundreds every day.

For conscientious German officers, such camps were a sad place to visit. They held

> thousands of Russian prisoners in a closely packed space with no protection from the hot sun or the torrential showers of rain. They seemed apathetic, their faces without expression. Their uniforms, which were simple but practical, were dull and further emphasized the impression of a gray mass. Because of the danger of lice, their heads had been close-cropped. They seemed resigned to their fate, for since time immemorial, they had only known oppression. Whether it was the tsar, Stalin, or Hitler, oppression remained oppression. In a pouch, they carried their "iron ration": dry bread . . .

"Now and again," a sympathetic German observer added, "someone would start up one of those Russian songs that reveal a corner of the Russian soul."

But to speak of a generic Russian soul was to romanticize the situation — which hardly made sense, given the diverse nature of the prisoners' reactions. Some were planning to escape and had already discussed it with the people sitting next to them. Some were scared to death, some just languished, and some (including a remarkable number of the Red Army generals) had already volunteered to collaborate with the Germans. Probably the only thing that held all the prisoners together was physiology — they were constantly thirsty and begging the guards for water. As often as not, there was not enough water for everyone. The Germans had not been prepared to deal with such a large number of captives.

As everywhere across Europe, Jews suffered the most. Before the war almost half of Minsk's population was Jewish. On June 28, when the German army took the city, about 80,000 Jews remained there. A barbed-wire ghetto was installed for them, and yellow stars of David became obligatory. Jews were no longer allowed to use public transportation or even sidewalks. The executions started soon after.

It wasn't long before the Germans selected Minsk as the extermination site for German, Austrian, and Czech Jews as well as Soviet ones. Out of all the German Jews deported to Minsk, only ten survived. As for the Minsk Jews, only a few hundred survived.

The Germans would never have been able to conduct such a massive purge in a foreign land without help, and the local police force, consisting mainly of volunteers, stepped in. Yesterday's Stalinists now searched the area for Jews and Communists, delivered captives into German hands, and occasionally performed the executions. Some of these men, desperate to provide food and safety for their families, simply sought a secure job. Others, of course, were looking for vengeance for personal reasons or were just as racist as their new rulers.

▪ ▪ ▪

It is difficult to generalize about Soviet civilians' feelings toward the Germans. In one abandoned settlement a dog ran up to some German soldiers, wagging its tail and whimpering. The soldiers tried to stroke it, but it crawled under an armored vehicle. "Suddenly we heard a bang, an explosion," a witness wrote. "The vehicle was damaged but luckily failed to catch fire. We ran up to it and discovered that the dead dog had had an explosive charge concealed in the fur of its back, with a movable pin as detonator." Some villagers, though, offered the invaders an egg and a piece of dry bread as a welcome, and women came out of their houses with icons held to their chests, crying, "We are still Christians. Free us from Stalin, who destroyed our churches."

Churches could indeed open now. Candles were burning again, and people were praying in front of the shimmering icons. Some churches were so packed that "there was not a corner left in the cathedral in which people were not standing, sitting, or kneeling." However, many Germans, moved by the sight of such devotion, failed to realize that people streamed to churches not only because there were no Communists to stop them any longer, but also because they felt shattered by the devastation of war and sought shelter from its fiery breath.

Another mistake the Germans made was to lump together all the gentiles in the Soviet western borderland. Just as the German high command referred to the Red Army as "the Russians," ignoring its remarkable ethnic diversity, German soldiers and officers rarely distinguished between Russians and Ukrainians, Byelorussians and Poles. Ironically enough, by refusing to accept each group's individuality, they actually missed an opportunity for effective collaboration, arrogantly believing that they wouldn't need Soviet citizens to help them defeat Stalin.

Even if the Germans didn't need the locals on the front line, they still needed them to carry out numerous mundane tasks throughout the conquered regions. The Wehrmacht was unwilling and unable to manage daily life on the vast occupied territories — someone had to take care of plumbing, electricity, and roads, to clear the ruins and the rubble, to deliver pork and bread to the army units, to police the streets and report anti-German terrorist plots. Fear and material incentives alone couldn't buy loyalty, but the Germans were reluctant to offer anything else.

Many Ukrainians, Latvians, Lithuanians, and Estonians longed for nations of their own and were willing to pay the Germans handsomely for it, but their aspirations seemed absurd to the invaders, who had come to crush the very notion of independent statehood in that part of the world, not to encourage nationalist movements. The occupying force cracked down on idealistic activists, and soon OUN started staging terrorist acts against the Germans, just as it had against the Soviets and the Poles.

However, even the core of the Soviet Union, the Russians, did not stand united in the face of German occupation. The revolution, the civil war, and the recent purges had put a great divide between those who had benefited from them and those who had lost something important, be it family, religion, or property. The millions of have-nots would probably have exchanged their cooperation and obedience for lenient laws and the promise of administrative autonomy. But the Germans were not ready to barter with the people their Führer called subhuman.

▪ ▪ ▪

In Minsk women dug in the debris, looking for dead bodies or belongings. The sweetish, nauseating smell of decomposing flesh drifted up from the rubble. Against every hope, people searched for relatives, and contrary to every supposition, they sometimes found them at the other end of the city, sheltered by acquaintances, distant family members, or kind strangers.

Food became everyone's obsession. The people of Minsk started planting vegetables right in the rubble, but there was not much chance that the vegetables would ripen before the frost, and they had to be guarded relentlessly. The black market thrived, but few could afford it. Money had become worthless, so people resorted to barter or, if they had it, to gold.

The Brest Fortress

In 1941 the fortress at Brest was one hundred years old but still sturdy. Its citadel, built in a ring shape and appropriately called Rondo, stood on an island between the Moukhavets and Bug Rivers. Its thick two-story forts, pierced by narrow embrasures, were also barracks that could house as many as 12,000 men. The warehouses were in the basement, and below that were tunnels.

Built in the shape of a star, the bastions protected all sides of the citadel. Canals guarded the bastions, dividing the fortress into three islands — Central, Southern, and Western. When the new border of 1939 was created, however, it passed along the Bug River and split the fortress. The citadel was taken over by the Soviets, and the forts on the western bank fell into German hands.

Spacious and well tended, the citadel had grown into a bustling community. Acacias and lilacs lined the canals, oaks towered over the walls, and neat lawns framed the alleys. Children happily roamed around, and teenagers arranged dates at bridges and gates, thinking themselves very lucky to dwell in such an exciting place.

Their fathers, however, officers of General Korobkov's Fourth Army, didn't share their sentiments. Conveniently for Stalin's preemptive strike plan, the Brest fortress stood right on the border. For the *vozhd,* it was an excellent base for an offensive maneuver, since Red Army soldiers could be on German territory in no time. However, the servicemen themselves were of a different opinion. Watching German troops gather just across the Bug, they knew that a few enemy tanks at the gates would turn the place into a trap. Soldiers asked their commanders, "When will we be taken out of this mousetrap?" Many officers attempted to send their families away but were stopped by their superiors. In the early hours of June 22, their fate was sealed.

Singled out by the Luftwaffe from the first second of the strike, the citadel suffered most. Many officers and their families died there in the apartments, which instantly crumbled. Some rushed their wives and children out and hastily escorted them to a nearby basement, while others, already with their men, cursed and yelled and ordered the soldiers about, in reality having no idea what to do. Meanwhile the blasts multiplied as the German artillery across the Bug joined in. Lights went out and telephones went dead. Instinct told people to flee.

The majority did exactly that, racing toward the gates, stumbling over rubble and corpses, whipped by shrapnel and felled by blasts amid the screaming. Many men wore just their boxers. One commander tried to stop the stampede, pleading, "It's just a German provocation — let's wait!" but it was as impossible to check the flight as it would have been to charm a falling rock back onto a ledge.

At the gates the stampede turned into a crush. The first to reach an exit were either dead and thus obstructing the way for the living or frantically trying to get back into the fortress, realizing that it would be impossible to make their way through the German firewall. Those in the rear were still desperately pushing forward, unaware of the fact that they were now bound to stay: the mousetrap had snapped shut.

▪ ▪ ▪

Late in the morning of June 22, fourteen-year-old Valia Zenkina was walking along the bridge leading to the fortress, unable to control an anxious shiver. She and her mother were part of the group that had miraculously escaped from the fortress unscathed — only to be captured by the Germans at the gate. Now she was going back. A German officer in charge of the prisoners had ordered her to return to deliver an ultimatum. The fortress was to surrender immediately. "Your mother will stay here until you return," she was told.

Like the other refugees and the Germans themselves, Valia didn't know what was going on inside the fortress walls, but it was clear that the panic had subsided. Nobody was trying to push through the gates, and the fortress machine guns were firing, preventing the Germans from approaching the walls. Valia felt hollow. Her father had been killed at dawn, her mother was now a hostage, and she herself was walking through a battlefield to deliver an ultimatum to people she knew well.

For some reason, as she entered the gate the shooting stopped. She couldn't see anyone, so she kept on walking between the shattered walls. The smoke rising from the rubble made her eyes water. She didn't know where she was supposed to go, and after some hesitation she headed for the one place she recognized, the barracks of the 333rd Rifle Regiment. Suddenly somebody called to her. Going into the basement from which the voice had come, she found herself in front of her father's friends. Knowing that she had nothing to lose, she blurted out the Germans' message.

"They are asking too much," one of the men said. "We'll see who will be forced to surrender . . . And you, you go back, your mother is there."

"May I stay?" Valia asked.

The men looked at each other in desperation.

"Yes, you may."

▪ ▪ ▪

On the afternoon of June 22, the men from the 333rd Rifle Regiment had no idea who else was left in the fortress. Rifle shots and machine-gun bursts exploding here and there suggested that they were not alone, but that was all they knew, since German shelling prevented them from reaching other ramparts.

Corpses had become so numerous that they had ceased to be shocking, and people paid attention only to exceptional things, like the body of a child in a cradle. It seemed unlikely that he had been abandoned, and the bodies of his father and mother no doubt lay somewhere nearby under the debris.

Throughout the day the Germans kept the fortress under relentless fire. The old structure proved its worth, however; it was hard to penetrate and very difficult to destroy. Its tunnels, basements, and corridors gave shelter to the besieged. The Germans didn't want to suffer unnecessary losses in a labyrinth of ruins, where every corner and every hole promised an ambush, so they advanced very slowly. The defenders suspected that they could hold out for several days, but they couldn't be sure that the Red Army would return in time to save them. They could only guess what was happening outside the fortress walls.

For example, they didn't know that the German armor now rolling past the gates belonged to General Guderian, who had stormed the citadel several years earlier, in September 1939, when Brest still belonged to Poland. The Polish soldiers then locked in the fortress, like the Soviets there now, had lasted for a few days and even inflicted heavy casualties on the Germans, including Guderian's favorite adjutant. According to the Stalin-Hitler deal, Brest had gone to Moscow, so Guderian had politely shaken hands with the Soviet commanders, held a farewell parade, saluted the Nazi and hammer-and-sickle flags, and departed. Now he was back. However, this time his tanks passed by the fortress on a more important mission. But even Guderian had to admit that the fortress once again "held out with remarkable stubbornness."

A group of soldiers assembled around a radio, attempting to tune in to Moscow, but all they could find was a broadcast from Kiev, in Ukrainian. They understood that the government was reporting an all-out war, but there were no Ukrainians in the group, so they could make out only a few key words, like *Chervonna Armia,* Red Army. Even if they had picked up a Moscow broadcast, they would have had a hard time discerning the truth from the rambling, bragging reports.

▪ ▪ ▪

It is unclear to this day how many people remained inside the fortress on the morning of June 22, but it was probably about three and a half thousand. Their instinct told them to leave — in some cases, their superiors did too — but they couldn't. The commander of the Forty-fourth Regiment, Peter Gavrilov, had rushed into the fortress intending to lead his unit out, but he had been trapped there with his men and now was in charge of the defenses at one of the outer bastions.

With the exception of Gavrilov, all the commanders of the troops were self-appointed. On the morning of June 22, rank ceased to matter, and whoever was able to issue a sane order and persuade others to carry it out was acknowledged as a leader. Gradually death and retreat created six groups in the citadel. Isolated and desperate, they refused to allow the Germans in. The fortress, now a maze of ruins, resembled a medieval walled town more than ever. Notwithstanding the power of bombs and artillery shells, each structure had to be besieged by ground troops before it could be taken, and the squeamish Germans were unwilling to commit themselves to such costly missions.

A number of women and children, including family members as well as several orphaned boys adopted by Red Army units before the war, were also in the citadel. Believed to be soldiers and regarding themselves as such, the orphans were now employed as scouts, and crossed the canals to reconnoiter the German positions. Sometimes they were sent into battle, where they died like adults. Girls searched for spare ammunition among the debris, tended to the wounded, and occasionally took over at the machine guns when the men had been killed.

■ ■ ■

On June 24 the commanders finally decided to meet. Their groups had started losing ground, and it was past time to unite forces. The person to initiate the conversation was Commissar Efim Fomin, a thirty-two-year-old Jew. He had lost his parents as a young boy, spent his childhood in orphanages, and become a political officer at the age of twenty-one. His only exposure to war had been the brief Polish campaign, yet now, in the citadel, he stood out as a determined leader, zealously loyal to the fading cause. Worshipping Communism as others worshipped God, he introduced a gruesome ritual: after a man was killed, his Party or Komsomol card, often covered with blood, was to be delivered to Fomin.

The conference took place in the barracks at Brest Gate. Many faces were unfamiliar, as the fortress garrison was huge, but even people who had met before didn't recognize each other at first. Two days of fighting had covered them with a thick coat of dust, soot, and sweat. Their eyes were bloodshot and their faces worn out by exhaustion.

"I need to see everybody's ID," Fomin said. After examining their papers, he ordered the commanders to report. There was not much they could say that others didn't already know. The Germans were bombing and shelling the citadel methodically and relentlessly; the units were running out of ammunition, food, and water; and their only real hope was a Red Army rescue.

Nevertheless, Fomin chose to sound upbeat. Friendly forces would reach the fortress soon, he promised, and meanwhile a centralized command would ensure better use of resources. Though he was the obvious candidate for the job of leader, Fomin unexpectedly declined. He pointed to a veteran of two wars, Captain Ivan Zubachev, eleven years his senior. Nonetheless, he didn't exactly step aside. A firm believer in Party leadership, he stayed next to Zubachev and shared in the decision-making. There were only a few decisions they could make: all supplies had to be accounted for immediately and from then on distributed with thrift, all men had to be encouraged to fight until the last bullet was used, and every effort had to be made to reach the outside world.

They knew there was fighting at the outer bastions, and they attempted to get in touch with those units, but the messengers failed to make it through the German blockade. At night they dispatched sixteen men to break through the siege and reach the Fourth Army headquarters at Kobrin. They couldn't have imagined that by then, those headquarters had moved 100 miles east. The band never returned, and shortly after they left, the men at Brest heard shooting at the Moukhavets River.

That didn't necessarily mean that all sixteen men had been slaughtered. However, the episode had a grave impact on Fomin and Zubachev. In the morning they acknowledged that help would not be forthcoming and decided that the whole group had to try to break through the German ring. It was unclear where they would go next, but Fomin, at least, didn't care — for him, the main thing was to leave the stone grave. Lieutenant Anatoly Vinogradov was to lead 120 soldiers across the bridge over the Moukhavets, and if this spearhead succeeded, the rest of the men would follow.

At midnight on June 26, Vinogradov took his men to the bridge. Fomin and Zubachev could hear that they were met with stormy fire, which continued throughout the next several hours. Since no soldier returned, it was fair to assume that the Vinogradov group had been killed. Fomin and Zubachev knew they were trapped.

They continued with their rather purposeless resistance, which was becoming more problematic with each day, as ammunition waned, food supplies thinned, and thirst mounted. There was no water left in the citadel or in any other area of the fortress. Two rivers and a few canals were tantalizingly close, but the soldiers could not reach them because the gloating Germans held them under constant fire. Their thirst had become so intense that many now put moist sand in their mouths, although of course that just added to their suffering.

Someone suggested digging holes in the damp basements, but the soil yielded only meager amounts of polluted water. In the fort, where Major Gavrilov was in charge, they tried digging for water too, but the result was maddening. For a century the fort had served as a stable, and now the moisture from the ground was undrinkable even for people dying of thirst.

In one of the basements, famished women and children had discovered barrels containing sauerkraut and couldn't stop themselves from eating some. The soldiers hated going into the basement now, as they couldn't stand the voices of the children crying for water.

As if to mock their suffering, the fortress's ancient gardens, now pocked with ruins, contained an amazing display of roses. Their sweet scent contrasted sharply with the stench inside the citadel's walls.

The Germans had set up loudspeakers, and a steely voice incessantly rang through the air: "Russians, surrender. German command guarantees your lives. Moscow has already capitulated." Once an imaginative German put an armored vehicle on a rampart, carrying a red Soviet banner with the Nazi swastika smeared across it.

Finally Fomin and Zubachev decided that the women and children had to leave if they were going to survive. The army wards were told to go as well, but they flatly refused. Fomin didn't argue.

The families were arrested by the Germans at the gate. Valia Zenkina was part of that group. The last person to enter the fortress, she was one of the last to leave it too. Fomin and Zubachev were captured a few days later in the ruins of their rampart. Fomin was shot at Kholmsk Gate for the double sin of being a commissar and a Jew; Zubachev was sent to a concentration camp.

Major Peter Gavrilov remained in the Eastern Fort for thirty-two days, until July 23.

Stalin, July 1–2

On July 1, Stalin resumed his office hours in the Kremlin. Beria was a daily visitor, delivering alarming reports about soldiers, officers, and even generals who were surrendering to the Germans or deserting. Occasionally he mentioned an angry officer who had attacked his superiors or shot a police patrol. But the *vozhd* was remarkably unperturbed. All those acts of treason did not amount to a popular revolt or a coup. No army unit had staged a mutiny, and no general had tried to assassinate him.

He remained depressed and uncertain about the future, however. The country he ruled was immense, and if he was forced to, he could take the Red Army to the Urals or even farther, into Siberia, making it virtually impossible for Hitler to catch him. He had already ordered hundreds of factories and plants to move east, where the Luftwaffe would not be able to hit them. The eastern wilderness still didn't have enough cleared land to accommodate the arriving machinery, but there were millions of men and women, an inexhaustible labor resource, in the gulag.

One of Stalin's worst fears was that Hitler's ally, Japan, would now strike too. With each passing day, though, that looked less and less likely. The Japanese seemed to prefer the richer, warmer lands of Southeast Asia. If Stalin's eastern flank remained quiet, he could move troops from the Far East and Siberia to the west, where they were badly needed.

On July 2, Leeb made a powerful thrust in the Baltics and the Northwestern Front lost the strategic city of Pskov and began its retreat toward Leningrad. The Western Front had surrendered Byelorussia and was barely holding the defenses at the Dnieper, the last natural obstacle between Bock's Army Group Center and Moscow. The Southwestern Front, exhausted by futile counterstrikes, had disintegrated and was unable to protect Kiev. In ten days the Germans had advanced 300 miles east, and all three major cities of the Soviet Union were in peril.

The war maps in Stalin's study announced new challenges, some of them potentially catastrophic. The Germans and the Finns had crossed the border north of Leningrad and were fast approaching the city. Not only Finland but also Italy, Hungary, Romania, and Slovakia had sided with Germany and were now at war with the Soviet Union. Of the latter four, only Romania could be expected to support the Wehrmacht actively — but that was in a strategically crucial area, southern Ukraine. The Southern Front, safe from German ground troops until June 26, collapsed as soon as the German offensive in the Black Sea area began in earnest. That meant that the coastal areas of Ukraine, the gateway to the Crimea and Caucasus, were now vulnerable. At the Barents Sea coast, the Wehrmacht struck from Norway, aiming at the only significant Soviet city in the Arctic, Murmansk.

It seemed that without the Far Eastern army group, the USSR would not have enough resources to save its European core. Only now were a number of armies that had been intended for the preemptive strike reaching the Dnieper area to shield Moscow. The new defensive arc was about 300 miles long, and only about 175 miles of it were protected by rivers. This meant that at least 200,000 land mines would be needed to seal the gaps and keep the defenses relatively secure. There was no way the Red Army could produce that many in such a short time.

Other arms were in short supply too. Belatedly, Stalin had increased production of T-34 and KV tanks, which had proved to be the only kinds of panzers fit for battle. On July 1 he told a number of military plants to start making them right away, even if they had to create production lines from scratch.

Since his regular troops had been battered, he now placed high hopes on saboteurs and partisans attacking the German rear. They destroyed bridges, railroads, and highways and put mines where the Germans were likely to go. Very soon, though, it became clear that the Soviet antitank mines could not inflict serious damage. Normally it took a German tank crew no more than half an hour to repair their tanks after hitting one of the mines. As for time bombs, amazingly enough, the army didn't have any at all, and the veterans of the Spanish civil war, hastily dispatched to the occupied territories, started making them from cans.

Guerrilla warfare had traditionally figured prominently in Soviet military doctrine, and Soviet saboteurs had been trained all over the country, so they had experience with every kind of terrain. Arms had been stockpiled in secluded places. However, during the 1937 purge Stalin had decided that trained saboteurs and their weapons were a security risk, so the cadres had been shot and the arms depositories had been turned over to the army or destroyed altogether. Now the whole network had to be built anew.

Also, there was little hope for guerrilla warfare in western Ukraine and the Baltics, where many people had greeted the Germans as liberators. Even if they hadn't, they were still unwilling to assist the Soviets, who didn't look any better to them than the Nazis. That limited the "people's war" to Byelorussia, but the loyalist republic counted for just one third of the lost territories.

▪ ▪ ▪

There was, however, one area in which the Soviet Union was making good progress: diplomacy. Interestingly, success in that respect had cost Stalin nothing at all. Two Western democracies, the United States and Britain, had no other choice than to embrace him, reluctantly, as an ally.

The British prime minister, Winston Churchill, learned about the German invasion of the Soviet Union at eight o'clock in the morning of June 22. His private secretary had received the news four hours earlier, but as he was under firm instructions not to wake the prime minister for anything but an invasion of Britain, he waited. When Churchill was finally told, his only comment was "Tell the BBC. I will broadcast at nine tonight."

Churchill was one of the most principled opponents Communism had. Two decades earlier he had led an unsuccessful crusade for full-fledged military intervention in the Russian civil war to nip the Communist state in the bud. The political U-turn he was now forced to make demanded an explanation. He began preparing his speech at eleven in the morning and finished it only twenty minutes before airtime.

"No one has been a more consistent opponent of Communism than I have for the last twenty-five years," Churchill said.

> I will unsay no word that I have spoken about it. But all this fades away before the spectacle which is now unfolding. The past, with its crimes, its follies, and its tragedies, flashes away. I see the Russian soldiers standing on the threshold of their native land, guarding the fields which their fathers have tilled from time immemorial . . . I see advancing upon all this in hideous onslaught the Nazi war machine, with its clanking, heel-clicking, dandified Prussian officers, its crafty ex-

> perts fresh from the cowing and tying-down of a dozen countries . . . It follows, therefore, that we shall give whatever help we can to Russia and the Russian people . . . The Russian danger is, therefore, our danger, and the danger of the United States, just as the cause of any Russian fighting for his hearth and home is the cause of free men and free peoples in every quarter of the globe.

Twelve hours before Churchill's address, at noon Moscow time, the British chargé d'affaires insisted on being seen by Molotov's deputy, Vyshinsky. He said that he hadn't received any instructions from his government yet but he was sure that cooperation between Britain and the Soviet Union was now imminent. The embassy had already sent British women and children from Moscow to Iran via Baku. He said that he had heard the Soviet government was preparing to leave the capital too, and he expressed the hope that the British embassy staff would not be left behind. Vyshinsky indignantly denied the rumor and remained noncommittal in general, but he promised to monitor the progress of the train taking the British families to the Caucasus.

Pravda published parts of Churchill's speech, but there was no other immediate response from Moscow. Churchill found the silence at the top level "oppressive," but he thought that Stalin was being understandably "shy," given the two countries' unfortunate relationship. The Soviet ambassador to London, Ivan Maisky, a talented intellectual who had survived the purge of the diplomatic corps by mere luck, was equally disheartened. He kept meeting with British officials on his own, having been given absolutely no guidance from Moscow.

In Washington the Soviet ambassador, equally confused and nervous, met with the acting secretary of state, Sumner Welles, who announced that the government of the United States was ready to consider giving material assistance to the Soviet Union. The Soviet newspapers reported the meeting, but again there was no official reaction from the Kremlin.

Cooperation with the Americans and the British still looked risky to Stalin. He wasn't sure that the offers of help weren't a trap set up to punish him for having stabbed the West in the back two years earlier, when he had sided with Hitler. He decided not to rush into any partnership, particularly since there wasn't much that Britain or the United States could do to check the progress of the German juggernaut aiming at Moscow.

▪ ▪ ▪

The catastrophe was having an unexpected effect on Stalin. Everything in his previous career — his vengefulness, his brutality, his obvious paranoia and obsession with conspiracy theories — suggested that his response would be to start another grand purge, to punish the generals for the calamity and to persuade the people that the initial phase of the war had been lost because of treason within the ranks. Under torture, the senior officers arrested in June had already supplied Beria with plenty of evidence against every military leader in the country, and it would have been logical for Stalin to put that to use. In spite of Beria's prodding, however, he refused to purge the military, deciding instead to limit his vengeance to the Western Front command. This looked like an act of unbelievable lenience on his part, but nobody could be sure how long his newfound tolerance would last.

The first thing everyone looked for in newspapers was word from the front. However, Stalin didn't allow the editors to mention the fronts' names in print. The Germans knew nearly everything, right down to the names of the corps commanders they faced, yet Stalin stuck to the outmoded and absurd concept of total secrecy. Throughout his whole life he had been a keen reader, and he knew that, in principle, a newspaper report should start with both a date and a location to give it credibility and a sense of immediacy, so he told the censors that the newspapers were free to use the names of military districts that had been abolished before the war started.

Very upset, the editor of the well-regarded army newspaper *Red Star,* David Ortenberg, called Zhukov to say, "People will laugh at us."

"I agree," Zhukov said. He kept silent for a while and then made a decision: "All right. Put 'Army in the Field' instead."

The episode was revealing. Zhukov was gaining in popularity within military circles. Until late June he had been just another benefactor of the Great Purge, the fourth chief of general staff in four years, an upstart whose star could fall as rapidly as it had risen. His new popularity couldn't be explained by his strategic genius, since he had not demonstrated any thus far. His recent stint at the Southwestern Front, which he bragged about now, hadn't saved the day. To the contrary, the Southwestern's troops, exhausted by the counterattacks he had sanctioned, were now retreating rapidly, jeopardizing Kiev. As for the two arcs of defense around Moscow, they had yet to be tested. He kept boasting about the strength of his character and his outstanding willpower, but had it demanded much of either to order General Riabyshev and his Eighth Corps to embark on a suicidal mission prescribed by the *vozhd*? Or to tell Ortenberg to put "Army in the Field" instead of "Western Military District"? The current pariah of the Red Army, the recently arrested General Pavlov, had demonstrated very similar tendencies, as well as a readiness to send subordinates to death without batting an eyelash. In all likelihood, Zhukov's recent rise in popularity was due to one single thing: for some inexplicable reason, after June 22 he became the *vozhd*'s favorite.

On the eve of war Stalin had been treating Zhukov with deliberate coldness, excluding him from important meetings, preventing him from reading sensitive intelligence documents, and occasionally snapping at him angrily in public — all of which seemed to indicate that he regretted promoting Zhukov in January and was planning to purge him, as he had purged his other new appointees. Shortly after the start of the hostilities, however, Stalin's attitude changed. On the afternoon of June 22 he dispatched Zhukov to salvage the strongest army group in the country. Four days later, before the general could achieve anything there, the *vozhd* called him back to Moscow in the hope that he would repair the overall strategic damage. Now the *vozhd* had sent People's Commissar of Defense Timoshenko to the Dnieper area to command the Western Front troops, as if Timoshenko were an ordinary general, and kept Zhukov at his side.

Notwithstanding his general misanthropy and paranoia, Stalin was endowed with outstanding managerial skills, and in times of crisis he instinctively assessed people according to their true merits, not the inflated or deflated rank he had bestowed on them in more peaceful times. Now he was reducing Timoshenko to the role that best suited him — that of a regional military leader — and elevating Zhukov to de facto chief of the armed forces. Timoshenko was already a spent man, obviously incapable of leading the army, and it was clear that he would lose his position soon.

Even when Timoshenko was still in Moscow, it was Zhukov who was truly in charge of central command. He dominated the cramped and noisy conference rooms of the General Staff headquarters, where all the senior officers now assembled, their desks lined up along the walls, the telegraph personnel and even the typists placed next to them to expedite communications.

However, in early July, Zhukov didn't feel much better than Timoshenko, who had just been sent on an impossible mission in the west. Zhukov was stunningly self-centered and vain, but nobody could say that he didn't care. With frustration and anger, he realized that he was virtually powerless in his new position of authority. His proximity to the *vozhd* had gained him the respect of his peers but very little influence over the army in the field.

Day after day the Red Army suffered defeat, not just in Byelorussia, Ukraine, and the Baltics but in Moscow too, because of the ludicrous decision-making process that Stalin had molded. The fronts' headquarters reported to Zhukov, Zhukov talked to Timoshenko, and then Timoshenko and Zhukov went to the Kremlin to report to Stalin — but Stalin never came to the office before late afternoon, and sometimes not until eleven o'clock at night. Often twelve hours would pass before Zhukov was able to deal with a desperate report from the Berezina River or Moghilev. He expected the *vozhd* to ask, "Why are we always late?" but the question did not come up.

Instead the *vozhd* would make some shocking decision at random, utterly oblivious of the consequences. When the daredevil test pilots, for whom he had always had a soft spot, told him that they wanted to create their own elite regiments and go to the front immediately, he enthusiastically approved. "They will teach the rank-and-file pilots," he said contentedly. Apparently he didn't realize that the best Soviet test pilots would be dead within a few weeks, having wasted themselves in a fit of reckless patriotism, thus making things worse for the rest of the Red Air Force.

Most probably, in July 1941 every top military leader, even the dimwitted Budenny and Voroshilov, would have liked to talk some sense into Stalin. His blunders were too obvious, his behavior was too erratic, and his vision was too blurred. The army still didn't have a commander in chief, and the country still hadn't heard anything from the *vozhd* that would explain the catastrophe or promise hope. Everybody had to wait, and nobody dared to hurry him. But surely no one was as frustrated as Zhukov. The old guard had been broken by fear long ago, and he, the only newcomer in the military hierarchy, was the only person still capable of indignation, however deeply he suppressed it. But he had to keep his feelings to himself, and in this regard Chief of General Staff Army General Zhukov was the same as a private sitting in a shallow trench at the Berezina.

■ ■ ■

The war continued, and the cocoon of lies that Stalin had spun around himself finally burst. He had to face hard facts. The only asset that remained undamaged was his people's compliance. In every other way the system had failed. While the smashing defeats in Byelorussia and elsewhere had occurred too far away to be properly investigated and analyzed and could therefore be blamed on treasonous elements, almost everything Stalin encountered in Moscow spoke of a grave malaise — and shocking ineptitude.

With the front line barely 300 miles away, the high command bunker at Kirovskaya subway station was still unfinished. Many air-raid shelters throughout the capital appeared inadequate, and there was no time to build better ones. To camouflage the Moscow airfield, the city authorities had decided to cover the surrounding streets with dark slag, but traffic had turned it into a thick dust that now clouded the air and made driving virtually impossible. The air defense still couldn't tell a Soviet plane from a German one and on a number of occasions shot down friendly aircraft.

Alarmed and angry, Stalin attended a war game for the senior officers of Moscow Air Defense. Predictably, and in sharp contrast to the chaos unfolding in the sky, the staff exercises ended in total victory for the Red falcons. Stalin liked war games to end that way, but this time he looked disappointed. He paced the room silently, contemplating the map of Moscow. Finally he lit his pipe and said quietly, "I don't know — maybe it's the way it should be . . ."

It was unclear what he meant, but obviously his statement reflected painful and totally uncharacteristic soul-searching. Then, just as pensively, he added, "We are short of smart people . . . Not enough of them, no . . ."

Some officials present at the game were hurt, but others were frightened. An aircraft designer named Alexander Yakovlev decided to use the *vozhd's* fleeting regret to save the life of a friend, Deputy People's Commissar of Aviation Industry Vassily Balandin, who had been arrested with other air force leaders on the eve of the war. "He can't be an enemy," Yakovlev said. "And we need him."

Stalin was familiar with Balandin's case. While Zhukov reported on the progress of German tanks, Beria briefed him on the interrogations of the arrested generals and captains of military industry.

"Yes, he has been in jail for forty days and he still hasn't admitted anything," Stalin replied. "Could well be that he is all right . . . Could be . . . Such things happen . . ."

The next day, Balandin, with a shaved head and a thin face, showed up in his old office.

A few days later, Stalin asked Yakovlev, "Well, how is he doing?"

"Working as if nothing had happened, Comrade Stalin."

"Yes, his arrest was a mistake." Realizing that such errors required an explanation and curious to try out his new, lenient approach, Stalin told the shocked Yakovlev, "Well, that's how it works. A capable man, he works well, other people are envious and decide to ruin him . . . Particularly if he is a bold person and says what he thinks . . . That makes people angry, and then the distrustful *chekists* that are worthless and feed on rumor and gossip get him."

Wary of casting too much doubt on Beria's *chekists,* however, the *vozhd* abruptly began discussing Beria's predecessor, Yezhov, this time feigning sincere indignation: "Yezhov was nothing but scum! A nasty character. You call him at the office — they say he has left for the

Central Committee. You call the Central Committee — they say he is in his office. Then you send people to his home and they find him there blind drunk, spread out on the bed. He destroyed many innocent people. We had him shot for that."

No Kremlin insider could be persuaded that 35,000 Red Army officers and a few million civilians had perished just because the head of the police had been a drunk. But remarks like this hinted that Stalin felt a certain remorse for the Great Purge. More proof of the *vozhd*'s somewhat repentant mood was his decision not to punish anyone except Pavlov and his generals for the continuing catastrophe in the west. Yet more evidence was the role he assigned to Zhukov.

Usually compliant and deferential in the presence of the *vozhd,* like everyone else, Zhukov still occasionally displayed stubbornness and rebelliousness, qualities long missed in the Kremlin. But instead of ruining him, these characteristics actually elevated him in Stalin's eyes. Chief among his episodes of defiance were his prodding in June about the impending German attack, his call to the *vozhd* at 3:45 in the morning on June 22 announcing the attack, and the explosive confrontation in the General Staff conference room on June 29 after the fall of Minsk. True, Stalin had reduced him to angry tears that day, but before that Zhukov had basically told the *vozhd* and other top leaders, Beria included, to mind their own business. For the first time in more than a decade, Stalin seemed ready to tolerate another strong male near him.

However, the *vozhd* left no doubt about his determination to squelch any real dissent or punish any criminal weakness. From the abyss of depression, on June 28, he sanctioned a directive concerning "traitors who had fled abroad," a euphemism for the hundreds of thousands of soldiers captured by the Germans. Not only were they all to be purged once they were repatriated; their families were to be punished for their disloyalty as well.

In the imperial Russian army, the death of an officer had to be reported to the czar. Stalin didn't want to be bothered with anyone whose rank was lower than general, but even the list of generals was becoming longer every day. By July 1 two top military commanders who had been present at the May 24 meeting in his Kremlin study had shot themselves, Commissar Vashugin and Commander of the Western Front Air Force Kopets. A number of generals had died on the battlefield, including Major General Semen Kondrusev, commander of the Twenty-second Corps, who was killed on June 24 on the southwestern front, and Major General Vladimir Borisov, commander of the Twenty-first Corps, who had been killed on the western front, leaving no grave nor even an exact date of death. The same was true of Major General Fedor Budanov, Major General Alexander Garnov, Major General Vassily Evdokimov, and Major General Alexander Zhurba.

Another list was much more worrisome to the *vozhd,* who was still vacillating between purge and lenience. Quite a few Red Army generals were now reported missing in action, and he couldn't be sure whether they had actually surrendered to the Germans. Among the suspected traitors were his emissary at the Western Front, Marshal Kulik, and Pavlov's deputy, General Boldin, both of whom had disappeared with the Tenth Army at Belostok.

General Boldin, Tenth Army, Western Front

In the first days of July, General Ivan Boldin was already 175 miles east of Belostok, in the woods near Minsk. A lucky star had delivered him from the pocket and led him through the Byelorussian forests unharmed. Yet if he could, he would gladly have forgotten the events of the previous ten days altogether.

He had flown to Belostok on the afternoon of June 22 to lead the Tenth Army out of the pocket. On the way his plane was attacked by a Messerschmitt, and shortly after it landed and he and his staff had disembarked, a Junker hit the plane with a bomb and it exploded. This was a sign of things to come.

The commander of the Tenth Army, Golubev, whom Boldin met shortly afterward, looked totally crushed. He said that the army had disintegrated and in all likelihood would not be able to leave Belostok. Later that night Pavlov called and cheerfully sent Boldin on an insane assignment to counterattack with the forces of the Sixth and Eleventh Mechanized Corps and the Thirty-sixth Cavalry Division.

The Eleventh Corps didn't answer Boldin's calls. The officers sent to locate them were never heard from again. The Thirty-sixth Cavalry Division had been severely hit by a Luftwaffe raid and was totally crippled. The Sixth Corps, sent into combat on its own, couldn't do much except temporarily halt the German advance, and the troops soon perished, together with their commander, General Khatskelevich. On June 27, General Boldin found himself on the run.

He walked east with a group of soldiers and officers from the Sixth Mechanized Corps and the Sixth Cavalry Corps. Occasionally they crossed the path of German tanks, and several times they were discovered by the Luftwaffe. However, there were too few of them to warrant German pursuit — just fifty men in all.

The scouts wore civilian attire and sneaked into villages to get food, sporadically stealing cans and crackers from German cars as well. The Germans were surprisingly careless. At one point they stopped Boldin's men, decided that they were local peasants, and let them go.

The closer the men got to Minsk, which was already occupied by the Germans, the more disbanded Red Army units they met. Nobody knew how many people were hiding in the Minsk woods. A colonel they came across estimated that about 20,000 were there.

Once Boldin saw two generals sitting on a felled log, involved in a quiet conversation. When they recognized the deputy commander of the front, they displayed neither zeal nor fear. "What are you doing here?" they asked with mild surprise.

"I wanted to see how you're commanding the troops," Boldin replied venomously.

"I think no one would've faired any better," one of the generals said.

Indignant, Boldin decided not to pursue the matter. He announced that he was going to assemble all the troops in the woods and attack the Germans at Minsk. Refusing to comment on this plan's strategic virtues, the bolder general simply remarked that he would not participate in such a campaign. Boldin felt powerless in the face of such blatant insubordination and did not object. Instead he started organizing the retreating troops. To his frustration, he discovered each morning that many of those he had gathered the previous day had quietly fled during the night.

Some semblance of an attack did take place on July 1 and 2, but even Boldin admitted that it was ineffective. After the senseless battle he had only about 5,000 men left. German planes showered them with leaflets saying that Moscow had already been taken, and many soldiers believed this. Having lost all resolve, the general decided to abandon the fight for Byelorussia and marched his ragtag army east.

Stalin Speaks, July 3

Late at night on July 2, a Central Committee secretary, A. S. Shcherbakov, called David Ortenberg, the editor of *Red Star.* "How are you doing on tomorrow's issue?" he asked.

"Almost there," Ortenberg replied. "We'll be sending everything to the printer soon."

"Hold on to the front page," Shcherbakov said. "An important piece is on its way."

Ortenberg immediately knew that it was Stalin's speech. The *vozhd*'s ten-day silence was equally inexplicable to generals, privates, and housewives, and the nation had been eagerly awaiting word from him since June 22. Ortenberg, well schooled in the Kremlin's innuendoes, got the message right away. Without delay, he summoned all available correspondents and dispatched them to the airfields, air defense posts, barracks, draft offices, and hospitals to be present during the historic broadcast and report on people's reactions.

By five o'clock in the morning, Stalin still hadn't delivered his address. Like every other apparatchik in the capital, Ortenberg knew that the *vozhd* worked late, but five A.M. was late even for him.

At about that time the USSR's best newscaster, Yury Levitan, was standing in front of Lavrenty Beria and Stalin's chief bodyguard, Vlasik. Virtually everyone in the country was taken with Levitan's ringing, captivating, sometimes tragic, sometimes triumphant, opera-quality

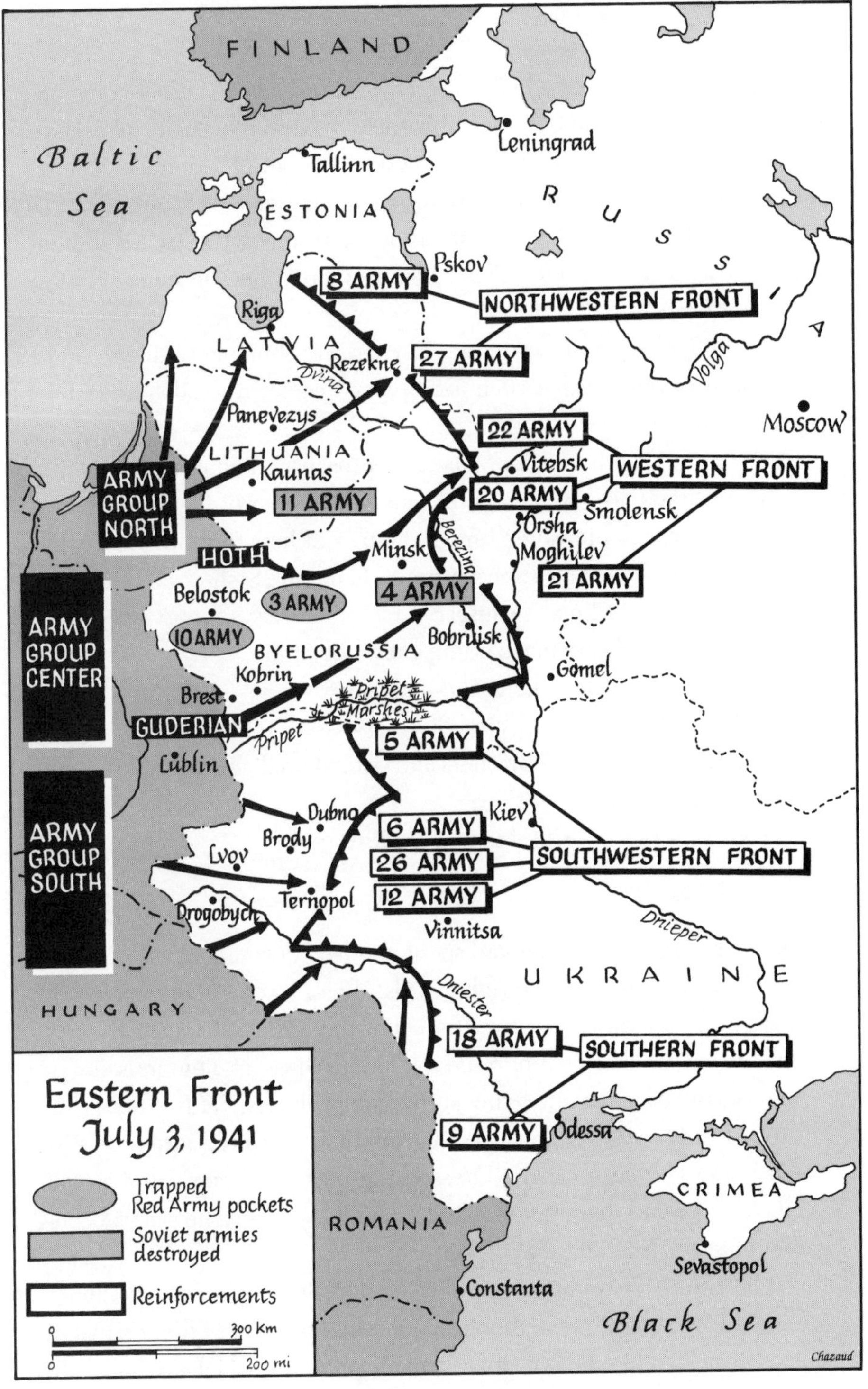

FINLAND
Leningrad
Baltic Sea
Tallinn
ESTONIA
RUSSIA
Pskov
8 ARMY
NORTHWESTERN FRONT
Riga
LATVIA
Rezekne
27 ARMY
Dvina
Volga
Moscow
Panevezys
22 ARMY
LITHUANIA
Vitebsk
WESTERN FRONT
ARMY GROUP NORTH
Kaunas
11 ARMY
20 ARMY
Smolensk
Orsha
HOTH
Minsk
Berezina
Moghilev
21 ARMY
ARMY GROUP CENTER
Belostok
3 ARMY
4 ARMY
10 ARMY
Bobruisk
BYELORUSSIA
Gomel
Kobrin
Brest
Pripet Marshes
GUDERIAN
Pripet
5 ARMY
Lublin
ARMY GROUP SOUTH
Dubno
Kiev
Brody
6 ARMY
Lvov
26 ARMY
SOUTHWESTERN FRONT
Ternopol
12 ARMY
Drogobych
Vinnitsa
Dnieper
UKRAINE
Dniester
HUNGARY
18 ARMY
SOUTHERN FRONT
Eastern Front July 3, 1941
9 ARMY
Odessa
Trapped Red Army pockets
CRIMEA
Soviet armies destroyed
ROMANIA
Sevastopol
Reinforcements
Constanta
300 Km
Black Sea
0
200 mi
Chazaud

baritone, and the *vozhd* had chosen to seek his advice before going on the air. Levitan's clothes — even his socks — were thoroughly checked, and he was issued one short instruction: "To all of Comrade Stalin's questions, answer yes or no, and don't ask him questions yourself."

Soon the newscaster was standing in front of the *vozhd*. Stalin seemed in a good mood. "*That's* how you look," he said benevolently. "I thought so."

In all likelihood this was a lie. Levitan was short and skinny, and it was hard to believe that such a rich voice came from such an unimpressive body.

"What do you think — how should I present?" Stalin asked.

To Levitan's dismay, he couldn't answer the question with a yes or a no, and so it took him some time to figure out how to reply. Finally he muttered shyly, "As you always present, Comrade Stalin."

"Where should I make pauses?"

"Where you always make them, Comrade Stalin."

Very much amused, the *vozhd* laughed.

At 6:30 A.M. he went on air — live.

"Comrades! Citizens! Brothers and sisters! Soldiers and sailors! I am addressing you, my friends!"

The country went still. Many wept with relief.

▪ ▪ ▪

Ten days earlier, Churchill had spent almost a dozen hours writing his speech, looking for just the right words. When Joseph Stalin finally addressed the nation on the twelfth day of the bloodiest war in Russia's long history, he merely rephrased the Party's internal memorandum of June 29, full of hollow bragging and vague promises. Yet for those who listened to his speech that morning, nothing mattered after the first four lines. The *vozhd* had addressed them as family for the first and only time, and to them that implied nothing less than a new social contract between him and the people.

The brand of Communism propagated by Stalin, a former seminary student from a small, xenophobic nation, was dogmatic in nature. Just as an esoteric cult has its own rituals and incantations, which are hollow to outsiders but supremely meaningful to the faithful, so the Soviet Union had its own language. A change in wording that was meaningless to non-believers looked overwhelmingly important to members of the group, as it seemed to be transporting them to an entirely different plane. That was exactly what occurred on the morning of July 3, when the Soviet people heard Stalin addressing them as "brothers and sisters."

A foreigner might easily have failed to notice this phrasing at all, and if he hadn't, he might have dismissed it as a cynical ploy used by a politician — a carrot instead of the more usual stick. In a way that was exactly what it was, but the very fact that they had finally been offered a carrot stunned the Soviet people. Stalin had been promising them better housing, better education, and better food for years; he had even been promising them democracy and freedom. However, he had never been on an equal footing with them, and the fact that this time he laid bare his humanity and mortality — he was their *brother* — meant more to them than all the previous promises combined. Even those who harbored no illusions about Stalin and his intentions — which were, after all, to save his skin and his regime — took the words seriously and interpreted them as a long-awaited sign of his weakness and perhaps eventual failure.

It is impossible to say how many free spirits opposed the regime, but all sources indicate that in July 1941 they were a minority. Most Soviet people took the *vozhd*'s calculated address for fatherly encouragement and the promise of a better life. They savored his calm, slightly muffled voice, the pronounced Georgian accent, the pause he made to pour some water into a glass (they heard how it splashed) as if they were witnessing a divine apparition.

In the speech, the *vozhd* announced that the "enemy's best divisions and aviation units have already been defeated and have found their graves on the battlefield" — but at the same time he admitted that the Germans had occupied Lithuania and parts of Latvia, Ukraine, and Byelorussia and that Murmansk, Orsha, Moghilev, Smolensk, Kiev, Odessa, and Sevastopol, among other cities, had suffered from enemy air strikes. Grossly understating the severity of the challenge, he acknowledged that "our motherland is being threatened by a serious danger." However, in a moment of bizarre hyperbole, he informed the Soviets that Hitler planned to restore the power of the czars.

Directly quoting from the June 29 Party memo, Stalin called for guerrilla warfare in the occupied territories and the destruction of all valuables there. He also suggested that those who could not be drafted because of old age or bad health should voluntarily join the militia headed for the front line. He thanked Churchill and the U.S. government for moral support and asked his people to close ranks around the Communist Party, which he modestly called "the party of Lenin and Stalin."

▪ ▪ ▪

The text of Stalin's speech reached *Red Star* an hour later, and at nine in the morning the first thousands of copies hit the street.

Zhukov eagerly listened to Stalin's speech in the hall outside his office, where the radio was. Throughout the previous thirty-six hours the *vozhd* had found no time to receive the chief of general staff, but that hardly seemed important now, as a new contract between the *vozhd* and the people had finally been signed.

Commissar Popel, Southwestern Front

On July 3, Commissar Popel and the soldiers of the maimed Eighth Corps who were still with him were unaware of Stalin's homily. The person who had sent them to almost sure death, Front Commissar Nikolai Vashugin, had shot himself, but Popel and his men knew nothing about that either. They hadn't been in touch with friendly forces for a week.

Vashugin had ordered them to take Dubno. Tired and angry, they did their best. The fight for Dubno was the worst they had ever seen. They fought on the streets, in cemeteries, in the fields, and in the woods. After a battle the branches of the trees around them were covered with bloody body parts. Popel's tanks were dark red, and water and sand couldn't wash the blood off the vehicles.

A few days later, battered and worn out, they were forced to withdraw. They hoped to join the main force of the Southwestern Front, but it wasn't long before they realized that they were stranded in a pocket.

On the night of July 2, when Stalin was still working on his speech, Popel found himself at the bottom of a wooded ravine. He was sitting on a large round glacial rock, shivering from the cold. He knew he had to remain watchful and could not allow himself the luxury of a nap, but he was incredibly tired after the difficult day. He wished he could stand up and walk around to drive the sleepiness away, but he couldn't — something was wrong with his right leg. He guessed it was the result of shell shock, when he had been buried under debris with General Riabyshev a week earlier.

The soldiers were restless as well — a thousand men talking in their sleep, fighting nightmares; the wounded moaning; the sentries calling to one another. The sentries were very busy that night, since more soldiers were constantly arriving alone and in groups. In the absence of a password (the retreating troops could have none, as they were from different units), the exchange — "Who is walking?" "Friendly forces." "What kind of friendly forces?" — was largely meaningless. If the Germans had bothered, they could have infiltrated Popel's troops by the dozen.

Popel didn't leave the rock until dawn. He was pondering his next move. They had no ammunition, no food, and almost no medicine. Water was scarce, and the little bog in the ravine stank and was probably full of germs. The only thing they had in abundance was weapons. The roads were studded with them, and each group of scouts brought back more than the unit could possibly carry.

By morning Popel had made up his mind. His decision demanded not compliance but commitment, so he convened a general meeting of the force. Having assembled his men, he told them that their consciences should be clean; they had taken Dubno, thus fulfilling the front headquarters' order. The unit, he emphasized, was fit for any mission. Now their task was to break through the German ring and reunite with the rest of the Red Army.

The reaction was unpleasant. Soldiers started asking what they were going to eat, which way they were supposed to walk, how they were going to fight the German tanks, and so on. Popel didn't have many answers. Instead he ordered the men to surrender all their food into a common fund. He suspected that some would hold on to their meager reserves, but there was nothing he could do about that. Now at least the wounded would each get a lump of sugar.

He also thought the unit needed a Party cell and resolutely created one on the spot. To improve morale, he suggested that volunteers could join the Party now. That was legitimate. A Party cell could authorize such a thing.

While they were discussing who was worthy of becoming a Communist, a German bomb hit the ravine. No one was hurt, but the explosion was so powerful that the fountain of dirt reached the tops of the trees. Exhausted and agitated, the soldiers panicked. Those among the wounded who knew they couldn't escape howled. Popel had to interrupt the meeting.

When the men finally reassembled, slightly ashamed of themselves, Popel decided to capitalize on their remorseful mood and said that the Party members had to give a special oath. No such thing existed in the Red Army, but the resourceful commissar now made the men repeat after him: "I swear to the Party, the people, and the motherland to be loyal to Lenin's banner. Never, under any circumstances, will I give up, panic, abandon my comrades, or give away military secrets, even under torture. I swear to do my duty as a Communist, as a citizen, as a soldier. I swear to avenge the deaths and misfortunes of my people, the rape of my land."

When the meeting adjourned, one question still remained: when should they leave the ravine? The scouts captured an SS soldier, who amazed them by having a black band with a white skull and crossbones on his sleeve. When interrogated, the German admitted that an SS division would soon start combing the woods for Red Army stragglers.

Still Popel lingered. The day was hot and muggy, and the night was even worse. Darkness fell early, and in the dusk fog arrived, covering the gorge with a thick veil. Even Popel felt uneasy.

In the morning he said to himself that the longer they stayed, the more likely it was that the SS troops would find them. There was no safe escape route. The ravine ran for just two miles, and then the rye fields opened up. Because the rye was exceptionally tall that summer, though, Popel decided to give it a try.

Before the troops left, they disabled the tanks, destroyed the documents or hid them in the ground, and entrusted the wounded to the care of a local farmer — in other words, abandoned them. Popel told his soldiers that nobody would be allowed to take his insignia off during the march, as that would be considered a sign of desertion; those who disobeyed would be court-martialed. Everyone knew what the court-martial would decide.

They didn't leave until the evening of July 4. Popel told them to march in a column and carry the red banner in front of them until they left the ravine and entered the rye fields. But the fog was so dense that night that the soldiers walking in the rear of the column could see neither the commissar nor his red banner. It took them three weeks to break through German lines and finally reunite with friendly forces.

EPILOGUE

When I was a boy, almost all the protagonists in this story were still alive. Marshal Zhukov was quietly writing his memoir in forced retirement, as were his rival, Marshal Rokossovsky, and less well known war veterans like Commissar Popel. The notable exception was, of course, Generalissimo Joseph Stalin, as he started calling himself after the war. Stalin died six years before I was born, yet one of our neighbors, a hard-drinking war veteran with the archetypal name of Uncle Vanya, kept a huge poster of the generalissimo in his shed. When asked why, Uncle Vanya would shrug his shoulders and answer in desperation, "To throw a *Stalin* away? I *can't.*"

We know now that the Soviet Union lost at least 8,668,400 Uncle Vanyas during World War II, about 600,000 of them during the first twenty days. Such casualties, virtually unprecedented in Russian history, should have doomed the nation. On July 3, the day Stalin spoke, the chief of the German General Staff, Franz Halder, wrote in his journal: "It is thus probably no overstatement to say that the Russian Campaign has been won in the space of two weeks." Hitler expected to take Moscow in August, and he had every reason to be optimistic. On July 3, only 300 miles separated General Guderian's tanks from the Kremlin. The Luftwaffe hit the Soviet capital on July 22. The German onslaught progressed robustly, and by the end of the year almost 40 percent of the country's population — 74,531,000 people — lived under German rule.

Even Stalin occasionally thought that the Soviet cause was irrevocably lost. Nonetheless, in July the Red Army managed to stall the German panzer armada at the Dnieper, at the arcs of defense designed by Zhukov in Stalin's study on June 26. In December the Germans were checked on the doorstep of Moscow. It was Hitler's first real defeat and Stalin's first real triumph. To his credit, and more or less true to the spirit of his July 3 "brothers and sisters" speech, the dictator hadn't abandoned the capital.

A year later, the monumental battle of Stalingrad took place. The Soviet victory there became a turning point of the war, and Hitler's army started to pull back. It is perhaps ironic that the greatest battle on the eastern front occurred in the City of Stalin, and the *vozhd* exploited the coincidence mercilessly. Tens of thousands of captured Germans were paraded through the streets of Moscow, displayed to the city's women and children as disarmed vermin, and cameramen obligingly took pictures of their total humiliation.

By the end of 1944, the Red Army had finally reached the prewar western border. In April 1945, Marshal Zhukov's armies entered Berlin.

Naturally, the months separating the horrendous defeats of June 1941 and the first victories over the Germans later that year were critical ones, and the turnaround requires some explanation. One factor, however prosaic, was the Russian climate. Hitler failed to finish the campaign before mud season arrived in September. The harsh winter that followed also worked in Stalin's favor.

Another factor was the vast size of the Soviet territory. Russia could afford to lose an immense amount of land without disappearing as a state. In principle, if worse came to worst, Stalin could take the heart of the resistance to Siberia and keep striking at the Germans from there until they collapsed under the burden of imperial overstretch. In the summer of 1941, he had already successfully transferred his industrial capability to the eastern wilderness, where the Luftwaffe could not reach it.

Yet another reason for Stalin's victory was Japan's decision not to go to war with the USSR. Japan could easily have attacked the Soviet Pacific coast, and if it had, the Soviet Union would have collapsed. But Japan chose to channel its energy toward Southeast Asia instead, thus allowing Stalin to transfer critically important military units from the Far East to the west by the end of 1941.

We are left to wonder why Hitler failed to capture Moscow in August, before mud season started, military production was moved, and the reinforcements from the Far East arrived. The answer is straightforward: he was delayed by the millions of Uncle Vanyas. On June 29 Halder wrote in his journal: "The Russians are fighting to the last man." Despite the appalling blunders of military leaders, Soviet soldiers rammed German planes in the air and jumped on top of German tanks with Molotov cocktails; they stayed in the trenches until they ran out of ammunition; they starved, they froze, they suffered — and eventually they won.

Ironically, perhaps, the seeds of Soviet victory grew out of the frustration and despair of the first weeks of war. Humiliation, pain, and anger forged the people's determination to fight. On August 24, 1941, Commissar Alexander Pankratov threw himself on the machine-gun embrasure of a German pillbox. Five other people did the same thing that year, and thirty-one more in 1942. If the beginning of the war had been less dramatic, the Soviets might never have fought their way to the heart of the Third Reich.

But this is not the end of our inquiry. The rank-and-file military could impede the Wehrmacht, but it couldn't defeat it without proper leadership. Stalin finally delivered that — but not until a few million had died. For this to happen, the country had to be transformed, starting with the corridors of power in Moscow.

Change did not come overnight. On July 14, near Leningrad, the undeniably stupid Voroshilov, with a pistol in his hand, led his infantrymen in a suicidal attack against German tanks. The imbecilic Budenny was appointed commander in chief of the Southwestern Strategic Sector, where his pathetic leadership led to the surrender of half of Ukraine, including Kiev, in a matter of weeks. But after a while some important lessons must have been learned, for in December the Germans were stopped. Eventually the Red Army became the Wehrmacht's toughest opponent.

So what changed after the summer of 1941?

The most crucial thing was that Stalin created a new military establishment based on meritocracy. None of the generals who commanded the victorious Soviet troops at a later stage of the war — Zhukov, Rokossovsky, Konev, Malinovsky, Vasilevsky, Meretskov — had been a part of Stalin's old guard. Two of them, in fact — Rokossovsky and Meretskov — had done time in the torture rooms, Meretskov as recently as the summer of 1941. A number of other leaders who had been arrested in June were freed and reinstalled in their high positions. True, most of the men arrested in the June purge had been shot, but this was the first time the *vozhd* had rehabilitated any state official at all.

Overall, Stalin took a more lenient stance toward the military. Except for the unfortunate Western Front command, no top officer was purged because of the June 22 debacle. Feeling that it was safer to take chances and even to make mistakes, no matter how costly, the generals began suggesting unorthodox strategic maneuvers. Initiative and ingenuity returned to the war room.

The role of the political officers — the notorious commissars — changed dramatically. They still shadowed every commander, but now they rarely dared to meddle in strategy, and the notion that a general was an independent leader, which had been undermined by the purges, was restored.

Forsaking his technological conservatism, Stalin promoted the introduction of innovative weapons. Although he had dumped the first Soviet rocket, the M-13, or *katiusha,* before the war, Stalin now ordered immediate testing. On July 14–15, 1941, the first M-13s reached the Western Front at Orsha, and they quickly proved to be a winning weapon.

The alliance with the anti-Nazi West that had looked so problematic in June had become a reality by August. Soon after, the Red Army started getting crucially needed American lend-lease supplies and equipment, delivered in most cases by heroic British northern convoys. The freighters, which were escorted by naval ships, traveled all the way around northern Europe to Soviet ports in the Arctic, and were frequently decimated by German U-boats and air strikes off Norway. Later in the war the Soviet Union, Britain, and the United States began coordinating their battle plans, thus ensuring the quick demise of Hitler's Germany. Between 1943 and 1945, Stalin held three summits with U.S. and British leaders — in Tehran, Yalta, and Potsdam. It was only in Potsdam that the wartime alliance began to crumble, with the cold war just around the corner.

Of course, Stalin wouldn't have been Stalin if his new lenience hadn't been accompanied by a carefully orchestrated terror. Between July and December 1941, 1,339,702 people were put on trial, and 67.4 percent of them were sent to the gulag — a nice injection of fresh slave labor. Those prisoners thought to be somewhat reformed were shipped in the opposite direction, to fight on the front. Often they were put in special kamikaze squads known as "penal battalions." Between 1942 and 1945, 975,000 men served in these squads. The dark lord of the police, Beria, zealously supplied the front line with special "holding units" that rounded up and often executed retreating soldiers. Though the nationwide witch-hunt had receded and fewer people were now arrested for nonexistent crimes, every dissent and every failure was still immediately punishable — often by death.

▪ ▪ ▪

Something has to be said about the fortunes of the characters in this narrative.

The heroic efforts of the men inside the Brest fortress were finally made public twenty years after the war, after Stalin's death. When the *vozhd* was still alive, the extraordinary feats at Brest were considered too compromising to the authorities, and official historiographers were busy praising the spectacular victories at Stalingrad and Berlin. In the mid-1960s, however, a group of people who had been lower-level officers in 1941 came to power. They had personally paid for Stalin's folly and were now willing to admit the drama of June 22 into the public record. The times demanded that the events in the Brest fortress be praised lavishly, and with much brouhaha it was awarded the title of "Hero Fortress" — which it certainly deserved.

The commander of another heroic unit, the Fourth Army, Korobkov, was shot along with Pavlov, while the commanders of the two other Western Front armies, the Third and the Tenth, Kuznetsov and Golubev, who had lost all their troops and failed to halt the German advance, were given new assignments. The Western Front's terminator, General Guderian, almost reached Moscow and in December 1941 established his headquarters at Tolstoy's manor house at Yasnaya Polyana.

The commander of the Southwestern Front, Kirponos, was killed in action in Ukraine. The valiant performance of the Eighth Mechanized Corps, so prominent in the abortive counterstrike in the southwest, caught Stalin's eye, and its leader, General Dmitry Riabyshev, was appointed commander of the Southern Front. However, he quickly lost this prestigious position because of the lack of any tangible success, and his performance remained undistinguished throughout the war.

Marshal Shaposhnikov, the classicist, was reappointed as the chief of general staff in July 1941. Two years later, because of poor health, he became the director of Voroshilov Military Academy, but he died shortly after. It must be noted that he was the only marshal who garnered universal posthumous praise from other military leaders.

Klim Voroshilov, the chief cavalryman, did nicely for himself. Although he kept saying that his short trip to the Western Front in June 1941 had cost "several years of his life," he lived to be eighty-eight. For seven of those years he held the fictional though highly notable post of chairman of the Presidium of the Supreme Soviet — in other words, president of the USSR.

Another cavalryman, Marshal Kulik, who had mysteriously disappeared in June 1941, popped up in Moscow in July. Together with what was left of the Tenth Army, he had spent weeks hiding in the woods. At that point Stalin didn't reward or punish him. However, nine years later, in 1950, in the midst of yet another purge, Kulik was accused of treason and shot.

Georgy Zhukov became *the* Soviet general of World War II. The two arcs of defense he designed in Stalin's study on June 26 did unexpectedly well, slowing the Wehrmacht's advance for several weeks, but they were just the first of his plans that worked. After a series of successful operations, he stormed Berlin in April 1945, and on June 24 he received a victory parade in Red Square. Ten months later, though, he was recalled from Germany and sent to Odessa to command a second-rate military district. In December 1947 he lost even that job. He packed a bag with some underwear, and while waiting to be arrested he had his first heart attack. Probably that's why Stalin showed mercy. The arrest never happened.

Right after Stalin's death, on March 5, 1953, the Politburo made Zhukov deputy minister of defense, and soon Khrushchev, now in power, invited him to join a conspiracy against Beria. With immense pleasure Zhukov walked into the Politburo room, grabbed Beria by the elbows, lifted him up, and announced, "You are under arrest!" Then, unable to control himself, he happily continued, "Now you've done it, scum! Wanted to have the whole country in jail, eh?"

Beria was proclaimed a foreign spy and executed, and Zhukov became the minister of defense. But Khrushchev was worried about his loyalty and sent him into permanent retirement in 1957. He even dismissed Zhukov from the Ministry of Defense Party organization, and until the end of his life the marshal belonged to the Party cell of an obscure machinery plant — a source of deep humiliation.

In modern Russia, Zhukov has become an icon, and an uninspiring statue of him on a horse stands at the entrance to Red Square. Some Russian monarchists say that his grandson, a Russian army officer, should be crowned czar to launch a new, patriotic dynasty. The descendants of soldiers whose lives Zhukov used as cheap currency during the war might have a different opinion, however.

The strangest fate of all befell Konstantin Rokossovsky, who had been through the torture rooms during the Great Purge. A brilliant strategist, he became one of Stalin's favorites during the war, second only to Zhukov, and in June 1945 he was in charge of Zhukov's victory parade. Stalin watched them both from the balcony of Lenin's tomb. Originally he had wanted to start the parade himself, but he failed to mount the horse during a secret nighttime rehearsal in the Kremlin, so he reluctantly delegated the honor to his young protégé.

Rokossovsky was Polish, and in 1949 the *vozhd* sent him to Warsaw as the minister of defense of Communist Poland. After Stalin's death, Poland rose from the dead, and in 1956 Polish students began to march in protest of Soviet rule. Rokossovsky angrily watched the members of the Polish Politburo calmly drink coffee and complain about the situation without doing anything to put a stop to it. "Finally," he recounted later, with ostentatious pride, "I went up to my office and summoned a tank corps to Warsaw."

That was a remarkable reaction in several respects. It was strange for a Pole to kill Poles for the sake of a foreign empire, and for a gulag survivor to kill gulag opponents for the sake of the gulag. Joseph Stalin had died three years earlier, but he would have been proud of his marshal, and even prouder that his Great Purge had had such a lasting effect. Nineteen years had passed since 1937, yet one of its victims was still so intimidated by the terror that he was willing to inflict it on others.

The episode is very telling. Dictatorial regimes can be terribly inefficient — they rarely feed their soldiers well, they're often slow in accepting new technology, they send army units to the wrong locations, they sometimes even fail to stop foreign commandos from dismantling their most vital communication systems. However, they do one thing extremely well: they deprive people of their will. Since the Enlightenment, mainstream Western thinkers have been arguing that an ineffective regime that destroys its people's initiative and brainwashes them instead of educating them will crumble in time of crisis. This may be true in some instances, but it was emphatically not the case in the Soviet Union in June 1941.

In Stalin's USSR, state brutality compensated for everything — impassable roads, broken tanks, ignorant generals, inadequate food. As long as the dictatorship was able to manipulate its own people, it *was* efficient and could sustain almost any challenge, despite a faltering economy and jamming guns. June 22 and the ten days that followed offer gruesome proof of that.

A NOTE ON SOURCES AND METHODOLOGY

NOTES

BIBLIOGRAPHY

A NOTE ON SOURCES AND METHODOLOGY

As of this writing, the flow of new archival material from Russia is slowing to a trickle. Overwhelmed by the damning historical evidence, apprehensive of the West and its scholars, and encouraged by the new, "enlightened" nationalism of President Vladimir Putin, the Russians are closing down their archives. The era of openness is coming to an end, and it is unlikely that we will learn anything important about the Russian perspective on World War II over the next several years, if not the next several decades. From time to time Russia lapses into a deep freeze; it happened after the period of liberal reforms of the 1860s and 1870s, and it is happening now.

It is therefore important to pause and reflect on the questions that still remain. What is missing from this narrative? My answer would be two things: the details of the preemptive strike plans of 1940–1941 and police reports detailing acts of insubordination and violence against authorities in the first days of war. We still know too little about Stalin's offensive plans, on the one hand, and the degree of popular resentment of his regime, on the other. It is to be hoped that future generations of historians (and readers) will have this information.

In any case, cross-examination of sources, both old and new, exasperates a conscientious writer. Marshal Rokossovsky contradicts Marshal Zhukov, both contradict Marshal Vasilevsky, and it is not possible to have the final verdict on the "truth" in the absence of the primary witness, Stalin, who left no memoir, no diary, no notebooks, and very few letters.

For obvious reasons, memoirists have a vested interest in painting the past in a certain way, and when treating this or that event, they almost invariably glorify themselves and badmouth others. The three marshals I've just mentioned, Rokossovsky, Zhukov, and Vasilevsky, disliked one another profoundly, almost like rival mob bosses in Chicago in the 1920s. During the prewar purge, Rokossovsky was imprisoned and Zhukov promoted. After 1941 things started looking brighter for Rokossovsky, and in time he almost equaled Zhukov, yet in 1945 Stalin stripped him of a critical command in the west and handed it to Zhukov. As a result, it was Zhukov, not Rokossovsky, who stormed Hitler's lair in Berlin in May 1945, thus bringing the war to an end and securing for himself a special place in history. However, a couple of years later, Stalin purged Zhukov and elevated Rokossovsky. Then, after Stalin's death, Zhukov again became the alpha male, only to be irrevocably purged by Khrushchev in 1957, with the gleeful support of his rival. The catalogue of their mutual offenses can be made much longer and more detailed, but I hope this suffices to show the difficulty of relying on Rokossovsky's memoir where Zhukov is concerned, and vice versa.

Again like Mafia dons, the marshals had their own clans — generals whom they promoted and who in turn (with the inevitable exception of a handful of opportunists) supported their cause. As a result, the memoirs of lesser generals are just as biased as the memoirs of their former bosses, and memoirs of colonels (of which there are only a few) are no better than the memoirs of the generals.

This isn't just a Soviet problem — memoirs as a whole are about as trustworthy as a bus station hustler, particularly when the writer is quoting dialogue he or she heard quite a while ago. Try to put on paper the words you said or heard only yesterday and you will end up recreating, if not inventing entirely. Take any particularly important day of your life — say, the day you proposed to your future spouse or announced your decision to leave the marriage. Can you be *sure* you actually said the words you now think you said?

Some authors tend to put more faith in documents than in records of human memory, but aren't we constantly reading newspaper reports about memos that have been doctored and those that contain blatant lies? Even if we know we can trust the person who composed a particular document — though how could we really? — how do we account for human error? When was the last time you disputed a credit card charge or a grocery bill?

All the difficulties endemic to historical research become more acute in the case of war, especially one as fierce as that on the eastern front in the summer of 1941. Let's imagine a typical Soviet army commander writing a report to his superiors after a day of heavy fighting. He knows that in the previous twenty-four hours his army has covered 30 miles, speedily retreating under German fire and losing a soldier every two seconds. He feels crushed physically and emotionally, just as his troops do. He has no idea where two thirds of his divisions are or what the front line now looks like. He cannot even be sure that the report he is writing will reach the headquarters, for he doesn't know whether headquarters has survived the atrocious day of bombing and shelling. Also he must send his report by messenger, and when a messenger is killed, the report is lost forever. If the document does reach his superiors, he wants it to sound appropriately brisk and businesslike, so in the absence of facts he applies hearsay, common sense, and — occasionally — straight-out lies, which he himself might prefer to describe as imagination or strategic instinct.

In all likelihood he is composing the report in his tent by the feeble glow of a flashlight. He hasn't slept for forty-eight hours and hasn't had a proper meal in days. The last time he heard from the troops fighting in the area was eight hours ago — and their commanders had prepared *their* reports six hours earlier. How in the world is he supposed to know whether the Germans or the Soviets control the town of Barrenhill right now? In the unlikely case that it is still controlled by the Soviets, which corps, the Twenty-first or the Forty-sixth? An air force pilot stopping by his tent believes he saw the Forty-sixth's tanks south of Barrenhill earlier in the day, but the chief of staff argues that the tanks must have belonged to the Twenty-first, as the commander of the Twenty-first mentioned Barrenhill in a scrambled radio exchange that afternoon. Now the army commander must be an arbiter of truth, and he has to pass judgment instantly. He thinks well of the commander of the Forty-sixth and doesn't like his chief of staff all that much, so he puts the Forty-sixth into the report.

That's the kind of document that finds its way into the archives. Now let's imagine this army commander thirty years later: a retired marshal, a national hero, a patriotic icon, a model of a successful military leader, for the Soviets did eventually defeat the Germans. He is writing his memoirs and has three concerns: censorship, his own sense of guilt, and his fading memory. The Party wants him to forget the painful retreat and focus on the victory, or at least on themes of heroic perseverance. But he still feels guilty, because millions of soldiers didn't survive the war and he did. As for memory, it can't be trusted. He obtains access to his report of June 1941 and happily quotes from it, pretending it provides his memoir with solid factual background. But deep in his heart he knows it doesn't. Regardless, his book is soon published, and historians weigh in, observing that his memoir supports his June 1941 report, and that the truth about who controlled the town of Barrenhill at 9 P.M. on June 24, 1941, has therefore been established. Obviously, nothing could be further from the truth.

Take one dramatic episode, the dismissal of Colonel General Dmitry Pavlov. Pavlov commanded the Western Front troops and did so poorly. Stalin needed a scapegoat for the crushing defeats, and as soon as Pavlov was arrested, his fate was sealed (he was shot). However, it is virtually impossible to establish *when* Pavlov actually surrendered his command.

Marshal Zhukov, who at that point was chief of general staff, says in his memoir that on the morning of June 30 Pavlov was still in the headquarters, and he even quotes from a lengthy telegraphic exchange with him ("Where is the cavalry corps?"). According to Zhukov, Pavlov was recalled to Moscow on the same day, June 30, and reached the capital on July 1 ("He had changed so much during the eight days of war that I hardly recognized him").

Yet the man who succeeded Pavlov on the Western Front, Marshal Andrei Yeremenko, insists in *his* memoir that Pavlov was dismissed on June 28 and claims to have delivered the news to him in person in the Western Front headquarters on June 29 ("The People's Commissar has ordered you to Moscow"). However, Yeremenko's first order to the troops is dated July 1, and it is highly unlikely that with the front crumbling he would have waited two full days before issuing a directive. So July 1 could be taken as the date of the change of command on the Western Front.

July 1 is also the date mentioned by the Fourth Army chief of staff, Leonid Sandalov. Another memoir, by Semen Ivanov of the Thirteenth Army, also indicates, albeit vaguely, that Yeremenko reached the Western Front headquarters on July 1.

In a newly released archival document, the minutes of Pavlov's interrogation by the police on July 7, Pavlov says that he was arrested on July 4 in the town of Dovsk. He does not say when he was dismissed.

This is a typical case. This dramatic event was witnessed and remembered by many — Pavlov was the only top commander shot during the war — and yet we are left with three different dates, June 29, June 30, and July 1.

What does an author do in this situation? He assumes that July 1 was the date for a number of important, but not necessarily definitive, reasons. First, the person who succeeded Pavlov at the Western Front, Yeremenko, was a chronic liar, and a number of dubious claims in his memoirs have already been proven false, so June 29 as the date for Pavlov's dismissal is by definition problematic. Second, Zhukov, who says Pavlov was dismissed on June 30, was not a liar but wrote his memoir when he was old and occasionally got dates confused; there are several examples of this in his memoirs. Third, we can have some degree of confidence that the two documents quoted by Yeremenko (his order to the troops of July 1) and Zhukov (the minutes of his conversation with Pavlov on June 30) are authentic. In Soviet times, editors were paranoid about quoting correctly, so we can assume that they did check the originals — and both documents suggest July 1 as the date. Fourth, two minor witnesses, Sandalov and Ivanov, also mention July 1. Sandalov's memoir is very detailed and generally credible and definitely stands out in this respect; one starts suspecting that he anticipated his place in history and began carrying a notebook in his pocket, meticulously documenting his every interaction.

So if we cannot fully trust our sources, is there any chance at all of recovering the past — in this case, the story of the first ten days of war on the eastern front?

Despite the challenges, this is indeed what I hoped to accomplish, by following a number of simple rules. First, determine the biases of a source and filter it accordingly. Second, if possible, find the source's enemy — in other words, a document or a memoir written by someone holding an opposite viewpoint — and try to establish the golden mean. Third, examine an event from a variety of social perspectives — for example, from the viewpoint of a General Staff leader, an army commander, and a newspaper correspondent. Fourth, be realistic; if a memoir contains, say, five pages of uninterrupted dialogue, dump it. Fifth — and perhaps most important — delete if necessary, but never add.

▪ ▪ ▪

Geographical names are another serious methodological challenge for any author writing about Eastern Europe. Borders in that part of the world kept changing throughout the twentieth century, and each major territorial shift resulted in a linguistic cleansing — as cities changed hands, their names changed too. The capital of Ukraine, still known to Russians as Kiev, is Kyyiv to Ukrainians; Belostok, where General Golubev's Tenth Army perished in 1941, is now called Bialystok by the Poles who live there; and so on and so forth. As this is a story told from the Russian perspective of 1941, I chose to keep the Russian transliteration that was then common in most cases. No political statement or insult to current ethnic sensitivities is intended.

Another terminological trap is the distinction between "Soviet" and "Russian." Westerners tend to use the latter as more recognizable and constant ("The Russians are coming!"), but the former is more appropriate for this book. Russians certainly made up the ethnic core of the Soviet Union, but in 1941 internationalism was taken seriously in the USSR and the Party attempted to create a metanational entity, "the

Soviet people." In June 1941 no Red Army leader would have referred to his "Russian troops." The country's elite was multiethnic: Stalin was Georgian, Beria was Mingrelian. Of course, in the course of the war the *vozhd* vigorously started promoting Russian nationalism, and at the celebratory reception in 1945 he toasted not the Soviet but the Russian people. Yet in 1941 the concept of Sovietness was still firmly in place, and this is why I talk about Soviet troops and Soviet people.

NOTES

Several abbreviations are used in the notes:

Rokossovsky 2002:	K. K. Rokossovsky. *Soldatsky dolg.* Moscow: Olma-Press, 2002.
VIZh:	*Voenno-istorichesky zhurnal* [Military History Journal]
Vypiska:	"Vypiska iz zhurnalov zapisi litz, prinyatykh I. V. Stalinym" [I. V. Stalin's office log]. In *1941 god. Dokumenty.* Vols. 1 and 2. Moscow: Demokratiya, 1998.
Zhukov 1971:	G. K. Zhukov. *Vospominaniya i razmyshleniya.* Moscow: APN, 1971.
Zhukov 2002:	G. K. Zhukov. *Vospominaniya i razmyshleniya.* Vols. 1 and 2. Moscow: Olma-Press, 2002.

PAGE

PROLOGUE

1 retired uncharacteristically early: Vypiska 2: 300.
Reports of German plans: Georgy Kumanev, *Ryadom so Stalinym* (Smolensk: Rusich, 2001), p. 24.

2 At least ten German planes: "Iz soobshcheniya NKVD SSSR v TsK VKP(b) i SNK SSSR o narusheniyakh sovetskoi granitsy inostrannymi samoletami s 10 po 19 iunya 1941 g." In *1941,* 2: 396–97; L. G. Ivashov. "Ot 'yunkersa' 1941 goda k 'cessne' 1987-go." VIZh 6 (1990), pp. 45–46.
On June 13 they started: Zhukov 2002, 1: 257; *Georgy Zhukov* (Moscow: Novator, 1997), p. 119.
But in a few days: Zhukov 2002, 1: 258.

4 After much hesitation: Vypiska 2: 300; Kumanev, pp. 336–37, 474; Meretskov, pp. 209–12; Ortenberg, *Iiun,* p. 5; Ortenberg, *Stalin,* p. 22; Zakharov, pp. 261, 270; Kiselev and Ramanichev, p. 17.

At 8 P.M. : Zhukov 1971, p. 251; Zhukov 2002, 1: 260.

But when Timoshenko and Zhukov: Vypiska 2: 300. Zhukov says that Vatutin was also present at the meeting (Zhukov 2002, 1: 260–61), but Stalin's log doesn't mention him.

"Could this be": Zhukov 1971, pp. 251–52; Zhukov 2002, 1: 260–61.

Stalin then learned: Zhukov 2002, 1: 260. It is unclear what the first draft of the plan specifically said and whether it actually suggested launching a preemptive attack on Germany immediately. Its exact content has never been revealed.

5 The troops' commanders: Ibid.

Driving back: Zhukov 1971, pp. 253–54; Zhukov 2002, 1: 261–63.

But at 11 P.M. : Vypiska 2: 300.

Stalin and his generals: Zhukov 1971, p. 256.

Almost five hours after Stalin left: Zhukov 2002, 1: 264.

6 When Zhukov and Timoshenko reached the Kremlin: Zhukov 2002, 1: 264–65; Vypiska 2: 300; "Strategicheskiye," p. 21.

7 "What have we done": Werth, p. 127.

9 In the first three weeks: *K 50-letiu,* p. 32; Krivosheev, pp. vii, 83.

According to even the most conservative estimates: Krivosheev, pp. 84–85, 235.

10 The total figures for both civilian and military: Bullock, p. 987.

It is also known: *K 50-letiu,* p. 31.

13 The variety of new sources: "Zapiska narkoma oborony SSSR i nachalnika Genshtaba Krasnoi Armii v TsK VKP(b) I. V. Stalinu i V. M. Molotovu ob osnovakh strategicheskogo razvertyvania vooruzhennyh sil SSSR na zapade i na vostoke na 1940 i 1941 gody" [People's Commissar of Defense and Chief of General Staff's memo to I. V. Stalin and V. M. Molotov on the principles of the USSR's armed forces deployment in west and east in 1940 and 1941], not later than August 19, 1940, in *1941,* 1: 181–93; "Zapiska narkoma oborony SSSR i nachalnika Genshtaba Krasnoi Armii v TsK VKP(b) — I. V. Stalinu i V. M. Molotovu ob osnovakh razvertyvaniya vooruzhennyh sil Sovetskogo Soiuza na zapade i na vostoke na 1940 i 1941 gody" [People's Commissar of Defense and Chief of General Staff's memo to I. V. Stalin and V. M. Molotov on the principles of the USSR's armed forces deployment in west and east in 1940 and 1941], September 18, 1941, in *1941,* 1: 236–53; "Zapiska narkoma oborony SSSR i nachalnika Genshtaba Krasnoi Armii v TsK VKP(b) — I. V. Stalinu i V. M. Molotovu" [People's Commissar of Defense and Chief of General Staff's memo to I. V. Stalin and V. M. Molotov], not earlier than October 5, 1940, in *1941,* 1: 288–90; "Zapiska narkoma oborony SSSR i nachalnika Genshtaba Krasnoi Armii predsedateliu SNK SSSR I. V. Stalinu s soobrazheniyami po planu strategicheskogo razvertyvaniya vooruzhennyh sil Sovetskogo Soiuza na sluchai voiny s Germaniei i ee soiuznikami" [People's Commissar of Defense and Chief of General Staff's memo to the Chairman of the Council of People's Commissars I. V. Stalin, considering the plan for the strategic deployment of the armed forces of the Soviet Union in case of war with Germany and its allies], around May 15, 1941, in *1941,* 2: 215–20; "Direktiva narkoma oborony SSSR i nachalnika Genshtaba Krasnoi Armii komanduyushchemu voiskami ZAPOVO" [People's Commissar of Defense and Chief of General Staff's directive to the commander of the Western Military District], in *1941,* 2: 227–32; "Direktiva narkoma oborony SSSR i nachalnika Genshtaba Krasnoi Armii komanduyushchemu voiskami KOVO" [People's Commissar of Defense and Chief of General Staff's directive to the commander of the Kiev Military District], in

1941, 2: 233–38; "Direktiva narkoma oborony SSSR i nachalnika Genshtaba Krasnoi Armii komanduyushchemu voiskami Odesskogo voennogo okruga" [People's Commissar of Defense and Chief of General Staff's directive to the commander of the Odessa Military District], in *1941,* 2: 239–44; "Vystupleniye Generalnogo sekretarya TsK VKP(b) I. V. Stalina pered vypusknikami voennykh akademii RKKA v Kremle" [I. V. Stalin's talk to the Red Army military academies graduates in the Kremlin], May 5, 1941, in *1941,* 2: 159–62; "Iz direktivy nachalnika Glavpura A. S. Shcherbakova o sostoyanii voenno-politicheskoi propagandy" [Chief of the Red Army Propaganda Directorate A. S. Shcherbakov's directive on current military and political propaganda] in *1941,* 2: 301–2. The two meetings in Stalin's study in the Kremlin, on May 24 and June 21, downplayed or even omitted by Soviet historiography, now look overwhelmingly important as the landmarks of his preemptive strike planning.

16 General Andrei Vlasov's Russian Liberation Army: Medvedev, p. 775.
"who had direct connections": Reshin, VIZh 1 (1993): 31–32.
The list of generals like Bogdanov: Ibid., 35–36; VIZh 2 (1993): 10–13.

1. WAR GAME

22 In the early evening: Vypiska 1: 499–500.
Throughout the week: See the highly contradictory evidence from four participants: Yeremenko, *Pomni voinu,* pp. 128–29; Kazakov, pp. 50–57; Zakharov, pp. 192–202; Zhukov 1971, p. 199; Zhukov 2002, 1: 198–200; *Georgy Zhukov,* pp. 64–65.

25 Lenin didn't like what he saw: Malkov, pp. 108–9, 114–22.

26 The generals walked into Stalin's office: Vypiska 1: 500.
From a distance: Zhukov 1971, p. 306.
By Soviet standards: Ibid., p. 303.

27 That night the *vozhd:* Zhukov 2002, 1: 199–200.
Timoshenko's concluding remarks: "Iz zakliuchitelnoi rechi narkoma oborony SSSR Marshala Sovetskogo Soiuza S. K. Timoshenko na voennom soveshchanii 31 dekabria 1940 g.", in *1941,* 1: 470–75.
At 9:45 the generals left: Vypiska 1: 500.
When Georgy Zhukov was nine: Mirkina, p. 69.

28 Like every other child: Zhukov's biography is drawn from Zhukov 2002, 1: 11–189.

31 Nineteen thirty-seven: "O masshtabakh," p. 73.

32 Vassily Bliukher had been tortured: "O masshtabakh," p. 74; Bliukher, p. 83.

33 All over the country: Details of arrests and the subsequent detainment, torture, and exile are taken from Gorbatov, pp. 120–34.

34 Almost all the division commanders: Karpov, pp. 80–90; Zhukov 2002, 1: 144–58.

35 Zhukov returned from the Far East: Zhukov 2002, 1: 186–89; Karpov, pp. 162–63.

36 On January 3 the war game: Yeremenko, *Pomni voinu,* pp. 128–29; Zhukov 1971, p. 199; Zhukov 2002, 1: 199–200; *Georgy Zhukov,* pp. 64–65; Kazakov, pp. 50–57; Zakharov, pp. 239–50.
Iosif Vissarionovich Stalin: Stalin's biography can be found in Conquest, pp. 1–221; Amis, pp. 97–180; Montefiore, pp. 3–193. Numerous books explore Stalin's life; these three are the most notable among the recent ones.

41 "We will disrupt": "Gulag," p. 14 [Stalin's remarks at the Supreme Soviet session, August 25, 1938].

42 a collector of wristwatches: Kumanev, p. 448.

"Still, it's a pity": Allilueva, *Twenty,* pp. 153–54.

He turned into an avid reader: Allilueva, *Only,* pp. 389–90.

43 On August 19: The text of Stalin's speech is reproduced in Doroshenko, pp. 73–75. The speech itself was discovered in the Special Kremlin Archive in 1994 by T. S. Bushueva.

44 250,000 Polish soldiers and officers: Lebedeva, p. 282.

45 "to respect each other's": "Perepiska," pp. 18–21; Berezhkov, p. 47.

demanding from Hitler: Berezhkov, p. 50.

46 As for a formal reply: Ibid., p. 51.

The man with the glistening: *Voenny entsiklopedichesky slovar,* pp. 1485–86.

47 The man with the carefully trimmed: Kardashov, *Voroshilov,* pp. 141, 171–73, 227; Rubtsov, pp. 26–67; Mirkina, p. 55. Marshal Semen Timoshenko quoted in Kumanev, p. 310.

"104 and a half days": *Tainy i uroki . . . ,* p. 426.

The man with the grotesque: Kardashov, *Voroshilov,* pp. 141, 171–73, 227.

48 The stooping dwarf: "Grigory Ivanovich Kulik," pp. 18–20; Vannikov quoted in *Stalin and His Generals,* p. 153; Voronov quoted in ibid., p. 159.

The sick-looking man: Shaposhnikov, pp. 559–62; Vasilevsky, p. 107; Kazakov, p. 45.

49 The conference started badly: Again, the memoirs of the participants in the conference contradict each other significantly. See Yeremenko, *Pomni voinu,* pp. 128–29; Yeremenko, *V nachale voiny,* pp. 45–49; Zhukov 1971, pp. 200–202; Zhukov 2002, 1: 201–4; Kazakov, pp. 57–62.

53 the summer of 1942: Mikoyan quoted in Kumanev, p. 22.

In Mongolia: *Voenny entsiklopedichesky slovar,* p. 1561.

The difficult victory: Krivosheev, "Nakanune," pp. 43–44.

The cavalrymen were devoted: Kardashov, *Voroshilov,* pp. 141, 171–73, 227; Rubtsov, pp. 26–67.

54 the precious sabers and daggers: Alliueva, *Only,* pp. 401–2.

Few people knew: Curtis, p. 70.

Like a model: Chuev, p. 273; Vasilevsky quoted in Kumanev, p. 279.

55 "Well, now": Vasilevsky, p. 108.

Like many other young people: Ibid., pp. 98–99.

56 In the summer of 1940: "Zapiska narkoma oborony SSSR i nachalnika Genshtaba Krasnoi Armii v TsK VKP(b) I. V. Stalinu i V. M. Molotovu ob osnovakh strategicheskogo razvertyvania vooruzhennyh sil SSSR na zapade i na vostoke na 1940 i 1941 gody" [People's Commissar of Defense and Chief of General Staff's memo to I. V. Stalin and V. M. Molotov on the principles of the USSR's armed forces deployment in west and east in 1940 and 1941], not later than August 19, 1940, in *1941,* 1:185–86. See also the memoir by a General Staff officer, M. V. Zakharov, in Zakharov, p. 217.

Barely a month later: "Zapiska narkoma oborony SSSR i nachalnika Genshtaba Krasnoi Armii v TsK VKP(b) — I. V. Stalinu i V. M. Molotovu ob osnovakh razvertyvaniya vooruzhennyh sil Sovetskogo Soiuza na zapade i na vostoke na 1940 i 1941 gody" [People's Commissar of Defense and Chief of General Staff's memo to I. V. Stalin and V. M. Molotov on the principles of the USSR's armed forces deployment in west and east in 1940 and 1941], in *1941*, 1: 241; also Zakharov, p. 217.

57 Now the army was expected: "Zapiska narkoma oborony SSSR i nachalnika Genshtaba Krasnoi Armii v TsK VKP(b) — I. V. Stalinu i V. M. Molotovu" [People's Commissar of Defense and Chief of General Staff's memo to I. V. Stalin and V. M. Molotov], not earlier than October 5, 1940, in *1941*, 1: 289.
Now, on the evening of January 13: Yeremenko, *Pomni voinu*, pp. 128–29; Yeremenko, *V nachale voiny*, pp. 45–49; Zhukov 1971, pp. 200–202; Zhukov 2002, 1: 201–4; Kazakov, pp. 57–62.

2. ON THE EVE

59 Stalin's military appointments: Zakharov, p. 221.
60 The situation was unacceptable: Zhukov 2002, 1: 206–29.
Soviet representatives: "Komandirovka," pp. 4–11.
Throughout the spring Soviet spies: In his memoir, Zhukov insisted that he had not been getting the spy reports at all (*Georgy Zhukov*, p. 116). But many spy reports did find their way to his desk, like "Soobshchenie NKGB SSSR Narkomu Oborony SSSR Timoshenko s preprovozhdeniem agenturnyh soobshchenii iz Berlina," in *1941*, 2: 25–27.
"You will be told": Zhukov 2002, 1: 255.
On April 16: "Neuslyshannye," p. 7.
62 Numerically, the Red Army: Zhukov 2002, 1: 212–13; Krivosheev, "Nakanune," p. 42.
Sometimes the weaponmakers: Zhukov 2002, 1: 208.
The Soviet Union had many more: Ericson, p. 98; Zhukov 2002, 1: 213–14; Krivosheev, "Voina," p. 36; Popel, p. 471; Beshanov, pp. 76–106.
63 Still, the new generation: Vannikov, pp. 79–80.
64 When the people's commissar: Ibid., p. 80.
Another revolutionary weapon: Zhukov 2002, 1: 215.
In general, Soviet artillery: Ibid., 1: 214–15; Krivosheev, "Voina," p. 36.
Aircraft fascinated the dictator: Zhukov 2002, 1: 219–22; Krivosheev, "Nakanune," p. 37.
65 Conservatism ruled: Zhukov 2002, 1: 220–21.
The average pilot: "Vypiska iz reshenii Politburo TsK VKP(b)" [Abstracts from the Politburo decree], May 10, 1941, in *1941*, 2: 191.
The aircraft, runways, and hangars: Zhukov 2002, 1: 221. The decision to camouflage the aircraft wasn't taken until June 19: "Postanovleniye SNK SSSR i TsK VKP(b)," "O maskiruyushchei okraske samoletov, vzletno-posadochnyh polos, palatok i aerodromnyh sooruzhenii, June 19, 1941," in *1941*, 2: 387.
Before the war began: "Vypiski iz protokola resheniya Politburo TsK VKP(b)" [Abstracts from the Politburo decree], April 9, 1941, in *1941*, 2: 54–55.
Roads in Byelorussia and Ukraine: Zhukov 2002, 1: 216–19.
Radio transmitters remained scarce: Ibid., 218–19.
66 a Goebbels propaganda film: Kazakov, p. 71.
70 percent of the current commanders: Ramanichev, p. 3.
"I cannot read the map": Maltsev, pp. 22–23.
Inspection of the Red Army's: "Zapiska S. K. Timoshenko i G. I. Kulika I. V. Stalinu" [Timoshenko and Kulik's memo to Stalin], June 19, 1941, in *1941*, 2: 393.

66 Zhukov found it particularly ominous: Shaptalov, pp. 52–54.
67 Once a commissar asked a soldier: Maltsev, p. 19.
68 To Zhukov's consternation: Zhukov 2002, 1: 202, 232–35.
Stalin ordered the construction: Ibid., 220–21.
Equally vulnerable: Vasilevsky, pp. 112–13.
69 Marshal Shaposhnikov: Biriuzov quoted in *Stalin and His Generals,* p. 239.
Worse, the placement of Soviet troops: Zhukov 2002, 1: 202.
70 Also, Hitler had told Molotov: "Telegramma Narkoma inostrannyh del SSSR V. M. Molotova Generalnomu sekretariu TsK VKP(b) I. V. Stalinu iz Berlina" [Molotov's cable to Stalin dispatched from Berlin], November 13, 1940, in *1941,* 1: 368.
On July 23, 1940: "Iz razvedsvodki upravleniya pogranvoisk NKVD USSR o voennykh meropriyatiyah Germanii i kontsentratsii germanskih voisk v pogranpolose SSSR, July 25, 1940," in *1941,* 1: 131.
supported their forecast: "Zapiska NKVD SSSR I. V. Stalinu i V. M. Molotovu o voennyh prigotovleniyah Germanii," July 1940, in *1941,* 1: 143.
In October they promised: "Soobshcheniye NKVD SSSR narkomu oborony SSSR S. K. Timoshenko," October 1940, in *1941,* 1: 328.
In December they said: "Soobshchenie "Meteora" iz Berlina ot 29 dekabria 1940 g.," in *1941,* 1: 466.
How was that misleading data: "Spravka o vstreche 'Zakhara' s 'Korsikantsem' i 'Starshinoi,'" April 11, 1941, in *1941,* 2: 60–61.
On April 3, the prime minister: Churchill, *The Grand Alliance,* p. 358.
71 Stalin was equally suspicious: Erickson, pp. 73–76.
72 "See how many of them": Simonov, *Glazami,* pp. 332–33, quoting Admiral I. S. Isakov.
At a conference: This probably took place around April 9. See "Vypiski iz protokola resheniya Politburo TsK VKP(b)" [Abstracts from the Politburo decree], April 9, 1941, in *1941,* 2: 54–55.
"Of course we will continue": Simonov, *Glazami,* pp. 339–40, quoting Admiral I. S. Isakov.
73 In the past, at parties: Khrushchev, 1: 287–89.
Before coming to Moscow: Kershaw, p. 364.
74 When they met: Zhukov 2002, 1: 237–38.
That conversation took place: "Beseda Generalnogo sekretarya TsK VKP(b) I. V. Stalina s ministrom inostrannyh del Yaponii I. Matsuoka" [Minutes of I. V. Stalin's talk with the Japanese foreign minister Matsuoka], April 12, 1941, in *1941,* 2: 71–74.
75 He was so elated: Werth, p. 121; Goebbels, p. 315.
On May 5, Stalin appointed: "Protokol plenuma TsK VKP(b)" [Party Central Committee plenum minutes], May 5, 1941, in *1941,* 2: 155.
76 "Is German army invincible?": "Vystupleniye Generalnogo sekretarya TsK VKP(b) I. V. Stalina pered vypusknikami voennykh akademii RKKA v Kremle" [I. V. Stalin's talk to the Red Army military academies graduates in the Kremlin], May 5, 1941, in *1941,* 2: 159–62.
"Let me introduce a correction": "Sovremennaya armiya," p. 30.
77 He was unable to read maps: Konev, p. 580.
It was a fifteen-page memo: Danilov, p. 139.
the document suggested striking: "Zapiska narkoma oborony SSSR i nachalnika Genshtaba Krasnoi Armii predsedateliu SNK SSSR I. V. Stalinu s so-

obrazheniyami po planu strategicheskogo razvertyvaniya vooruzhennyh sil Sovetskogo Soiuza na sluchai voiny s Germaniei i ee soiuznikami" [People's Commissar of Defense and Chief of General Staff's memo to the Chairman of the Council of People's Commissars, I. V. Stalin, considering the plan for the strategic deployment of the armed forces of the Soviet Union in case of war with Germany and its allies], around May 15, 1941, in *1941,* 2: 215–20. In a 1965 interview, Zhukov said Stalin hadn't approved the plan and even got angry at the generals' initiative (Shaptalov, p. 35), but in all likelihood this comment, made in hindsight, was intended as yet another criticism of Stalin — a popular activity in the early 1960s.

80 In all likelihood, he had been unnerved: Speer, pp. 174–76; Churchill, *The Grand Alliance,* p. 48; Bullock, pp. 713–14.

"supernatural powers": Speer, p. 176.

Since Stalin had always subscribed: Bullock, p. 714.

Reinforcing his suspicions: "Spravka vneshnei razvedki NKGB SSSR, May 22, 1941," in *1941,* 2: 248–49.

A few times Stalin had hinted: Zhukov 2002, 1: 230, 260.

81 He notified his defense industry: "Iz protokola soveshchaniya zamestitelei narkoma aviatsionnoi promyshlennosti ot 16 iunia 1941 g.," in *1941,* 2: 378; "Vypiska iz dispetcherskogo otdela narkomata aviatsionnoi promyshlennosti SSSR 'Dinamika proizvodstva samoletov,'" in *1941,* 2: 490–91.

Five armies started secretly moving: Vasilevsky, p. 119; Zakharov, p. 259.

The armies were to be in position: Zakharov, pp. 259–61.

Two more armies: Vasilevsky, p. 119; Zhukov 2002, 1: 241; Shtemenko, p. 26; Ivanov, *The Initial,* p. 181.

The move was to remain top-secret: Bobylev, "Tochku," p. 51.

By May 20, Timoshenko: "Direktiva narkoma oborony SSSR i nachalnika Genshtaba Krasnoi Armii komanduyushchemu voiskami ZAPOVO," in *1941,* 2: 227–32; "Direktiva narkoma oborony SSSR i nachalnika Genshtaba Krasnoi Armii komanduyushchemu voiskami KOVO," in *1941,* 2: 233–38; "Direktiva narkoma oborony SSSR i nachalnika Genshtaba Krasnoi Armii komanduyushchemu voiskami Odesskogo voennogo okruga," in *1941,* 2: 239–44.

The Western Military District: "Direktiva narkoma oborony SSSR i nachalnika Genshtaba Krasnoi Armii komanduyushchemu voiskami ZAPOVO," in *1941,* 2: 228.

The Kiev Military District: "Direktiva narkoma oborony SSSR i nachalnika Genshtaba Krasnoi Armii komanduyushchemu voiskami KOVO," in *1941,* 2: 234.

The Odessa Military District: "Direktiva narkoma oborony SSSR i nachalnika Genshtaba Krasnoi Armii komanduyushchemu voiskami Odesskogo voennogo okruga," in *1941,* 2: 240.

82 800,000 reservists were quietly drafted: Vasilevsky, p. 119; Bobylev, "Tochku," p. 51.

All military schools: Zakharov, p. 262.

The seven armies were expected: "Zapiska VRID nachalnika mobupravleniya Genshtaba Krasnoi Armii nachalniku operativnogo upravleniya Genshtaba Krasnoi Armii," not later than May 20, 1941, in *1941,* 2: 244–48.

The frontier military districts: Zakharov, p. 263; Bobylev, "Tochku," p. 51.

The commanders of those districts: Zhukov 2002, 1: 241–44.

Three million servicemen: Ibid., 242.

True to form: Vypiska 2: 144–45.

83 Around the same time he started: "Dokladnaya zapiska NKGB SSSR v TsK VKP(b), May 16, 1941," in *1941*, 2: 221–23; Montefiore, p. 334.
"with minimal losses": Volkogonov, p. 369.
When Chief of General Staff Marshal Yegorov: Pavlenko, p. 101.
84 As early as April 24: Nevezhin, p. 125.
"keep propagating socialism": Meltiukhov, p. 97.
In the beginning of June: "Iz direktivy nachalnika Glavpura A. S. Shcherbakova o sostoyanii voenno-politicheskoi propagandy," in *1941*, 2: 301–2.
"war is the time": Meltiukhov, p. 95.
By June 20: Ibid., p. 99.
85 "totally fantastic": "Oproverzheniye TASS," in *1941*, 2: 178–79.
People flying: Kazakov, p. 64.
"Shtern has proved": Kuznetsov, "Krutye povoroty," p. 79.
Shtern was arrested: Reshin, p. 18; "O masshtabakh," VIZh 5 (1993): 62; Medvedev, p. 473.
Among the latter: Vannikov, p. 85.
86 Yet on June 15: N. D. Yakovlev, pp. 55–59.
"Zeus": "Soobshcheniye 'Zevsa' iz Sofii ot 14 maya 1941 g.," in *1941*, 2: 198–99.
87 "Dora": "Soobshcheniye 'Dory' iz Zuriha ot 19 maya 1941 g.," in *1941*, 2: 224.
"Extern": "Zapiska 'Arkadiya' s preprovozhdeniem agenturnogo istochnika 'Extern' o voennykh prigotovleniyakh Germanii," in *1941*, 2: 225.
"ABC": "Soobshchenie Eshchenko iz Bukharesta ot 28 maya 1941 g.," in *1941*, 2: 271.
"Mars": "Soobshcheniye "Marsa" iz Budapeshta ot 23 maya 1941 g.," in *1941*, 2: 252.
"Ramzai": "Agenturnoye soobshcheniye 'Ramzaia' is Tokyo," in *1941*, 2: 252.
"Maybe we should tell": quoted in Karpov, p. 211.
A few months earlier: Fediuninsky quoted in *Stalin and His Generals*, p. 241.
More important, German planes: "Iz soobshcheniya NKVD SSSR v TsK VKP(b) i SNK SSSR o narusheniyakh sovetskoi granitsy inostrannymi samoletami s 10 po 19 iunya 1941 g.," in *1941*, 2: 396–97; Ivashov, pp. 45–46.
Even the servile and opportunistic Beria: "Neuslyshannye," pp. 9–15.
88 "Hitler and his generals": Zhukov's draft quoted in *1941*, 1: 500.
The British had evacuated Crete: Churchill, p. 301.
London suspected: Ibid., pp. 57, 321–32.
The sole British success: Ibid., pp. 305–20.
89 On June 7 he told: Kuznetsov, *Kursom k pobede*, p. 466.
If the *vozhd*'s wavering: Zhukov 2002, 1: 244–50.
At the end of May: *Georgy Zhukov*, pp. 68–69; Zhukov 2002, 1: 230.
90 "Please do not worry": *Georgy Zhukov*, p. 114; Zhukov 2002, 1: 250.
91 Kremlin insiders: Amis, p. 197; Conquest, p. 176.
In mid-June, German diplomats: "Iz zapiski narkoma gosbezopasnosti SSSR I. V. Stalinu, V. M. Molotovu i L. P. Beriya o massovom otezde iz SSSR sotrudnikov germanskogo posolstva i chlenov ikh semei, i ob unichtozhenii arkhivov posolstva, June 18, 1941," in *1941*, 2: 384–85.
Soviet trains continued to take strategic raw materials: "Zapiska A. I. Mikoyana v SNK SSSR i TsK VKP(b) — I. V. Stalinu, June 16, 1941," in *1941*, 2: 367–74.
On June 13: Zhukov 2002, 1: 257; *Georgy Zhukov*, p. 119.
For two days: Vypiska 2: 299.
92 The next day, June 14: "Soobshcheniye TASS," in *1941*, 2: 361.

92 Judging by Stalin's schedule: Vypiska 2: 298–99.
As soon as they had a chance: Zhukov 1971, pp. 249–50; Zhukov 2002, 1: 257–59.
Concerned about the safety: "Postanovleniye SNK SSSR i TsK VKP(b) "O maskiruyushchei okraske samoletov, vzletno-posadochnyh polos, palatok i aerodromnyh sooruzhenii, June 19, 1941," in *1941,* 2: 387; "Prikaz Komissara Oborony Soiuza SSSR, June 19, 1941," in *1941,* 2: 392–93.
Exasperated and tired: Goebbels's diary entry for June 21, 1941, in Goebbels, p. 420.
93 On Thursday, June 19: Vypiska 2: 300.
His old colleague Mikoyan: Mikoyan quoted in Kumanev, p. 24.
He called General Ivan Tiulenev: Tiulenev, p. 140.
However, he did not call: Vypiska 2: 300.
The first measure he took: Simonov, *100 sutok voiny,* p. 5.
The second step: Berezhkov, p. 55; Erickson, pp. 103–4.
The night was sultry: Chadaev quoted in Kumanev, p. 474.
Vorontsov had arrived: Kuznetsov, *Nakanune,* p. 355.
94 The meeting lasted for seventy minutes: Vypiska 2: 300; Kuznetsov quoted in Kumanev, pp. 336–37; Meretskov, pp. 209–12; Ortenberg, *Iiun,* p. 5; Ortenberg, *Stalin,* p. 22; Zakharov, pp. 261, 270; Kiselev and Ramanichev, p. 17; Chadaev quoted in Kumanev, p. 474.
95 At 8 P.M., while the meeting: Zhukov 1971, p. 251; Zhukov 2002, 1: 260.
When the generals walked in: Vypiska 2: 300. Zhukov says, Vatutin was also present at the meeting (Zhukov 2002, 1: 260–61), but Stalin's log doesn't mention him.
His concerns were obvious: Zhukov 1971, pp. 251–52; Zhukov 2002, 1: 260–61.
96 To his immense displeasure: Zhukov 2002, 1: 260.
a photograph of the young Stalin: Kuznetsov, *Nakanune,* p. 370.
Poskrebyshev tried to figure out: Chadaev quoted in Kumanev, pp. 474–75.
At ten o'clock the storm came: Kuznetsov, *Nakanune,* p. 355.
Zhukov and Timoshenko were dismissed: Vypiska 2: 300.
97 When the car stopped: Zhukov 1971, pp. 253–54; Zhukov 2002, 1: 261–63.
By then many officers: Ortenberg, *Stalin,* p. 23.
As for Stalin, he spent just forty minutes: Vypiska 2: 300.
Earlier that night Molotov: Erickson, pp. 103–4.
The situation was dire: Vypiska 2: 300.
At about midnight: Bagramian, *Zapiski,* p. 55.
At 0:30 A.M., Zhukov called Stalin: Zhukov 2002, 1: 263.

3. THE ATTACK

98 Discreetly and effectively blockaded: Zhukov 1971, p. 256.
As Zhukov and Timoshenko had predicted: Gorkov, p. 17.
No, Timoshenko responded: Nekrich, p. 203.
99 "Never mind": Boldin, pp. 64–65.
On the night of June 21: Ibid.
100 That same night: Sandalov, *Na moskovskom,* pp. 71–74.
101 The evening of June 21: Azarov, pp. 12–17; Rybalko, pp. 63–66; Kuznetsov, *Nakanune,* pp. 357–64; Kuznetsov quoted in Kumanev, p. 337; Eroshenko, pp. 6–

7; Zhukov 2002, 1: 264; Borisov, pp. 32–33. In his memoir, Borisov says that the person who didn't believe Oktiabrsky's report was not Kuznetsov but Zhukov.
104 The war first reached people: Kudelin, in *Geroi Bresta,* p. 109; Korovchenko, in ibid., p. 112.
105 "lead hail": Kudelin, in ibid., pp. 109–11.
Boys climbed the trees: Marlen Robeichikov, in Alexievich.
pitch-black plumes of thick smoke: Sisin, in *Geroi Bresta,* p. 78.
Parents hastily escorting their children: Zinaida Prikhodko, in Alexievich.
some people felt: Sisin, in *Geroi Bresta,* p. 78.
A border guard: Sisin, in ibid., p. 77.
Another soldier, trapped: Sachkovskaya, in ibid., p. 102.
like a flock of rooks: Sisin, in ibid., p. 78.
The Fourth Army headquarters: Sandalov, VIZh 12 (1988): 15; Sandalov, *Na moskovskom,* pp. 74–77.
106 Right before the Junkers: Boldin, p. 65; Irinarkhov, p. 243.
107 "No actions": Boldin, p. 65.
At six A.M.: Starinov, pp. 167–68.
108 The bulk of the Fourth Army: Sandalov, VIZh 12 (1988): 16–18.
The streets of Brest: Usherov, in *Geroi Bresta,* p. 90.
The railway station: Grechneva, in *Geroi Bresta,* p. 240.
At five o'clock: Sandalov, VIZh 12 (1988): 17, 19; Beshanov, p. 244.
Six-year-old Lenia Bobkov: Bobkov, in *Geroi Bresta,* pp. 186–89.
110 "We should order": Zhukov 2002, 1: 264–66; Vypiska 2: 300; "Strategicheskiye," p. 21.
After Zhukov and Timoshenko left: Ponomarenko quoted in Kumanev, pp. 109–40.
111 By the time Zhukov: Zhukov 2002, 1: 266.
The worst news: Kurochkin, pp. 192, 197; Tersky, pp. 227–32.
113 "What's the location": Tiulenev, pp. 141–42.
the generals decided to call: Zhukov 2002, 1: 267. Zhukov says that Stalin saw them at 9 A.M., but Stalin's log proves that they didn't meet with him until 2 P.M. (Vypiska 2: 300–301).
Stalin said: Zhukov 2002, 1: 267.
114 One person followed another: Vypiska 2: 300–301.
Shortly after eleven o'clock: "Vystupleniye po radio zamestitelya predsedatelya SNK i narkoma inostrannykh del SSSR V. M. Molotova," in *1941,* 2: 434–36. The opening line of the address actually read, "Citizens and citizenesses" — a Communist nod to gender equality, hard to render in English.
Fighting his stutter: Skrjabina, p. 4.
115 When the brief broadcast: Ibid.
A Moscow student: Khokhlova quoted in Noggle, p. 117.
116 In the Far East: Karlo Stajner quoted in Applebaum, p. 412.
In western Ukraine: Pyskir, pp. 13–14.
"You sounded too nervous": Chadaev quoted in Kumanev, p. 477.
The only general: "Vypiska," 2: 300–301.
Concerned about the developments: Ponomarenko quoted in Kumanev, pp. 141–42.
117 It was 2 P.M.: Vypiska 2: 301.
Sullenly he read: Zhukov 2002, 1: 267–68.
118 That augured: Ibid.

118 "Our front commanders": Ibid.; "Strategicheskiye," p. 24; Vypiska 2: 301. Zhukov says in his memoir that Stalin just called him, and he doesn't mention the second interview in the Kremlin. Also, the timing he gives is wrong when compared to Stalin's office log.
At 4 P.M.: Vypiska 2: 301.
They did not know: Chadaev quoted in Kumanev, pp. 478–79.
The cable announcing nationwide mobilization: Gorkov, p. 18.
119 The only institution: "Moskovskie chekisty," pp. 10–110.
At 4:25 P.M.: Vypiska 2: 301.
He had already spent: Ibid.
An Italian author: Malaparte, pp. 19, 27–28.
120 Still undecided in November: Goebbels, p. 174.
"Everything else": Ibid., p. 414.
121 "with one stroke": Ibid.
Hitler was not sure: Fugate, pp. 61–98; Cooper, pp. 203; Bullock, pp. 697–714.
122 "severest famine": Ibid., p. 697.
On June 21: Goebbels, p. 423.
The first reports: Halder, pp. 412–13.
"Tactical surprise": Ibid., pp. 410–11.
Over 3.2 million German soldiers: Erickson, p. 98.
123 If the three German army commanders: Brett-Smith, pp. 15–76.
124 "we hardly bothered": von Luck, p. 53.
The only piece of weaponry: Ibid., p. 54.
Pavlov faced off: Brett-Smith, pp. 66–70.
Heinz Guderian: Ibid., pp. 243–44.
Hermann Hoth: Ibid., pp. 273.
The Soviets had: Semidetko, p. 23.
126 Among the strongest units: Beshanov, p. 186.
To make things worse: Sandalov, VIZh 10 (1988): 7.
one thing was clear: Semidetko, p. 27.
The commander of the Western Front's air force: Meretskov, *Na sluzhbe,* pp. 204–5; Vypiska 2: 144–45; Simonov, *100 sutok voiny,* p. 344.
127 "in a trembling voice": Irinarkhov, p. 210.
Hoth soon captured: Halder, p. 413.
That was the worst choice: Boldin, pp. 65–66.
128 He dismissed the last visitor: Vypiska 2: 301.
In the evening he decided: "Direktiva voennym sovetam Severo-zapadnogo, Zapadnogo, Yugo-zapadnogo i Yuzhnogo frontov," in *1941,* 2: 439–40.
It was sent: Ibid., p. 440.

4. DISASTER IN THE WEST

130 In the Baltics: Krivoshein, p. 40.
Finally it dawned: Irinarkhov, pp. 211, 273.
132 One more of Stalin's representatives: Ponomarenko quoted in Kumanev, pp. 144–45.
He was still struggling: Sandalov, VIZh 2 (1989): 36–37.
133 Pavlov's order: Sandalov, *Na moskovskom,* p. 91.
he didn't know where: Ibid., p. 79.
"as if they had gone": Ibid.

133 "Do you want them": Ibid., p. 91.
"destroy the enemy": Sandalov, VIZh 2 (1989): 37.
During the night Korobkov grew restless: Sandalov, VIZh 6 (1989): 8.
134 The roads that Korobkov traveled: Sandalov, *Na moskovskom,* pp. 93–94.
Grim, exhausted, and scared: Evgenia Bilkevich, Taisa Nasvetnikova, Natalia Grigoryeva, Emma Levina, Lidia Melnikova, Elena Kravchenko, Rimma Pozniakova, in Alexievich.
135 At 6 A.M. the Fourth Army: Sandalov, VIZh 6 (1989): 9–11; Sandalov, *Na moskovskom,* pp. 94–98.
136 He asked Pavlov: My account of Korobkov's movements between June 23 and June 26 is taken from Sandalov, *Na moskovskom,* pp. 95–119.
140 The counteroffensives ordered by Stalin: Irinarkhov, p. 274.
The bombing of Minsk: Ibid., p. 291.
As early as June 22: Zaitsev, pp. 24–25.
On June 24 the evacuation of Minsk began: Ponomarenko quoted in Kumanev, pp. 144–46.
In the morning: Ekaterina Korotaeva, Inna Levkevich, in Alexievich.
141 On the night of June 25: Irinarkhov, p. 318.
Borovoi had no communications center: Ibid., p. 279.
142 Marshal Shaposhnikov finally warned Moscow: Ibid., pp. 298–99.
Timoshenko magnanimously allowed: Zhukov 2002, 1: 284.
The Thirteenth Army: Ivanov, *Shtab,* pp. 40–48.
When Filatov reached Molodechno: Ibid., pp. 48–53; Irinarkhov, pp. 293–94.
143 The area was in total disarray: Ivanov, *Shtab,* pp. 53–61.
144 Filatov decided to ignore: Ibid., p. 56.
When Filatov and his officers: Ibid., pp. 61; Sandalov, *Na moskovskom,* p. 118; Irinarkhov, pp. 318–19.
Coincidentally, June 26 was the day: *Na linii fronta,* p. 42.
145 As a result, Pavlov and his officers: Irinarkhov, p. 319.
Some Red Army units: Beshanov, pp. 266–67.
146 Filatov felt helpless: Ivanov, *Shtab,* pp. 64–68.
From his new headquarters: Ibid., 73–74.
According to Stalin's preemptive strike plan: "Zapiska narkoma oborony SSSR i nachalnika Genshtaba Krasnoi Armii predsedateliu SNK SSSR I. V. Stalinu s soobrazheniyami po planu strategicheskogo razvertyvaniya vooruzhennykh sil Sovetskogo Soiuza na sluchai voiny s Germaniei i ee soiuznikami" [People's Commissar of Defense and Chief of General Staff's memo to the Chairman of the Council of People's Commissars, I. V. Stalin, considering the plan for the strategic deployment of the armed forces of the Soviet Union in case of war with Germany and its allies], around May 15, 1941, in *1941,* 2: 218.
147 Peter Kurochkin was a hardworking: Kurochkin, pp. 191–94.
"Elephant": Ibid., pp. 194–95; Poluboyarov, p. 114.
148 That was Stalin's directive #1: Kurochkin, p. 198.
It took General Kuznetsov: Ibid., 193–99.
On the night of June 21: *Na linii,* pp. 44–45.
Others had felt secure: Hetagurov, p. 51.
Leaders of a Soviet republic: "Pravitelstvo," pp. 103–6.
150 he didn't know where his armies were: Kurochkin, pp. 200–201; Beshanov, pp. 210–15.
Nobody in the Northwestern Front: Kershaw, p. 395.

150 On June 25, realizing: Kurochkin, pp. 202–3.
Several hours later: Ibid., p. 205.
151 He suggested moving: Ibid.
The last week of June: Khvaley, p. 311.
152 "Read this": Kurochkin, pp. 206–9.
153 The only army: Beshanov, pp. 219–20.

5. HOPE IN THE SOUTH

154 A full twenty-four hours: "Postanovleniye SNK SSSR i TsK VKP(b) 'O Stavke glavnogo komandovaniya vooruzhennykh sil Soiuza SSSR'" in *1941,* 2: 441.
155 The men jumped from their seats: Kuznetsov, *Nakanune,* pp. 370–71; Simonov, *100 sutok,* p. 309.
156 He saw fewer people: Vypiska 2: 428–29.
Between June 23 and June 25: Ibid. Zhukov's deputy, Vatutin, got thirteen hours and fifty-five minutes, but always in the presence of Timoshenko; People's Commissar of the Navy Kuznetsov had ten hours and fifty minutes, almost as much as the Red Army chief commissar, Mekhlis (nine hours and thirty-five minutes). Next came the people's commissar of transportation, Lazar Kaganovich, with seven hours and fifty-five minutes, and Stalin's economist, Voznesensky, with six hours and forty minutes. The Moscow Party boss, Shcherbakov, almost equaled that, with six hours and twenty-five minutes, as did the commander of the air force, Zhigharev.
157 On June 23, Kirill Meretskov: Meretskov, pp. 202–5, 209–14.
Instead of going to the front: Mikoyan's uncensored memoir in *1941,* 2: 497.
The airy house: Allilueva, *Twenty,* pp. 21–22; Gusliarov, pp. 244, 253.
158 His elder son: Allilueva, *Twenty,* pp. 157, 160; Gusliarov, p. 342.
He hesitated: "Agenturnoye donesenie, NKO SSSR, 14 June 1941," in Gusliarov, p. 313.
159 The commander of the Southwestern Front: Bagramian, *Tak,* p. 48.
Vashugin was handsome: Ibid., p. 43; Popel, p. 138.
Vashugin had spent: Bagramian, *Tak,* pp. 43–44, 47; Popel, p. 139.
161 "You just wait": Fediuninsky quoted in *Stalin and His Generals,* p. 241.
The resilient terrorist underground: Pyskir, p. 12.
Combined, the two fronts: Beshanov, pp. 194–99.
Both Kirponos and Vashugin: Vypiska 2: 145.
On June 15, Kirponos was instructed: Bagramian, *Tak,* pp. 77–78.
162 On June 19: Ibid., p. 83.
The staff's automobile column: Ibid., pp. 84–86.
On that day alone: Beshanov, p. 299.
German bombers arrived: Moskalenko, p. 28.
It was in the evening: Ibid., p. 32.
Kirponos couldn't get: Bagramian, *Tak,* pp. 88–89.
"I cannot": Ibid., p. 90.
At about eleven o'clock: "Direktiva voennym sovetam Severo-zapadnogo, Zapadnogo, Yugo-zapadnogo i Yuzhnogo frontov," in *1941,* 2: 439–40.
163 Kirponos read and reread: "Zapiska narkoma oborony SSSR i nachalnika Genshtaba Krasnoi Armii predsedateliu SNK SSSR I. V. Stalinu s soobrazheniyami po planu strategicheskogo razvertyvaniya vooruzhennykh sil Sovetskogo Soiuza

na sluchai voiny s Germaniei i ee soiuznikami" [People's Commissar of Defense and Chief of General Staff's memo to the Chairman of the Council of People's Commissars, I. V. Stalin, considering the plan for the strategic deployment of the armed forces of the Soviet Union in case of war with Germany and its allies], around May 15, 1941, in *1941*, 2: 218.
"What are we to do": Bagramian, *Tak*, pp. 113–19.
164 "shred them into pieces": Chuev, p. 324.
"Tell me": Ibid., p. 328.
When his photo: Ortenberg, *Stalin*, pp. 59–60.
165 "You are not a general": Chuev, p. 316.
He still mourned: Zhukov 2002, 1: 145–58.
166 The person meeting him: Ibid., 268; Khrushchev, 1: 265, 272, 300–302.
167 They reached the Southwestern Front: Khrushchev, 1: 302.
The news was dire: Zhukov 2002, 1: 268–69.
168 To Zhukov's immense displeasure: Ibid., 269; Bagramian, *Tak*, p. 118.
Konstantin Rokossovsky, a classmate: Bagramian, *Tak*, p. 14.
He wasn't able to resist: Khrushchev, 1: 303.
An avowed cavalryman: Popel, p. 21; Riabyshev, p. 5.
He spent the morning of June 22: Popel, p. 21.
At ten o'clock: Ibid., p. 28; Riabyshev, p. 13.
169 an awkward assortment of 932 tanks: Popel, p. 337; Riabyshev, p. 5.
To boost morale: Details of the corps's march can be found in Popel, pp. 30–39.
171 The soldiers sought refuge: Ibid., p. 38.
When they reached their compound: Popel, p. 43; Riabyshev, pp. 15–16.
172 There its commander: Popel, pp. 45–54; Riabyshev, p. 16.
Kirponos ordered them: Riabyshev, p. 18.
its fighters ambushed the Eighth: Popel, pp. 56–57.
173 They didn't realize: Applebaum, p. 416.
In the suburbs: Popel, pp. 60–62.
174 At dusk: Zhukov 2002, 1: 269–70; Riabyshev, pp. 20–21.
175 "Good guys": Zhukov 2002, 1: 269.
At the end of the day: Popel, p. 65.
On June 25: Riabyshev, pp. 21–22; Popel, pp. 65–66.
In a while the scouts: Popel, pp. 66, 70; Riabyshev, pp. 22–23.
Riabyshev knew what that meant: Popel, p. 71.
He sent the scouts out again: Ibid., pp. 76–77.
176 While the tanks were struggling: Ibid., pp. 80–84.
Moving in and out: Ibid., pp. 84–88.
his KV's wheels jammed: Ibid., p. 89.
Exploring the liberated town: Ibid., p. 90.
177 "This is a war": Ibid., pp. 93–95.
While Riabyshev tried: Ibid., pp. 95–97.
178 fodder for the torture mill: Kuusinen, p. 173; Rubtsov, pp. 228–42.
Almost straight from the camp: Rokossovsky, *Soldatsky dolg*, p. 24.
179 He spent much of the spring: Rokossovsky, VIZh 4 (1989): 52–55, 5 (1989): 60; Rokossovsky, *Soldatsky dolg*, p. 30.
He was unhappy with his corps: Rokossovsky, *Soldatsky dolg*, pp. 30, 37.
One of the regiments: Karpov, p. 255.
The Kiev Military District: Rokossovsky, *Soldatsky dolg*, pp. 26–29.

180 At four o'clock on the morning: Ibid., pp. 30, 35.
he had to figure out: Bagramian, *Tak,* p. 135.
181 The corps didn't depart: Rokossovsky, VIZh 4 (1989): 55–57; 5 (1989): 60–62; Rokossovsky, *Soldatsky dolg,* pp. 30–39, 458.
182 On the evening of June 23: Rokossovsky, VIZh 5 (1989): 59; Rokossovsky, *Soldatsky dolg,* pp. 39–41.
By the end of June 25: Rokossovsky, VIZh 5 (1989): 59–60; Rokossovsky, *Soldatsky dolg,* pp. 41–49.
184 To Rokossovsky's indignation: Karpov, p. 257.
"the left-handed": Rokossovsky, VIZh 6 (1989): 52.
The insane counteroffensive : Bagramian, *Tak,* pp. 129–30.
Its futility: Ibid., p. 131.
Tank units got stuck: Beshanov, pp. 308–11.
185 The Germans advanced: Moskalenko, p. 34.
186 Instead he went through his deputy: Zhukov 2002, 1: 277.
But another piece of information: Pavlenko, p. 125; Mirkina, p. 54.
At one point an interrogator: Pavlenko, p. 125.
In another cell: Ibid.
Zhukov didn't know: Mirkina, pp. 54–55, Pavlenko, p. 99.
Early in the morning: Zhukov 2002, 1: 278.
Later in the day: Ibid., p. 284.
187 When Zhukov reached: Vypiska 2: 429.
Stalin barely nodded: Zhukov 2002, 1: 284–85.
They told Stalin: Ibid.; Zakharov, p. 261.
189 However, that afternoon: Vypiska 2: 429.
again Beria was there: Ibid., pp. 429–30.
Beria's secure convoys: "Operatsiyu," p. 107.
Stalin ordered Beria: "Iz obiasnitelnoi zapiski P. A. Sudoplatova v Sovet Ministrov SSSR" [P. A. Sudoplatov's affidavit for the Council of Ministers of the USSR], August 7, 1953, in *1941,* 2: 487–90. In his memoir published in the West in 1994 (Sudoplatov, pp. 145–46), Sudoplatov says he got the instructions from Beria on July 25. Yet in a memo written forty years earlier, in 1953, Sudoplatov gives the date as between June 25 and June 27 (*1941,* 2: 487). Khrushchev says the attempt to sign a separate peace was made in the autumn of 1941 and notes that he heard about it from Beria and Malenkov (Khrushchev, 1: 348–49).
191 General Riabyshev spent the night: Riabyshev, p. 29.
At four o'clock: Ibid., p. 31.
At 6:40 in the morning: Popel, p. 131–33; Riabyshev, p. 31–32.
Almost immediately after Zhukov: Bagramian, *Tak,* pp. 140–41.
192 He was sitting in the woods: Popel, pp. 136–41.
Vashugin was plotting: Khrushchev, 1: 305–6.
193 Vashugin returned: Bagramian, *Tak,* pp. 144–45.
194 At the front headquarters: Ibid.
The next day: Ibid., p. 149.
On June 28, Kirponos: Ibid., p. 150.
They reported that the Eighth: Ibid., p. 151.
When he heard this news: Khrushchev, 1: 306–7.
195 By June 29: Popel, pp. 188–89; Riabyshev, pp. 36–43.
196 On the night of June 29: Riabyshev, pp. 43–47.
Riabyshev didn't recognize: Popel, pp. 190–91; Riabyshev, pp. 47–48.

Soon Riabyshev ran across: Popel, p. 194.
At about the same time: Ibid.
In Vinnitsa: Ibid., pp. 194–95.
General Zhukov claimed: Zhukov 2002, 1: 276.
197 The Southwestern Front had lost: Beshanov, p. 334.
at least 160,000 men: *1941*, 2: 481.

6. THE LOSS OF BYELORUSSIA

198 Trenches: Simonov, *100*, p. 37.
like a downed but intact Messerschmitt: Ibid., p. 39.
A hungry unarmed soldier: Ibid., p. 38.
199 There was a young female pilot: Raisa Zhitova-Yushina quoted in Noggle, p. 87.
A village cemetery: Ivan Titov, in Alexievich.
A deranged teenage infantryman: Simonov, *100*, pp. 18–19.
Virtually every witness: Ostashenko, in *Geroi Bresta*, p. 120.
Fear gave rise: *Na linii fronta*, p. 43.
A civilian: Simonov, *100*, p. 13.
More and more soldiers: Ibid., p. 96.
Officers started: Ibid., pp. 96, 16.
A Commissar Grigorenko: Karpov, p. 257.
200 Sometimes, having run out: Simonov, *100*, p. 54.
201 Occasionally planes with red stars: Ibid., pp. 40–43.
Sometimes the Red Air Force: Ibid., p. 12.
The roads had dried up: *Effects*, pp. 45–60.
202 The woods could be silent: Simonov, *100*, pp. 10, 17.
The Moscow railway stations: Ibid., pp. 6–7.
203 all the trains now stopped: Zhadov, pp. 7–8.
Junction authorities: Simonov, *100*, pp. 28.
The roads west of Orsha: Zhadov, pp. 7–10.
Children suffered: Marina Karyanova, David Goldberg, in Alexievich.
204 The puffs of white smoke: Gryaznov, p. 131.
The Commissariat of Defense didn't know: "Soobshcheniye 3 Upravleniya NKO SSSR v GKO SSSR — V. M. Molotovu o nedostatkakh v organizatzii zheleznodorozhnykh perevozok," in *1941*, 2: 453–55.
205 On the night of June 26: Sandalov, *Na moskovskom*, pp. 118–19.
Guderian's guns: Ibid., pp. 119–21.
At the end of the day: Ibid., pp. 122–24.
207 Leonid Sandalov: Ibid., pp. 124–25.
208 General Pavlov's headquarters: Zhadov, pp. 9–10; Sandalov, *Na moskovskom*, p. 125; Starinov, pp. 174–75; Simonov, *100*, pp. 30–33.
Pavlov took Sandalov: Sandalov, *Na moskovskom*, p. 125.
209 The night before, Zhukov had cabled: Zhukov 2002, 1: 285–86.
on June 26 alone: Simonov, *100*, p. 341.
210 "The main thing": Kardashov, *Voroshilov*, p. 135.
Voroshilov drove up: Simonov, *100*, pp. 30–31.
As soon as he glanced: Ivanov, *Shtab*, p. 61.
At 2 A.M. on June 28: Zhukov 2002, 1: 286–87.
211 Completely oblivious: Starinov, p. 176.

211 Pavlov decided to go to Bobruisk: Zhadov, p. 10.
Pavlov kept promising: Irinarkhov, p. 340.
General Filatov commanded: Ivanov, *Shtab,* pp. 78–79.
212 At his own risk: Ibid., pp. 79–81.
The Germans informed: Ibid., pp. 81–82.
As they left: Zhadov, pp. 11–12.
Stalin became flushed with rage: Molotov quoted in Karpov, pp. 285–87; Mikoyan quoted in Kumanev, pp. 30–31; Zhukov 2002, 1: 287–88; Mikoyan's uncensored memoir: *1941,* 2: 497. The evidence for Stalin's visit is rather controversial. Zhukov, for example, says that Stalin visited the Commissariat of Defense twice that day.
217 At 6:45 A.M.: Zhukov 2002, 1: 288–89.
218 The surrender of Minsk: Vypiska 2: 430.
he refused to answer the phone: Chadaev quoted in Gusliarov, p. 350.
219 Late in the afternoon: Mikoyan's uncensored memoir in *1941,* 2: 498; Mikoyan quoted in Kumanev, pp. 31–34; Beria quoted in Khrushchev, 1: 301. The primary source for the episode is Mikoyan, who says that Voroshilov was among the leaders to visit Stalin at his dacha. In reality, Voroshilov was at that point at the Western Front headquarters.
221 Young pilots: Yekaterina Musatova-Fedotova, in Noggle, p. 147.
so many letters from female pilots: Klavdiya Terekhova-Kasatkina quoted in ibid., p. 191.
Those who had been far away: Galina Drobovich quoted in ibid., p. 189.
Still in doubt: Zhukov 2002, 1: 289.
222 "I've been waiting for you": Yeremenko, *Pomni voinu,* pp. 131–32.
Two years earlier: Ibid., pp. 8–128.
223 Now, driving toward Moghilev: Ibid., p. 132.
Yeremenko sent Malandin: Ibid., pp. 132–33; Yeremenko, *V nachale,* pp. 78–80.
224 Earlier in the day: Ivanov, *Shtab,* p. 83.
He had already switched: Starinov, p. 179.
The third dignitary, Ponomarenko: Yeremenko, *Pomni voinu,* p. 133; Yeremenko, *V nachale,* p. 80.
Notwithstanding the mayhem: "Znachitelnye," pp. 115–16.
225 After interviewing all three men: Yeremenko, *Pomni voinu,* pp. 133–34.
After Sandalov returned: Sandalov, *Na moskovskom,* p. 128.
The next day, before dawn: Ibid., pp. 129–30.
226 The front headquarters rushed: Simonov, *100,* pp. 336–37.
"Comrade Yeremenko": Yeremenko, *Pomni voinu,* p. 135.
227 The former commander: "Protokol doprosa arestovannogo Pavlova D. G.," in *1941,* 2: 455–86; Starinov quoted in *Stalin and His Generals,* p. 236.
On July 1: Sandalov, *Na moskovskom,* pp. 131–32.
A few days later: Ibid., p. 136.

7. THEIR MASTER'S VOICE

228 According to Hitler's: Guderian, p. 145.
A week before the war had started: Ibid., pp. 153, 150.
229 "there are enemy forces": Halder, p. 445.
"stubborn enemy resistance": Ibid., p. 444.

Guderian thought: Guderian, p. 161.
Between June 26 and June 30: Ibid., p. 161.
The Novogrudok pocket: Halder, p. 445.
The advance of Army Group North: Ibid., pp. 445–46.
the situation remained "tight": Ibid., pp. 424–34.
230 "The enemy's withdrawal": Ibid., p. 446.
Hitler answered the question: Bullock, p. 720.
"the layout of the Soviet forces": Manstein, p. 181.
"morale of our troops": Halder, p. 433.
"vast forests": von Luck, p. 54.
231 "Please take me": Ibid., p. 58.
"gruesomely mutilated": Manstein, p. 180.
"after throwing up their hands": Ibid., pp. 180–81.
"sparsely furnished": von Luck, p. 56.
"take a quick plunge": Manstein, pp. 190–91.
"were very hard": Ibid., p. 191.
232 Many villages were so poor: von Luck, p. 56.
Someone had to bury: Vasily Baikachev, in Alexievich.
The Germans herded: Liudmila Andreeva, in Alexievich.
233 Where POW columns: Yury Karpovich, in Alexievich.
Minsk was subjected: Gartenschlager, p. 14.
234 "I kept talking": Ekaterina Korotaeva, in Alexievich.
Many German officers were bothered: Manstein, p. 179.
235 Such people said: Ibid., p. 180.
"safety measures": Nolte, p. 34.
Many bookshelves: Kima Murzich, in Alexievich.
In Minsk, the Germans created: Gartenschlager, pp. 16, 23.
thousands of Russian prisoners: von Luck, p. 57.
236 Some were planning to escape: Kozlov, in *Geroi Bresta*, p. 180.
including a remarkable number: Reshin, VIZh 1 (1993): 31–32, 35–36; 2 (1993): 10–13.
Before the war almost half: Gartenschlager, pp. 21–22; Nolte, p. 47.
237 "Suddenly we heard": von Luck, pp. 57–58.
"We are still Christians": Ibid., p. 56.
Churches could indeed: Ibid., p. 58.
238 soon OUN: Pyskir, p. 17.
In Minsk women dug: Gartenschlager, pp. 16–18; Nolte, p. 35.
239 When the new border: Guderian, p. 146.
Their fathers: Sinkovsky, in *Geroi Bresta*, pp. 125–26.
The majority did exactly that: Sisin, in ibid., p. 77.
240 "It's just": Kozlov, in ibid., p. 178.
fourteen-year-old Valia: Sachkovskaya, in ibid., pp. 100–102.
241 the men from the 333rd: Sandalov, VIZh 12 (1988): 20–21; Irinarkhov, pp. 222–27.
Corpses had become: Tereshchenko, in *Geroi Bresta*, p. 84.
The Polish soldiers then locked: Guderian, pp. 81, 83.
242 "held out": Ibid., p. 154.
A group of soldiers: Sisin, in *Geroi Bresta*, p. 78.
it was probably about: *Great Soviet Encyclopedia*, vol. 4, p. 66.
The commander of the Forty-fourth: Sandalov, VIZh 12 (1988): 20–21.

242 several orphaned boys: Sachkovskaya, in *Geroi Bresta,* p. 103.
243 Girls searched: Khodtseva, in ibid., pp. 158–60.
The person to initiate: Glyazer, in ibid., pp. 41–42.
introduced a gruesome ritual: Khodtseva, in ibid., p. 51.
The conference: Glyazer, in ibid., pp. 41–42.
244 There were only a few: Ibid., p. 45.
At night they dispatched: Khodtseva, in ibid., pp. 78–79.
At midnight on June 26: Glyazer, in ibid., pp. 45–46.
They continued: Kolesnikov, in ibid., p. 184.
There was no water: Sisin, in ibid., p. 79.
Their thirst had become: Leonovets, in ibid., p. 68.
245 Someone suggested: Glyazer, in ibid., pp. 46–47.
In the fort: Sisin, in ibid., p. 80.
In one of the basements: Tereshchenko, in ibid., p. 83.
an amazing display of roses: Sachkovskaya, in ibid., p. 100.
The Germans had set up: Sisin, in ibid., p. 79.
Valia Zenkina: Sachkovskaya, in ibid., pp. 104–6.
Fomin and Zubachev: Abramov, in ibid., p. 136; Sisin, in ibid., pp. 79–81.
Major Peter Gavrilov: Sisin, in ibid., p. 81.
On July 1: "Zhurnal poseshchenii I. V. Stalina v ego kremlevskom kabinete" [Stalin's office log], in Gorkov, pp. 228–30.
246 The Southern Front: Tiulenev, pp. 142–45; Beshanov, pp. 349–51.
247 Only now were a number: Zakharov, p. 262; Zhukov 2002, 1: 304–5.
This meant that at least: Starinov, p. 172.
Belatedly, Stalin had increased: Gorkov, p. 32.
As for time bombs: Starinov, pp. 177–78.
However, during the 1937 purge: Ibid., pp. 182–83.
248 The British prime minister: Churchill, pp. 370–71.
"No one": Ibid., p. 371.
249 Twelve hours before: "Beseda pervogo zamestitelya narkoma inostrannykh del SSSR A.Ya. Vyshinskogo s vremennym poverennym v delakh Velikobritanii v SSSR G. L. Baggaleem," in *1941,* 2: 438.
Churchill found the silence: Churchill, p. 380.
The Soviet ambassador: Maisky, p. 143.
In Washington: "Beseda K. A. Umanskogo s ispolniayushchim obiazannosti gossekretaria SShA S. Wellesom," in *1941,* 2: 444.
250 However, Stalin didn't allow: Ortenberg, *Stalin,* pp. 59–60.
Very upset, the editor: Ibid.
252 Even when Timoshenko was still in Moscow: Shtemenko, p. 29.
Stalin never came to the office: "Zhurnal poseshchenii I.V. Stalina v ego kremlevskom kabinete" [Stalin's office log], in Gorkov, pp. 228–29.
He expected the *vozhd:* Simonov in *Marshal,* p. 211.
When the daredevil test pilots: A. S. Yakovlev, p. 249.
253 To camouflage the Moscow airfield: Ibid., p. 241.
Alarmed and angry, Stalin attended: Ibid., pp. 262–64.
255 "traitors who had fled abroad": "Prikaz narkoma gosbezopasnosti SSSR, narkoma vnutrennikh del SSSR i prokurora SSSR 'O poriadke privlecheniya k otvetstvennosti izmennikov rodine i chlenov ikh semei'," in *1941,* 2: 445–46.
256 Major General Semen Kondrusev: "Otdali," VIZh 4 (1993): 2–3.

Major General Vladimir Borisov: "Otdali," VIZh 6–7 (1992): 2.
Major General Fedor Budanov: "Otdali," VIZh 8 (1992): 3.
Major General Alexander Garnov: "Otdali," VIZh 9 (1992): 3.
Major General Vassily Evdokimov: "Otdali," VIZh 11 (1992): 2.
Major General Alexander Zhurba: "Otdali," VIZh 12 (1992): 3.
In the first days of July: Boldin, pp. 65–72.
258 Late at night: Ortenberg, *Iiun,* pp. 21–24.
At about that time: Levitan quoted in Gusliarov, p. 352.
260 At 6:30 A.M.: Ortenberg, *Iiun,* p. 24.
"Comrades!": "Vystuplenie I. V. Stalina po radio 3 iulya 1941 g." [I. V. Stalin's radio broadcast, July 3, 1941], in *1941,* 2: 448–52.
Many wept: Simonov, *100,* p. 50.
Ten days earlier: Churchill, p. 371.
When Joseph Stalin: "Direktiva SNK SSSR i TsK VKP(b) partiinym i sovetskim organizatsiyam prifrontovykh oblastei" [Council of People's Commissars' and Party Central Committee's directive to the Party and state authorities of the areas adjoining the front line], June 29, 1941, in *1941,* 2: 446–48.
261 They savored his calm: M. Dokuchaev quoted in Gusliarov, p. 354.
262 The text of Stalin's speech: Ortenberg, *Iiun,* p. 24.
Zhukov eagerly listened: Zhukov's security officer Nikolai Bedov quoted in Karpov, pp. 296–97.
Throughout the previous thirty-six hours: "Zhurnal poseshchenii I. V. Stalina v ego kremlevskom kabinete" [Stalin's office log], in Gorkov, pp. 228–29.
The fight for Dubno: Popel, pp. 142–96.
263 On the night of July 2: Ibid., pp. 197–202.

EPILOGUE

266 We know now: Krivosheev, pp. 84–85.
"It is thus probably": Halder, p. 446.
Hitler expected: Ibid., p. 437.
The Luftwaffe: Shtemenko, p. 33.
267 almost 40 percent: *K 50-letiu,* p. 24.
268 "The Russians are fighting": Halder, p. 433.
On August 24: *Voenny entsiklopedichesky slovar,* p. 1111.
On July 14: Kardashov, *Voroshilov,* p. 297.
269 A number of other leaders: Vannikov, p. 85.
Although he had dumped: Yeremenko, *Pomni voinu,* pp. 139–40.
The alliance with the anti-Nazi West: Churchill, pp. 381, 383–84.
270 Between July and December: "Gulag," p. 23.
Between 1942 and 1945: Ibid., p. 20.
271 The commander of another: Beshanov, p. 296.
The Western Front's terminator: Brett-Smith, pp. 80, 251.
The commander of the Southwestern Front: *Voenny entsiklopedicheskii slovar,* p. 705.
General Dmitry Riabyshev: Pokrovsky, p. 70.
Marshal Shaposhnikov: Shaposhnikov, p. 562.
Klim Voroshilov: Kardashov, *Voroshilov,* p. 292.
Another cavalryman, Marshal Kulik: *Voenny entsiklopedicheskii slovar,* p. 801.
The two arcs of defense: Zhukov 2002, 1: 304–5.

272 Ten months later: Chuev, p. 320; Markov in *Marshal,* pp. 21–34, Semin in *Marshal,* pp. 43–45, Mirkina in *Marshal,* pp. 49–60.
Right after Stalin's death: Markov in *Marshal,* p. 30.
Originally he had wanted: Stalin's son Vassily quoted in Karpov, pp. 80–83.
273 Rokossovsky was Polish: Chuev, p. 352.
"Finally": Ibid.

A NOTE ON SOURCES AND METHODOLOGY

280 "Where is the cavalry corps?": Zhukov 2002, 1: 288.
281 "He had changed": Ibid., p. 289.
"The People's Commissar": Yeremenko, *Pomni voinu,* pp. 131–33.
However, Yeremenko's first order: Yeremenko, *V nachale,* p. 83.
July 1 is also the date: Sandalov, *Na moskovskom,* pp. 131–32.
Another memoir: Ivanov, *Shtab,* p. 83.
In a newly released archival document: "Protokol doprosa arestovannogo Pavlova D. G. 7 iulya 1941 g." [Minutes of D. G. Pavlov's interrogation, July 7, 1941], in *1941,* 2: 455–86.

BIBLIOGRAPHY

PRIMARY SOURCES

1941 god. Dokumenty [1941: A collection of documents]. Vols. 1 and 2. Moscow: Demokratiya, 1998.

Alexievich, Svetlana. *Posledniye svideteli.* www.alexievich.promedia.by/poslsvidrus.doc (2002).

Allilueva, Svetlana. *Only One Year.* New York: Harper & Row, 1969.

———. *Twenty Letters To a Friend,* New York: Harper & Row, 1967.

Arkhipov, V. *Vremia tankovykh atak.* Moscow: Voenizdat, 1981.

Azarov, I. I. *Osazhdennaya Odessa.* Moscow: Voenizdat, 1962.

Bagramian, I. Kh. *Tak nachinalas voina.* Moscow: Voenizdat, 1971.

———. "Zapiski nachalnika operativnogo otdela." *Voenno-istorichesky zhurnal* 3 (1967).

Berezhkov, Valentin M. *At Stalin's Side: His Interpreter's Memoirs from the October Revolution to the Fall of the Dictator's Empire.* New York: Birch Lane, 1994.

Bialer, Seweryn, ed. *Stalin and His Generals. Soviet Military Memoirs of World War.* New York: Pegasus, 1969.

Biriuzov, S. S. *Surovye gody, 1941–1945.* Moscow: Nauka, 1966.

Bliukher, Glafira. "S Vasiliem Konstantinovichem Blukher — shest' let." *Voenno-istorichesky zhurnal* 3 (1990).

Boldin, I. V. "Sorok piat dnei v tylu vraga." *Voenno-istorichesky zhurnal* 4 (1961).

Buslaev, A. A., Mazur, K. A., and Shumeiko, Y. I. "Neoplachenny dolg." *Voenno-istorichesky zhurnal* 9 (1992).

Churchill, Winston. *The Grand Alliance.* Boston: Houghton Mifflin, 1948.

Egorov, G. M. "Katastrofy predotvratit ne udalos." *Voenno-istorichesky zhurnal* 3 (1992).

Eroshenko, V. N. *Lider "Tashkent."* Moscow: Voenizdat, 1966.

"Frontoviki otvetili tak! Piat voprosov Generalnogo Shtaba." *Voenno-istorichesky zhurnal* 3, 5 (1989).

Galai, M. I. "Pervyi boi my vyigrali." *Novyi mir* 9 (1966).

Georgy Zhukov. Moscow: Novator, 1997.

Geroi Bresta: novye dokumenty, svidetelstva ochevidtsev. Minsk: Belarus, 1991.
The Goebbels Diaries, 1939–1941. Edited by Fred Taylor. London: Hamish Hamilton, 1982.
Gorbatov, A. V. *Gody i voiny.* Moscow: Voenizdat, 1980.
"Gotovil li SSSR preventivny udar?" *Voenno-istorichesky zhurnal* 4, 5 (1992).
"Grigory Ivanovich Kulik." *Voenno-istorichesky zhurnal* 3 (1990).
Guderian, Heinz. *Panzer Leader.* New York: Dutton, 1952.
Gusliarov, Evgeny, ed. *Stalin v zhizni.* Moscow: Olma-Press, 2003.
The Halder War Diary, 1939–1942. Edited by Charles Burdick and Hans-Adolf Jacobsen. Novato, Calif.: Presidio, 1988.
Ivanov, S. P. *Shtab armeisky, shtab frontovoi.* Moscow: Voenizdat, 1990.
Karpov, Vladimir. *Marshal Zhukov.* Moscow: Veche, 1994.
Kazakov, M. I. *Nad kartoi bylykh srazhenii.* Moscow: Voenizdat, 1965.
Khetagurov, G. I. *Ispolneniye dolga.* Moscow: Voenizdat, 1977.
Khrushchev, N. S. *Vospominaniya. Vremia, liudi, vlast.* Vols. 1–3. Moscow: Moskovskie novosti, 2000.
Khvaley, S. F. "202-ya strelkovaya diviziya i ee komandir S. G. Shtykov." In *Na severo-zapadnom fronte, 1941–1943.* Moscow: Nauka, 1969.
"Komandirovka v Germaniyu pod 'kryshei' Aeroflota. Otchet Mayora N. V. Chistyakova. May 1940." *Istoricheskii arkhiv* 3 (1995).
Konev, I. S. *Zapiski komanduiushchego frontom.* Moscow: Olma-Press, 2003.
Kumanev, Georgy. *Ryadom so Stalinym.* Smolensk: Rusich, 2001.
Kurochkin, P. M. "Sviaz Severo-Zapadnogo fronta." In *Na severo-zapadnom fronte, 1941–1943.* Moscow: Nauka, 1969.
Kuusinen, Aino. *The Rings of Destiny.* New York: William Morrow, 1974.
Kuznetsov, N. G. "Krutye povoroty. Iz zapisok admirala." *Voenno-istorichesky zhurnal* 12 (1992), 1 (1993), 2 (1993), 3 (1993), 4 (1993), 6 (1993).
———. *Kursom k pobede.* Moscow: Olma-Press, 2003.
———. *Na flotakh boevaya trevoga.* Moscow: Voenizdat, 1971.
———. *Nakanune.* Moscow: Voenizdat, 1969.
———. "Pered voinoi." *Oktiabr* 11 (1965).
———. "Voenno-Morskoi Flot nakanune Velikoi Otechestvennoi voiny." *Voenno-istorichesky zhurnal* 9 (1965).
Lutsky, Igor. *More i plen: tragediia Sevastopolia (1940–1945).* New York: All Slavic Publishing, 1975.
Maisky, I. M. *Vospominaniya sovetskogo posla.* Moscow: Nauka, 1965.
Malaparte, Curzio. *The Volga Rises in Europe.* London: Alvin Redman, 1957.
Malkov, Pavel. *Zapiski komendanta Kremlia.* Moscow: Molodaya gvardiya, 1967.
Maltsev, E. E. *V gody ispytany.* Moscow: Voenizdat, 1979.
Markov, S. P. "Poslevoennye gody." In *Marshal Zhukov: polkovodets i chelovek.* Edited by A. D. Mirkina and V. S. Yarovikov. Moscow: APN, 1988.
Meretskov, K. A. *Na sluzhbe narodu.* Moscow: Politizdat, 1970.
"Mikhail Petrovich Kirponos." *Voenno-istorichesky zhurnal* 7 (1989).
Mirkina, A. D. "Ne skloniv golovy." In *Marshal Zhukov: polkovodets i chelovek.* Edited by A. D. Mirkina and V. S. Yarovikov. Moscow: APN, 1988.
Molotov Remembers: Inside Kremlin Politics. Conversations with Felix Chuev. Chicago: Ivan R. Dee, 1993.
Moskalenko, K. S. *Na yugo-zapadnom napravlenii.* Moscow: Nauka, 1969.
"Moskovskie chekisty v oborone stolitsy, 1941–1942 gg." *Voenno-istorichesky zhurnal* 1 (1991).

"Na linii fronta." *Istorichesky arkhiv* 2 (1995).
"Neuslyshannye signaly voiny. Dokladnye zapiski L. P. Berii i I. I. Maslennikova I. V. Stalinu, V. M. Molotovu, S. K. Timoshenko, G. K. Zhukovu, A. Y. Vyshinskomu. Aprel-iiun 1941 g." *Istorichesky arkhiv* 2 (1995).
Noggle, Anne. *A Dance with Death.* College Station: Texas A & M University Press, 1994.
"O masshtabakh repressii v Krasnoi Armii v predvoennye gody." *Voenno-istorichesky zhurnal* 2 (1993), 3 (1993), 5 (1993).
"Operatsiyu provesti v trekhdnevny srok," *Istochnik* 2 (1995).
Ortenberg, D. I. *Iiun — dekabr sorok pervogo.* Moscow: Sovetsky pisatel, 1986.
———. *Stalin, Shcherbakov, Mekhlis i drugie.* Moscow: Kodeks, 1995.
"Otdali zhizn za rodinu." *Voenno-istorichesky zhurnal* 4 (1993), 6–7 (1992), 8 (1992), 9 (1992), 11 (1992), 12 (1992).
Pavlenko, N. G. "Razmyshleniya o sudbe polkovodtsa." In *Marshal Zhukov: polkovodets i chelovek.* Edited by A. D. Mirkina and V. S. Yarovikov. Moscow: APN, 1988.
"Perepiska V. M. Molotova s I. V. Stalinym. Noyabr 1940 goda." *Voenno-istorichesky zhurnal* 9 (1992).
"Pervye dni voiny v dokumentakh." *Voenno-istorichesky zhurnal,* 5, 6, 7, 8, 9 (1989).
"Pogibli za Rodinu." *Voenno-istorichesky zhurnal* 9 (1991).
Pokrovsky, A. P. "Na Iugo-Zapadnom napravlenii (iiul-sentiabr 1941 g.)." *Voenno-istorichesky zhurnal* 4 (1978).
Poluboyarov, P. P. "Krepche broni." In *Na severo-zapadnom fronte, 1941–1943.* Moscow: Nauka, 1969.
Popel, Nikolai. *V tyazhkuyu poru.* Moscow: AST, 2002.
"Pravitelstvo i TsK Litvy pozorno bezhali." *Istochnik* 2 (1995).
Pyskir, Maria. *Thousands of Roads.* London: McFarland, 2001.
Riabyshev, D. *Pervy god voiny.* Moscow: Voenizdat, 1990.
Rokossovsky, K. K. *Soldatsky dolg.* Moscow: Olma-Press, 2002.
———. "Soldatsky dolg." *Voenno-istorichesky zhurnal* 4, 5, 6, (1989), 2 (1990), 7 (1991), 3 (1992).
Russiyanov, I. N. *V boyah rozhdennaya.* Moscow: Voenizdat, 1982.
Rybalko, N. F. "V pervyi den voiny na Chernom more." *Voenno-istorichesky zhurnal* 6 (1963).
Sandalov, L. M. *Grif sekretnosti snyat.* Moscow: Voenizdat, 1961.
———. *Na moskovskom napravlenii.* Moscow: Nauka, 1970.
———. *Perezhitoe.* Moscow: Voenizdat, 1963.
———. *Pervye dni voiny.* Moscow: Voenizdat, 1989.
———. "Stoyali nasmert." *Voenno-istorichesky zhurnal* 10, 11, 12 (1988), 2, 6 (1989).
Semin, V. P. "Vstrecha zemliakov." In *Marshal Zhukov: polkovodets i chelovek.* Edited by A. D. Mirkina and V. S. Yarovikov. Moscow: APN, 1988.
Shaposhnikov, B. M. *Vospominaniya. Voenno-nauchnye trudy.* Moscow: Voenizdat, 1980.
Shtemenko, S. M. *Generalny shtab v gody voiny.* Moscow: Voenizdat, 1968.
Simonov, Konstantin. *Glazami cheloveka moego pokoleniya.* Moscow: Pravda, 1989.
———. "Marshal Zhukov (zametki k biografii)." In *Marshal Zhukov: polkovodets i chelovek.* Edited by A. D. Mirkina and V. S. Yarovikov. Moscow: APN, 1988.
———. *100 sutok voiny.* Smolensk: Rusich, 1999.
Skrjabina, Elena. *Siege and Survival: The Odyssey of a Leningrader.* Carbondale: Southern Illinois University Press, 1971.
"'Sovremennaya armiya — armiya nastupatelnaya.' Vystupleniya I. V.Stalina na prieme v

Kremle pered vypusknikami voennykh akademii. Mai 1941 g." *Istorichesky arkhiv* 2 (1995).
Speer, Albert. *Inside the Third Reich.* New York: Macmillan, 1970.
Starinov, I. T. *Miny zhdut svoego chasa.* Moscow: Voenizdat, 1964.
"Strategicheskie proschety Verkhovnogo?" *Voenno-istorichesky zhurnal* 8 (1992).
Sudoplatov, Pavel, and Sudoplatov, Anatoly. *Special Tasks: The Memoirs of an Unwanted Witness — A Soviet Spymaster.* Boston: Little, Brown, 1994.
Tainy i uroki zimnei voiny 1939–1940. St. Petersburg: Poligon, 2002.
Teremov, P. A. *Pylayushchie berega.* Moscow: Voenizdat, 1965.
Tersky, R. S. "Aviatsionnye svyazisty fronta." In *Na severo-zapadnom fronte, 1941–1943.* Moscow: Nauka, 1969.
Tiulenev, I. V. *Cherez tri voiny.* Moscow: Voenizdat, 1972.
"Upriamye fakty nachala voiny." *Voenno-istorichesky zhurnal* 2 (1992).
Vannikov, B. I. "Iz zapisok narkoma vooruzheniya." *Voenno-istorichesky zhurnal* 2 (1962).
Vasilevsky, A. M. *Delo vsei zhizni.* Moscow: Olma-Press, 2002.
"Voennye razvedchiki dokladyvali . . ." *Voenno-istorichesky zhurnal* 2, 3 (1992).
Von Luck, Hans. *Panzer Commander.* New York: Praeger, 1989.
Von Manstein, Erich. *Lost Victories.* Chicago: Regnery, 1958.
Yakovlev, A. S. *Tsel zhizni.* Moscow: Respublika, 2000.
Yakovlev, N. D. *Ob artillerii i nemnogo o sebe.* Moscow: Voenizdat, 1981.
Yemelianov, V. S. "O vremeni, o tovarishchakh, o sebe." *Novyi mir* 2 (1967).
Yeremenko, A. I. *Pomni voinu.* Donetsk: Donbass, 1971.
———. *V nachale voiny.* Moscow: Nauka, 1964.
Zaitsev, N. M. "Vmeste s Altoi." *Voenno-istorichesky zhurnal* 4, 5 (1992).
Zakharov, G. N. *Ya — istrebitel.* Moscow: Voenizdat, 1985.
Zakharov, M. V. *Generalny shtab v predvoennye gody.* Moscow: Voenizdat, 1989.
Zhadov, A. S. *Chetyre goda voiny.* Moscow: Voenizdat, 1978.
Zhukov, G. K. *Vospominaniya i razmyshleniya.* Moscow: APN, 1971.
———. *Vospominaniya i razmyshleniya.* Vols. 1 and 2. Moscow: Olma-Press, 2002.
"Znachitelnye tsennosti vyvezeny polnost'iu." *Istochnik* 2 (1995)

SECONDARY SOURCES

Amis, Martin. *Koba the Dread. Laughter and the Twenty Million.* New York, Hyperion, 2002.
Andreyev, Catherine. *Vlasov and the Russian Liberation Movement: Soviet Reality and Émigré Theories.* New York: Cambridge University Press, 1987.
Anisimov, N. L., and Oppokov, V. G. "Proisshestviye v NII-3." *Voenno-istorichesky zhurnal* 10, 11 (1989).
Applebaum, Anne. *Gulag: A History.* New York: Doubleday, 2003.
Aptekar, P. A. "Opravdany li zhertvy?" *Voenno-istorichesky zhurnal* 3 (1992).
Beshanov, Vladimir. *Tankovyi pogrom 1941 goda.* Moscow: AST, 2002.
Bezymensky, Lev. *Gitler i Stalin pered skhvatkoi.* Moscow: Veche, 2002.
Bobylev, P. N. "Repetitsiya katastrofy." *Voenno-istorichesky zhurnal* 6 (1993).
———. "Tochku v diskussii stavit' rano. K voprosu o planirovanii v Generalnom Shtabe RKKA vozmozhnoi voiny s Germaniei v 1940–1941 godakh." *Otechestvennaya istoriya* 1 (2000).
Borisov, N. V. "Pobratimy A. Matrosova." *Voenno-istorichesky zhurnal* 6–7 (1992).

Brett-Smith, Richard. *Hitler's Generals*. San Rafael, Calif.: Presidio, 1977.

Bullock, Alan. *Hitler and Stalin: Parallel Lives*. New York: Knopf, 1992.

Chuev, Felix. *Soldaty imperii. Besedy. Vospominaniya. Dokumenty*. Moscow: Kovcheg, 1998.

Conquest, Robert. *Stalin, Breaker of Nations*. New York: Penguin, 1991.

Cooper, Leonard. *Many Roads to Moscow: Three Historic Invasions*. New York: Coward-McCann, 1968.

Curtis, J.A.E. *Manuscripts Don't Burn: Mikhail Bulgakov. A Life in Letters and Diaries*. Woodstock: Overlook, 1992.

Dzeniskevich, Andrei R. "The Social and Political Situation in Leningrad in the First Months of the German Invasion: The Social Psychology of the Workers." In *The People's War: Responses to World War II in the Soviet Union*. Edited by Robert W. Thurston and Bernd Bonwetsch. Chicago: University of Illinois Press, 2000.

Effects of Climate on Combat in European Russia. Washington, D.C.: Department of the Army, February 1952.

Eliseev, V. T., and Mikhalev, S. N. "Tak skolko zhe liudei my poteryali v voine?" *Voenno-istorichesky zhurnal* 6–7 (1992).

Erickson, John. *The Road to Stalingrad*. New York: Harper & Row, 1975.

Erickson, John, and Dilks, David, ed. *Barbarossa: The Axis and the Allies*. Edinburgh: Edinburgh University Press, 1994.

Fugate, Bryan I. *Operation Barbarossa: Strategy and Tactics on the Eastern Front, 1941*. Novato, Calif.: Presidio, 1984.

Gartenschlager, Uwe. "Living and Surviving in Occupied Minsk." In *The People's War: Responses to World War II in the Soviet Union*. Edited by Robert W. Thurston and Bernd Bonwetsch. Chicago: University of Illinois Press, 2000.

Gavrilov, Leonard. "Marshal pobedy." In *Marshal pobedy: K 100-letiu G. K. Zhukova*. Moscow, Voenizdat, 1996.

Gorkov, Yury. *Gosudarstvenny komitet oborony postanovlyaet. 1941–1945. Tsifry, dokumenty*. Moscow: Olma-Press, 2002.

Gorodetsky, Gabriel. *Grand Delusion: Stalin and the German Invasion of Russia*. New Haven, Conn.: Yale University Press, 1999.

Great Soviet Encyclopedia. Vols. 1–31. New York: Macmillan, 1973–1983.

Gryaznov, B. *Dorogoi soldata*. Leningrad: Lenizdat, 1968.

"Gulag v gody Velikoi Otechestvennoi voiny." *Voenno-istorichesky zhurnal* 1 (1991).

Herring, George C., Jr . *Aid to Russia, 1941–1946*. New York: Columbia University Press, 1973.

Irinarkhov, R. S. *Zapadnyi osobyi*. Minsk: Harvest, 2002.

Ivanov, S. P. *The Initial Period of War: A Soviet View*. Washington, D.C.: U.S. Government Printing Office, 1986.

Ivanov, S. P., and Shekovtsev, N. "Opyt raboty glavnyh komandovanii na teatrakh voennykh deistvii." *Voenno-istorichesky zhurnal* 9 (1981).

Ivashov, L. G. "Ot 'yunkersa' 1941 goda k 'cessne' 1987-go." *Voenno-istorichesky zhurnal* 6 (1990).

K 50-letiyu pobedy v Velikoi Otechestvennoi voine, 1941–1945 gg. Statisticheskii sbornik. Moscow: Mezhgosudarstvenny statistichesky komitet, 1995.

Kardashov, V. *Rokossovsky*. Moscow: Molodaya gvardiya, 1972.

———. *Voroshilov*. Moscow: Molodaya gvardiya, 1976.

Kershaw, Ian. *Hitler, 1936–45: Nemesis*. New York: Norton, 2000.

Khorkov, A. G. *Grozovoi iiun*. Moscow: Voenizdat, 1991.

Kiselev, V. N., and Ramanichev, N. M. "Posledstviya otsenok (deistviya voisk Yuzhnogo fronta v nachalnom periode Velikoi Otechestvennoi voiny)." *Voenno-istorichesky zhurnal* 7 (1989).

Kosenko, I. N., and Shapovalov, N. I. "Kogda rodina zvala v boi." *Voenno-istorichesky zhurnal* 11 (1992).

Krasnov, Valery. *Neizvestny Zhukov. Lavry i ternii polkovodtsa.* Moscow: Olma-Press, 2002.

Krivosheev, G. F., ed. *Soviet Casualties and Combat Losses in the Twentieth Century.* London: Greenhill, 1997.

———. "Nakanune." *Voenno-istorichesky zhurnal* 6 (1991).

———. "Voina broni i motorov." *Voenno-istorichesky zhurnal* 3 (1991).

Kuznetsov, P. G. *General Chernyakhovsky.* Moscow: Voenizdat, 1969.

Medvedev, Roy. *Let History Judge.* New York: Columbia University Press, 1989.

Meltiukhov, Mikhail I. *Upushchenny shans Stalina. Sovetskii Soiuz i borba za Yevropu, 1939–1941.* Moscow: Veche, 2000.

Montefiore, Simon Sebag. *Stalin: The Court of the Red Tsar.* New York: Knopf, 2004.

Nekrich, Alexander. *1941, 22 iunya.* Moscow: Pamiatniki istoricheskoi mysli, 1995.

Nevezhin, V. A. *Sindrom nastupatelnoi voiny.* Moscow: Airo-XX, 1997.

Nolte, Hans-Heinrich. "Destruction and Resistance: The Jewish Shtetl of Slonim, 1941–44." In *The People's War: Responses to World War II in the Soviet Union.* Edited by Robert W. Thurston and Bernd Bonwetsch. Chicago: University of Illinois Press, 2000.

Petrov, B. N. "Kak byl ostavlen Pskov." *Voenno-istorichesky zhurnal* 6 (1993).

Ramanichev, N. M. "'Krasnaya Armiya vseh silnei'?" *Voenno-istorichesky zhurnal* 12 (1991).

Repko, S. I. "Tsena illuzii." *Voenno-istorichesky zhurnal* 11 (1992).

Reshin, L. E., and Stepanov, V. S. "Sudby generalskie." *Voenno-istorichesky zhurnal* 12 (1992), 1, 2 (1993).

Rubtsov, Yu. V. *Marshaly Stalina.* Rostov-on-Don: Fenix, 2002.

Semidetko, V. A. "Istoki porazheniya v Byelorussii (Zapadnyi osoby voenny okrug k 22 iunya 1941 g.)." *Voenno-istorichesky zhurnal* 4 (1989).

Shaptalov, Boris. *Ispytaniye voinoi.* Moscow: AST, 2002.

Smirnov, S. S. *Brestskaya krepost.* Moscow: Molodaya gvardia, 1965.

Stepanov, V. S. "K istorii odnogo perezahoroneniya." *Voenno-istorichesky zhurnal* 8 (1992).

Suvenirov, O. F. "Vsearmeiskaya tragediya." *Voenno-istorichesky zhurnal* 3 (1989).

Suvorov, Viktor. *Den "M".* Moscow: AST, 2003.

———. *Icebreaker: Who Started the Second World War?* London: Hamish Hamilton, 1990.

———. *Ledokol.* Moscow: ACT, 2002.

Thurston, Robert W. "Cauldrons of Loyalty and Betrayal: Soviet Soldiers' Behavior, 1941 and 1945." In *The People's War: Responses to World War II in the Soviet Union.* Edited by Robert W. Thurston and Bernd Bonwetsch. Chicago: University of Illinois Press, 2000.

Tucker, Robert C. *Stalin in Power: The Revolution from Above, 1928–1941.* New York: Norton, 1990.

Vaneev, G. I. *Chernomortsy v Velikoi Otechestvennoi voine.* Moscow: Voenizdat, 1978.

Voenny entsiklopedichesky slovar. Moscow: BRE, 2002.

Volkogonov, Dmitry. *Stalin: Triumph and Tragedy.* New York: Grove Weidenfeld, 1991.

Weeks, Albert L. *Stalin's Other War: Soviet Grand Strategy, 1939–1941*. New York: Rowman & Littlefield, 2002.

Werth, Alexander. *Russia at War, 1941–1945*. New York: Dutton, 1964.

Wieczynski, Joseph L., ed. *Operation Barbarossa: The German Attack on the Soviet Union, June 22, 1941*. Salt Lake City: Schlacks, 1993.

Zaitsev, A. D. "Khronika vozdushnykh taranov." *Voenno-istorichesky zhurnal* 3 (1989).

INDEX